Practical Co...p

Practical Computer Graphics 2/e

Malcolm Richardson
Department of Innovation Studies
University of East London

THE McGRAW-HILL COMPANIES

London · Burr Ridge, IL · New York · St Louis · San Francisco
Auckland · Bogotá · Caracas · Lisbon · Madrid · Mexico · Milan
Montreal · New Delhi · Panama · Paris · San Juan · São Paulo
Singapore · Sydney · Tokyo · Toronto

Published by
McGraw-Hill Publishing Company
SHOPPENHANGERS ROAD,
MAIDENHEAD,
BERKSHIRE,
SL6 2QL, ENGLAND
Telephone +44 (0) 1628 502500
Fax: +44 (0) 1628 770224 Web site: http://www.mcgraw-hill.co.uk

---

A catalogue record for this book is available from the British Library

Further information on this and other McGraw-Hill titles is to be found at
http://www.mcgraw-hill.co.uk

Author's Website address:
http://www.mcgraw-hill.co.uk/textbooks/richardson

Publishing Director: Alfred Waller
Commissioning Editor: Elizabeth Robinson
Produced by: Steven Gardiner Ltd
Cover by: Kate Hybert Designers

Typeset by Malcolm Richardson

Printed and Bound in Great Britain at the University Press, Cambridge

Contents

1

Some Important Ideas

1.1 Introduction

This book is intended as an introduction to the whole field of computer graphics. It covers hardware, graphics languages and graphics applications. It concentrates on the sort of graphics which can be done by anyone on a personal computer – and it is increasingly true that there is very little that cannot be done on such equipment. It is designed to be as practical an introduction to the subject as can be achieved without becoming a handbook for one particular computer or specific pieces of software. Wherever possible, examples are given from real computers and real software packages, rather than imaginary ones postulated for teaching purposes, but in such a way that general principles are established that will apply to most other situations. The two machines which are referred to, in most cases, are the IBM-PC and the Apple Macintosh, since these are the two computers most widely used in business and education.

Because of the breadth of coverage attempted in this book it is impossible, and probably undesirable, to try to discuss in depth some subjects that have a largely theoretical interest, like graphics algorithms. These are well covered elsewhere (see the list of further reading at the end of the book) and so only one chapter is devoted to an area that, for some writers, is the whole of the subject. The purpose of this chapter is to give the reader a feeling for what lies 'behind the scenes' when a computer creates a graphic on a screen – to show that what might seem like 'magic' is, in fact, based on a series of logical processes. An attempt has been made, however, to include material which is usually missing from many traditional books on computer graphics. These are subjects like scaleable fonts, graphics file types and professional printing technologies – all of which have great practical importance to the user of computer graphics systems.

If the first emphasis is breadth, the second emphasis of the book is that it is directed to the user of graphics rather than the specialist computer scientist or engineer. Computer graphics, which was once the province of the computer specialist, has become an everyday tool in the same way that word processing has. This book is therefore primarily aimed at the would-be user of computer graphics who has some general background in computing or is prepared to acquire one. It is designed to lay a sound foundation in all the important concepts which lie at the heart of computer graphics and will enable those readers who wish to use computer graphics in their own area of interest, to make intelligent choices amongst both hardware and software, and to get the best use out of whatever is available to them. At the same time everyone, even the specialist must start somewhere and so it is hoped that the book will also be of value to the specialist student of computing science who wishes to obtain a bird's eye view of computer graphics before exploring the details which are to be found in more specialized texts.

This first chapter sets the scene by introducing many of the main ideas of the subject – ideas which will recur over and over again throughout the book and will find application in both hardware and software.

1.2 The Basic Question

The computer is often thought of as a high-powered number-crunching machine, a device which is able to perform a huge number of calculations at immense speed, and with legendary accuracy. While this picture is essentially correct, it fails to demonstrate why the computer has had such an impact on society. It seems to suggest that the computer is no more than a device to help mathematicians and accountants add up numbers, faster and more accurately than ever before. In fact the extraordinary impact of the computer stems not only from the rapid advances in the technology but from the ingenuity of software designers in finding ways to represent almost any human activity by means of numbers.

Though usually hidden from the user, computer applications involve the representation of some aspect of the physical world by a set of numbers, numbers which are then manipulated in such a way as to simulate or represent some meaningful set of events that could take place in the real world. For example, a financial spreadsheet program stores and manipulates data concerning such quantities as the prices of raw materials and products, stock levels, sales and profits of a company. These data can then be used not only to represent the current financial state of the company but also to predict what would happen to the affairs of the company if one or more of those figures, like the profit margins or the sales figures, were to change in a particular way. To take a second example, more relevant to the subject of computer graphics, a flight-simulator program stores and manipulates data which represent the appearance of an airfield in order to show what a pilot would see in a real aircraft at a real airfield when he handles his controls in a particular way.

Now, it is easy to see how numbers representing prices and sales figures can be manipulated in a computer for a useful purpose because these are the sort of numbers we are used to handling in our own financial transactions. The computer is simply performing the sort of operations we might perform using a pencil and paper or a pocket calculator. But how can an image be represented in a computer? Secondly, what sort of useful manipulations can be performed on a computer-representation of an image? Thirdly, given that it is possible to store a description of an image in a computer, how can that description be converted into visible form on a computer screen or the printed page?

This chapter begins to answer question like these and, in particular, describes the two basic methods used for representing images by numbers and gives a brief introduction to three other important areas: how these representations are created, how and why they are manipulated and how they are made visible to the human eye. All of these topics are elaborated throughout the book but certain fundamental ideas are vital and form the basis for everything that follows. First, however, it is useful to review how conventional images – images not created by a computer, such as drawings, painting and photographs, for example – are created.

1.3 Conventional Images

We are so familiar with images like paintings, photographs and printed pictures that we probably never reflect on the processes that are used to create them. We may not even know exactly how a photograph or a printed image is actually made. It is not necessary to have a detailed understanding of the technical processes involved in creating a photograph or printed picture but it is helpful to have an overview of the principles behind these processes in order to see how images display colour and form.

1.3.1 Images made with lines

It is useful to make a distinction between images created by hand (painting and drawing) and those created by machine (printing and photography). The basic difference lies in the way that the ink is applied to the paper. It should be noted here that the term 'ink' is used as a generic term for any coloured medium such as oil paint, water colour and pencil 'lead'. In hand-made images the coloured ink is

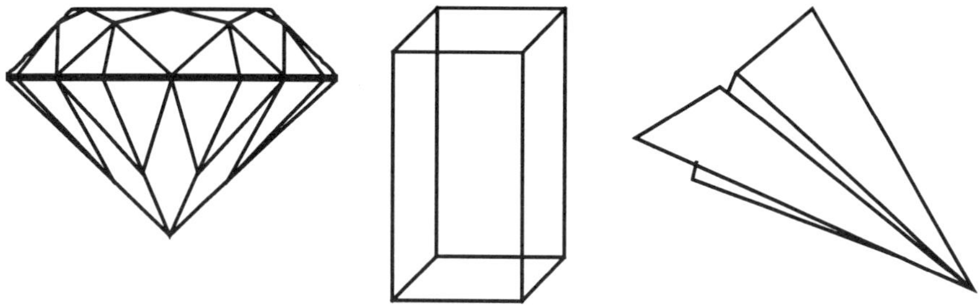

Fig. 1.1 *Examples of images made from lines*

applied by stroking a pen, pencil or brush across the paper leaving behind lines of colour, the width of the lines depending on the thickness of the brush, the pressure applied by the artist in making the stroke and the way that the brush is manipulated (see Fig. 1.1 for examples of simple line drawings). Larger areas of colour are made by adding more lines, side by side or overlapping. With the notable exception of the late-nineteenth century 'pointillist' style of painting (painting with dots) colour is applied in continuous strips. The colour is 'solid' and there are no gaps between the ink. Different colours are made by using different inks, these inks often being created by the artist by mixing other inks to obtain the right shade, either on or off the canvas.

1.3.2 Naming colours

It is important, as early as possible, to clear up a possible confusion in the use of the word 'colour'. The obvious, everyday, use of the word is to restrict its meaning to pigments which have names (for example, red, blue, green). On that basis, when white light is split into a spectrum, using a prism, it is often said to contain seven colours: red, orange, yellow, green, blue, indigo and violet. The eye, though, can detect a much wider range of intermediate shades and it is clear that it is arbitrary to say that there are only seven colours present. In fact, it seems that the number seven was originally chosen because it was felt that there should be seven basic colours in the spectrum because there were seven notes in the western musical scale. Whatever the reason, there are very few named colours. As a result, difficulties arise when trying to distinguish the many thousands of recognizable but subtle differences in colour that the eye can detect. One solution is to differentiate many 'shades' of a colour; a wide range of colours are given the same basic name but distinguished as a 'bright' red or a 'dark' red, for example. Occasionally a shade is popular enough to be given a name of its own – for example, a particular variety of pale red is called 'pink'. A variation on this theme is to try to distinguish a colour as a mixture of two others – 'brownish-red', for example. Another approach is to use the name of an well-known object to give a label to its characteristic colour – 'salmon pink', 'pillar-box red' or 'navy blue'. Using this approach, manufacturers of paint or cosmetics give fanciful names to colours ('misty peach') in an attempt to identify and popularize particular shades, but it is inevitable that millions of colours will never have an agreed name and that even well-established names have no exact definition.

In the technical context, then, the common usage of the term colour and the common names are not sufficiently precise and so each of the hundreds of recognizably different shades of red (or any other colour) must be considered to be a different colour, even though most have no name to distinguish them. Some of the different, more scientific, ways that are used to distinguish them are described in the chapter on colour. The same basic principle must also apply to the many shades of black. Black may not be considered to be a colour in normal speech (we talk about 'black-and-white' pictures as opposed to 'coloured' pictures) but for the sake of consistency black and white are treated as colours and so each possible grey (a mixture of black and white) must also be considered to be a different 'colour'.

1.3.3 Images made with dots

Unlike hand-made art, machine-made images are almost always created as a series of dots rather than continuous patches of colour. These dots are normally sufficiently small that the eye does not see any individual one – it sees only the overall effect (see Fig. 1.2). The reasons for this will be explained in the chapter on hardware but they partly derive from technological considerations and partly from the way that printing and photography create the effect of colour. The artist creates colour effects by carefully choosing and mixing inks to obtain the desired shades – one ink (one colour) for each portion of the image – and sometimes the printer does the same. If, for example, a brochure is to be printed in only two or three colours (say, black, blue and yellow) then the three appropriately coloured inks are carefully chosen, pre-mixed and then printed on the paper, one after the other, to produce the desired result. These printing inks are termed 'spot colours' and this approach is suitable as long as only a very few colours are required.

On the other hand, if hundreds of colours are to be printed, as in the reproduction of a coloured photograph (or even a black-and-white photograph), this spot colour technique is impractical and a completely different approach is needed. Paradoxically, when a larger number of colours are required, the technology which is adopted uses, not a larger number of colours, but a much smaller number of 'primary' colours – as few as three or four in some cases. The desired effects are produced by printing millions of tiny dots – the different colours being produced by changing the relative proportions of these primary colours in any particular area of the image. The effect depends on the fact that the eye cannot see any of the

Fig. 1.2 *Images made from dots: an enlarged portion of a photograph reveals that it is made up of rectangular dots*

individual dots because they are too small. Even the smallest area on the paper that the eye can detect contains a very large number of these coloured dots. The colour that the eye sees at any point depends on the precise mixture of the primary coloured dots in that region. The eye, in fact, sees a composite colour effect by averaging the effect of the component primaries and not the individual primary colours themselves. This effect is treated in more detail in the chapter on colour. This technique of fooling the eye by the use of extremely tiny dots is essentially the one used in photographs also. Photographs consist of millions of tiny silver crystals and primary-coloured dyes, laid down by the chemical development process.

To summarize, conventional (non-computer based) images are created using two completely different approaches to creating colours. One uses specially created inks and dyes – one for each shade or colour. The other uses mixtures of tiny dots, each dot being one of a very few 'primary' colours'. Now for the question of how computers deal with images.

1.4 Computer Images

In discussing computer images we must deal with two extra processes. In addition to producing permanent copies of images on paper, a computer must also be able to store a representation of those images, electronically, in its memory, and also be able to display them on some sort of screen for immediate, interactive purposes. The former obviously corresponds to the process of painting or printing in conventional images. The other two processes, though, have no technological equivalent in conventional pictures like paintings since the storing and 'viewing' of the images are done in the mind of the artist. It is reasonable to expect that the first process – the printing process – will have similarities with conventional printing methods and this is in fact the case. The details are explored in the chapter on hardware. Here we are principally concerned with the storage and display of computer images.

At this stage three general points need to be made about display devices. First, all modern displays, like most printing systems, create images using tiny dots, laid down in parallel lines (called a 'raster' pattern). Second, displays actually generate light, unlike printed inks which produce their colours by selectively absorbing and reflecting the light which illuminates the printed page. The third point follows from the second: because of the way that displays actually generate coloured light it is possible to control the amount of light that is produced at each point and this gives direct control over the brightness of these primary colour components. These three features of display all have important consequences and so will be discussed further, but for the moment we are principally concerned with their relationship to the way that images are stored in computers.

There are, in fact, two fundamentally different approaches to this question of representing an image in a computer. The first one uses a method which mimics the way that human beings draw pictures using a pencil or paint brush, in a series of lines. This means that the lines have an obvious natural relationship with the shape of the object being drawn – the lines follow the shape of the object. The second is a method whose logic is much less obvious but relates to the way that television-style monitors operate – using dots laid down in a rectangular, grid-like raster pattern. The differences are best illustrated by imagining the process of converting an existing image, like a drawing or photograph, into the two computer-based forms.

1.4.1 Vector (or line) images

In the first method, an image is considered to be made up of a collection of lines, both straight and curved, each with its own properties like thickness and colour. This method is best suited to the representation of such two-dimensional images as pencil-drawings (for example cartoons and technical illustrations), graphs and architectural or engineering drawings – in fact, any illustration or plan whose elements consist of simple, single-thickness, single-coloured lines with clear edges (see Fig. 1.1).

While such images are usually of two-dimensional objects, simple three-dimensional objects can also be represented using the 'wire-frame' approach. The edges of the surfaces of the object are represented as thin lines so that, for example, a solid cube is depicted as if it were made from twelve straight wires, surrounding the six faces. This method can produce fairly realistic impressions of simple geometrical solids and manufactured objects and is acceptable for many engineering and scientific applications where a stylized, semi-abstract image is acceptable.

These type of images are sometimes called 'calligraphic', a term which is used of handwriting, and implies an image composed of lines, as in written text created by the use of a pen. An alternative, more mathematical, name is a 'vector' image. A vector is a mathematical term for an entity which is usually visualised in terms of lines or arrows and which represents a quantity which has both magnitude and a direction of action. Another term used of this type of drawing, particularly when applied to one created by a mechanical plotting device, is 'stroke-writing'. Other terms which are used are 'line images' or 'line art'.

Storing vector images

The function of any computer display, whether graphic or not, is to give a visual representation of data which is stored in its memory. Many computer users would be unable to say exactly how a set of numbers (in a spreadsheet, for example) was actually stored in a computer's memory but it is taken for granted that a computer can store and process numbers. Given this fact, it follows that any image could also

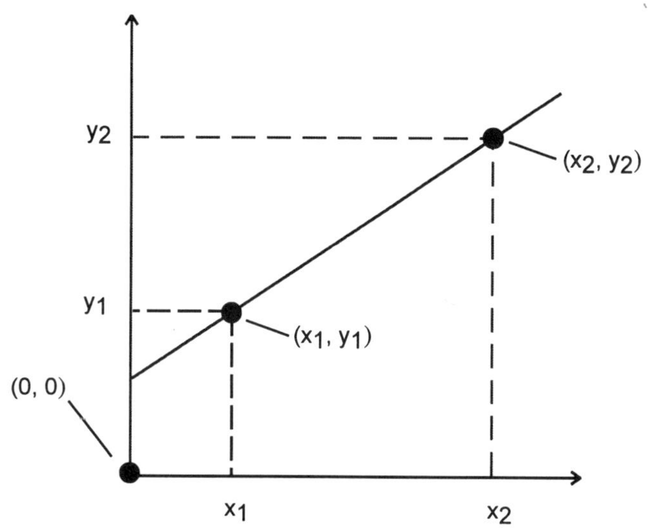

***Fig. 1.3** Cartesian co-ordinates*

be stored if a suitable method of describing the image can be devised which uses a set of numbers. In fact no new technique is needed for storing vector images because a simple method has been used for many years by mathematicians and others for describing line graphs. For example, a straight line can be represented in a computer simply by measuring the positions of its two ends and storing those numbers. The positions of the ends are specified by their 'co-ordinates'. The same general approach is used to specify positions on a map or atlas, where they are called map references.

The term co-ordinate refers to a standard method of fixing a position in space with respect to a system of axes. This involves two or three measurements of distance from some arbitrary system of reference lines (called the axes, and normally taking the form of two or three mutually perpendicular lines in space). Two co-ordinates are sufficient if we are working in two-dimensional space; three co-ordinates (and three axes) are necessary if we are defining a position in three dimensional space. Fig. 1.3 illustrates the widely-used system of two dimensional 'Cartesian' co-ordinates which uses as its axes two mutually perpendicular lines. The co-ordinates of a point are defined as the distances to those lines from the point in question, these distances to be measured along a line perpendicular to the axes and usually designated x and y. Two points in the figure, marked by horizontal and vertical dotted lines, have co-ordinates x_1, y_1 and x_2, y_2. Curved lines can be approximated by treating them as if they were made up from a very large number of very short straight lines or can be matched to a mathematical formula which describes the shape of that curve.

One, early, method of displaying these images used a special type of monitor (called a vector-scan monitor) in which the lines which made up the image were drawn directly on a fluorescent (glowing) screen by an electron beam, in much the same way that an imaginary artist might have drawn them by hand. Copies of the image could also be made on paper by means of a plotter – a device in which a system of motorized moving parts controlled a pen, which drew the lines onto the paper. Details of these and other display and plotting devices are discussed in the chapter on hardware. This, vector, system was a compromise between a fully digital approach and a traditional analogue method. Thus, while the data representing the lines were stored and manipulated in the computer in the usual manner (as digital quantities), displaying the lines involved the computer converting these quantities to suitable analogue (that is, smoothly varying, non-digital) voltages in order to 'drive' the writing process in the monitor – by steering the electron beam which draws the lines on the screen. A similar process went on in the pen-plotter. Vector display systems of this sort are no longer used and yet an increasing proportion of modern images are stored in vector form. In order to display them on the modern raster-scan display they must be converted into a suitable form – a process called scan-conversion or 'rasterization'.

Creating vector images

Although vector images are defined mathematically it would be impractical to expect most users to be able to create them from scratch by specifying these mathematical parameters. Most users do not have the mathematical knowledge and it would, in any case, be a time-consuming process to create circles, rectangles and more complicated shapes like curves in this way. In fact, the shapes must somehow be stored in the computer – either in a permanent form or by loading the description as a piece of software – and in such a way that a user can place them on the screen and make any modifications that might be required. This is usually done by means of applications software, like a drawing package, details of which are discussed in the chapter on application software. The general principle is that the software contains a mathematical description of a whole range of shapes and all that the user does is to choose a shape and provide such details as the dimensions and exact position where the shape is to be placed. For example, if a circle is required, the user chooses that particular shape, probably by clicking on an icon or choosing from a menu. The software 'knows' how to draw a circle – that is, it contains a mathematical 'algorithm' (a series of steps) which will produce a circle on a screen or a printer. The user specifies where the circle is to be, how big it is to be and what colour and thickness of line is required and the software then does the rest. Some examples of such simple graphics algorithms are provided in a later chapter to illustrate the principles that are used.

Not all vector images have a simple geometrical shape like circles and rectangles. Text characters, like the printed letters on this page, can also be considered to be vectors. Early computer systems used to operate in two 'modes' – text mode or graphics mode – but in modern systems all the modes that are commonly used are graphics modes and the commonest graphic object of all is the text character. In that sense, all users of computers are using graphics applications without realizing it. Thus, the handling of text characters has become sufficiently important to the general user of computer systems to deserve a whole chapter to itself and it is treated in some detail later in the book. It is also used later in this section to illustrate some of the basic advantages and dizadvantages of vector images.

Editing vector images

The big advantage of vector images over those created from dots (discussed in the next section) is the ease with which they can be edited. Take the simple example of a circle which has already been discussed. Suppose the user decides that a circle that has been drawn on the screen is in the wrong position, or is the wrong size. The user simply 'edits' the circle. This process of editing takes its name from the term used in the production of books and newspapers where an editor (a person) makes changes to work which has been submitted. In the computing context the term editing is used of any operation in which some existing text or graphics are altered. (The term editor, in computing, however, often describes a piece of software, rather than a person.)

The reason that the editing of vector objects is so simple is that the object was created using an in-built algorithm, based on information provided by the user. This means that editing is simply a matter of removing the old version of the object (the circle, in our example) and then creating a new version of the same object, using the same algorithm, but with different information – say its size, or its position, or the colour of the line. For the computer to be able easily to remove the old version of the object, it is necessary for it to have a record of all the component objects that make up the vector graphic image and maintaining such a list is an important part of the function of such vector software. It can therefore be seen that, strictly speaking, editing is not so much a process of altering an object as removing the object entirely and replacing it with a new one. It is only because of the speed of the computer that graphic objects, when edited, usually appear as if they were being transformed gradually and smoothly from one state to another. In fact, the old object is completely removed and a new one put in its place and this might occur many times in the course of an editing operation where, for example, an object is apparently being 'stretched' by the user to a new size.

Printing vector images

Vector images can be printed as vectors (lines drawn directly on the paper) using a vector hard-copy device which has already been mentioned briefly and which is called a pen plotter. The principal advantage of the this type of printer is that these devices can draw images on very large sheets of paper whereas most desktop printers are restricted to A4 or A3 size. Pen plotters are ideally suited for producing engineering drawings and architectural plans. However, most vector images are printed using exactly the same printers as those used for bit-mapped images, the computer having previously 'scan-converted' the image into a bit-map. Since this is the first occasion in this book that the term 'bit-map' has been used, it is a good place to discuss this very important idea.

1.4.2 Dot-matrix (or raster) images

The second method of representing an image in a computer, using dots instead of lines, can be thought of as a process rather like that of 'sampling' an original analogue image. To explain this idea at its simplest – for a black-and-white image – imagine taking an existing image, say a pencil-drawing, and then placing a

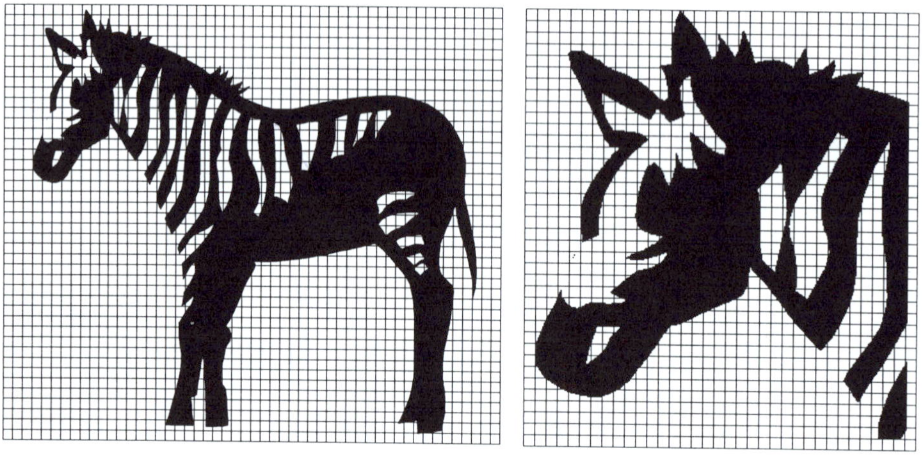

Fig. 1.4 *An image with a grid-like structure placed on top. The second image shows a detail, taken from the first. In the second image, the grid is finer than the one in the first.*

rectangular grid (like a piece of graph-paper, printed on transparent material) over the picture. The next stage is to make some measurement of what is found in each cell of the grid, representing that by a number and recording the result separately for each cell. The simplest way of doing this is to record whether the picture is light or dark in each cell and representing this by a 0 or a 1. Fig. 1.4 shows this process applied to a simple representation of a zebra, and in detail to part of the image. In the second image, each square has been further subdivided in order to make the grid finer since this will lead to a more detailed representation of the original, when digitized. Imagine, now, that, every cell in the grid is 'coded' with 0's and 1's. A '0' is recorded whenever a cell is mostly, or entirely, light. A '1' is recorded whenever a cell is mostly, or entirely, dark. Because the dots are recorded in a rectangular grid, this system is often referred to as a 'dot-matrix', since in mathematics a rectangular array of rows and columns is called a matrix. These dots are called 'picture elements', a term which is usually shortened to 'pixels' or even 'pels'.

It will be seen, in the chapter on graphics hardware, that the document scanner performs exactly this sampling process, described above, though most modern scanners can record colour and grey-level images as well as two-level monochrome ones. The scanner has become an extremely important way of creating digitized images for use in computers and recently-developed digital cameras perform a very similar task. It will also be seen later that most modern display and print-out devices use the same dot-matrix approach also. One particular type of printer has become popularly known as a 'dot-matrix printer' but in fact virtually all computer printers print dots in a rectangular matrix. What this means is that the dot-matrix format can be used, not just for storing images, but for inputting them, displaying and printing them also. When images are stored as vectors, on the other hand, it is usually necessary for them to undergo a conversion process – either from the vector format to the dot-matrix format for display or printing, or from a digital format to an analogue format if analogue devices like pen-plotters are used to print the images. It should be recognized, however, that though the term 'dot-matrix' is a perfectly logical one for a wide range of printers and display devices it has, for historical reasons, become associated only with a largely, obsolete printing device and the terms used are usually the 'bit-map' (defined later in the text) and the raster.

In that the digitization process, described above, starts with a smoothly-varying (called an 'analogue') picture and produces a series of dots – each represented digitally by a number – it is similar to many other modern technologies, like the recording of music on a compact-disc (CD). In the production of a CD, a sound wave is converted by a microphone to an electrical wave-form, which is a smoothly varying analogue of the original sound waves. This is then repeatedly sampled by a high-speed electronic circuit, at short time intervals, and converted into a stream of digits which are then stored in the form of tiny pits in the surface of the disc. Increasingly, because of the importance of the computer as an all-purpose information processor, many technologies are using a variation of this technique of sampling analogue data and storing the results in digital form.

Creating raster images

One obvious way of creating raster images has already been described – that of digitizing an existing image like a photograph using a device like a document scanner or digital camera. Existing lines and other regions of colour of many shapes are sampled and converted into numbers. There are two other techniques, however. The first is very similar to the method discussed for creating geometrical shapes in the section on vector images: the shapes are stored as mathematical algorithms and drawn on the screen under user control in a drawing package. This raises an obvious question – how is this different from a vector image, if it is created in the same way? The answer is that, though created in the same way, the image is stored in a different way – in fact, as a 'bit-map'.

The third method is very simple. Images can be drawn freehand using a pointing device like a mouse or light-pen. In fact, vector images can also be drawn freehand but the techniques are different and the details must be reserved until the chapter on graphics application software. In the case of raster images the movement of the mouse is detected and translated by the drawing software into dots on the screen.

Storing raster images – 'bit maps'

It has been seen that vector images are stored as a list of the various geometrical shapes which make up the image, together with information such as the position of each shape, the line thickness and colour. Clearly raster images cannot be stored in the same way. Raster images are defined as a set of dots – pixels – which are arranged in parallel lines and so the storage method must reflect that fact. The simplest image would be one where all parts of the image are either black or white – a monochrome image. In this case all that has to be recorded is whether a particular

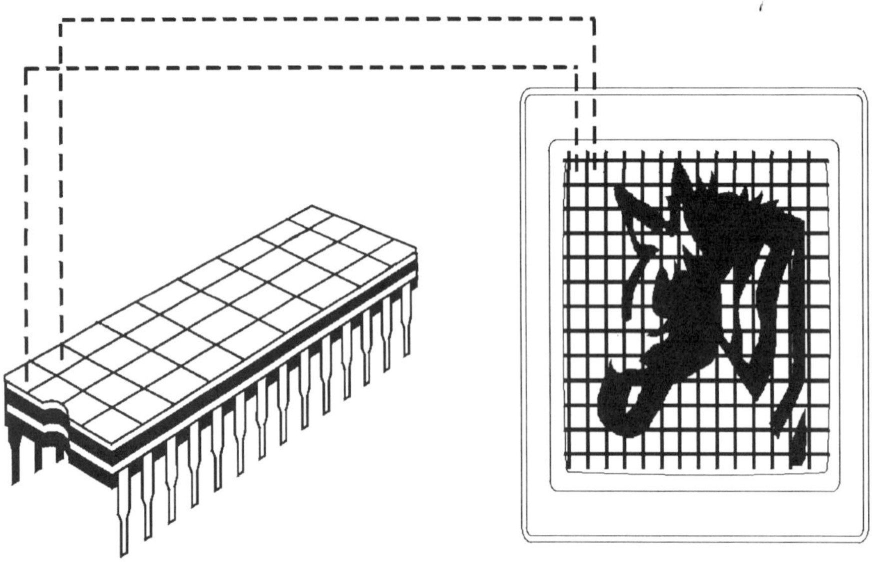

Fig. 1.5 *Bit mapping: each pixel on the screen is 'mapped' to a corresponding region of memory – one or more bits per pixel*

pixel in the matrix is black or white and in a computer memory this can be represented using only one 'bit' of information. A bit can, of course, have one of two states – usually represented as 0 or 1 – and so 0 can be used to represent black and 1 to represent white. This means that a byte of memory (eight bits) can be used to store the graphic content of eight pixels and the simplest method is to record in one byte the state of eight consecutive pixels in a raster-line (see Fig. 1.5). This way of storing information is called 'bit-mapping'. The portion of computer memory which is set aside to store the image is called by a variety of names such as the 'refresh buffer', the 'display memory', the 'frame store' and the 'video RAM'. The process can be thought of as storing an electronic map of the image – one or more bits in the map representing the state of each pixel in the image. A map, of course, is a diagrammatic representation of a real object – usually a geographical region – in which there is a simple one-to-one relationship between the object and the map, though normally drawn to a reduced scale. Here, the object is the image and the map is the electronic state of a series of memory locations.

Editing raster images

Because of the completely different way that raster images are stored it is inevitable that editing processes will be of a different kind. At its simplest, raster images are stored as a collection of bits in a bit map and editing can take place only at the level of the individual bits – that is pixel-by-pixel. Take the example of a drawing package which offers the facility to draw curved lines, of any shape, by freehand sketching, using a mouse. If the software were creating vector images then the shape of the curve, once drawn, would be stored as a mathematical description in the list of objects which constitute the whole image. Editing could then be done in the way described in an earlier section. If, on the other hand, the software is designed to create bit-mapped images then the shape of the curve will be stored simply as a collection of pixels on the screen (and therefore bits in the refresh-buffer) of a particular colour, and in a particular shape, as determined by the drawing process. There is no easy way to isolate them from all the other pixels, of various colours, which make up the picture. In many cases the human eye is probably the best way of separating the pixels which specify the curve from those that make up the rest of the image. Often the only way of editing such a shape – for example, to remove it from the picture – is for the user laboriously to change the colour of each pixel back to the original colour (the background colour). This can be done with the aid of a 'zoom' facility that enlarges the image in such a way that each pixel is easily identified and changed (see Plates 1a and 1b). An alternative method which is available where there is plenty of computer memory, is for the software to keep temporary copies of the picture at various stages of the drawing process so that it can 'restore' an earlier state of the image when something goes wrong. This is rather like keeping back-up copies of a document, in addition to the latest version, when word-processing, so that the author can go back to an earlier version if necessary.

In addition to changing individual pixels by hand, as just described, a whole array of mathematically-based editing techniques has arisen, largely for the purpose of modifying scanned photographs and some of these are described under the section on Photo-retouching software in the chapter on applications software.

1.5 Digital Fonts

The use of digital fonts has become sufficiently important to all users of computer graphics for the subject to be treated in some detail in a later chapter but a brief introduction can serve as a useful example of the value of vector image storage. It should stressed at this stage that although early computer graphic systems used a special type of display (the vector-display) that was ideally suited to drawing vector images directly on a fluorescent screen, all modern systems now use raster displays. These are obviously ideally suited to the display of bit-mapped images because there is a direct correspondence between the state of the bits stored in computer memory and the colour of the pixels in the raster pattern on the screen. It might seem to be obvious that the storage of images as vectors would quickly become as redundant as the vector display hardware, and yet the opposite has happened. Vector-based images have actually grown in importance over the years. Why?

The simple answer is that in many areas of application, vector images are much more flexible and can produce much higher-quality results and digital fonts provide a good example. Early computers used fonts which were stored as collections of dots ('bit-mapped' fonts) and this was fine as long as the user didn't want either to

Fig. 1.6 When a character is digitized, each rectangular pixel must be either all black or all white and so the original smooth outline is lost in a series of steps

display a larger version of the font or to print the font. For example, let us suppose that the font was '10 point'. Points are a measure of the size of the font – used by typographers – and 10 point corresponds to the sort of size used in a printed book. It is inevitable that when small characters are composed using dots which are spaced at about 72 per inch (the sort of spacing that is used in a computer display) that many compromises have to be made which affect the quality of the character (see Fig. 1.6). However, there is no reason why these compromises need be as deleterious to the quality of the final result if the character is scaled up to, say, 60 points, for a large headline. A much larger character will include many more dots and so a much higher quality character can be created because the finer details of the shape can be more precisely matched by the dots. Fig. 1.7 illustrates this effect. The letter 'n' is displayed using very few pixels (6 × 5), then with more pixels (9 × 10) and finally with even more pixels (32 × 32). The first corresponds to the character displayed at a very small point size and the other two with the same character at larger sizes – using more pixels. The results have been scaled to the same size for comparison. Clearly the higher quality of the third example would not be achieved simply by magnifying the first character – enlarging the dot size in the process. And yet, this is all that could be done if the character were stored as a single bit map.

One solution – used in the early days – is to store many different bit-maps of the characters, one for each size that might be needed, but this uses a lot of memory and in fact only a few popular sizes are likely to be available – 8 point, 10 point, 12 point, 16 point, 20 point, 36 point, 48 point, 60 point for example. The, much better, alternative is to store the basic shape of the letters as a set of vectors and to create a bit-map of a particular size of letter when it is needed – 9.5 point, for example. This is a process known as scan-conversion – converting a vector description into a set of bits (and therefore pixels) to fit a raster-scan. The disadvantage of this method is that it takes time to do this conversion but modern computers are well able cope with this even though early ones would have taken too long for it to be a practical proposition.

The advantages outlined here – in terms of quality – also apply when it comes to printing the result. Printers use many more dots per inch than displays (a minimum of 300 per inch, as compared with 72) and are therefore inherently capable of higher-quality output. It would be absurd to use a bit-mapped font which has been designed for a 72-dot-per-inch (dpi) screen when printing at 300 or more dpi using a laser printer. Of course, as with screens, it is possible to create separate printer-fonts,

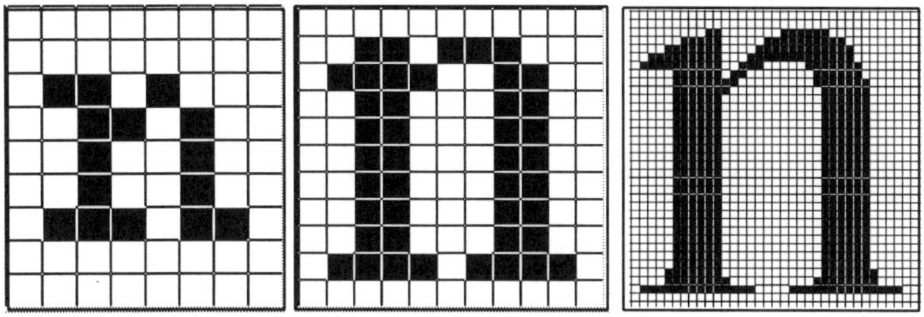

***Fig. 1.7** The quality of a character improves as more pixels are used*

designed for the larger number of dots, and this system has been used, but the same approach of creating the fonts from a basic vector description is much more satisfactory. This feature of vector fonts (and vector images generally) is sometimes described as 'device-independence'. This means that the description of the graphic object, because it is held as a mathematical formula, is stored in a form that is independent of any particular display or printing device. When the time comes for it to be displayed or printed it then acts as the starting point for the scan-conversion process and this then produces a bit-mapped version of that shape that is the best that that particular device can handle.

1.6 Printing Raster Images

In an earlier discussion on colour an important point was made concerning the use of primary-coloured dots to simulate many other shades and colours, as an alternative to the use of 'spot colour' (specially mixed colours). This technique, known as 'dithering', is fundamental to the production of all 'tonal' images and is discussed in greater detail in the chapter on colour. At this stage it is enough to say that virtually all computer raster-style printers are restricted to placing dots of black, or one of three (or more) primary colours, on the paper and that any other colours or grey-levels can be simulated only by dithering.

1.7 Digitization and Colour

'Sampling' an image to create a bit-map has been discussed, so far, largely in terms of monochrome pictures – the pixels are either white or black. The process of digitization – turning a smoothly changing (analogue) image into numbers – can be thought of, in this case, as 'spatial digitization' (digitizing, or chopping-up space into little units called pixels). There are however, two extra complications which must be mentioned. One is that many images are 'tonal' – made up from many shades of grey or other colours. The other is that the process of chopping up space into little lumps and representing those lumps by a single number inevitably results in a loss of detail.

Table 1.1 A truth table for a three-colour display system

Red	Green	Blue	Resultant Colour
0	0	0	Black
0	0	1	Blue
0	1	0	Green
0	1	1	Cyan
1	0	0	Red
1	0	1	Magenta
1	1	0	Yellow
1	1	1	White

The first complication can be dealt with by adding to the idea of spatial digitization that of intensity digitization. Strictly speaking, we have already done that without perhaps noticing it. Even a monochrome image already has both forms of digitization because each pixel (the 'chopped-up' region of space) has also been digitized into values of intensity; it is just that we have only allowed for two intensity states – all or nothing, white or black, 1 or 0. To cope with tonal and 'coloured' images we must allow for a greater range of intensity values in each pixel. For example, a black-and-white photograph can be digitized by allowing every pixel to have, say, one of 16 intensity values, or 'grey-levels'. Two of these will still be the extremes of black and white but the other 14 will be intermediate values of grey. The same principle can be used on 'coloured' images (i.e. images which use colours other than black, grey and white). In this case each pixel is considered to be made up from three primary colours and the digitization process specifies the intensity of each of these primary colours, for each pixel – producing three different numbers instead of one. What is clear is that these processes will generate more numbers (and also bigger numbers) than the digitization of monochrome images. For example, a 16 grey-scale image will require that we store any number from 0 to 15 for each pixel, not 0 to 1, and this will need more memory. In fact it takes four bits to store a number in the range 0 to 15 (decimal) and so, such an image will need four times as much memory as a monochrome image with the same number of pixels.

This requirement for more memory, if more colours were to be stored, was one of the factors that restricted the use of colour in early computer systems. It is only fairly recently that thousands, and even millions, of colours have become normal in desktop computer displays, though as the hardware chapter will show, memory limitations were not the only limiting factor.

1.7.1 How many colours?

The earliest computers didn't offer colour displays but this was more to do with the cost of the hardware than memory restrictions because, when colour was introduced on the IBM-PC, for example, only four colours were provided, compared with a larger number of grey-levels which were already available, and which required more memory. It was soon established that an absolute minimum for a colour system should be at least eight colours, which are provided by assigning one bit to each of the three primary colours (red, green and blue). With a very simple colour system like this each pixel can exist in one of eight states – according to whether or not each of the three primary colours is present. This is most easily seen in a truth table (see Table 1.1). This is still a simple on-off system, like the monochrome system first discussed, except that the on-off now applies to each of the three primary colours independently. In the table, a *zero* signifies that the primary colour is absent and a *one* that it is present. For more colours, each of the primary colour components must be digitized into more than two levels, as in the eight-grey level system discussed. Top end, 'photo-realistic' colour systems which are increasingly available even on ordinary desktop computers are systems where each of the primary colours is digitized into 256 levels which produces 256 × 256 × 256 colours = 16,777,216 (often referred to as 16.8 million) colours.

1.8 Loss of Detail

The second problem mentioned above is that of the loss of detail when an analogue image is represented as a series of pixels. Consider again the case, discussed earlier, where an imaginary grid is placed over an image and for each grid cell we record what is found in the cell. Originally we recorded only whether the contents of a cell were white or black. Now we know that we could equally well have recorded a level of grey or a colour but the problem still applies and we will, for simplicity, continue to use the example of a monochrome image.

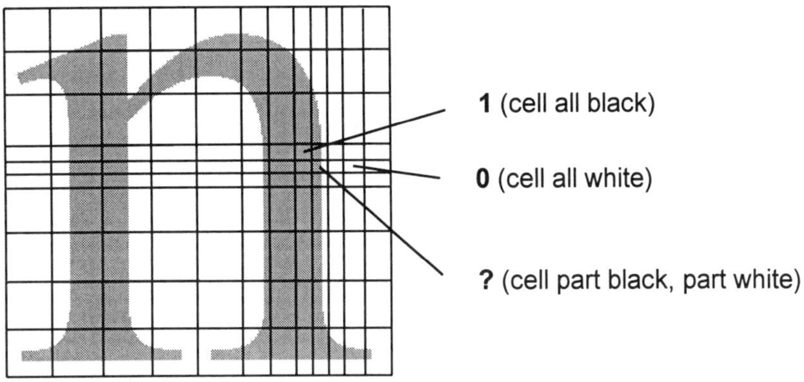

Fig. 1.8 Problems in deciding how to 'code' pixels that are neither all black nor all white

It is obvious that it is not likely that the intensity will be always be completely uniform within a cell, though it may be in many. Where it is not uniform – as in the cell labelled with a question mark in Fig. 1.8 – neither of the values 1 or 0 is really appropriate and yet some value must be given. In these cases the only solution is to treat the cell as if it were all black, if there is more black than white in it, or all white

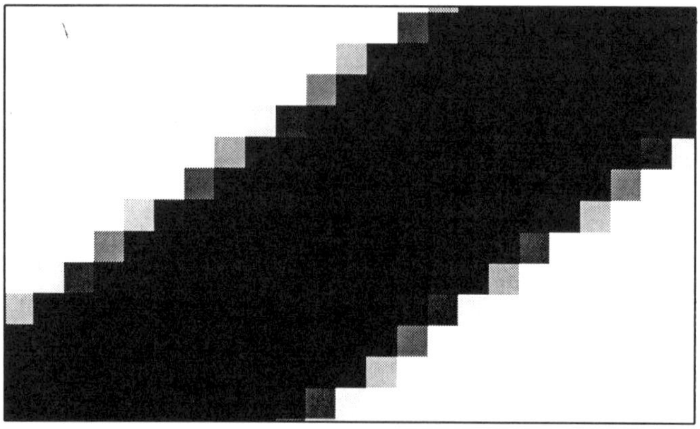

Fig. 1.9 *A straight line, highly magnified, showing the use of grey pixels in anti-aliasing*

if there is more white than black. This process inevitably results in the loss of fine details in the image since a cell, though it contains both black and white portions in the original, is reduced to a single intensity value, as if it had only one of those colours in it. What this means is that when an analogue image is digitized, as in a document scanner, the result is never a completely faithful copy of the original. A similar problem often exists even when the final image has not been created by scanning an existing analogue image. The simplest example is that of a diagonal straight line which might be created by any drawing package. Because the line is represented by a series of square pixels on a rectangular grid it appears on the screen, not as a nice smooth-sided straight line, but as something which resembles a staircase. This effect of lines appearing rather jagged, like the teeth on a saw, is sometimes referred to as 'the jaggies'.

The aesthetic effects associated with this problem can be improved by the use of grey-levels. The technique is called 'anti-aliasing'. It involves filling in the angular, step-like, edges of a jagged line, straight or otherwise, with pixels which are displayed at a lower intensity than the line itself. This has the effect of producing a smoother transition across the boundary of the object and removing the harsh angular step-like edges (see Fig. 1.9).

The best way to improve the quality of the digitized image – at least in principle – is to use more cells in the sampling grid, so producing more pixels. Imagine drawing a broad diagonal line in three sections, each one being drawn with smaller pixels than the previous one (by splitting each pixel into one of half the length and half the breadth) – see Fig. 1.10. It is clear that the quality of the line improves as the pixels get smaller and the digitized line gets closer and closer to its ideal. It also becomes clear why printed output often looks so much better than that displayed on the computer screen. It is simply because laser printers, for example, use 300 – 1200 pixels per inch whereas screens operate at about 72 per inch. The printed output has hundreds or even thousands of times more dots (which are correspondingly much smaller).

1.8.1 Precision and resolution

In the last section we arrived at a very important general principle of computer graphics which relates to the precision with which an image is stored and the amount of information contained in it. We saw that an image which is digitized using a large number of small pixels is of better quality than one which uses fewer,

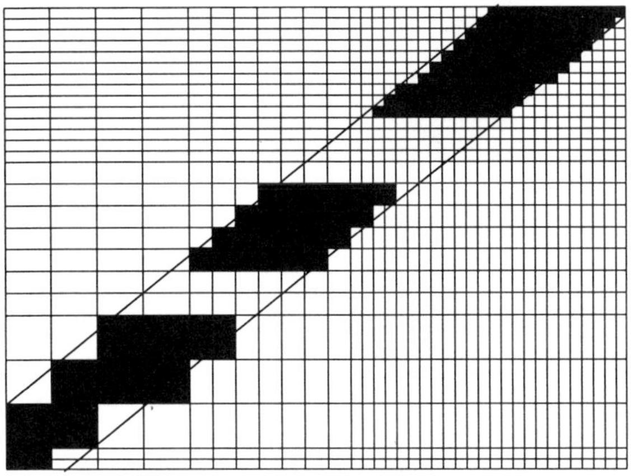

Fig. 1.10 The effect of jagged edges is reduced when more, smaller, pixels are used

larger pixels. The term quality, here, relates to the amount of detail in the original or 'perfect' image, which is preserved in the digitized version. In passing, it is worth pointing out that exactly the same principle applies to intensity and colour digitization as to spatial digitization. The term that is used to refer to the amount of detail in an image is 'resolution'. Strictly speaking the term should be 'spatial resolution' since the general idea of resolution is used in many areas of science and here it is being applied to space or distance but it could equally be applied to 'colour resolution'. Its general meaning is that of the degree of fine detail which is measurable in some quantity. In this case spatial resolution is a measure of the fine differences in position in space and this translates into the number of pixels per line or per unit length of image. A computer image which is made up from a large number of pixels contains more information than one which is made up of a few and will be a better approximation to the original (or ideal) image it represents.

The general principle is familiar to most readers through the computer graphic manipulation of images, widely used on television, called pixelling. In this effect a normal TV image is progressively displayed in a smaller and smaller number of (larger and larger sized) picture elements. The picture is progressively less and less recognizable. Sometimes the effect is applied selectively to a person's face in television interviews so that he or she cannot be recognized. In Fig. 1.11 the same picture is reporoduced three times – one using 250 × 206 pixels, one using 100 × 83 pixels and one using 30 × 25 pixels.

It is worth asking the question – how small do the pixels need to be? If using smaller pixels produces a better quality image then how small ought they to be? The answer can only depend on the context. If it is necessary to preserve every feature of the original then it is necessary to choose pixels which are as small as the smallest feature of the original. This begs the question – 'how small is that?' – and the answer, again, depends on the particular case. In general, all images, though we may

***Fig. 1.11** An image becomes progressively less recognizable as fewer and fewer pixels are used*

think of them as analogue (i.e. smoothly varying; having no step-like structure) must in fact be made up of basic units of a finite size, though they may not be visible to the unaided eye. A helpful example from the field of images can be found in photography. A photograph examined under a suitable microscope can be seen to be made up of fine crystals or grains – the density or blackness of the picture at any point being a reflection of the number of these grains per unit area. If the photograph is over-enlarged we can often see a 'grainy' image even with the naked eye. This is because the excessive enlargement has produced grains which are so large as to be visible. Normally the grains are not detectable and so the unaided eye sees only a continuous image. Similarly, high quality printed images of both text and photographs also consist of a very large number of tiny dots too small for the eye to notice but in cheaper versions of the printing process such as those used to reproduce photographs in newspapers the dot structure can easily be seen with the aid of a magnifying glass. Even in the world of art, not all painting has been done by the continuous processes described earlier in the chapter – the 'Pointillist' school of Impressionists quite deliberately created their pictures from a very large number of dots.

All this has a bearing on our question – how small should the pixels be? Clearly a digitized image will look like a continuous image if the pixels are smaller than the eye can detect. If, on the other hand, there is any intention of magnifying the image at any stage, it is necessary to reduce the size of the pixels to the point where they cannot be seen even when magnified. The context will determine how big the pixels should be. It might seem sensible to simply use the smallest possible pixel size at all times and so be 'on the safe side'. The objection to this is that the smaller the pixels, the more there are and therefore the more information which has to be stored. This is a classic 'trade-off' for computer graphics – quality versus quantity. High quality implies a greater quantity of data which means, for example, that fewer images could be stored on a floppy disc. As will be seen in the chapter on hardware, there are other, related problems with high quality images. If they contain more information it will take longer to move them from one place to another, for example, which means that it takes longer to load a high quality image from a disc, for display on the screen. As a result, some systems for storing digitized photographs on CD-Roms, for example, actually store six different versions of the photograph, digitized in different amounts of detail. This means that if it is necessary to display the image highly magnified the more detailed image can be used; if it is to be displayed in a small 'snap-shot' size then a less detailed one can be loaded instead – saving time.

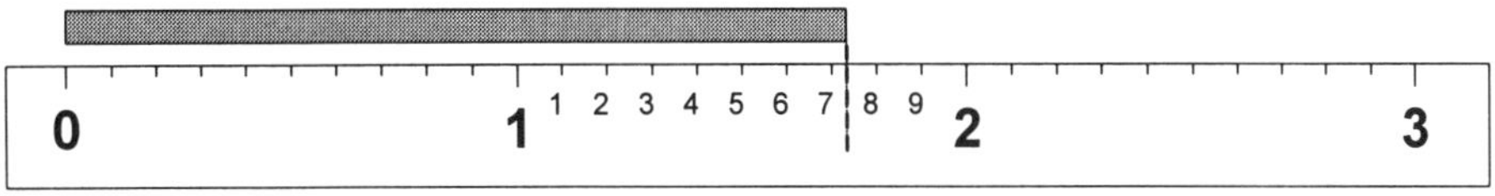

Fig. 1.12 Estimating the length of a rod using a ruler

1.8.2 Precision and accuracy

The previous section implies that when a continuous image is digitized, information is lost – unless the pixels that are used are so small that they correspond to the smallest basic unit of the original image. It is worthwhile extending this discussion to make two important points – one concerns a matter of terminology and the other asks a basic question – 'what information is actually lost in the process of digitization?'.

The question of terminology relates to two words which are often confused – precision and accuracy. Measurements of any kind can only be done with limited precision and many measurements are quite deliberately performed with a precision which is less than could be achieved. The term 'inaccurate' as it is used in common parlance, on the other hand, carries with it the suggestion of fault or mistake either in the measuring device or in the operator. An inaccurate measurement seems to be one in which the measured result differs from the ideal or 'true' result more than is necessary – and by mistake or carelessness. It implies that the true or correct result could be achieved with sufficient care. The precision of a measurement, however, is a more neutral term and is simply a quantity which describes how near a measured result is to the ideal; it carries no suggestion of fault or error.

These distinctions can be clarified by two simple examples. Suppose we are asked to say how many people live in a certain village and by mistake we give the result as 113 when there are really 115. This would be an inaccurate answer – it is 'not true'. On the other hand, we might have been asked to give the number 'to the nearest ten', in which case the correct answer would be 110 or 'about 110'. The implication of quoting a value 'to the nearest ten' is that only limited precision is needed for a particular purpose; the exact figure is not needed. Suppose, now, we are now asked to measure the length of a steel rod (Fig. 1.12). We could measure it with a variety of different instruments and obtain many different answers simply because some instruments are capable of greater precision than others. One instrument will measure the length with a precision of one part in ten, another with a precision of one part in a thousand and another with a precision of one part in a million. The answers come out to : 1.7 cms, 1.73 cms and 1.72947 cms respectively. Which of these three is correct? Assuming no careless operator errors, the answer is that all are correct, but some are more precise than others.

The important difference between the two cases is that in the first case it is possible to give the answer with complete accuracy (because it is a whole number – an integer) and in the second case there is no completely accurate answer. All scientific measurements are made with a specified precision but there is virtually no limit to the precision which might, in principle, be used.

1.8.3 What level of precision is needed?

Let us now look at the effect of a particular level of precision in the digitization of images. The two measurements to which the question applies are those of position and intensity level (or colour). First, consider measurements of position.

Clearly there is no point in defining or measuring the lengths of the components of an image with a precision greater than that with which they can be displayed (or printed). Let us assume that we wish only to display the digitized image. The precision with which positions are measured or specified usually depends on the

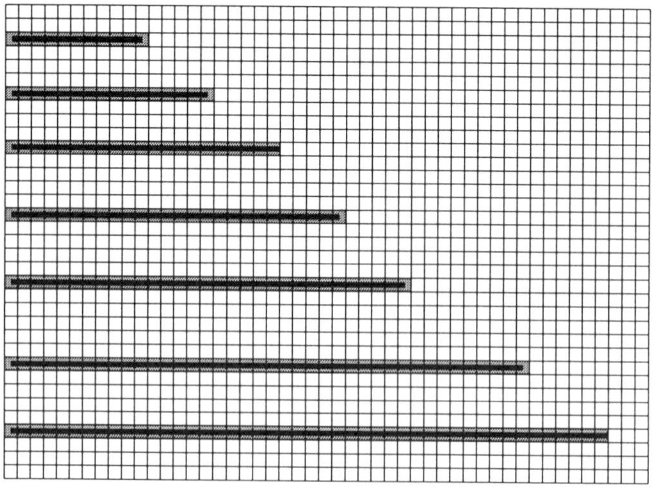

Fig. 1.13 Longer lines can be represented more precisely than shorter lines

number of squares in the grid used to display the pixels. These will vary from something like 640 × 480 in a home computer to something like 1600 × 1200, or better, in a professional graphics workstation. Fig. 1.13 shows a number of 'ideal' straight lines (the dark lines) together with a digitization grid. Most of the lines have ends which do not coincide exactly with the grid boundaries and so there must be some loss of precision when they are displayed as pixels (the grey squares). Each line can be represented only by a whole number of pixels and so whether the pixels at the two ends are counted as 'on' or 'off' depends on the proportion of the pixel which is occupied by the ideal line. Thus if the grid has 1000 × 1000 cells then a line which is as long as the image can be represented to an accuracy of about one part in 1000 as a result of the rounding process. On a display based on 500 by 500 pixels the precision can only be half this – one part in 500. A line which is only half as long as the whole image can be represented with only half the precision of the longer line – one part in 500 and one part in 250 respectively. A very short line, equivalent to, say, 50 pixels, can be represented only with a precision of about 1 part in 50. The same effect can be seen by referring back to Fig. 1.6. The smoothly curving edge of the original character must be approximated by a number of square pixels, each of which can be only on or off.

The same principles apply when measuring the intensity or colour of the pixel. The precision with which intensities and colours are measured depends on the display (or printing) system. The minimum precision, of course is two levels – usually, but not necessarily, black and white. This may be sufficient for the display of text but is not adequate for graphics except for line drawings. Some computer systems use 'grey-level' monitors, meaning monochrome devices, but most modern displays are colour devices. The number of colours depends very much on the particular display 'graphics adapter' (see next chapter) but thousands of colours have become the norm and this might seem to be quite enough for all practical purposes. To explain why this is not necessarily so, is left for an extended discussion of colour later in the book. The maximum normally encountered is 256 levels for each of the three primary colour components, giving over 16 million possibilities.

1.9 Windows and zoom effects

One way of coping with this problem of limited precision in the display of an image is to store sufficient data for a larger or more detailed image in the computer but to display only partial views of it. There are two ways of doing this. If the image is stored as a set of pixels then the screen normally displays only a part of that complete stored image – a sub-set of those pixels – corresponding to a rectangular region in any part of the complete image. It is as if the screen acts as a window, revealing part of the outside world but obscuring the rest. To see other parts of the image, either it (the image) or the window, must be moved – it amounts to the same thing – but the whole image can never be displayed at one time except by the use of an output device like a printer which is able to display more dots per line, or by discarding much of the detailed information.

The other approach is practical only if the image is stored in vector form so that measurements of the components of the image can be stored with considerable precision. This method offers images which are displayed in varying degrees of detail according to the proportion of the total picture which is being displayed. The views can either be large areas, perhaps the whole of the image, shown with limited detail or they can be small areas shown in much fuller detail, perhaps with the precision of the original measurements. Thus, for example, architectural data might be stored about a building. The detail needed to specify the whole building would be too much to display in a single view and so the software would be designed to give a view of the whole building with relatively little detail – such as an observer would see from a distance. There would be a facility, however, to 'zoom-in' on part of the building and see that part in more detail. Even if more detail cannot be seen, the quality does not deteriorate; there is no sign, in Fig. 1.14, of the sort of pixellation seen in Fig. 1.2. See also Plates 2a and 2b.

This sort of facility cannot easily be provided when the image is stored simply as a collection of pixels, unless a number of different versions of the image are created – at different values of resolution. This approach has been used to store digitized photographs. A format created by Kodak to archive images on a CD stores five versions of each image : 'Wallet' (128 × 192 pixels), 'Snapshot' (256 × 384 pixels), 'Standard' (512 × 768 pixels), 'Large' (1024 × 1536 pixels) and 'Poster' (2048 × 3072 pixels). An alternative would be to store only the highest resolution version of the image and then use special software to generate lower resolution versions as required. This would save storage space but increase the time required before any particular image could be seen.

Fig. 1.14 *Image quality does not deteriorate when a vector image is 'zoomed'*

In contrast, the vector approach requires that full details concerning the component parts are stored in vector form and that conversion to pixel form is performed only when the view has been selected. Fortunately printing and plotting devices are able to produce pictures with much more detail than display devices and so when the design of the building is complete it is still possible to produce a final hard-copy of the whole image even if it is not possible to obtain such an image using the interactive display device.

The same technique is used in desk-top publishing and other graphics software where a zoom image may display a portion of a page exactly as it will appear when printed – with diagrams, photographs and text in whatever typeface has been selected. To see the complete page, however, the best that can be managed with a moderately-good, medium resolution display (say 800 × 600 pixels) is a rough approximation in which it may not even be possible to read individual words but nevertheless the overall layout of the page is apparent.

Exercises for the Reader:

(1) *The following is a question which arises naturally from some of the material in the first chapter but a complete answer cannot be found in that chapter. It is designed to make you think about a simple but important matter; part of the answer is to be found later in the book.* A computer stores all its data – whether spreadsheet files, word processor documents or pictures – as a set of numbers in binary format. How then does it 'know' how to interpret a sequence of binary bits in a file (such as 01101010 10001101 etc) ? How is it possible to tell if such a sequence is a picture, and not a document, and if it is a picture, how is that picture re-constructed from the binary bits?

(2) Look at a monochrome newspaper photograph through a good magnifying glass. Describe what you see. How, exactly, are the dots used to simulate a variety of shades of grey? Now, do the same exercise with a coloured photograph, as printed in a newspaper, to see how colours are simulated. If you have a very strong magnifying glass or a low-powered microscope, repeat the exercise a third time, with a photograph printed in a glossy magazine (where the dots are smaller). Look also at any areas of a single colour to see if they are created by primary-coloured dots or are 'spot' colours.

(3) If you have access to a colour printer, print a coloured image and then compare the print with the original image, as displayed on the screen. What differences can you see? Now, change the settings (for example, the contrast and brightness) on the monitor and also alter the viewing conditions (for example, the amount of light falling on the screen). What conclusions do you come to about the relationship between images which have been printed on paper and those which are viewed on a screen?

(4) Take a piece of graph paper and draw a thick, straight line on it using a felt-tip pen or marker. Imagine that the paper represents a computer screen and that the small squares on the graph paper represents pixels. Now, count the number of pixels in the line you have drawn and calculate how many bytes of memory would be needed to store this line as a bit-map. Now compare this with the storage requirement of the same line if it were stored as a vector, using co-ordinates.

(5) Using another piece of graph paper, draw a simple picture. The picture should either be a line-image using a thick felt-tip pen (one which is a few pixels wide) or an image with dark shaded areas. Now, identify which 'pixels' are clearly made up entirely of one colour (black or white) and which pixels contain both colours. For each of the latter, decide whether it is to be considered as black or white, on the basis of which is the majority colour. Now draw a new version of the picture with those pixels in the new state (entirely one colour or the other). What proportion of the total number of pixels did you have to change in this way? How might this proportion change with a different type of picture?

(6) Look carefully at the way that bit-mapped characters are defined – using the 'Paintbrush' package supplied with Microsoft Windows 3.1 (re-named 'Paint' in Windows-95). Follow these steps. Open a DOS window while running MS-Windows (Windows provides a DOS icon for this purpose). Maximize the window so that the characters are at maximum size. Press the PrtScr

(PrintScreen) key while holding down the Alt key (this 'grabs' a copy of the active window into the clip-board area of memory). Close the DOS window and run the Paint program. Press the Crtl-V key combination to paste the contents of the clip-board into Paint. Magnify a portion of this image using the zoom facility so that you can see the individual pixels that make up the characters. In Windows 3.1 this effect is very clear because with zoom setting a grid is placed over the image automatically. In Windows-95, switch on the grid (using the View/Zoom menu) to see the same effect. Copy a few of the characters onto graph paper. This is a simple bit-mapped font.

(7) Again, using graph paper as a model of a bit-mapped screen, show the effects of pixelling on an image. Find a simple piece of monochrome clip art (for example, from those supplied with MS-Word or some other word processor). Display it on screen and 'grab' it as before. View it in 'Paint'. Zoom into a portion of the image, switch on the grid and copy some of it to graph paper. Now make a pixellated version by amalgamating each 2 × 2 group of pixels into one pixel (four times the size of the original pixels). The colour of the new pixel will be the majority colour of the four constituent pixels. This exercise can then be repeated a number of times to see the progressive deterioration in image quality.

2

Graphics Hardware

2.1 Introduction

Stunning examples of computer graphics can be seen almost daily on television and there seems to be almost no limit to the effects that can be achieved, other than the limits which are imposed by time and the imagination of the designer. However, it should be remembered that these brilliant effects are achieved with the use of equipment costing hundreds of thousands of pounds and that most practitioners of computer graphics are limited by the much cheaper hardware at their disposal (to say nothing of the limits of their imagination!).

In the previous chapter we discussed the digitized image using such general concepts as pixels, colours and grey-levels. In this chapter we shall look in more detail at the equipment used to create, record and display digitized images, to see how in practice these general concepts are realized and to discover how the characteristics of this equipment impose practical limitations on the quality of computer graphic images. The limitations imposed by the software will be explored in later chapters.

The most important piece of hardware in a computer graphics system – other than the computer itself – is the display device, since it is through the screen that images are seen in an interactive manner. The use of the term interactive here is important because although it is perfectly possible to create representations of an image in the computer without a display device, images which can then be permanently recorded on paper, film or video, if there is no immediate display of the image then there is no chance to make changes or correct mistakes and no way to respond to the image in 'real time'. Many of the advantages of computer graphics and many of its important applications are therefore lost. Thus we shall begin by discussing display devices.

2.2 Display Devices

2.2.1 The cathode ray tube

The commonest type of display device, the standard monitor or VDU (visual display unit), uses what is essentially the same technology as a television set and at the heart of this is the cathode ray tube (CRT). Cathode rays are in fact beams of electrons travelling in a vacuum. The term 'cathode ray' was coined before the identity of the rays was discovered and the terminology has remained in use – at least in this particular context. The fundamental principle of the cathode ray tube is that a beam of electrons is fired at a flat screen coated with a luminescent substance which glows at the spot where the beam is absorbed (Fig. 2.1). The beam is rapidly scanned across the screen, its intensity varying in such a way that an image is created. Since the luminescent glow fades quickly, the image is continually re-drawn. This allows a new version of the image to replace an earlier one, very rapidly, so giving the illusion of a smoothly changing picture.

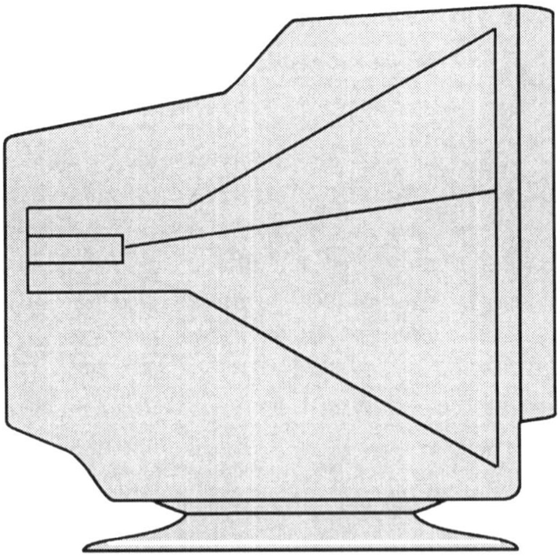

Fig. 2.1 *In a CRT an electron beam is projected onto a phosphor-coated screen*

The simplest way in which an electron beam can be created is by electrically heating a suitable metal filament (a wire rather similar to that in an electric light bulb) and then accelerating the electrons rapidly to a high velocity by means of a strong electrostatic field causing them to be fired, as if out of a gun, in the form of a continuous beam. This must be done in a vacuum – usually in a glass vessel (the television tube) from which the air has been removed – since electrons are easily scattered and absorbed in air. The simple device used to produce the beam is called, naturally, an 'electron gun'. Because electrons carry an electrical charge they can be forced to change direction under the influence of magnetic or electrostatic fields and this provides the principle by which the beam is scanned. The charge on the electron creates a problem, however, when the beam is used in this way for creating an image. It is essential for the creation of a good image that the beam should form a tiny spot when it hits the luminescent screen; it certainly should be no larger than the size of the pixels. But because of their charge the electrons repel each other and so naturally drift apart.

The answer to this problem is to use the same method as is used for scanning the beam. A magnetic or (usually) an electrostatic lens is fitted inside the vacuum tube which is used to focus the beam. The electron beam is constantly being moved by magnetic fields, generated by two sets of magnetic deflection coils which are mounted on the outside of the cathode-ray tube. By their means the beam is swept in a regular fashion across the flat, front surface of the tube on which is deposited the special luminescent layer. In modern designs a regular and repeated pattern of parallel horizontal lines – the raster – is used. One set of deflection coils is arranged so as to sweep the beam regularly from left to right and the other is set at right-angles to the first so as to push the beam down one line's width at the end of each scan (Fig. 2.2). When the whole screen has been filled the beam flies back to the beginning and starts the process all over again. Thus the image is created in much the same way that a page of text from a book is built up from separate horizontal lines.

The function of the luminescent layer is to generate the light needed to make an image. Luminescence is a useful property possessed by certain materials that causes them to absorb the energy of radiation, such as an electron-beam, and then re-emit at

Fig. 2.2 *In a raster, the electron beam scans the screen in a series of horizontal parallel lines*

least some of it as visible or near-visible light. If the emission process is instantaneous then the phenomenon is called fluorescence. If the light is emitted over a longer period of time (anything longer than a hundred millionth of a second) then the process is termed phosphorescence. The two effects are grouped together under the general title of luminescence. When the light is not emitted instantaneously then its intensity decays steadily and the time taken for this to happen can vary widely from one material to another. The process is measured by a quantity called the material's 'persistence'. The persistence of a phosphorescent effect is the time taken for the emitted light intensity to drop to one tenth of its original value. A suitable value of persistence for a monitor screen is of the order of one tenth of a second. Anything much longer will interfere with the rapid refreshment process – causing the images to overlap in time. This means that they are visible longer than they should be, which causes a 'smearing' effect when the image changes, instead of the clean-cut effects we expect. Anything much shorter may produce a flickering effect as one image fades before the next one takes its place. A material which produces phosphorescent effects is referred to as a 'phosphor'.

The colour of light emitted depends on the particular phosphor chosen by the manufacturer of the monitor. Monochrome monitors usually emit green, amber or white light. Green is often chosen because the eye is more sensitive to that colour than any other and this results in an image with the maximum contrast to the eye. Amber is sometimes used in the belief that this colour is more restful to the eye. White is chosen by some manufacturers in order to create the black-on-white appearance of a typewritten sheet of paper, for monitors used in word-processing applications and desktop publishing.

Cathode ray tubes are inevitably rather large and heavy, for two reasons. Because the electron beam can be created and used only in a vacuum the glass tube must be very strongly made in order to withstand the enormous pressure exerted by the atmosphere. Secondly, the geometry involved in using a single fixed source of electrons to produce a beam which can be swept over the entire face of the tube requires that it be placed well behind that face. If this condition is not met the beam has to be bent through large angles and this tends to introduce distortion into the image. This second factor leads to a tube with a considerable depth and therefore a large volume and the first factor determines that the tube be made from heavy gauge material. Together these considerations lead to a large heavy device. As computer technology has consistently led to smaller and lighter devices efforts have intensified in order to create smaller, lighter monitors. These have taken two directions : efforts to reduce the size of the cathode ray tube and attempts to produce alternative flat-screen devices not based on CRT technology. Two modern flat screen display devices, used widely in portable computers, are described later.

A further disadvantage of the CRT is the need for a high voltage power supply which is relatively large and cannot be supplied by batteries as the rest of the computer could. This stems from the fact that the electron beam must be given sufficient energy to ensure that when it is absorbed in the phosphor layer it can produce light of a reasonable intensity. This is done by accelerating the electrons to a high velocity by means of a high voltage DC supply.

Vector-scan devices

The raster-scan method (described in more detail the next section), is used in television sets and all modern computer monitors, but it is not the only way of using a cathode ray tube to create images. It is of some interest to describe briefly the vector-scan devices which were first used in computer graphics because this offers some interesting insights into the relative advantages of vector, as against bit-mapped, storage of images. Although vector display devices are now obsolete, vector images are of increasing importance.

In vector-scan devices the electron beam was directed so as to draw the lines which make up the image on the screen directly, rather than as a series of dots or pixels on parallel raster lines (Fig. 2.3). This approach was a direct development of the cathode ray oscilloscope, used by engineers to give a pictorial representation of electrical wave-forms and it is, in principle, the same method used by plotting devices where a pen is steered by a system of mechanical arms so as to draw lines on a sheet of paper. This type of monitor was sometimes called a 'random-scan' device. The term 'random' indicates that in operation the beam may be directed to any part of the screen in any order, unlike the regular, predictable scanning pattern of the raster device. This type of device was particularly appropriate to applications which consist mostly of straight lines or simply-defined curves, such as architectural plans and engineering drawings. An important point to grasp is that the image which was created was not made from dots or pixels. The beam was switched on, and left on, as long as it was drawing a line. It was switched off when the beam was being steered to the starting point of a new line (so as not to draw anything) just as the pen is lifted off the paper in a pen-plotter.

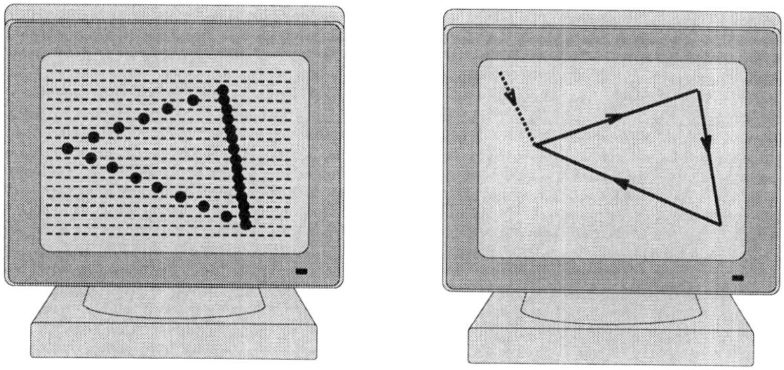

Fig. 2.3 Drawing a triangle using the modern raster technique (first diagram) and using the obsolete vector hardware (second diagram)

The two principal virtues of this approach were the economical use it made of memory and the high quality of lines which it could draw. First, let us look at the use of memory in the two display methods. By their very nature both raster-scan and vector display devices must be constantly refreshed. It would be wasteful of computing power if this were done by a continual process of repeating all the calculations which had gone into constructing the image, so a store is needed to keep a record of the current state of the image. In the raster-scan device this store (the refresh buffer) contains information on the state of every pixel in the display whether it is a part of the image or only the background. In some images this is a very wasteful use of memory since large areas of the image contain no useful information. A minimum of one bit per pixel is needed and a coloured or grey-level image will need anything from 3 to 24 bits per pixel, and possibly even more. In the vector-scan device the only information which must be stored (in the simplest case of images composed entirely of straight lines) is the position of a pair of end-points for each line. Take, for example, an image consisting of 500 lines. These need 1000 sets of endpoint co-ordinates (two endpoints per line in a 2-D image) and each endpoint needs two co-ordinates to specify its position. If the resolution of the screen is better than 256 pixels in each direction then each number will need two bytes to store that number (because the numbers will be, potentially, greater than 256). Thus $1000 \times 2 \times 2 = 4000$ bytes of memory are needed to store what is quite a complicated image (500 lines). Now, compare this with the memory requirements of a raster-scan device. This needs a refresh buffer of nearly 40,000 bytes even in the case of a 640×480 pixel monochrome display ($640 \times 480 \times 1 / 8 = 38{,}400$). In the early days of computer graphics this sort of memory was not available at an economic cost simply for use as an image bit-map.

The quality of straight line images in a vector-scan display was noticeably better than that with the raster-scan display because of the jagged-line problem of dot matrix displays, mentioned in Chapter 1. This effect can be reduced only by improving the spatial resolution – using more, smaller, pixels – or by special anti-aliasing techniques. Anti-aliasing, mentioned briefly in Chapter 1, involves the use of grey pixels to fill in some of the steps in a jagged line. The clearest difference between the two methods is that the raster-scan method can only place pixels in certain pre-determined positions – the cells of the grid. The vector-scan method can, in principle, place the beam anywhere. However, although the vector method does not address individual pixels there is a limit to how precisely the electron beam can be positioned. On this basis it is possible to calculate a value for precision in line-drawing in terms of equivalent pixels which means the number of pixels which would be necessary in a raster display to obtain a similar quality of image. Typical vector displays offered the equivalent of about 4000 pixels per line although displays were available at up to 8000 pixels per line (equivalent). This was another reason for the universal use of vector displays in the pioneer days. No raster scan monitors of anything like this quality were available. The television broadcast standard of that time was of 405-line images in the UK. Even today, colour raster scan monitors with 2000 pixels per line or better are extremely expensive and the highest resolution monochrome monitor offers 4096 by 3300 pixels (no grey-levels) and is also extremely expensive. The vector display device did however have disadvantages. Although vector monitors offered the highest spatial resolution they were not good at applications which require colour and shading effects. Because the images were not composed from regularly spaced scan lines the shadow-mask technique for producing colour in raster displays (discussed later in the chapter) was not a practical proposition. Vector monitors were usually monochrome devices and those that did offer colour usually provided only three (red, green and yellow) by a beam penetration method. In this, the screen was coated with two phosphors, one green-emitting and the other red-emitting, laid down on top of each other. According to the energy of the electron beam it penetrated largely into the first layer (low energy), into both layers (medium energy) or into the second layer (high energy). This produced light from the first, both or the last layers, respectively, resulting in three different colours. This is clearly no rival to a system which can now produce 16.8 million colours!

2.2.2 Raster scan computer monitors

It has been said that the principles of the raster scan monitor are essentially the same as those of a television set but there are two important differences. A television set is designed to pick up broadcast television signals with the aid of an aerial and contains circuitry which tunes in to the particular television channel required. A computer monitor does not need such tuning circuits and neither does it need a demodulating circuit to separate the picture signal from the carrier wave used in broadcasting. The video signal which contains the image information is received directly from the computer itself, via a signal cable. The second difference lies in the way that the image itself is generated. A television image is essentially an analogue image – the signal which controls the brightness of the image varies smoothly and continuously as it scans along the line. The only sense in which it can be said to be digitized arises from the fact that the image is chopped up into a series of horizontal lines; no object smaller than the width of the scan lines can be displayed. It is therefore discontinuous, if not strictly digitized, in the vertical direction and

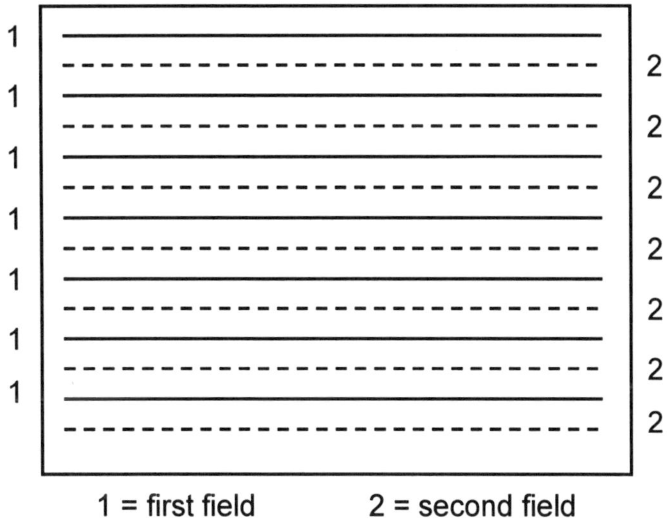

Fig. 2.4 *Interlacing*

analogue or smoothly varying, in the horizontal direction. Early raster scan computer images were, however, fully digitized, as described in the last chapter and normally displayed as a series of dots or pixels. In the simplest case these dots were either fully on or fully off. What this means is that as the electron beam scans across the raster lines it is rapidly switched on and off by means of a control electrode in the electron gun. (Modern systems, in fact, do use analogue monitors, like TV sets, even though the images are stored in the computer in digital form. The reason for this will be discussed later.)

Refreshing the image

An essential feature of the raster scan display, whether a television or a computer monitor, is that the raster, when complete, is immediately repeated to create the illusion of a smoothly changing image. In the UK television system images are repeated 25 times per second; in the US they are refreshed 30 times per second. An interesting question to consider is, how frequently should this refreshment process take place? The lower limit for the refresh frequency is set by the characteristics of the human eye. The eye will detect the change-over if it takes place less often than about 30 times per second. This sets a lower limit to the refresh frequency of about 30 Hertz (1 Hertz = 1 cycle per second). It might seem that there is no necessary upper limit to the refresh frequency – but in practice this will be set by engineering limitations and, more important in most cases, economics (cost).

An important engineering restriction is that it is convenient to use a simple multiple of the mains electricity alternating frequency. In the UK this is 50 cycles per second and as a result the UK television system uses a refresh frequency of 50/2 = 25 times per second. The reason for using half the mains frequency lies in an economic compromise – it keeps the rate of information flow down to the absolute minimum, thus reducing engineering costs and making most economic use of the available broadcasting frequencies – while reducing flicker by a technique called interlacing (Fig. 2.4). Interlacing means that only alternate lines of the image are displayed in the first half of the refresh cycle (taking 1/50 second) followed by the missing lines in the second 1/50 second. Each half of the process is called one field and so two fields make up the complete picture (one frame). This means that complete images are transmitted at only 25 Hertz but the eye is fooled into seeing a refresh cycle of 50 Hertz because the updating process is occurring every 1/50 of a second.

Another way of looking at it, using the idea of resolution introduced in Chapter 1, is that the eye is presented with low resolution images (containing only half the number of lines) at a frequency of 50 Hertz, and so sees no noticeable flicker, and because alternate images fill in the spaces left by the previous image the eye also receives high resolution information (though at half the frequency – 25 Hertz). The frequency with which an image is refreshed on a monitor is called the vertical frequency. The frequency with which individual lines are redrawn is called the horizontal frequency and is discussed in more detail later in the chapter. One way of reducing any flicker effects that might still persist and produce eye strain to the computer operator is to use a long persistence phosphor. The term ‘long’ as used here is relative to the tenths to hundredths of a second normally used – it still means a fraction of a second. This was sometimes done in monochrome monitors intended primarily for text applications like word-processing. It tended to produce a slight smearing effect when the text was scrolled as a result of the old image not clearing sufficiently rapidly and was therefore not suitable for true graphics applications.

The system described so far is that used in the UK domestic television service and because the first computers were designed to operate with television sets as their display devices it was the system used in computers and the first raster-scan monitors also. Two factors have led to the use of higher refresh rates in modern computer systems. One is that, although interlacing (as a way of making low refresh rates acceptable) is quite effective with moving images of the sort seen on TV sets, it is less effective with static images and flicker is therefore more likely to be noticed on this type of cheaper computer monitor. The move to non-interlaced systems has come from an acceptance that low refresh rates are not really acceptable except when combined with long persistence phosphors which are not suited to graphics systems. The other factor is that flicker is more noticeable at the periphery of one’s vision and since there is a trend to the use of larger monitors this also can lead to more noticeable flicker. About 50% of users notice flicker when the screen is refreshed at 60 Hz but this reduces to only about 5% at 72 Hz and so modern, non-interlaced, monitors now use refresh rates of 70 Hz and above. Since no modern computer is designed to be used with a TV set there is no need for the designers of computer monitors to adhere to the standards set for broadcast TV (standards that will themselves be replaced shortly in the move to higher definition pictures and digital signals). Modern computer monitors, in fact, operate at a number of different refresh rates – depending on the screen mode. In general the highest refresh rate will be available in the lower resolution modes, and vice versa.

2.2.3 Bandwidth

Another variable affecting the quality of the image is the bandwidth of the monitor. The term bandwidth is used by engineers as a measure of the quantity of information which a system can receive or transmit in a given time. In the case of a two-colour image the quantity of information is simply the number of pixels which can be transmitted and displayed per second – which depends, in part, on the frequency with which the electron beam can be turned on and off. Since information is transmitted electronically via the medium of alternating electrical signals, the rate of information flow will also depend on the frequency of the carrier wave. The bandwidth of a system can therefore be defined as the range of signal frequencies that can be transmitted by a system with an acceptable level of signal loss or distortion. Early computer systems stored images digitally and also transmitted them to the monitor digitally. This meant that the monitor had to be designed to work with a digital signal also. However, as images improved, both in resolution (number of pixels) and in the number of colours, it was necessary for the systems to cope with the increased bandwidth (information flow) that followed. It is, in fact, more economical for high bandwidth signals to be transmitted as analogue signals than as digital signals. As a result, modern computers convert the digital information generated internally into a analogue signal before feeding it to the (analogue) monitor. This is beginning to a cause a problem now that Liquid Crystal (LC) screens (described later) are being offered as an alternative to CRT displays. LC screens are driven directly by a digital signal. Since, in the standard computer, the output is converted internally from digital to analogue, any LC screen designed to take the place of a CRT screen must contain analogue to digital circuitry to convert it back again. The only alternative, at the moment, is to replace the normal video card (again, see later for details) with one generating digital signals.

Clearly with these differences it is important to match the monitor to the computer. A television or monitor with too low a bandwidth will simply degrade the image. The most important match must be that of line-scan frequency. The IBM-PC, for example can be fitted with a variety of different graphics-output boards and each might require a monitor with a different line-scan frequency. To overcome this problem of compatibility, monitor manufacturers now produce monitors which will automatically adjust to a wide range of line-scan frequencies.

2.2.4 Colour monitors

Coloured images are obtained by a system which uses three different types of phosphor which emit red, green and blue light respectively. These materials are arranged on the inside surface of the screen in a regular pattern – in small circular spots arranged in a triangular pattern (Fig. 2.5) or, as in many modern TV tubes, in short thin stripes. Red, green and blue are primary colours from which it is possible to create all the other colours but it is necessary to be able to control the intensity of the spots independently of each other and this means using three different electron beams from three different electron guns.

To ensure that each gun only excites its corresponding colour, traditional designs of tube are fitted with a 'shadow' mask containing circular holes arranged in a triangular pattern (Fig. 2.6). The phosphor dots on the viewing screen are arranged in groups of three, in a triangular arrangement and the three electron guns are also arranged in a triangle. The geometry of this system ensures that each gun only 'sees'

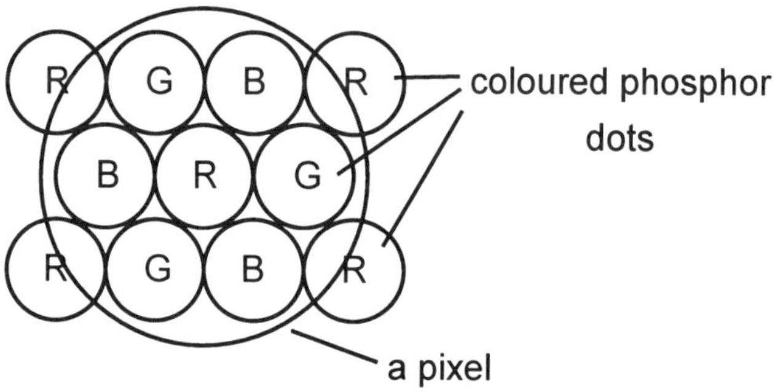

Fig. 2.5 *A pixel contains a number of coloured phosphor dots*

its correct colour of phosphor dots through the holes in the mask. Clearly if any pixel on the screen can be set to any of the available colours it is necessary to have a minimum of three different coloured phosphor spots for each pixel. The greater the number of dots (and therefore, the smaller the dots) the larger the number of pixels which can be displayed. This quantity is referred to as the pitch of the screen and is measured in millimetres. The pitch of a screen is the distance between repeating elements – for example, the distance between the red spots in two adjacent 'triads' (triangular sets of spots). Most modern colour monitors have a dot pitch in the range 0.25 – 0.28 mm. Confusion can sometimes arise when a manufacturer uses a different method of measuring dot pitch – for example, by quoting the distance between holes in the shadow mask, rather than the distance between similar phosphor dots.

An alternative system, designed to reduce the complexity of the tube, uses dots which are arranged as thin parallel stripes and guns which are in a line, instead of a triangle (see Plates 3a and 3b). One advantage of this geometry is that the 'mask'

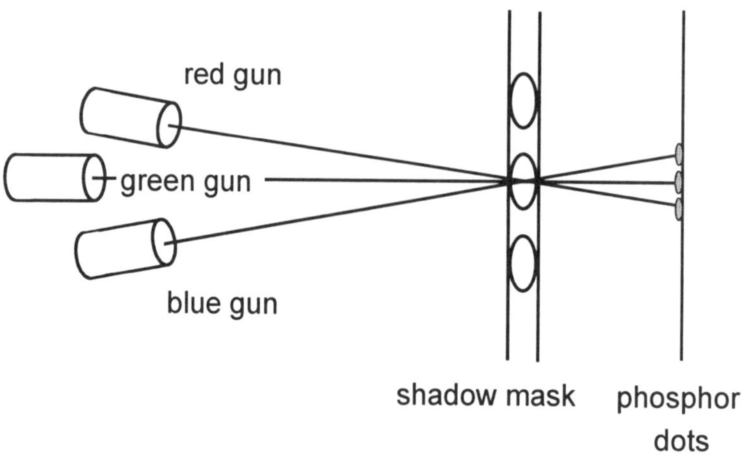

Fig. 2.6 *The holes in the shadow mask line up with the coloured phosphor dots*

uses slits rather than holes – in fact the slits are simply thin parallel wires, rather like a harp. These absorb fewer electrons than the conventional mask which means that more electrons are absorbed in the phosphor stripes, producing more light, and the result is a brighter picture. The disadvantage is that the larger size monitors need a supporting structure to keep the wires in the correct position. This takes the form of two fine horizontal wires which can sometimes be seen as two black, out-of-focus, lines crossing the screen. Some of these designs use only one electron gun instead of the usual three. This design involves a method of rapidly bending the beam so that it approaches the shadow mask from three different directions, in turn – behaving as if it were three different beams.

2.2.5 The shape and size of monitors

The steady move towards larger monitors, which has been mentioned above, is worthy of further comment. Larger monitors are increasingly needed because of the move to graphical interfaces and graphic applications. The term 'interface' is discussed in some detail later in the book but for our immediate purposes the term is taken to refer to the design of the material displayed on the screen, through which the user interacts with the computer. Early, text-only, software interfaces were

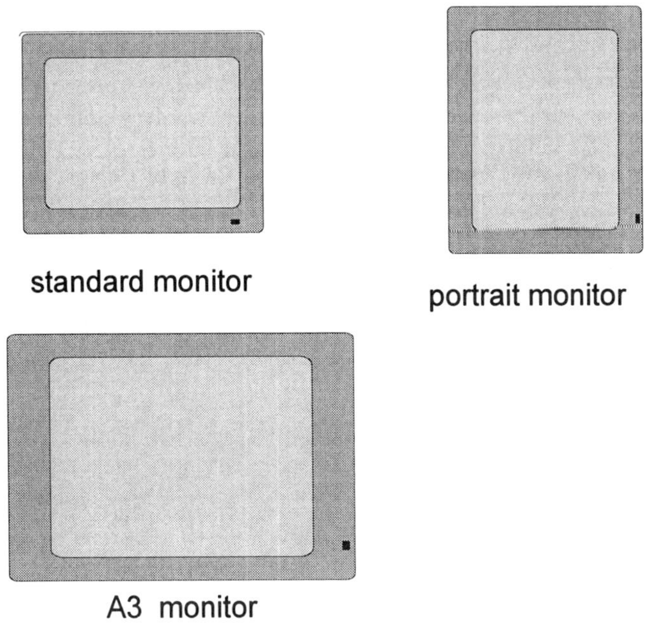

Fig. 2.7 *Monitors come in a variety of sizes and shapes*

required only to be able to display a limited number of text characters, as the user typed in commands and read the computer's response, again in a few lines of text. These interfaces have given way to graphically-based ones, like the Apple Macintosh '*Desktop*' and Microsoft's '*Windows*'. Graphical interfaces, because they are based on pictures, benefit from a larger viewing space simply because much more, detailed, information is being offered to the user. Scientific and engineering workstations, which were using graphical interfaces a long time before they became common on ordinary desktop computers, have always been equipped with large monitors as a standard feature. In order to pack more information onto the screen, monitors have been developed which are capable of much higher resolution than the early models but there is a limit to this process – imposed by the limits of the human eye. Modern computers are capable of displaying details which are simply too small for the unaided eye to see when displayed on, what was, the standard, 14 inch monitor. Short of viewing a monitor through a magnifying glass, the only way to take advantage of this extra detail is to make larger screens with more of the same-size pixels – rather than using small screens with smaller pixels.

It is also important to realize that the pitch of the phosphor dots is not the only factor which determines the quality of a colour monitor; the size of the screen is also important. At first sight the size of a display might seem irrelevant, within reasonable limits. Large monitors are often viewed from a greater distance than smaller ones and the apparent size of the image is therefore similar, so if the image is made up from the same number of pixels it would seem that the quality of the image must be similar. However, a large monitor will have a larger number of coloured stripes or dots than a smaller one *if they have the same dot pitch.* For example, a 36 cm wide monitor (corresponding approximately to a 17 inch diagonal) with a pitch of 0.25 mm will have about $36 \times 10 \times 4 = 1440$ sets of phosphor dots across its width as compared with the figure of 960 for a 24 cm monitor (13 inch diagonal), of the same pitch. This could potentially improve the quality of the image by enhancing its ability to display detail, but there will only be a difference if the computer hardware can generate an image using more pixels (that is, produce more detailed images). This ability to generate images with differing resolutions will be discussed later.

The earliest CRT-based devices were round because this is the easiest shape for a glass-blower to make and this shape was used for some of the first televisions and for many cathode ray oscilloscopes. We have now come to expect all such displays to be rectangular because that is the traditional shape for most images, including paintings and photographs. Such images are rarely square, however, since it is usually considered that a rectangular shape is more pleasing to the eye. The proportions of a rectangular image are defined by its 'aspect ratio' which is the ratio of its width to its height. Television sets and standard computer monitors have an aspect ratio in the range 4 : 3 (1.33) or 3 : 2 (1.5). The result of using a rectangular screen is that the number of pixels in the x (horizontal) direction is more than that in the y (vertical) direction and this is not suitable for all applications. Graph plotting might benefit from a square display with equal numbers of pixels in each direction. Word processing would benefit from monitors with more pixels in the vertical than in the horizontal because printed pages are almost always taller than they are wide. In fact special monitors, with more suitable aspect ratios, are available for some of these applications (see Fig. 2.7). A 'portrait' monitor, for example, has the same aspect ratio as an A4 sheet of paper with the longer dimension vertical. Some monitors can actually be rotated in use, in order to suit the application – so getting the best of both worlds.

Because of the historical connection between TV screens and computer monitors the plans for a new system of high definition, wide screen TV sets are likely to have an impact on future computer systems. 'High-definition' (which means the same as high-resolution) is likely to mean a TV system based on twice as many lines as the current systems (625 lines in Europe). The purpose of this is to offer TV pictures of similar quality to that experienced in the cinema. 'Wide screen' implies a different aspect ratio (16 : 9), nearer to that of the cinema, so that films can be shown without clipping off the edges – as is common now. A few manufacturers are already making wide-screen monitors for both desktop and portable computers.

Until recently the standard computer monitor was a 14 inch model. The measurement (14 inches) refers to the diagonal measurement of the screen (as on TV sets) but some of the screen cannot actually be seen. Because of the curvature of the screen the edges, which are not suitable for the viewing of an image, are masked off by the case and so it becomes rather arbitrary exactly where the measurements are taken. A 14inch screen will not actually have 14 inches worth of image and there can be significant variations among manufacturers in the way these measurements are made. In a typical monitor, sold as a 15 inch, there might be only about 14 inches of tube which are viewable and 13.5 inches of actual picture because it usually has a narrow black surround to it. In fact, a 13.3 inch flat-panel display on a laptop computer might have the same viewing area as a so-called 15 inch CRT display on a desktop computer.

The trend is towards larger screens and so 15 inch models have become the standard with 17 inch models much commoner than before – and much cheaper. For some applications, 19 inch, 21 inch or 23 inch models are to be preferred, though the price rises rapidly with size. At the time of writing the largest commercially available colour screen based on CRT technology is a 37 inch. Some applications, like desktop publishing of documents which are to be printed in monochrome, do not require a colour display and for these, larger monochrome monitors are available at a reasonable price. A typical example is an A3 (or dual-page) screen – the size and shape of two A4 sheets of paper, in portrait mode, placed side-by-side as they might be in an open magazine (see Fig. 2.7).

2.2.6 Image distortion

The basic technology of the CRT inevitably produces some distortions in the image – both geometrical distortions and colour distortions. Geometrical distortions result from the fact that the electron beam, though it originates from a single point, is made to sweep over a large area of the screen which means that it must be bent by the magnetic fields produced by the scanning coils. In addition, though it travels a shorter distance when it illuminates the centre of the screen – in the middle of its raster scan – than when it illuminates the edges of the screen, it must stay in focus all the time. Increasingly, monitors are provided with special controls to allow the user to correct, by eye, the common geometrical distortions – pincushion and barrel – as well as to fine-tune the size and position of the image (see Fig. 2.8). Less common are corrections for skew (or 'trapezoidal') and rotation distortions. Some geometrical problems produce colour effects. For example if the three electron beams do not focus on exactly the right spot, over the whole of the screen, then the result can be a 'convergence' problem – the electron beams are not converging (meeting) properly. This produces red fringes on one side of an object and blue fringes on the other side. Some of the subtler geometrical problems cannot be

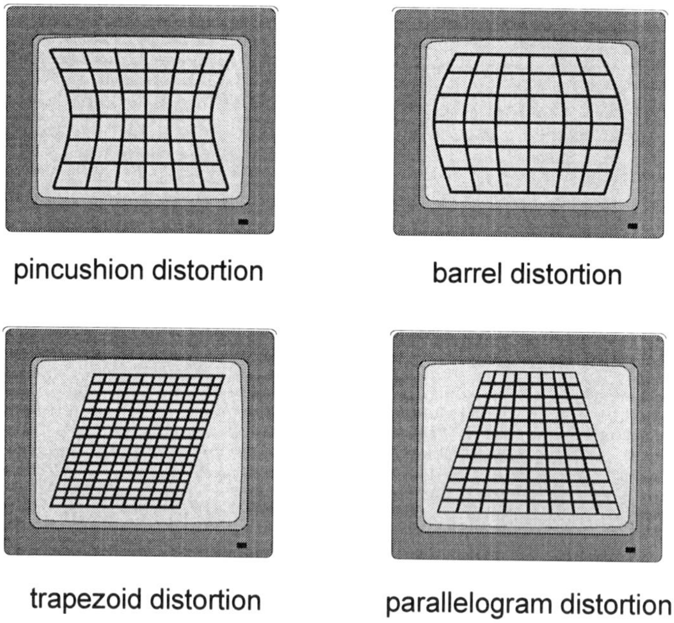

***Fig. 2.8** Four types of geometrical distortion in CRT monitors*

corrected by the user; they are a function of the design and manufacturing process and depend, in part, on how well the factory adjustments have been made. One of the most attractive features of flat screen systems – discussed later – is that the pixels are built into the screen (created in the manufacturing process) and do not depend on the geometry of moving electron beams.

Some monitors allow for the correction of some colour distortions – by changing the balance between the red, green and blue components – and for altering the 'colour temperature'. Colour correction is discussed in more detail in a later chapter.

2.2.7 Graphics adapters

In early computers the graphics capabilities were fixed. They were determined by the graphics interface chips and their associated circuitry which were a permanently installed part of the computer. However, most modern systems handle all their output through a system of plug-in adapter cards which are small circuit boards equipped with edge connectors which plug into special sockets inside the computer. This gives them considerable flexibility since cards can be installed and replaced at will and in the case of the IBM-PC this has led, over the years, to many different graphics standards. The first, the Monochrome Display Adapter (MDA) was a monochrome, text-only system. This was soon supplemented by a third-party 'Hercules' system with the same characteristics as the MDA but which also supported bit-mapped graphics. All the subsequent systems provided both colour and graphics – each one improving on the previous one by offering more colours and better resolution. These included the Colour Graphics Adapter (CGA), Enhanced Graphics Adapter (EGA), Video Graphics Adapter (VGA) and the super-VGA (an enhanced VGA) – see Table 2.1

Table 2.1 *Some of the graphics standards used on IBM-PCs*

Name	Resolution	Colours	Text
Monochrome Display Adapter (MDA)	720 × 350	2	9 × 14
Hercules (also monochrome)	720 × 350	2	9 × 14
Colour Graphics Adapter (CGA)	640 × 200	2, 4	8 × 8
Enhanced Graphics Adapter (EGA)	640 × 350	16 from 64	8 × 14
Video Graphics Adaptor (VGA)	640 × 480	256	9 × 16
Super-VGA (SVGA)	1280 × 1024	16.8 million	9 × 16

Some manufacturers have, however, returned from time to time to the practice of putting the chips which are normally on the display adapter on to the main board of the computer in order to reduce manufacturing costs. This obviously reduces the flexibility which the plug-in card was designed to create unless it is possible to 'switch off' the built-in graphics chips at some later date and add a newer graphics interface card.

A modern graphics chip set will be able to produce the full range of current graphics standards for 2-D displays, and will therefore suit most users, but there is a rapid growth in specialist graphics cards which accelerate video and 3-D images and these are not currently part of the 'standard'. The major characteristics of these standards are listed in Table 2.1. In reading the table it should be appreciated that most of the graphics standards have a number of modes, usually including the older ones in order that older software can still be run, and in general the graphics mode with the best resolution will have the least colours and vice-versa. A complicated story has been made more complicated by the fact that although the early graphics standards in the IBM-PC were set by IBM itself the running in recent years has been set by the manufacturers of graphics cards and so 'standards' have not been so tightly controlled. For example, the original VGA standard was for a 640 × 480 pixel display with 16 colours but card manufacturers soon started to offer enhanced versions (called super-VGA) with increased resolution and more colours (at least 800 × 600 pixel resolution, with at least 256 colours) and now the super-VGA is the lowest specification version of VGA available.

The changes which have taken place in graphics standards over the years can be judged by comparing the characteristics of the first and the most recent graphics cards. The first (for IBM-PCs), called CGA, offered 320 × 200 pixels with 4 colours (or 640 × 200 with two colours – black and white!). Modern cards offer 640 × 480, 800 × 600 and 1024 × 768 pixels at least – with most going to higher resolutions of 1280 × 1024 and even 1600 × 1200 pixels. The number of colours at any particular resolution will depend on how much refresh-buffer memory is fitted to the card and will vary from 256 to 16.8 million. Most modern cards have a minimum of 2 – 4 Mbytes and many can be upgraded to 8 Mbytes or more.

Graphics chips

The subject of graphics cards leads naturally to the subject of graphics chips (video or display controller chips). The graphics standards described above grow naturally from the design of the graphics chips which are used on the cards. A number of types of graphics chip exists. The earliest type of card used only a specialized chip designed to generate a suitable video signal based on two types of instruction which originated from the main processor. The first type of instruction related to the graphics mode which was to be used. The second type of instruction was that which defined the image structure and came directly from the computer's refresh-buffer (for bit-mapped graphics) or from the character generator ROM in response to the ASCII codes stored in the refresh-buffer (for text-only displays). The function of the chip, then, was to take the stored image information in the computer and to produce a video signal which contained that information and repeated this process at the refresh rate of the monitor. In other words, the computer, using its central processor, did all the work in creating the image and translating it into a bit-map. The graphics card did the absolute minimum – which was to translate this image into a signal which was suitable for the monitor. For example, all the graphics commands, such as those to draw a line or a circle, involved the central processor in calculating which of the bits in the refresh-buffer must be set. These tasks had to be accomplished in addition to all the normal functions of a central processor.

Graphics work is computationally intensive and there is usually a requirement that fresh images be created quickly. As a result, the move to ever higher resolutions and greater numbers of colours threatened to overload the main processor when this type of card was used. The reason for this is that lines drawn at higher resolution require more calculations because they contain more pixels. In addition higher resolution images are likely to contain more lines because they offer the scope for more detail. A third effect is that images with more colours imply pixels which have more memory assigned to them. Ultimately the point was reached where the central processor could not make changes in the image in a reasonable time.

This led to the use of a second microprocessor, dedicated to the video output, and acting as an intermediary between the host processor and the display controller. In its earliest form this was a standard, general purpose, microprocessor like the computer's main processor but in its modern form it is a specially developed graphics processor. This type of processor is often called a co-processor because it is designed to accept instructions from the main processor which delegates specialist functions to it. Another example of such a device which is often used in graphics applications is a mathematics co-processor. This has instructions for doing floating-point calculations (calculations on decimal rather than integer numbers) – something which the early processors could do only relatively slowly through software. The maths co-processor used to be a separate chip which was fitted on the main board of the computer but has now been incorporated into the design of the main processor.

Graphics co-processors, however, are usually part of the graphics card, which has its own memory chips also, to be used as the refresh-buffer. The function of this second, graphics, processor is to relieve the main processor of almost all its graphics functions. All the main processor is required to do is to send simple codes to the graphics processor. For example, to plot a straight line it sends the appropriate plot command, followed by the necessary parameters – the co-ordinates of the two end points, line colour and style (continuous or dotted) etc. The plot command activates the special graphics instruction set of the graphics co-processor which contains routines for all the standard tasks such as line, circle and polygon drawing. All the rest of the computation, to place bits in the correct locations in the refresh-buffer, are performed by the co-processor. In addition to the usual line and arc drawing functions, many co-processors also provide 'bit-BLT' (Bit-Block Transfers) operations. This is a facility for copying blocks of pixels from one part of an image to another and to make logical operations on the destination image, and is described in a later chapter. Modern graphics cards also offer facilities for image transformations like scaling, zooming, panning and rotation, together with colour look-up tables (see the chapter on colour). Many graphics processors have graphics commands which are particularly suited to the sort of operations used in graphical user interfaces like Microsoft Windows and are sometimes advertized as 'Windows accelerators'. Standard resolutions offered are 640 × 480, 800 × 600, 1,024 × 768, 1,152 × 864, 1,280 × 1,024 and 1,600 × 1,200 pixels. It should be noted that, usually, the higher the resolution selected, the lower the refresh rate that will be supported and the smaller the number of colours – though the number of colours may depend on the amount of memory fitted to the card. In some cases using a very high resolution may induce flicker on some monitors and so whether it is possible to make use of the full range of capabilities of the card will depend on the quality of the monitor.

Modern graphics cards have to cope with enormous amounts of data. Consider a monitor operating at 1,280 × 1,024 pixels and 24-bit colour. Each image consists of 1,280 × 1,024 × 3 bytes = 3,932,160 bytes. If the screen is to be refreshed at 75 Hz then this corresponds to 275.2 Mbytes per second. To cope with this, special 64-bit or 128-bit buses are needed on the card (together with the appropriate graphics processors) and very fast memory for the refresh buffer. Special types of RAM chips are used in graphics cards. One type (called VRAM – video RAM) is dual-ported which means that data can be written to it from the processor and read from it to the screen in one operation using two ports.

Another specialized chip to be found on a graphics card is the RAMDAC chip which converts the digital data from the graphics processor to analogue form suitable for the monitor (DAC = digital to analogue converter).

3-D cards

The standard desktop computer is still equipped with a graphics adapter which is designed to process 2-D images but 3-D and video images are of increasing importance in multimedia applications and games. Currently these markets are catered for by specialist graphics adapters, though experience suggests that such functions are likely to be served in the future by incorporating the appropriate chips into the central processor. Assistance for multimedia data has already been added to the current Intel Pentium chips in the form of the MMX extensions. These are additions to the instruction set of the processor that are designed to speed up activities associated with multimedia data.

Co-processors able to perform 3-D operations such as shading and hidden-surface removal have long been a feature of graphics workstations – a specialist niche market of high-powered computers used for engineering design – but now mass produced, low cost chip sets are available, offering increasingly realistic 3-D images on the desktop computer. As a result some 2-D graphics cards also have some 3-D features as well. Others are specialist 3-D cards, designed to connect to existing 2-D graphics cards and so they act as co-processors to the main graphics co-processor! This is simply a way of keeping costs down by not duplicating the functions of the existing graphics card – one of which is already supplied with every computer. In time one might expect this situation to change and all graphics cards to have fully-featured 3-D accelerator chips as standard. The main problem with these types of specialist cards, as with all specialist hardware, is that in the early stages software designers have to write special 'drivers' (software links) for each type of card. This type of problem is resolved only when software standards are established. These standards are called an Application Programming Interface (API) and initially they tend to be defined by specialist software houses or by chip makers but ultimately they become part of the computer's operating system. Both Microsoft and Apple now have their own preferred 3-D APIs for their operating systems.

Finally a word about terminology. Graphics cards (or boards) have in the past often been referred to as 'video cards', using the term video to mean a card that generates a video signal – that is a signal which feeds a visual display. Using this definition, any graphics card is a video card. However, the word 'video' has a range of other meanings. In everyday language it can mean a domestic VCR recorder or a video cassette, for example, and it can also refer any recorded moving images which are stored magnetically instead of on photographic film. As a result 'video' in the computer world, has gradually come to mean digitized moving images, as opposed to conventional stationary images. As a result the term 'video card' is now more likely to mean a special type of graphics card which is designed to speed up the display of moving images ('videos'). This type of graphics card will be covered in a later section since they are often used in conjunction with input devices.

2.2.8 Flat-panel displays

Displays based on the cathode ray tube are very bulky and very heavy, consume a large amount of electrical energy and require high electrical voltages (thousands of volts). High voltages are needed in order to give the electron beam enough energy to produce a bright spot of light when it is absorbed in the phosphor. Relatively large currents are needed to power the electromagnetic deflection coils. Considerable effort has therefore gone into the quest for much less bulky, flat-panel, displays which consume less energy and do not need high voltages – and not only for use with computers. So far two devices have reached the stage of commercial application as computer monitors, mainly for use with portable computers. In the earliest portable computers both gas-plasma screens and liquid-crystal devices (LCD's) were used but advances in technology have resulted in LCD systems dominating this particular market. Until recently neither had been able to rival the best that the CRT screens could offer in terms of image quality – particularly resolution and numbers of colours – but now the LCD display has reached the stage of being as good as a standard monitor, failing only to match up in terms of price. Both technologies offer what the CRT devices cannot – small size and portability – and LCD's can operate on batteries for reasonable periods of time. Early flat-panel screens for computers were monochrome-only and both plasma and LCD screens were common, but problems in developing colour screens led to the plasma panels falling out of the race. Colour plasma panels are now back in the race again, though resolution problems seem to be limiting their use to large panels (25 inches and upwards).

2.2.9 Gas-plasma displays

This type of flat-panel display is based on the fluorescent properties of certain inert gases (such as neon and argon) and is distantly related to the fluorescent light tubes used in shops and offices. It has the structure of a sandwich consisting of two flat glass plates, sealed at the edges, with a thin layer of a neon-gas mixture trapped

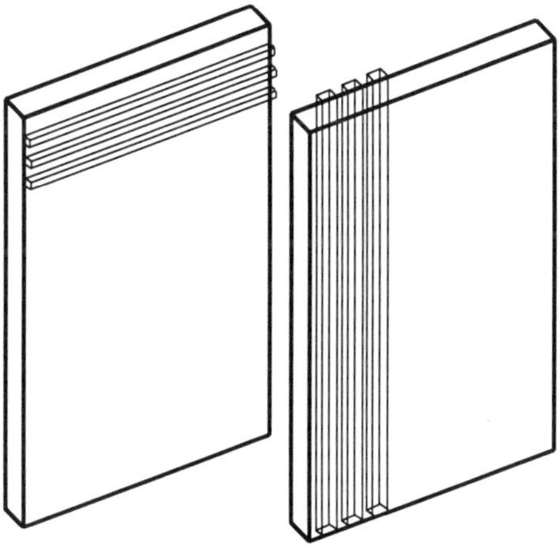

Fig. 2.9 *The plasma-panel display: the two glass plates and sets of mutually-perpendicular electrodes. Only three are shown on each plate for simplicity*

between, in tiny pockets or cells. The gas fluoresces when a suitable electrical voltage is applied between a pair of electrodes. These take the form of a large number of very thin, transparent 'wires' (electrically conducting substances; not made of metal) – one set running at right-angles to the other set and attached to the glass plates (Fig. 2.9). This means that, though very close together, they are nevertheless in separate, parallel planes. When a suitable voltage is applied to a pair of electrodes, one in the vertical set and the other in the horizontal set (see Fig. 2.9), the gas glows at the intersection of those two electrodes producing ultra-violet (UV) light. As in the fluorescent lamp, this UV light is absorbed in a fluorescent phosphor on the glass plates and visible, coloured light is emitted.

Unlike the CRT where every pixel is excited by the one, moving, electron beam, most flat-panel technologies have large numbers of light-emitting (or transmitting) zones – the pixels – which are permanent features of the panel and which must be activated by means of an electrically-conducting connector. It is necessary to be able to switch pixels on and off independently of each other but it is clearly impractical to connect a separate electrode to every pixel because this would require hundreds of thousands of electrodes. Flat-panel systems, therefore, use a much more limited number of electrodes – one for each column and one for each row of pixels. This is called 'multiplexing'. For a VGA display this still needs a large number of electrodes = 640 + 480 = 1,120 but this is nevertheless a considerable reduction on a system where every pixel had to have its own electrode. This would need 640 × 480 = 307,200 which is nearly 300 times as many.

In one type of plasma panel – the DC type – a voltage is applied at only half the necessary 'firing' level to a row electrode but in addition an equal voltage is also applied to a column electrode. A 'firing' voltage is a voltage high enough to cause the gas to suffer electrical breakdown, turn into a plasma and emit light. All the pixels in both the row and the column receive half the firing voltage but only the one at the intersection receives two pulses which add together and cause the pixel to glow. Unfortunately the glow soon begins to fade and must be refreshed, which means that the screen's brightness is not very high. In the other type of plasma panel – the AC type – no refreshment is needed to keep the pixels glowing. They have an in-built 'memory' effect and must therefore be turned off when not required but no effort is needed to keep them 'on'. This is a big advantage since in most screen technologies the pixels begin to fade immediately after being energized and must be continually refreshed.

There are two main drawbacks of this type of display. One is that the voltages needed (together with the fact that alternating current is needed in an AC system) mean that they have not really been suitable for battery operation. The second problem is that the size of the gas pockets means that the pixel pitch is currently more than 1 mm with little hope of this being reduced to less than 0.3 mm. This means that the technology is not suitable for small monitors – currently the smallest size available is about 20 inch diameter. However, plasma panels are simpler to make than LCD panels and so have a much better future for large screens – particularly large flat TV screens – and screens up to 55 inches in size are planned. Another advantage of plasma screens, in some applications, is the transparency of the screens which means that static information, like maps, can be permanently mounted behind and seen in conjunction with dynamic, constantly-updated information (e.g. the movement of vehicles).

2.2.10 Liquid-crystal displays

One of the most widely used graphics display technologies of the modern world is the liquid crystal display (LCD) – used in digital watches, calculators and hand-held games and manufactured by the millions. The inherent advantages of this type of display are that it is lightweight, compact and robust and uses very little (low-voltage) power. The display is based on the polarizing property of certain types of semi-crystalline liquids and in particular the fact that this property can be switched on and off. In early displays the number of crystals was severely limited and so displays were restricted to a few numerical characters, each made from 7 separate crystals (a seven-segment display – see Fig. 2.10). This was acceptable for calculators or digital watches but for computer displays a much larger number of crystals is required – one for each pixel in the image.

A few words of explanation about the meaning of the term 'polarized' light are necessary here. Light is an electromagnetic wave form and is often represented as a smoothly undulating ripple, represented by the mathematical function 'sine'. The wave is classified as a transverse wave which means that its electromagnetic vibrations are in a plane which is at right angles to the direction of the wave motion. Normal, unpolarized, light has vibrations in all possible directions in this plane but

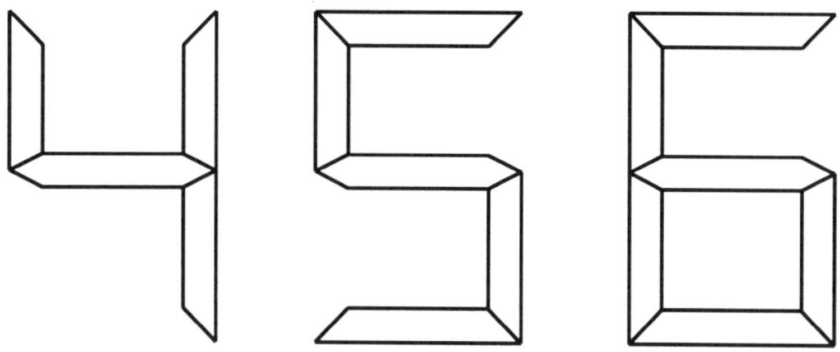

Fig. 2.10 *The simplest form of LCD display, with only seven segments (seven liquid crystals) per character*

certain materials ('polarizers') have the property of preferentially absorbing vibrations in one particular direction but not in the direction which is at right-angles. One of these materials ('Polaroid') is used widely in sunglasses to absorb glare – light which is reflected from the road, beach, snow etc. and which is partially polarized in the horizontal plane. If two lenses from such a pair of glasses are placed together, one turned through 90 degrees to its normal direction, it can be seen that almost all the light is absorbed (top diagram in Fig. 2.11). The reason is simply that one lens only allows that light to pass through it which vibrates in one direction, say the vertical, and the other only allows light through which vibrates in the other direction. Between the two, they absorb all the light. This principle of two rotated (or 'crossed') polarizers absorbing light forms the basis of the LCD display.

Certain liquid crystals, called 'nematic' because they have thread-like, rod-shaped molecules, have the useful property that their molecules tend to line up in the same direction and this direction can be determined by the manufacturing process. This is done by means of grooves in a coating on the inside of the glass sheets. 'Twisted' nematic crystals are liquid crystals which have been made as a thin sandwich between two sheets of glass, but in such a way that their molecules line up with one sheet in one direction and with the other sheet at right angles. This means that the molecules in between the two extremes are twisted into a spiral shape and if polarized light is passed through the sandwich it tends to follow the twist. As a result its plane of polarization is gradually rotated as its passes through. In this state, if crossed polarising sheets are attached to the sandwich (that is polarizers with their planes at right angles) light will pass through the sandwich (bottom diagram in Fig. 2.11). If, however, an electric field is applied across the sandwich (using thin transparent electrodes on the glass sheets) the molecules line up with the lines of electric force, the twisting effect of the liquid crystal is lost, and the light is not transmitted (middle diagram in Fig. 2.11).

There are three basic drawbacks with this system of liquid crystals. One is that is that even the light areas of the display are produced by polarized light, which is at a reduced intensity because of the light which is absorbed in the polarizers, acting like the lenses of a pair of sunglasses. This tends to lead to poor contrast images, contrast being the difference between the lightest and darkest regions in the picture. This can be improved only by the use of high-intensity illumination, to compensate for the light absorbed in the polarizers. In the original LCD displays the illumination of the crystals was provided by normal ambient light, which passes through the display

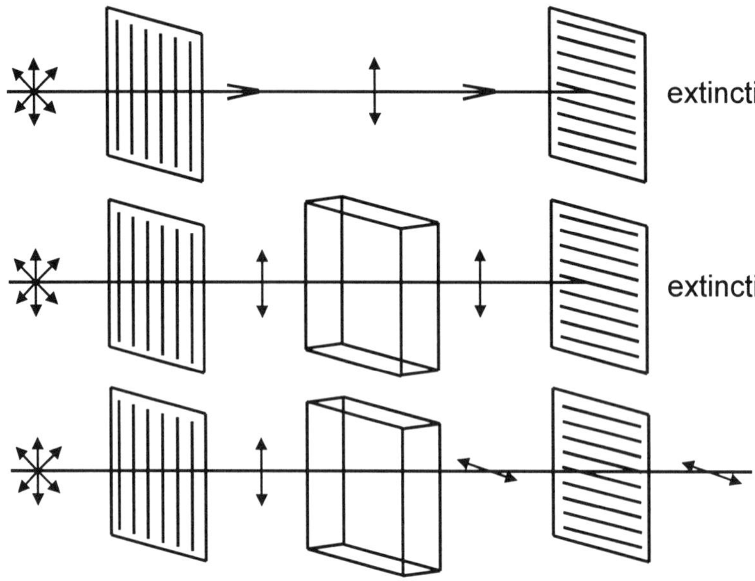

Fig. 2.11 *Liquid crystals rotate the plane of polarization of light*

and then is reflected back out again, as is still the case in a digital watch or calculator display. In more modern displays in computer screens, better contrast and more consistent visibility has been achieved by installing a light behind the panel. This system is able to produce a more consistent and brighter illumination and the final effect is not so subject to the vagaries of variable room lighting. Unfortunately it also means that such a panel consumes much more electricity (in powering the light) and so reduces battery life.

The second problem is that of 'cross-talk' which is a by-product of the method of 'addressing' (switching on and off) the crystals. Multiplexing (introduced in the section on plasma displays) relies on the technique of addressing a crystal by sending two signals – one up the vertical electrode and the other along the horizontal electrode – in such a way that they intersect at one particular crystal and switch it on or off. In practice, a voltage is applied to one row and all the pixels in that row which should be on (or off) are given an increased (or decreased) voltage in their column electrodes. This is then repeated with the next row and the process sweeps down the screen in about a sixtieth of a second. Unfortunately this means that there are many crystals that receive the column voltage ('cross-talk' voltage) which partially turns them on, or off, even though they are not selected and this inevitably reduces the contrast of the system.

Of course, only a few crystals can be addressed at any one time (those that are on the same row). This, however, is the same situation that exists in the CRT monitor where only one point on the screen is being excited by the electron beam at any one time. The answer in both situations is the same – a constant process of refreshment. Just as the phosphorescent spot on a CRT monitor begins to fade as soon as the electron beam passes, so the liquid crystal begins to relax (untwist) as the electrodes are used to address other crystals. Although the refreshment process means that a crystal is constantly being turned on again, the average effect is of a crystal that is only partly on since it is only fully on for a small proportion of the total time and this is the third problem with basic liquid crystal systems.

Continual improvements are being made, however, both to the formulation of the crystal material and the method of manufacture of the sandwich arrangements which holds the minute spots of crystal between sheets of glass. Improved liquid crystals, which are more effective in rotating the plane of polarization of the light, have been developed, and called 'super-twist' crystals. These will rotate the plane of polarization of the light using much thinner crystals and so the crystals absorb less light. The result is better contrast between the light and dark areas because the light areas are lighter. The other advantage of 'Super Twisted Nematic' (STN) – as opposed to the cheaper Twisted Nematic displays – lies in the higher voltages associated with twisting the molecules through 270 degrees (as compared with 90 degrees). When lower voltages are used the molecules twist through a smaller angle and this produces a grey-level effect. Modern STN displays can offer 16-bit colour using grey levels in the red, green and blue crystals (see later for a discussion on colour). A third advantage lies in a reduction in the cross-talk problem since there is a bigger difference between the polarization produced by the addressing voltage and the cross-talk voltage.

Another improvement in contrast is provided by the 'dual-scan' screen. A screen is divided into two halves and two separate refreshment circuits are provided. From an electronic point-of-view they are two screens, not one. The two halves can then be refreshed simultaneously, in half the time that would normally be taken. This means that the crystals have only half the time to fade between one refreshment and the next and so produce brighter, more contrasty images than a single-scan screen. Such screens have become the standard, basic LCD screen.

The screens which have been described so far are referred to by a variety of names – principally Super-Twist Nematic (STN) or Passive-Matrix devices. The term 'passive' is best understood with reference to the another technique for improving contrast – 'active' screens. An active screen is one in which every pixel is fitted with a tiny semiconductor 'switch' in the form of a transistor. In this type of screen the function of the electrode system is to provide the current to charge the crystal and also to switch the transistors on or off. Once turned on, the transistor stays on, until another signal is sent to turn it off, and while on, it ensures that the crystal is fed with electrical power. There is therefore no relaxing of the crystal and it transmits light all the time it is on – producing a higher contrast, brighter screen. This system also eliminates cross-talk problems. The price is the increased complexity of such screens, which have been very difficult to manufacture consistently, resulting in a price which is about two to three times that of the passive screens. These screens are usually referred to as TFT (Thin-Film Transistor) or Active-Matrix devices.

All early LCD screens were monochrome and such screens are still made, but a high proportion of modern screens are colour displays. As in all colours systems the colour is made by the use of three primaries. Each pixel consists of three liquid crystals, each of which is covered with an appropriate filter – red, green or blue. This means that a VGA screen, with 640 × 480 = 307,200 pixels must have three times that number – 921,600 – liquid crystals. It is hardly surprising that it is only recently that super-VGA screens with 800 × 600 pixels have started to appear at a reasonable price and that higher resolution LCD's have appeared at any price. The many improvements that have been made in LCD technology over recent years have led to the position that the best TFT screens match CRT technology in colour quality, brightness, contrast, viewing angle and response times while weight, size and power requirements are all much lower. They also have the advantage that all flat-screen systems have in focus and registration over CRT vacuum tubes. The main disadvantage is still price – four to five times that of a comparable CRT system.

LCD screens have always been smaller than CRT monitors – partly because of the expense and partly because of problems in manufacturing. The commonest size has been about 10 inches (diagonal measurement) but larger screens are now available – mostly 11 inch and 12 inch diagonal but 13 and even 14 inch panels are also being made. Most screens have been used in portable computers and since the designer's aim here has been to reduce the size and weight of these computers, small screen size has not been seen as a major drawback. When it becomes possible to make significantly larger screens at a reasonable cost there is no doubt that LCD screens will start to compete with CRT screens for use on desktop computers, where 15 inch screens have become the norm and 17 inch screens increasingly common. Currently desktop LCD screens with 16-bit colour and a resolution of 1,024 × 768 are available, the size being about 14 inches, which probably compares with a 15 – 16 inch (so-called) CRT screen.

In active (transistor-controlled) systems, variable intensity levels (grey-levels) in the crystals, which are needed to obtain a large number of colours, are obtained by rapidly switching the crystals on and off; the ratio of time spent 'on' to the time spent 'off' determines the level of intensity for a particular primary colour. Considerable effort has also been put into increasing the speed of response whereby the crystals can be turned on and off. In the early screens this response was not fast enough for rapidly changing images and so led to a 'smearing' effect of the sort that was also characteristic of long-persistence phosphors in CRT systems.

2.2.11 Other flat-panel technologies

Another consequence of the push towards replacing CRT-based screens with flat-screens is the search for rivals to the LCD system and also for alternative versions of the well-established STN and TFT screens. Examples of newer technology under development or being used in specialist applications include:

- TFT screens based on low temperature poly-silicon transistors, which are cheaper to produce and can be made in higher resolutions than transistors made from amorphous silicon (used in normal TFT screens);

- Ferro-electric LCD's which are very fast in switching (up to 1,000 times faster) and don't require any electrical power once switched;
- Field-emission displays;
- Electro-luminescent displays;
- Plasma-switched LCD's;
- Light-emitting diodes.

The last four are the most radical departures from current LCD technology. Field-emission displays (FEDs) are closer to the CRT in concept and could be classed as flat-panel CRTs. A FED consists of a grid-like array of electron-emitters – groups of which can be individually addressed – mounted on a flat surface and a second flat

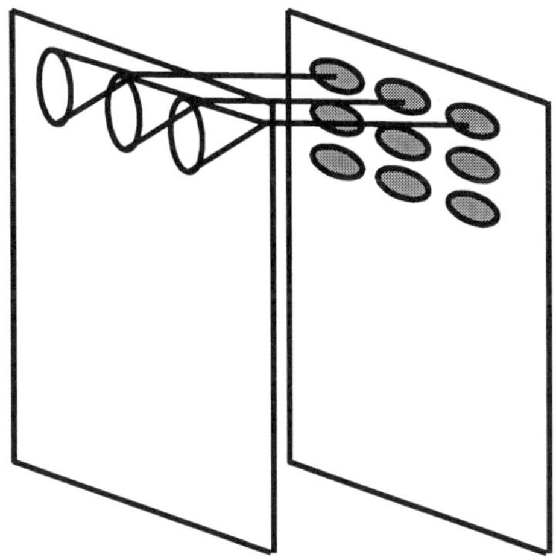

Fig. 2.12 *One of the radical alternative flat-screen technologies under development – each phosphor dot has its own tiny electron gun*

surface containing coloured phosphors, all mounted in a flat sandwich configuration (see Fig. 2.12). One electron gun (in the conventional CRT) is replaced by thousands of solid-state electron emitters (tiny spikes) – between 10 and 100 for each pixel. No bulky vacuum bottle or magnetic scanning coils are needed. The electron emitters are sometimes called 'cold cathodes' because they do not need to be heated (like an electron gun in a CRT) and require only about 1,000 volts to operate rather than the 25 – 30,000 volts of a CRT. The narrow space between the emitters and the phosphor dots on the faceplate, like the CRT, is a vacuum to enable the electrons to travel between the two. One version of this technology involves making the electrodes so small (a few hundred nano-metres across) that they will operate at only 20 volts. At this size there are many thousands of electrodes per pixel which means that the system will work even if many electrodes are not functional. One major problem with this technology is that of making the panels strong enough to withstand the force of atmospheric pressure.

Electro-luminescent (EL) displays, unlike LCDs, actually emit light rather than acting as a gate to transmit or block light from another source. In this sense they have considerable similarity to gas-plasma displays (see previous section). Instead of applying a voltage to a gas cell to cause it to emit light they apply a voltage to a solid substance to produce the light (hence the name 'electro-luminescent' which implies electricity producing luminescence – light emission). These are the only truly solid-state display devices, in that the whole device is fabricated from a single solid substrate rather than as an assembly of materials, gases, crystals etc. One of the problems has been to find substances which will emit brightly in the blue portion of the spectrum in order to create acceptable colour systems.

Plasma-switched (sometimes called Plasma-addressed) LCDs use gas plasma instead of transistors to switch the liquid-crystal pixels on and off. The main advantage of this unlikely-sounding system is that because solid-state transistors are replaced with plasma pockets only low-grade clean rooms are needed to manufacture the panels and this lowers the production costs. The resolution of these systems, like that of true plasma panels, is severely restricted. One company, however, plans to make TV sets and monitors using this approach, incorporating screens in the range 20 to 50 inches diagonal.

The restriction on the use of light-emitting diodes (LED's) for anything other than simple indicator lights has long been the problems of efficiency in converting electrical energy to light and limited range of colours (red, yellow and green). However, both these problems are being solved and this seems to be another technology with great potential.

2.2.12 Projection displays

There are many occasions when it is required to demonstrate computer output to a group of people rather than an individual. One approach is to use large CRT monitors, or a number of separate monitors connected to the same computer, or both. The alternative to this approach is some form of projector which will project an enlarged image on to a screen and there are currently four different ways of doing this. If there is no need to see the images as they are created then it is possible to make photographic slides or overhead-projector transparencies in advance and use conventional projectors. This photographic method is discussed in a later section.

If it is desirable to be able to interact with the computer and show the images as they are created then there are special projectors which show an immediate image – two types based on the LCD display, just described, and another based on CRT technology. One of the LCD displays is in the form of a large transparent panel which can be fitted on top of a normal overhead projector. The projector focuses an enlarged image of the display onto a screen in exactly the same way that it does with normal transparencies. The contrast in these devices is quite low and the colours rather pale. Currently VGA resolution (640 × 480 pixels) is standard with a limited number of colours (up to 64). A variation on this theme is also provided by a device which looks like a standard 35 mm slide projector but which is fitted internally with small transparent LCD in place of the usual transparency. This removes the need for an OHP projector and produces a much brighter image than an OHP.

For a good range of colours and strong contrast, however, a projector based on CRT tubes is needed. These projectors contain three high intensity monochrome CRT tubes which are used in conjunction with coloured filters to produce the three primary colours. Because of their very high intensity it is possible to project enlarged images onto a screen in a darkened room. The three images must be carefully focused so that they coincide on the plane of the screen to produce a full-colour single image.

An exciting recent development in this field – the Digital Micro-mirror Device (DMD) – is based on a special chip, about 0.5 inch square, which has a large number of microscopic mirrors fabricated on its surface (see Fig. 2.13). These mirrors are set on hinge-like supports which enable the mirror to be rotated by about

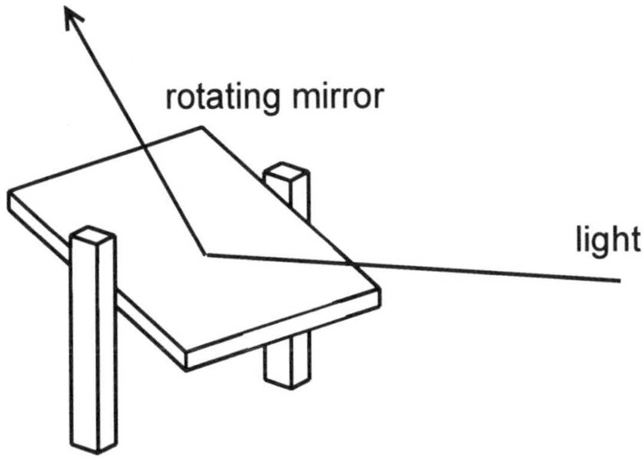

Fig. 2.13 *A digital micro-mirror*

10 degrees in either direction under electronic control (from a transistor sitting immediately underneath each mirror). A bright light is shone onto the DMD and pulses of electricity are used to flip the mirrors so as to reflect the light onto (or away) from a lens system. Each mirror, therefore is used to form a pixel in the final image. Coloured images are created by shining red, green and blue lights onto the chip in very rapid sequence. The mirrors are capable of flipping in 10 micro seconds (that is 100,000 times per second) so it is possible to blend the three primary colours together using only one mirror per pixel. This system is capable of high intensity, high-contrast images and looks very promising.

2.3 Buses And Storage

It is sometimes forgotten that modern graphics systems place great demands on the computer, in terms of its ability to move data around, and these have led to significant design improvements in the 'bus' system. A bus is the internal electronic data highway which carries bytes of digitized information to and from the central processor and its 'peripherals'. In this context the graphics display is a peripheral, connected to the bus via the graphics card. Early IBM-PCs had a bus that operated at 8 MHz and carried 8 bits of information. This was replaced with a 16-bit bus (the AT bus – later named the ISA, the Industry Standard Architecture) that then became standard for a long time (in computer terms). This specification was adequate for 8- and 16-bit microprocessors operating in the range 8 – 16 MHz, when graphic images contained 320 × 200 pixels and 4 colours (and therefore contained 16 K of data). It has become totally inadequate when processors are 32-bit, and more, and operate in the range 300 – 400 MHz – particularly when images contain at the very minimum, 640 × 480 pixels and 256 colours (and therefore contained over 300 K of data).

Over the years improvements have been made in bus design, not simply to deal with the increased information content of graphics, but the needs of graphics peripherals were high on the agenda. A number of attempts have been made to produce a new standard but they have tended to fail because of lack of backward compatibility. The first to succeed in the IBM-PC world was the VESA bus. VESA stands for Video Electronics Standards Association and their VL-bus was designed for the benefit of manufacturers of graphics cards. The problem of compatibility was avoided by fitting computers both with the traditional (ISA) bus and the newer VL bus – which was used only for graphics cards, and often referred to as a 'local bus' (connecting the microprocessor only with the graphics card). Other, fast, buses have been fitted to computers, including an extended version of the ISA (the EISA) and one devised by IBM – the MCA bus, but finally one seems to have become accepted as the new standard – the PCI (Peripheral Component Interconnect) bus. This can operate at 33 or 66 MHz and carry either 32 or 64 bits of information. It also has the advantage that it is being fitted to Macintosh computers, which have for long used their own NUBUS system and this means that manufacturers can more easily make cards for both types of computer. Because of the perceived need to offer customers the ability to plug in older interface cards, the new standard is still being fitted alongside the ISA bus (two or three of each) but unlike the VL bus manufacturers are adopting the PCI system for cards other than graphics cards – disc controller cards for example. The speed of the new buses, like the PCI, is a very important ingredient in the modern graphics-oriented computer and will play the same important role in coping with other data types, like sound, in multimedia computers. The latest development in this area is the AGP (Accelerated Graphics Port). This is a dedicated 66 MHz bus which connects the graphics co-processor directly to the computer's normal RAM, without having to pass through the main microprocessor, and with up to four times the bandwidth of a normal PCI bus.

High-speed processors and high-speed buses are valueless if they are connected directly to low-speed RAM and even lower-speed disc drives. The situation is rather like a motorway which feeds into a country lane. The slow lane acts as a bottleneck which limits the overall speed of traffic. All modern computers, therefore, make use of a variety of memory cache systems. A cache is a temporary storage area which acts as a buffer between a fast component and a slow one. In the case of the slowest components – disc drives – this takes the form of RAM, either a designated portion of the system RAM or special RAM fitted to the drive. When a piece of data is requested from the drive, for example, a section of the data that immediately follows it is automatically read at the same time and stored in RAM. In most cases as soon as the original data has been processed more is requested – usually that which follows the original data – and this is now already available from the much faster RAM chips. The same thing can happen in reverse when data is to be saved to the drive. In the case where the slow component is the RAM itself – feeding a much faster processor – the cache must be made from high-speed (expensive) static RAM. In modern processors some cache (called primary cache) is built into the processor itself. Secondary cache is fitted to the motherboard. Because of the cost of static RAM other types of RAM chips and memory addressing have also been developed to speed up transfer rates – including a type of RAM called EDO ('Extended Data Out').

2.3.1 Storage

The other general-purpose component of the computer which is affected by the growth of graphics is the storage system. The first computers used audio cassettes for storing programs and data files but these were soon superseded by floppy discs (of about 100K capacity) and hard discs (of about 10 Mbytes capacity). The current standard for floppy discs is still 1.44 Mbytes, until one of the newer 100 – 120 Megabyte systems takes its place. Hard discs normally range from about 4 – 12 Gigabytes (but up to more than 20 Gigabytes, at a price). In part this increase has been driven by the increasing size of applications software but a major factor has been the size of data files, in particular graphics files, sound and video files. Other high-capacity storage systems which have been developed for the reasons discussed, include a variety of optically-based disc systems such as read-only CD systems and a variety of read-write disc technologies. There seems no end in sight of the pressures for increased data-handling capacity as the demands of digital sound, animation and video are added to traditional graphic files.

Another response to the problem of increasing file sizes has been the increasing use of file compression. This is important enough to merit a chapter of its own – along with some associated topics – later in the book.

2.4 Hard-Copy Devices

Images which have been created interactively with the help of display devices can be stored in coded form on normal computer storage devices such as magnetic tape or floppy and hard discs and re-displayed when necessary. Because of the size and weight of computers and monitors it is important to have other ways of viewing their output and so it is convenient be able to make copies of computer images on paper or film. The rest of this chapter is devoted to a discussion of 'hard-copy' devices, which do this, together with a resume of the main types of input device. These provide alternatives to the usual computer input device – the keyboard – and, while not strictly necessary in many applications, do provide much more convenient ways of entering information relevant to images rather than text characters.

Hard-copy devices are perhaps the second most important piece of hardware in a graphics system – after the display device. These devices are generally called printers or plotters according to whether they are primarily designed for use with bit-mapped images or vector images, though this definition is not watertight since so many images, which are stored as vectors, are scan-converted and then printed using bit-mapped printing devices. It will be seen later that plotters were originally mechanical devices for the output of vector drawings and the term is still used for any device which fulfils the same purpose even though it may not strictly be a vector output device.

Some early printers – like the daisy-wheel printer – were satisfactory only for text and some – like the pen-plotter – only for line graphics (with a limited amount of text) but virtually all modern devices – like the inkjet and laser printers – are suitable for both, since they use the dot-matrix method of representing images with a high resolution – at least 300 dots per inch (dpi).

One of the earliest devices, the daisy-wheel printer, is now obsolete but another early device – its rival as a cheap printer (the dot-matrix printer) – still survives and a brief description is justified in that, for the home user on a budget, it can be used as a proofing device and for unsophisticated applications.

2.4.1 Dot-matrix printers

This device uses the basic principle of an impact printer – like a typewriter – using a typewriter-style ribbon, but the large number of individual type-bars are replaced by a single head containing a vertically-mounted row of tiny metal pins. These pins can be independently struck by small electro-magnetically operated hammers, so producing a dot-matrix pattern. The simplest and cheapest printers have a row of

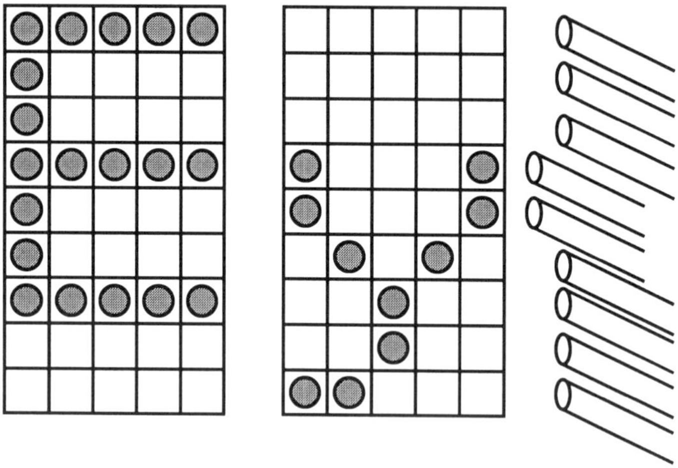

Fig. 2.14 Characters are created using a set of movable pins

only nine pins; more modern designs use a larger number to produce better quality results but all work on the same principle. A single character is created by a process in which the head is advanced horizontally over the paper, printing simultaneously one vertical column of dots and then going on to print the next column and the next until after five of more, the character is complete.

Figure 2.14 illustrates the way that characters are created on a 9 × 5 dot matrix. Many characters utilize only six or seven of the nine vertically-mounted pins though most symbols are made up from the full five columns and therefore involve five separate printing operations as the head rapidly traverses the paper from side to side. The explanation for this apparent waste of the pins lies in the need for descenders. These are those parts of a character which hang down below the line, as in the lower-case letter 'y' for example or as in some punctuation marks like the comma or semi-colon. Figure 2.14 compares an upper-case letter 'E' with a lower-case 'y' to illustrate the point.

The quality of these characters is not as good as those produced by a modern typewriter but the dot-matrix method has considerably greater flexibility in being able to produce a copy of any raster display. Even for text-only copy it has some advantages in that italic script, double height letters, alternative typefaces and sizes are easily obtained, usually from in-built software. Some matrix printers are able to produce a limited form of colour printing using a three or four colour ribbon with yellow, cyan and magenta stripes. The particular colour is selected by the activation of a motor which moves the ribbon up and down so as to bring the head into line with the correct stripe of colour on the ribbon. By a process of overprinting – that is, printing the characters more than once, in different primary colours – this system can produce the standard seven colours plus white (the colour of the paper). Some printers use a four-colour ribbon, the fourth colour being black. This produces a better quality black than is obtained by overprinting the three primary colours as well as being much faster. The problem of the overprinting method is that small quantities of ink are carried over from one coloured stripe to another and so the quality of the colours gradually deteriorates, leading to dirty-looking colours.

Improvements to the resolution of dot-matrix printers are achieved using two simple effects. One involves a slightly more sophisticated form of overprinting in which the head makes two or more passes over each line of text, the paper being advanced (shifted very slightly in the vertical direction) between passes. This means that on the second or third pass the sets of dots which are added to the image fit in between the dots printed earlier. This produces a similar result to that which would be obtained if the head had two or three times as many pins as it actually has, thereby improving the resolution of the image at the expense of slowing down the printing process. The second approach is actually to fit the printer head with more pins – usually 24 but in some cases, as many as 48 – and so gain the improved resolution without loss of speed and without the necessity of advancing the paper by small amounts between passes. In the case of 18- and 24-pin printers the pins are usually in two staggered rows (of 9 or 12 pins) which can be thought of as a compromise between the two approaches. Each column of dots is printed twice, once with each set of pins, producing the equivalent of 18 or 24 slightly overlapping dots. Some 24-pin printers claim 300 dots per inch but this doesn't imply the same quality as a 300 dpi laser printer since the dots in a dot-matrix printer are much larger than those in a laser printer. There is a lower limit to the size of the pins which can be used and which can sustain the hammering process involved in their operation.

Dot matrix printers are fast and cheap, both to buy and to run, but there is a limit to the fine detail they can display – lines show the jagged effect seen in most raster-scan displays – and they are also noisy and lack sophisticated colour and grey level facilities.

2.4.2 Thermal printers

These can be thought of as a variation on the impact dot-matrix printer. They use a ribbon with a special waxy ink which is transferred to the paper using a system of pins, but the transfer is by a heating process rather than by mechanical impact. The pins are heated electrically while the head is in contact with the ribbon. The result is a much quieter printer and, in the case of colour ribbons, much stronger and more saturated colours. The improved quality of the colour is a result of the fact that the melting of the ink transfers most of it to the paper – which means that the ribbons can only be used once (it is a 'single-strike' ribbon). Because of this, in a number of modern colour printers the 'ribbon' is actually a broad sheet of material – enough to cover the whole piece of paper. This type of printer often needs special paper to ensure that the melted ink does not smudge and to ensure that the heat is quickly conducted away from the printer-head to prevent it overheating. Special paper and special ribbons, together with the fact that ribbons can only be used one, make the system much more expensive than ordinary dot matrix printers.

Thermal dot matrix printers which produce coloured images, do so by multiple passes of each line, while the three primary colours are laid down. This system, like all multiple-pass systems, requires accurate registration to achieve good results – any small slippage of the paper between passes reduces the quality of the image considerably. One of the advantages of thermal printers is their quietness in operation; impact printers are so noisy that they are often operated inside sound-absorbing hoods. Because there are cheaper alternatives to the thermal process for monochrome output, thermal printers are exclusively used for colour printing.

2.4.3 Sublimation printers

These are a development of the colour thermal printer – already described – which use special inks to produce a vast number of colours. These special inks have the unusual property that when heated they do not melt to produce a liquid, as might be expected, but change directly to the gaseous state. This phenomenon is called 'sublimation'. Not many substances exhibit this effect at normal temperatures and pressures. The best-known example is 'dry-ice', which is solid carbon dioxide, and which changes to the gaseous form at room temperatures. It is often used on stage to produce a cloud-like effect. The advantage of using inks that sublime is that the primary colours can mix in the paper to produce intermediate shades which can be an enormous improvement over the dithering techniques used in all other colour printers. Dithering has been briefly introduced in Chapter 1 and will be discussed in detail in the chapter on colour but a brief discussion is given here.

All colour effects are the result of mixing primary colours – yellow, cyan and magenta in the case of printing techniques. The question is – how is the mixing to be done ? In Chapter 1 the term 'spot colour' was introduced as the printer's term for colours which are specially mixed before printing – as oil paints are mixed by an artist. However, most colour effects are obtained by the use of only three primary colours and the 'mixing' is done in the eye. The primary colours are laid down as a series of tiny dots, side-by-side, and the three colours of light so produced are mixed in the eye (or, more correctly, the brain) because the eye cannot actually see the individual dots of colour. It responds to the mixture of colours. This technique is called 'dithering' and is used by all colour printers, except sublimation printers. The disadvantage of dithering is that to produce a pixel (a picture element) in one of a series of colours that pixel must consist of a number of printed dots, and therefore the pixel can never be as small as the printed, coloured dot itself. Increasing the number of colours inevitably decreases the spatial resolution (and the detail) of the image.

The beauty of the sublimation technique is that this compromise is not necessary. By careful controlling the heating of the pins, variable quantities of the primary colours are released and mixed in the paper to produce a pixel of the required colour without dithering, and without loss of resolution. This type of printer can produce pictures of 'photographic quality'.

2.4.4 Pen-plotters

The principles of the pen-plotter have already been briefly described. It is a vector device in which a pen is driven over a piece of paper by means of some mechanical system, drawing lines directly on the paper in a single colour. There are two basic approaches to the mechanics of moving a pen over a piece of paper – flat bed geometry and drum geometry.

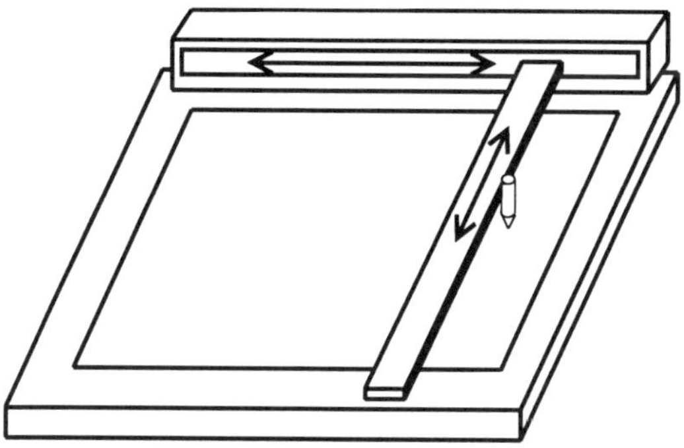

Fig. 2.15 *The principle of the flat-bed plotter*

In the flat-bed plotter, paper is fixed to a stationary flat surface (the bed) which might be of any size from a table-top model using A4 size paper (30 × 21 cm) to 2 × 3 m or larger (about the size of a billiard table). The paper is held firmly in place by one of a variety of methods, including simple sticky tape, electrostatic attraction and vacuum suction through tiny holes in the bed. The pen is carried on a holder which slides up and down a long straight gantry arm which in turn moves on rails at one or both ends of the flat bed (Fig. 2.15). This provides the two (X and Y) movements needed to move the pen to any part of the paper. In order to draw any desired line, including smooth curves, the two movements are driven by very accurate stepper motors which, together with suitable gears, mean that the pen can be moved in very small steps. These steps are typically 0.1 mm but can be as low as 0.01 mm in some devices.

The alternative approach to achieving the desired movements, used in the drum and belt plotters, is to divide those movements between the pen and the paper. The paper is mounted either on a horizontally-mounted drum or, if longer sheets of paper are to be used, passes from one roller to another on a loosely-mounted belt. Rotation of the drum or rollers provides one direction of movement and the other is provided by the pen in its holder sliding over a fixed arm at right-angles to the movement of the paper (Fig. 2.16). This second approach results in a much more compact device and provides a space-saving alternative to the larger flat-bed plotters.

Although at any time only one colour can be used, a wide variety of colours and line-thicknesses can be achieved in a diagram by the simple process of changing the pen. In modern plotters this is automated – the pen holder moving to a carousel or

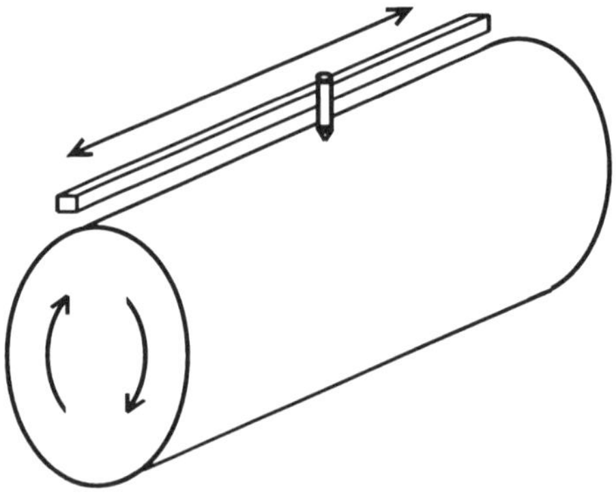

Fig. 2.16 *The principle of the drum-plotter*

other device and exchanging pens with one of the others held there. This type of device is ideal for plotting diagrams which consist of lines rather than blocks of colour and which require only a few colours (say six to twelve, rather than the minimum of 256 colours which are used in all modern monitors).

Within these restrictions a large flat-bed plotter is probably the most precise hard-copy device available, able to draw lines which are faultless to inspection by the naked eye by virtue of the fact that the pen can be moved by tenths or hundredths of a millimetre in drawing lines up to metres in length. The main drawback of the pen-plotter, other than its limited number of colours and unsuitability for large blocks of colour is that of speed. Plotters are very slow, but this is a natural characteristic of a device with relatively heavy moving mechanical parts. Early plotters also had the disadvantage that their slowness resulted in the computer's being occupied for a long time, particularly if the diagram involved a lot of computationally intensive activities such as driving a pen round curves or drawing text characters. In the modern plotter most of this software is resident in the plotter itself in the form of stored graphics primitives which can be called up from the host computer by simple, usually standardized, plotter codes.

Some modern devices sold as 'plotters' are not pen-plotters at all. The pen and sliding pen holder has been replaced with a long inkjet head (the width of the paper).

2.4.5 Electronic printing techniques

There are a number of printing technologies that use electronic methods of transferring ink to paper, the best-known of which – the laser printer – has been developed from the Xerographic methods used in the normal office photocopier.

The photocopier depends for its operation on the photo-conductive properties of substance like selenium and cadmium sulphide. The term 'conductivity' refers to the ability of a substance to conduct electricity. A substance is said to exhibit 'photo-conductivity' if its conductivity is affected by photons of light absorbed by its surface. Selenium, for example, is normally an electrical insulator, but becomes a

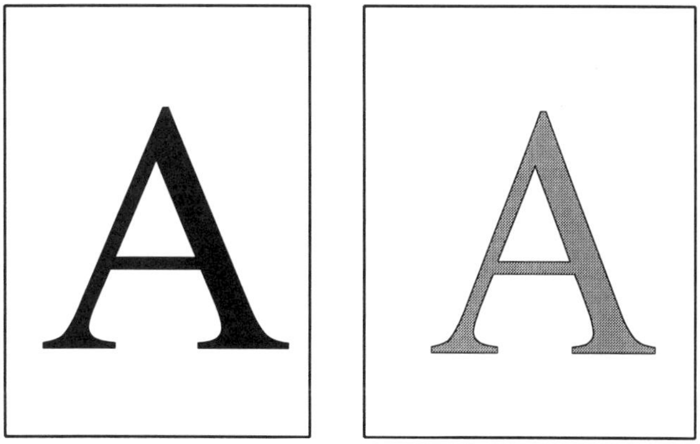

Fig. 2.17 *A photocopier converts a black-and-white image into a charge pattern*

conductor when bright light of the right wavelength shines on it. The same property is shared by certain organic compounds which are increasingly replacing selenium for this purpose. Selenium is a toxic chemical and this creates disposal problems when the photo-conductive drum has to be replaced, as it is from time to time.

The principle of operation is this. The selenium takes the form of a coating on an aluminium drum. This is initially sprayed with a layer of electrical charges from a high-voltage generator and the charges remain on the surface because the selenium is behaving as an insulator. A bright light in the form of a high intensity tube then progressively illuminates the document which is to be copied, steadily scanning it from top to bottom, and the light reflected from this is focused by a lens to produce an image of the document on the drum. The image of the document takes the form of some areas which are brightly illuminated (corresponding to the white portions of the original) and others which are not illuminated (corresponding to the black text or other printed parts of the document). Where light shines on it, the selenium layer becomes a conductor allowing the charge in those areas to leak through it and be lost via the earthed aluminium drum. In the dark areas the selenium remains an insulator and the charge is retained. In this way an electrostatically-charged (but invisible) copy of the original image is created on the drum (see Fig. 2.17).

In the next stage of the process the rotating drum passes over a trough of a special 'ink' (called toner) which is made up from minute particles of a black organic compound. These tiny particles are attracted to those regions of the drum which are charged and stick there. Next the drum rotates past a sheet of paper which is on an electrically-earthed plate and a high proportion of the toner particles (about 70%) transfer to the paper. The sheet of paper is then rapidly heated as it passes between heated rollers to fuse the toner on to the paper. The charge on the drum is then neutralized so that excess toner can be removed from it by a scraper assembly and the process repeated.

A variety of printers have been designed which all use this principle that electrostatic charge will attract tiny particles of ink and so can ensure ink particles are placed on paper where they are required. What distinguishes the different types of printer is the exact mechanism for manipulating the electrostatic charge.

2.4.6 Laser printers

The laser printer is an adaptation of the photo-copier which allows images, stored as bit-patterns in a computer, to be transferred to the photo-conductive drum using a laser. The purpose of the laser is to provide a bright focused spot of light which illuminates the drum and takes the place of the document-light-lens system in a photo-copier. The image is built up on the photo-conductive drum pixel by pixel by

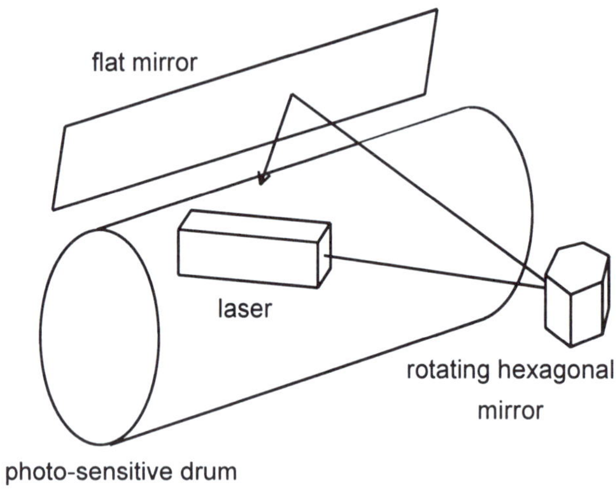

Fig. 2.18 *The principle of the laser printer*

scanning the focused light beam from the laser. The scanning device is a rotating hexagonal mirror and the scanning mechanism is simply illustrated in Figure 2.18. It begins with the laser beam being reflected off the edge of one of the mirrors on to the photosensitive drum. Because the mirror-system is rotating, the beam is scanned across the drum as the current face of the mirror changes its angle to the beam. When, because of the rotation of the hexagon, the beam comes to the far edge of the first mirror it then strikes the adjacent edge of the next mirror which is at an angle of 60 degrees to the first and this immediately switches the beam back to the beginning of a new line. Rotation of the drum at this point provides the necessary movement, perpendicular to the first, so that the second line is a short distance below the first. The individual pixels are obtained by rapidly switching the laser beam off and on as it scans. By this means a single fixed laser is able to scan a large number of lines on a rotating drum with a density of at least 300 dpi. A laser printer is therefore essentially a photocopier in which the analogue input via a document and lens has been replaced by a digital input via a switched laser. The cheapest laser printers give a resolution of 300 dpi and this was the standard for some years but it has given way to a new 600 dpi standard for professional work, leaving the 300 dpi machines as cheap home or small office devices, competing with inkjets. Even the 300 dpi standard produces a result which is far superior to the ordinary impact dot-matrix printer. Three hundred dots per inch on an 8 inch wide A4 size paper are the equivalent of 2400 dots per line. A dot-matrix printer using a 9 × 8 dot character matrix and 60 to 70 characters per line is using only about 500 – 600 dots per line.

More expensive laser printers are available which offer up to 3000 dpi and which rival the quality of traditional printing processes. In addition to a conventional text output, all laser printers have a graphics capability including grey-levels, obtained by dithering, a method which is acceptable when very high dot densities are possible. This can produce very acceptable results when printing monochrome photographs, for example, at 1200 or 1600 dpi. Most high-resolution laser printers have a capacity to vary the power of the laser beam when printing a dot, which therefore produces dots of variable size. This has two advantages. One is that a wider range of grey-levels can be simulated by dithering techniques (as already mentioned). The other is that for areas of uniform black, fewer, larger dots can be used – which improves the speed of printing – but for the edges of complicated shapes the smaller dots can be used, to obtain better fidelity to the desired shape.

In recent years colour laser printers have become available and, though initially very expensive, are already coming down in price to compete with the better quality inkjets. As in all colour printing devices, colour laser printers lay down three or four separate colours, in separate operations. In some designs the paper passes over three (or four) separate drums and coloured toner is deposited on the paper one colour at a time. Because of the ever-present problem of colour-registration (placing the different coloured dots in exactly the right position) other designs place the colours, in sequence, on an intermediate belt which finally transfers all the colours onto the paper in one final operation.

Laser printers, are sometimes described as 'page printers'. The name emphasizes the fact that a whole page of text or graphics is downloaded to the printer as a bit-image and printed in one single, smooth operation, utilizing a rotating drum. In contrast, many other designs form the final image one character or one line at a time, usually by means of some sort of printer head which passes over the paper, depositing ink in a narrow band, after which the paper is advanced by an equal amount and the next band of ink laid down underneath. The key to the success of this operation is that the paper must be advanced by a very precise amount. If the page advances by too much, a set of narrow white stripes appear, crossing the image. If it advances too little, then parts of the image overlap and a series of dark bands appear where the two batches of ink have been printed at the same place. The advantage of the page printer is that it is much less prone to this type of irritating fault.

2.4.7 LED and LCS printers

The LED (Light Emitting Diode) printer uses the same basic photo-copier mechanism as the standard laser printer but illuminates the photosensitive drum by means of tiny solid-state devices which generate light (the LEDs). Because they can be manufactured relatively cheaply and are very small it is possible to dispense with the rotating mirror and laser system and simply install a row of about 2400 LEDs – one for each pixel (corresponding to 300 dpi and the 8.27 inch width of A4 paper). These LEDs are mounted on an arm which is close to, and parallel to the main axis

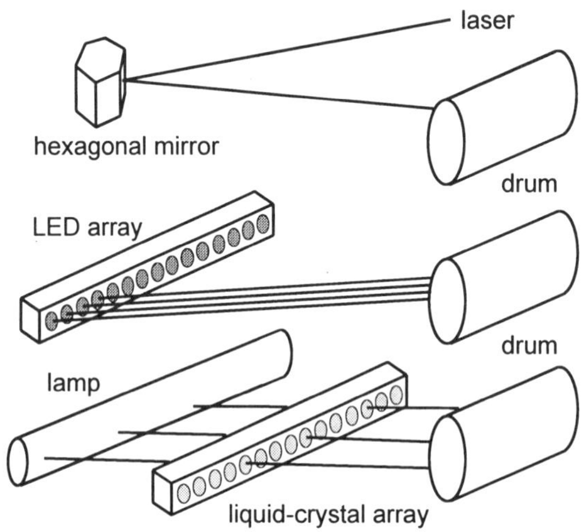

Fig. 2.19 *The principles of laser, LED and LCS printers compared*

of the photosensitive drum (Fig. 2.19). As the drum rotates beneath them the individual light-sources are switched on and off so as to lay down the appropriate charge pattern. Such a system does not have the mechanical complexity of a laser printer but clearly involves considerably greater electronic sophistication.

A variation on this theme is the Liquid Crystal Shutter (LCS) printer. The light in this printer is provided by a single rod-shaped source – in fact, a fluorescent tube. The separate pixels are achieved by means of a row of about 2000 tiny liquid crystal devices each about 1/300 of an inch in diameter. These are similar to the crystals used in the LC Display described in the previous section describing flat-panel displays. Their function here is to act as shutters or light-gates. In the LC Display the individual liquid crystal's function is to block the light so as to produce dark pixels against a light background. Here they act in a similar way to shut off light and prevent (or allow) it reaching the photosensitive drum.

The advantage of both the LED and the LCS printer is that they are mechanically and optically simpler than the laser printer. In addition it is much easier to achieve linearity across the full width of the line of pixels. In the laser printer the shape and separation of the individual pixels depends not only on the laser beam but on the optical characteristics of the mirror system which must sweep the focused spot across the width of the photo-conductive drum. In the LED and LCS printers the size and shape of the pixels depends on the uniformity of the LEDs and LCSs which are determined in the manufacturing process.

2.4.8 Image-setters (type-setters) and professional printing

All the printers discussed so far have been desktop devices, suitable for the production of single copies or short runs (up to a few hundred copies, at the most). When large numbers of copies are required (thousands, for example) different types of printer are needed. A desktop laser or inkjet printer cannot compete with professional printing technology because of their speed (they are too slow), the running costs and the relatively large size of the dots they create. Professional printing is mostly done now by a process called lithography – 'litho'. This is based on an 18th Century discovery that wax on the damp surface of a flat stone attracted ink whereas the wet areas repelled the ink. This meant that an image could be made with wax on the flat surface which would retain ink which could then be transferred to a sheet of paper. Although printers using flat stones were used until the turn of the century, modern printers use a metal plate, coated with a light-sensitive emulsion. This is exposed to a negative (reversed) image of a master document. The black regions in the original document (say, the text) become transparent so that the light shines onto the emulsion – making it hard. When developed, the hardened areas remain while the unexposed areas are washed away. The image area is then coated with a chemical that attracts ink but repels water. The other areas are coated with a substance that attracts water but repels ink. This plate is then attached to a rotating cylinder and water and ink are applied. The plate is then rolled against a rubber blanket (the offset roller), transferring the image to it and the image, in turn is then transferred to paper. The offset roller serves two purposes – it is flexible enough to make a good contact with the paper and it ensures that the printing plate is not subject to the abrasive qualities of the fibres in the paper – so making it last longer.

Until litho techniques were developed all printing processes involved surfaces which were not flat – either the best-known technology of moveable type ('letter-press') in which the shapes of characters protrude above the surface or gravure (intaglio) in which images are scratched into the surface. In the first the ink sticks to the raised areas and is then transferred to paper. In the second the ink sticks in the etched lines, below the surface. The first was pre-eminent for text; the second was developed in the last century for hand-drawn illustrations. Tonal images are a problem for both techniques. In litho printing, however, when the original is a tonal image (like a photograph) the master can be made by re-photographing the original through a special 'screen' – a finely-ruled grid of lines engraved on a glass sheet. The scattering of the light as it passes through this grid produces a dither-like pattern of dots in the photograph, of variable size and density which reflect the tones of the original image. Because the masters are created photographically the resolution of the final image depends on the resolution of the photograph (and the fineness of the grid). Now, the silver crystals used in photographic emulsions are of microscopic size and so this technique can create very high resolution images. The resolution of a printing process is often best judged by the quality of reproduction of tonal images, like photographs, because grey-scales involve some form of dithering. Very high-resolution processes can afford the loss of detail caused by this process in a way that the lower-resolution methods cannot.

We have seen that litho printers need an original, from which the master printing plate can be created and have seen how that is done when tonal images are needed, but what about text? A high-resolution printing system is needed to create the original, which seems to bring us back to where we started. We have seen that laser printers are restricted by the size of the toner particles used and the accuracy with which they can be placed by the electrostatic processes. However, if the end product is to be a master plate, produced by photography, there is no reason to use toner particles at all. An image-setter (early models were called type-setters) is essentially a modified laser printer, with no electrostatic drum and no toner particles. Instead, the laser beam exposes a photographic emulsion directly. A laser beam can be focussed to form a very fine spot and so an image-setter is capable of creating very high resolution images. The highest-quality image-setters can operate at up to 4,000 dpi which means that not only is text of the very highest quality but that half-tone images, like photographs, can be at very high resolution with a large number of grey-levels.

2.4.9 Inkjet printers

This type of printer does not use the electrostatic method of attracting toner to the paper which was common to previous devices. Instead, it sprays tiny droplets of ink on to the paper. In the earliest designs a continuous spray of up to 50,000 droplets of ink per second from a single nozzle was directed around the paper to produce the characters or other shapes required using electric fields, in a manner reminiscent of the way that an electron beam is steered in a CRT. To obtain blank regions the beam was simply allowed to fall, before reaching the paper, into a receptacle. Most modern monochrome inkjet printers, however, use a bank of up to 50 tiny nozzles – each about half the thickness of a human hair to produce the individual pixels on a drop-on-demand principle. The ink is ejected as droplets either by an electromechanical (piezo-electric) device which squeezes them out of the nozzle or by a rapid heating and expansion technique. The bank of nozzles, in two overlapping rows of 25 each, is packed into a distance of 1/6 inch and so can produce a dot density of 300 dpi or more. Each nozzle ejects about 6,000 droplets of ink per second

Colour inkjet printers use between three and six sets of nozzles, each set producing ink droplets of different colours. The basic colours are cyan, magenta, yellow and, usually, black; in some cases these are supplemented with light cyan and light magenta. For example, one current printer has 32 nozzles for each of six colours. The resolution obtained is either 360, 720 or 1440 dpi depending on the setting. Higher resolution images take longer to print than lower resolution images and it can take quite a few minutes to print a single page. One of the benefits claimed for the piezo-electric method of ejecting ink drops is that it is claimed that it offers greater control over this process which can result in smaller ink drops (and therefore improved resolution). Special coated paper is normally necessary for the best results. The coating is designed to stop the ink from spreading too much into the paper and so ensures maximum brightness and best resolution.

Some high-quality inkjet printers use ink which is solid at room temperature and takes the form of small cylindrical blocks. When the printer is in use the ink is heated to its melting point and maintained in liquid form in the printer but solidifies again when sprayed on to the paper, thus reducing the amount of spreading or diffusion into the paper. By this and other improvements to the properties of the ink, excellent results are increasingly possible with many ordinary types of paper from most modern inkjet printers. An early problem, that of the nozzles becoming blocked by dried ink, was solved by the simple expedient of replacing them frequently. The nozzles, together with an ink reservoir, are often provided in a single unit which is replaced when the ink runs out, though some colour inkjets use three or four separate nozzle units – one for each unit. This has the advantage that if one of the primary colours is used more than the others, its unit can be replaced without discarding the other colours at the same time.

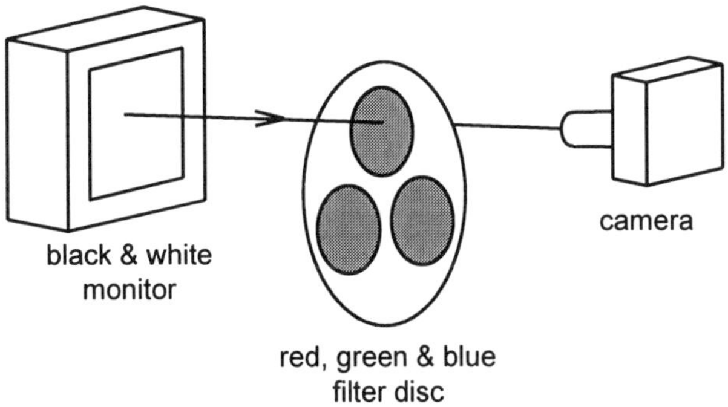

Fig. 2.20 *The principles of photographic recording*

One advantage of the piezo-electric technique has been that it is possible to apply very precise control to the process of squeezing out the ink droplets, so producing smaller droplets and therefore better resolution. Although the standard resolution of inkjet printers has been in the range 300 – 360 dpi for some years, some modern printers can now offer 1440 × 720 dpi. One spin-off of this is that a better range of colours can be created by dithering without sacrificing detail in the image. Early ink jet printers were used mainly for applications that did not require many colours – like printing bar-charts and architectural plans but the advent of digital cameras has spurred interest in 'photographic-quality' images with a large range of colours and shades. Smaller dot sizes provide one answer to this demand but some printers meet this challenge by the use of six-colour systems. The three primary colours can be mixed with intermediate shades to produce more natural effects.

2.4.10 Photographic methods

In principle, the simplest way of recording a computer-generated image is to take a direct record of the display by photographing the monitor screen. For someone who already owns a camera and tripod this can be a very economical method of producing occasional hard copy. It is particularly cheap when compared with those high-quality (and expensive) colour printers which are needed to produce the wide range of colours needed for photographic-quality results. There are two main problems with this approach, apart from the inconvenience of setting up the camera and the delay in obtaining prints. One is caused by the shape of the normal CRT screen which is often not very flat. This can lead to distorted images. The other is the problem of getting the correct colour balance since colour films are designed for use either with artificial tungsten lights or sunlight. A final irritation can be that of room lights reflected from the glass face of the display which mean that the monitor and camera need to be covered with blackout material.

To solve these problems and to make the technique more convenient, special photographic recording devices have been developed. These use special flat-face high resolution monitors – together with a system of coloured filters when colour images are required. Oddly enough a monochrome monitor provides a better way of obtaining coloured photographic images than a colour monitor. The problem with the colour monitor lies in the individual phosphor dots or stripes which are needed to produce the coloured image. The pitch of the screen (the size of the coloured phosphor dots) restricts the number of pixels which can be displayed and therefore the resolution of coloured images obtained this way. However, when the image is to be recorded on film a relatively cheap monochrome monitor, together with suitable colour filters is all that is needed. The flat-face monitor is built into a light-proof box which contains the filters on a rotating wheel together with a camera which is focused on the face of the monitor (Fig. 2.20). The whole device is connected to the computer and acts in the same way as a conventional monitor except that only one primary colour signal is displayed at any one time. Thus the, say, red portions of the image are displayed on the monitor and photographed through the red filter. The process is then repeated for the two other primary colours, each being photographed through the appropriate filter. This process of multiple exposures produces a complete colour image on the film without the need for a colour monitor and without any restrictions which might result from an inadequate phosphor-dot pitch. Another improvement is obtained by generating high resolution images with anything from 700 to 4000 lines on the screen. This can be necessary if the final slide is to be projected onto a large screen at high magnification. This number of lines is much easier to generate when it is not necessary to produce a complete image in 1/25 second. A high resolution system like this may take a few minutes to produce an image. One advantage of this technique is that it provides full control over the colour balance of the final image by alterations to the relative exposure times of the three primary colours – a process which can produce an almost unlimited number of colours.

2.4.11 Video output

The growth in interest in multimedia, the advances in processor speed and the development of new storage technologies in the gigabyte range have all stimulated an interest in the use of digitized videos. These are moving images which are originated on conventional video cameras but then digitized, frame by frame, for computer storage and processing. Because of the huge information content involved, specialized hardware and software are needed, both to capture the video (that is to digitize it) and to display it. The software contribution lies in compressing and decompressing the images so as to reduce the size of the video files and to reduce the necessary 'throughput' (the bandwidth) as the video files are moved around the computer. This aspect of the subject is reserved for the chapter on graphics files. Hardware devices take the form of two types of specialist adapter cards. One type is a capture card which is connected to a video input (the camera, typically, but it could be a video recorder) and digitizes the analogue video image. The other is a display card which assists the display of digitized video clips on the computer screen.

Capture cards digitize the video signals into 768 pixels per scan line – taking three measurements at each point, one for the red, one for the green and one for the blue components of the image at that point. The origin of the number 768 lies in the fact that the European (PAL) TV system uses 625 lines, of which 50 are not used for the picture (but are utilized for Teletext information). Since the aspect ratio of the image is 4 : 3 then to obtain square pixels the number per scan line = $(625 - 50) \times 4 \div 3 = 766.6$. To obtain a more convenient whole number the scan lines are increased by 1 to 576 so that the number then becomes $576 \times 4 \div 3 = 768$. The total amount of information per frame thus comes to $768 \times 576 \times 3$ bytes = 1,327,104 bytes (1.3 Mbytes) for 24-bit colour. This corresponds to 1.327×25 = over 33 Mbytes per second (since the TV image is refreshed at 25 frames per second). This sort of detail is necessary for 'broadcast-quality' but that level of quality is not always required. One type of saving can be achieved by digitizing at less than 24-bit colour. Another approach is to digitize only every alternate line. This produces perfectly acceptable images if the intention is to use them in a multimedia setting where the final image will not fill the whole screen.

The above calculations have been based on the European TV systems. The equivalent calculations for the US are based on a 525 line, 30 frames per second, system. In both cases, these figures will become redundant in a few years because of immanent moves to a new, higher resolution standard (or standards). In any case, new standards are likely to be digital and so the current equipment for digitizing analogue signals will become redundant.

Video display cards are cards which accelerate the handling of video files. Since these are normally compressed files the special function of the card is to decompress the files rapidly using hardware. In the absence of hardware decompression any graphics card can handle video files using software to produce the decompression but hardware-based solutions are usually faster. This type of card is likely to vanish before long as hardware video file decompression becomes a standard feature of all graphics cards.

2.5 Input Devices

Finally, and in what might seem a reverse of the natural order, we consider input devices. The majority of these are pointing devices which enable the operator to indicate choices and to draw shapes, but there are also automatic input devices to convert existing images into the appropriate digital form. However, it should not be forgotten that the traditional keyboard is still necessary as an input device even in graphics applications, for the entry of text and numeric data. Some keyboards are also available with special graphics input facilities of the sort to be described (such as joysticks and thumbwheels) incorporated into them.

2.5.1 Joysticks, mice, rollerballs, thumbwheels

All of these are simple mechanical devices, connected by a cable to the computer, which enable the operator to enter simple directional information. The joystick takes its name from the steering device on early aeroplanes and consists of a stick, mounted in the top of a box, which can be moved in any direction, these movements being detected by the fact that the joystick is connected to variable resistors inside the box. The value of the small voltage drop across the resistor is digitized by circuitry in the joystick container or in the computer to provide signals indicating which way the joystick is pointing. Most joysticks, unlike a mouse, only allow the user to indicate a direction and not a distance. This can be overcome, however, if the software is designed to measure how long the joystick points in a particular direction and the time is taken to represent a distance. When released, springs return it to the neutral position.

The mouse consists of a small plastic box containing, in the bottom, a ball which enables the mouse to be smoothly rolled around the desk or table in the vicinity of the computer. This movement is used to represent both direction and distance. In some designs – the cheapest – the movements of the ball in four directions are detected by means of simple electro-mechanical sensors (small friction rollers touching the ball which generate pulses as they rotate). In others the mouse is rolled over a special pad which is ruled with a large number of lines and movement over the pad is detected by means of electro-optical sensors fitted to the bottom of the mouse. The latter is a better system because the movement which is measured is that of the mouse relative to the pad rather than of the ball itself and so any slipping of the ball on a smooth surface will not affect the result. Slipping of the ball can often be eliminated by using the mouse on a special surface – a mouse pad. A commonly-used compromise design is one in which movement of the ball is detected by optical sensors – tiny light source (an LED) shines a beam of light through the slots in a small wheel and the light pulses which are generated as the wheel turns are detected by a light-sensitive chip.

A roller-ball or tracker-ball is really a mouse turned upside down – a box with a ball projecting from the top which is rolled in the desired direction by the hand – and can offer more sensitive control for small movements as well as being useful for situations where there is no room to use a mouse. Thumb-wheels serve a similar purpose but take the form of two small wheels set at right angles to each other, often incorporated into a keyboard, which can be rotated by the thumb. All of these devices are usually used in conjunction with software which drives a graphics cursor displayed on the monitor. Movement of the mouse or joystick produces movement of the cursor on the screen, so giving constant visual feedback. None of them is designed to be used to input very precise information and their purpose is usually to indicate direction of movement and approximate position, as when choosing an option from a screen menu, but with practice a good-quality mouse can be used for drawing as an alternative to the light pen or graphic tablet (see later in the chapter). The positional information provided is usually relative rather than absolute. When a mouse is picked up, for example, and placed down elsewhere on the table the cursor on the screen does not move because movement is detected only when the ball is rotated or when the optical sensors are close to the ruled surface of the pad.

2.5.2 Touch-sensitive screens

These are used in a similar way to allow the operator to indicate choice by pointing directly at the screen. They are particularly useful when the operator is inexpert in the use of a computer system or finds it inconvenient to use an ancillary device like

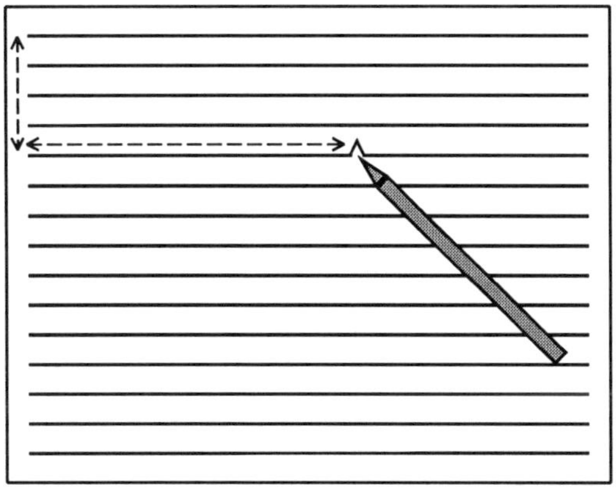

Fig. 2.21 A light pen detects the brief flash as a point is refreshed and calculates its position using the synchronization pulses at the beginning of each scan line

a mouse. Usually they take the form of a special transparent overlay screen, added to the front of a conventional monitor, which the operator touches to indicate a choice from a variety of coloured menu boxes displayed on the screen. The position of the finger is detected by one of a variety of methods. In some systems the finger presses onto and distorts a plastic sheet and the stresses so produced are detected by strain gauges attached along the edges of the sheet. Another method detects the position of the finger when it breaks one of a number of parallel infra-red beams. This method involves placing a row of infra-red emitters along two edges of the screen together with two rows of corresponding detectors along the opposite edges. Some work by detecting the capacitative changes when one sheet of plastic, covered with a thin transparent conducting coating, is pushed slightly closer under the pressure of the operator's finger to a similar sheet mounted close to it. These devices can offer only approximate information about position and so are used only to indicate choice from a limited number of options

2.5.3 Light pens

These can provide a much more accurate way of indicating position on a monitor, as compared with a mouse or joystick, and have the advantage that the operator can point directly at the screen – like the touch-sensitive systems just described. A light pen consists of a stylus (a pen-shaped object) which contains a light-sensitive device in the tip and which is connected to the computer via a cable. When placed on the screen this detects the momentary flash caused by the electron beam as it passes and refreshes that point, thus temporarily giving a boost to the intensity of the light emitted from that region of the screen. This sends a signal to the computer and precise timing measurements relative to the synchronization signals at the beginning of each raster line establish the location of the beam at the time the signal originated (Fig. 2.21). The number of synchronization signals received since the beginning of the frame indicate the value of y (vertical distance). The time since the last synchronization signal indicates the value of x (horizontal distance).

This type of device provides the most direct method of drawing on the computer screen, though used over a long time it can be tiring because of the need to hold one's arm up to the screen. One way to solve the problem of fatigue is to mount the monitor in a working surface such that the screen is flush with the desk-top or at a small inclined angle to it. The problem with this device is that the pen can be used only for pointing to areas which are being refreshed and which are emitting light – unless special hardware is fitted to the monitor to refresh regularly the whole display area in flashes between the normal image refreshment. The alternative is to use software which enables the user to steer a special cursor around the screen, thus providing an illuminated area constantly in association with the pen.

2.5.4 Graphics tablets

These provide a less tiring and more accurate alternative to the light pen in which the stylus is used in conjunction with a special flat tablet which is placed on a table in a normal drawing position. The location of the stylus on the tablet can be detected by many different methods but the commonest are electro-magnetic, electrostatic, magnetostrictive and sonic. The most widely used, the electro-magnetic, uses a tablet which contains embedded in it a grid made of a large number of parallel wires acting like the reference lines on a piece of graph paper. Either the grid is energized and the stylus serves as a receiver or the other way round but in either case the position detection mechanism is via the magnetic fields produced by electric currents. The electrostatic tablet is designed in a similar way but the detection mechanism here is the capacitative effect of two adjoining metal surfaces. The sonic device relies on measurements of the time taken for pulses of ultrasonic sound to travel from the stylus to long ribbon microphones on the edge of the tablet.

Tablets can be operated in a number of different ways. In point-mode the stylus is placed on the tablet and when a button incorporated into the stylus is pressed, the co-ordinates of that position are entered into the computer. In stream-mode a continuous stream of co-ordinates is sent to the computer as the stylus is moved over the surface of the tablet, thus allowing the normal drawing of continuous lines. Resolution can be very high in such systems, varying from about 100 to 1000 lines per inch. The most precise tablets, which are used for the input of data for such applications as mapping, use a puck instead of the usual pen-like stylus. A puck is a small flat plate-like object containing a transparent portion marked with fine cross-hairs for accurate registration. This is normally used only in point-mode for accurate entry of positional data.

2.5.5 Document scanners

All the devices discussed so far are designed to input digitized information which is based on the movements of the human hand. The rest of this chapter is concerned with devices which are used when it is necessary to input a pre-existing image such as a photograph, a handwritten document or drawing, for analysis, processing or archiving. The document scanner is probably the most common digitising device and has been developed specifically for documents; it is often referred to simply as a scanner.

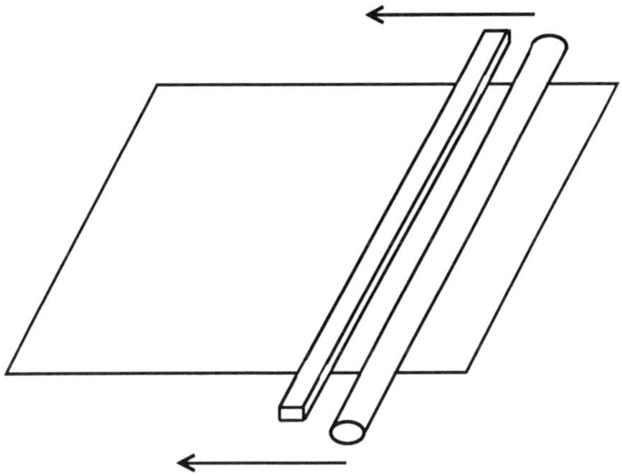

Fig. 2.22 *The two basic components of a flat-bed document scanner: an array of light-sensitive elements (CCDs) and a rod-shaped light source*

The most widely-used type of document scanner takes the form of a flat-bed with a window in the top surface – looking like a small photocopier. The document is placed face down on the window and a composite strip-light and detector arm then scans slowly below the window (see Fig. 2.22). Strips of the document are progressively illuminated and the reflected light detected by an array of photosensitive detectors – one per pixel. In most cases, these are CCDs (charge-coupled devices) which are tiny photo-sensitive semiconductor devices. They are arranged in a long array of about 2,400 or more (giving 300 + dpi in a document width of 8 inches). High-end systems use 5,100 CCDs and give 600 dpi resolution. The voltage which is generated by each CCD is proportional to the amount of light which is falling on it (that is, is reflected from the paper at that point). This is amplified and digitized (by an ADC – an analogue-to-digital converter) to produce a digitized copy of the document. The horizontal resolution of this technique depends on the number (and therefore the size) of the CCDs; the vertical resolution depends on how small a movement the CCD array can make, which depends on the precision of the stepper-motors and the gearing system which drive the detector assembly as it scans across the document. Many scanners use software to improve the apparent resolution by interpolating values between the measured ones. This means that, in a smoothly-varying image it is possible to calculate what intensity values must exist in-between the measured ones. Such a scanner might have a claimed resolution of 600 dpi when it is actually measuring 300 dpi. High-end systems might have a true ('optical') resolution of 600 × 1200 dpi and an interpolated resolution of 1200 × 1200 dpi. The reason that the optical resolution can be higher in one dimension than the other lies in the fact that the horizontal resolution depends on the size of the CCDs and the vertical resolution depends on how small the movements are as the CCD head scans down the paper.

It might seem that in scanning, the better the resolution, the better the results but in many cases this is not true. High resolution images produce large files that are slow to load and slow to process. In fact the optimum scanning resolution depends entirely on what is to be done with the final image. There is no point in scanning an image at 600 dpi if it is to viewed on a monitor at only 70 dpi – unless, of course, it is essential that the image be capable of being magnified without loss of quality. Even when the image is to be printed high resolution the data may well be wasted. Many colour printers operate at 300 – 600 dpi but create their colour effects by dithering – which reduces the effective resolution of the final image very considerably. Thus, for an image which is to be printed using 600 dpi the scanning process may only need to be at 200 – 300 dpi at most.

Colour scanners use three light sources (red, green and blue). These may be created by means of a set of filters and a single white light, or may be three separate coloured sources. The older, multiple-pass devices scan the document three times, each time with a different coloured filter. This is slow and there can be problems of aligning the three passes; if slight inaccuracies in the mechanical assembly which moves the CCD head and light cause any of the scans to be 'out-of-register' then the results will be unsatisfactory. If three separate coloured lights are used, they can be switched on and off in sequence to obtain the three measurements, in only one 'pass'. The only problem with this technique is that the three lights may decay over time in a different way, so altering the relative intensities of the illumination and therefore the reflected light readings. Another approach is to shine one white light onto the document but split the reflected light up into the three colour components using special ('dichroic') filters. This method needs three separate CCD assemblies but allows the quickest single-pass operation. A variation of this technique involves placing the coloured filters over the 3 rows of CCDs.

The detail (spatial resolution) of a scanner has been discussed already; what about the colour or grey-level detail? Even relatively cheap scanners will now claim to measure the intensity of each of the primary colours to an accuracy of 1 part in 256 (8-bits per primary colour) producing images with 24-bit colour depth (16.8 million colours) but in reality some of them are better than others at doing this. In some, the electronic noise in the circuits swamps the lowest measurements, effectively making the least-significant bits meaningless. In addition, when images are processed some grey-levels are effectively lost. Better scanners, therefore, scan into between 30 to 36-bit colour to allow for colours correction before saving a processed image as 24-bits.

In a document-feed scanner the document feeds into the device as it might into some photocopiers. These devices use the same technology but a different geometry. Sheet-fed devices keep the CCD assembly and light fixed and feed the paper past them. Some early desktop models worked this way (as did many early photocopiers) but the disadvantage is that only separate sheets of paper can be used, not books or magazines. Most full-size modern desktop systems are now flat-bed except where it is designed specifically for archiving large numbers of documents via an automatic sheet-feeder like that on a photocopier. Simple sheet-fed systems have, however, been revived recently to produce very compact, low-cost devices which look like a rather fat plastic sausage. These are compact enough to be fitted into a keyboard if necessary.

Hand-held scanners are devices which are about the size and shape of a large mouse and in which the light and CCD system is rolled over the paper. They are really only suitable for images up to about 4 inches across, though they are sometimes supplied with software which will 'stitch' together images of separate parallel strips of a larger picture. It is best if these strips are carefully made, using a frame and ruler device, designed to ensure that the strips really are parallel, but the 'stitching' software does attempt to rotate the images by small amounts when they are not quite parallel and to remove any redundant information when the strips overlap.

Drum scanners use a drum geometry for the same reason that professional image-setters do – to ensure that the geometry is as near ideal as possible. This is because the highest quality scanners use a photo-multiplier system rather than the array of CCDs used in all the other scanners. A photo-multiplier is an analogue electronic detector that is sensitive to light and which provides a better tonal range than CCDs. Because it is a single detector it must be optically scanned over the paper which is best done by putting it at the centre of a drum, the paper being wrapped round the inside of the drum and at a constant distance from the detector. The two scanning motions can be obtained by rotating the drum (or the detector) and by moving the detector steadily along the axis of the drum.

Film scanners are specialized systems designed for scanning photographic transparencies. The two differences between them and ordinary scanners are that they operate using transmitted rather than reflected light and that they concentrate the whole of the CCD array on a small picture size, producing resolutions of over 1,000 dpi. These high values of resolution are necessary because the final images will be considerably enlarged, as compared with the 35 mm, or so, originals. Modern Hollywood special effects depend on special versions of these devices which will digitize large numbers of movie frames, for processing in a computer, before the final images are returned to photographic material by means of a specialized device which will scan three coloured laser beams over the film to expose the new image.

2.5.6 Digital cameras

Digital cameras use a conventional-style camera body with a special back, which contains a two-dimensional array of CCDs, to replace the usual film holder. For colour images, each pixel needs three CCDs – one for each primary. The CCDs generate a continuous electrical current and this current is then passed to an ADC, as in a document scanner. Early cameras were very low-resolution devices but the bottom level cameras currently produce a VGA (640 × 480 pixel) image which is suitable for display on a computer monitor, particularly if the image will not be used to fill the screen. There are many applications, such as web pages and CD-ROMs where such images are more than adequate. The cameras will usually also have lower resolution modes where smaller or lower resolution images are acceptable, which means that more images can be stored in the camera before downloading. Such cameras will increasingly be used also for amateur photography where the final image will be printed at a small size (for example, postcard size) and the lack of detail will not be noticeable. For professional work higher-resolution systems are needed and 1,280 × 960 pixel cameras are available, at a price. Because of the file sizes produced, most cameras compress the images before storage. Images are usually stored in 'flash cards' or small removable discs and can also be downloaded directly to a computer, via a cable, for processing and printing. Flash cards are small removable cards which contain RAM chips that are non-volatile (they do not need power to retain data). In some cases the camera is connected directly to a printer if the user does not have access to a computer. Some cameras are fitted with an LCD viewer and this can be used to inspect the pictures that have been taken. This means that faulty images can be deleted immediately and so allows the user to take maximum advantage of the limited memory.

Digital cameras are a very convenient way of obtaining digitized photographs and have many advantages but the highest quality (and the cheapest) results are still obtained by digitising conventional photographs using a document scanner or film scanner. A 35 mm negative contains about 80,000 million photo-sensitive crystals (compared with about 6 million pixels in the very best digital camera system) a factor of 10,000 difference. Of course, the scanning process is what imposes the limit on the resolution of a digitized photograph but a drum scanner has a resolution of between 10,000 and 20,000 dpi and so a scan of a 6 inch photograph would produce about 60,000 pixels per scan. There is clearly no comparison if resolution is the most important factor.

2.5.7 Video digitizers

An alternative approach to digitising a wide range of images is to view the object with a video camera and then digitize the camera's video output with a 'frame-grabber' – see the earlier section on video input and output. The advantage of this approach is that the source object can be a three-dimensional object like a house or a car or a two-dimensional object like a document or drawing. This approach is likely to be superseded by the digital camera but can, in the mean time provide a very cost-effective approach to the owner of a conventional video camera.

Exercises for the Reader:

(1) A monochrome engineering drawing, consisting of 600 straight lines and 80 circles, is to be stored as a vector image and displayed on an old-style vector screen with an effective resolution of 1,000 × 750 pixels. The straight lines are to be stored by their end-point co-ordinates and the circles by their centres and radii. Calculate the memory requirements and compare them with those of a modern bit-mapped system.

(2) A modern bit-mapped screen has a resolution of 1024 × 768 pixels and can display 16.8 million colours. It is refreshed at 75 Hz (non-interlaced). Calculate the number of Mbytes of picture data per second that must be supplied to the screen.

(3) A 15 inch colour monitor has a viewable area which is 28 × 21 cm and has a dot pitch of 0.26 mm. How many phosphor dots does it have ?

(4) The earliest colour adapter for the IBM-PC (the CGA) had a resolution of 320 × 200 pixels (4 colours). Currently the highest resolution is 1600 × 1200 pixels (16.8 million colours). Calculate the data content of images in these two systems (in bytes).

(5) A field-emission display panel has 50 tiny spike-electrodes per phosphor spot. Calculate the number of spikes-electrodes needed for a VGA (640 × 480 pixel) colour display. How small must they be if the screen is 25 cm wide?

(6) Based on data in this chapter, calculate how much faster a modern PCI bus is compared with the original bus fitted to the first IBM-PCs.

(7) A flat-bed pen-plotter can draw on paper sizes up to 3 × 2 metres with an accuracy of 0.1 mm (that is, it can put dots on the paper at this separation). Compare this with a modern display screen and translate this into 'equivalent pixels'. For figures on displays see the relevant section of this chapter. Now do a similar exercise and compare it with a basic laser printer, operating at 300 dots per inch on A4 paper (210 x 297 mm). How many dpi can the plotter produce and how many total dots on its sheet of paper, compared with the laser printer on its sheet of paper?

(8) Laser printers produce grey-scales by dithering. Compare two different printers – one operating at 300 dpi and the other at 1200 dpi. Each produces dots of only one size and each is to print a photograph with 9 grey levels. For each printer in turn, calculate :
   - how many dots must be used to produce a 'grey pixel';
   - how many 'effective pixels' per inch are available when the printer dots are used in this way;
   - what is the smallest detail which the printer can show.

3

Graphics Applications Software

3.1 Using Graphics to Improve Human-Computer Interaction

3.1.1 Graphical interfaces

The earliest graphics application software predated the desktop computer and was of a very specialized nature, requiring expensive peripheral equipment, and mainly aimed at engineering design. 'Standard' computers used monochrome, text-only displays with a typewriter-style keyboard as the only input device. The major users of computers were in the business world where the storing and processing of text and numerical data didn't seem to require the use of graphics. The breakthrough occurred when the Apple Macintosh desktop computer was launched as a graphics-only computer and the modern computer is very much the logical descendent of this machine.

Although the Macintosh swiftly became the computer of choice for typographers and graphics designers the original design had not been aimed at graphic applications but rather at office and business tasks, areas where graphics had been considered largely irrelevant – a luxury at best. The Macintosh, however, was the offshoot of pioneering research and development work at the Xerox Palo Alto Research Centre (PARC) which was first used in Xerox's STAR system (itself developed from an earlier machine – called Bravo). These systems were based on a belief in the importance of graphics as a general tool for the user, independently of whether or not the task might be considered to be a graphic one. This tool we now call a graphic environment or graphic interface (GUI – graphic user interface). The basic belief was that if computers were to leave the world of the specialist – the scientist, the engineer, the computer expert – and enter the ordinary world of work then they would have to be designed to be used as easily as any other consumer-oriented machine, like a car, washing machine or video player. In a GUI the user is confronted with tiny pictures (icons) which represent objects that are familiar. If the software is for business use these objects would be in-trays and out-trays, filing cabinets, waste-baskets etc. A carefully designed GUI allows the user to manipulate representations of familiar objects using familiar skills.

To illustrate how different all this is from the traditional world of computers, consider a simple task like 'deleting a file'. In computer jargon a collection of data, saved on a magnetic disk is called a file. If the data is not needed any more and the space on the disk is to be made available for other uses it is said to be 'deleted'. To do this, and similar tasks in a non-graphic environment, the user must learn a series of commands which must be typed correctly at the keyboard. Part of the learning process involves understanding something about the filing system – the hierarchical storage method used to keep track of large amounts of information on a disk. In the

Disk Operating System used in IBM compatible computers the command would have looked something like this :

DEL C:\maindocs\northeas\smith2.doc

where all the symbols like ' C : ' and ' \ ' and ' .doc ' have a meaning for the initiated but can look very intimidating to those who prefer to inhabit a jargon-free zone.

Fig. 3.1 *Three icons representing (left to right) a document, the mouse cursor and a folder*

In contrast, in the STAR interface (mentioned above) and its successors, the Mac OS and Windows-95 for example, a file is represented by a small picture of a document and it is deleted by dragging it to a picture of a wastebasket, using a mouse. The principle is that everyone knows what a document and a wastebasket look like and everyone knows what it means to put one into the other. The objects are familiar and so are the actions. The pictures may not be very life-like because of the restrictions imposed by the display system but simple, stylized representations (icons) can still be recognized, and if not, at least easily learned. The abstract representations of a filing system, traditionally shown in mathematical-style symbols like **'C:\maindocs\northeas\smith2'**, can also be have their own visual symbols using pictures of cardboard folders, stored one inside the other, like Russian dolls. Simple mouse actions can be used to open and close these files ('folders') and documents can be dragged in and out. The designers of the original STAR system discovered that the dragging action is a universally powerful symbol. It can be used to delete by dragging over a wastebasket, to move by dragging from one folder to another, to send an E-mail by dragging into an Out-Tray symbol and to print by dragging it over a printer. In Fig. 3.1, the middle cursor (the mouse) is available to drag a document into a folder. Dragging becomes a general technique for moving an object from one environment to another, the environment often implying an action without further explanation.

Representing objects and actions by means of icons was not the only radical change introduced in these early GUIs. Two other important concepts were the 'menu' and the 'window', the first of which was already being used in text-only systems. In common speech a menu is a list of food items available in a restaurant and a computer menu is similarly a list of commands or actions available to the user in a particular piece of software. The major problem with the 'Command-Line' system (illustrated above in the file deletion example) is that the user must remember and type commands, both of which activities are prone to error. The beauty of a menu system is that the user need only recognize a command and then select it, both of which are easier and less prone to error than remembering and typing. A further advantage is that the items on the menu indicate the full list of possibilities that are available to the user – a useful teaching aid for those exploring the possibilities that the software offers.

The window is simply a rectangular region in the display area which contains a

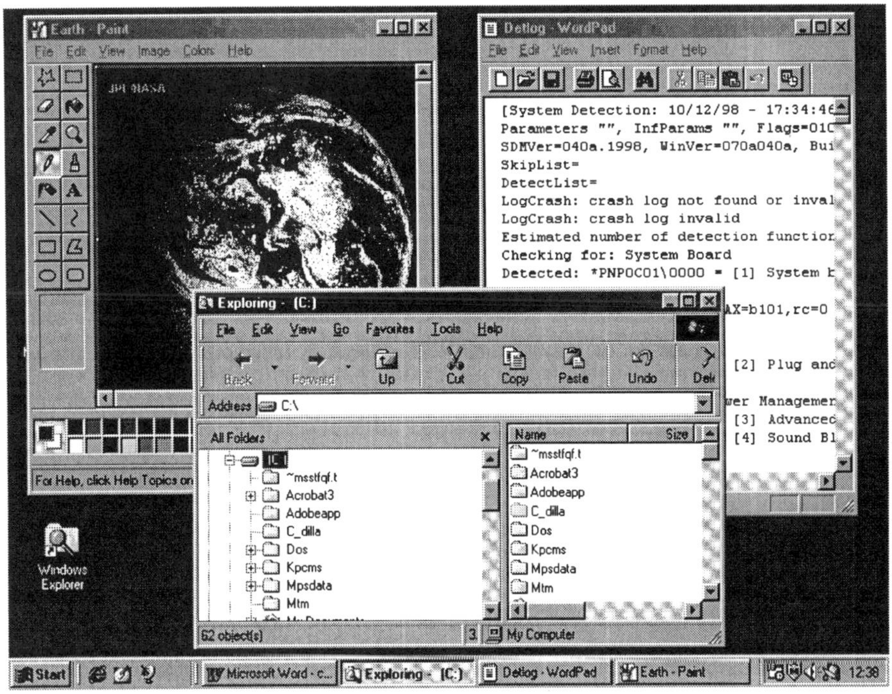

Fig. 3.2 Microsoft's Windows 98, a modern GUI with overlapping windows

separate set of information. In its most flexible form, multiple windows can be created which can be moved, re-sized, overlapped and easily brought to the top of the pile (see Fig. 3.2 and Plate 4). Because of the limitations of computer displays – both in size and resolution – it is important to be able to remove and replace windows easily and this is usually done by closing down to a minimum size (icon size) which can be blown up to the former size at any stage by a click (usually a double-click) of the mouse. This window-like property is shared by the modern, graphic menu which has a minimum size as a menu header but which can be expanded into a full menu by a mouse click. Although the menu is usually thought of as being like a roller-blind, to be 'pulled down' when required, it can also be thought of as a specialized type of window. Both are discussed in more detail in the next section.

These mental pictures, like a roller-blind or a window, which utilize the properties of everyday objects are sometimes referred to as 'metaphors' and the best GUIs are those that can successfully create an easily understood metaphor that encompasses the whole of the software interface. Users find it simple to work in the environment because they already feel that they know how to perform computer tasks, based on their everyday experience. The metaphor of the first GUI was of the office environment and the icons were pictures of office equipment and the tasks simulated the activities of a traditional office. Other metaphors have been developed since then, as will be clear from the rest of this chapter. Metaphors as diverse as the artist's paint palette and the thermometer have all been successfully developed to communicate ideas about the computer's state or the way that a task should be performed. Though the GUI was designed as a tool to aid any computer user in any sort of task it quickly became the preferred environment for graphics applications and one of the first successful ones was desktop publishing – described later in the chapter.

3.1.2 The principles of HCI

The design of the first Apple Mac interface (and its predecessor, the STAR), depended heavily on a high-resolution bit-mapped display – something of a revolution for desktop computers at the time – and without good graphics it would have been impossible to make sensible use of icons and other pictorial representations of computer-based tasks. Much of the thinking behind this first GUI was based on a fundamental re-think of the whole question of the human-computer interface. HCI (human-computer interaction) is the study of how people interact with computers and is primarily concerned with the question of how to make such interaction easier. Because of the fundamental importance of graphics in this early design some observers have come to the rather superficial conclusion that 'HCI equals graphics', that is to say that good interfaces are created simply by adding pictures. In fact HCI has a lot more to say on the subject than this simplistic formula and many lengthy books have been written on the subject, which can't be adequately summarized here, but a few words on the principles of HCI are in order.

Improvements in the design of the human-computer interface came about when designers began to recognize that a number of assumptions about the typical computer user were increasingly out of date. Early software had been designed by computer scientists for people like themselves but for the computer to take its place as a tool in the mass market, software would have to be designed for a much wider range of users. In fact three broad categories of user are now envisaged. One is the 'naïve' or inexpert, one is the experienced and the third is the traditional expert. The target group for whom the Star was designed – office workers with no knowledge of computers – is a good example of the first category. The major principle used here was that of skill-transfer. Office workers already have a set of skills which are appropriate to the traditional office equipment and tasks and the STAR interface was designed to provide a metaphor of the office, using computer graphics (as described in the previous section).

This approach illustrates two important HCI principles : 'Know the user' and 'Reduce cognitive load'. The first principle means, in this case : 'Recognize that the user knows nothing about computers and computerized filing systems but does know about offices, cardboard files, waste-baskets and – just as important – what to do with them'. The office metaphor makes maximum use of the user's existing skills and avoids making the user learn new skills and new jargon. The second principle means 'Reduce to the minimum the need to memorize'. In the text-based

MS-DOS interface (illustrated in the last section) the user must remember that the command to get rid of an unwanted file, for example, is 'Delete' and this must always be used in the shortened form DEL. The user must also remember that a space must be left between the command and the name of the file, and many other technicalities besides. In the graphic equivalent, all that must be remembered are two very generalized pieces of knowledge: that actions are achieved by dragging icons and that dragging involves holding down the mouse button. The only skills specific to deleting are those of recognising what a wastebasket looks like and remembering what it is for.

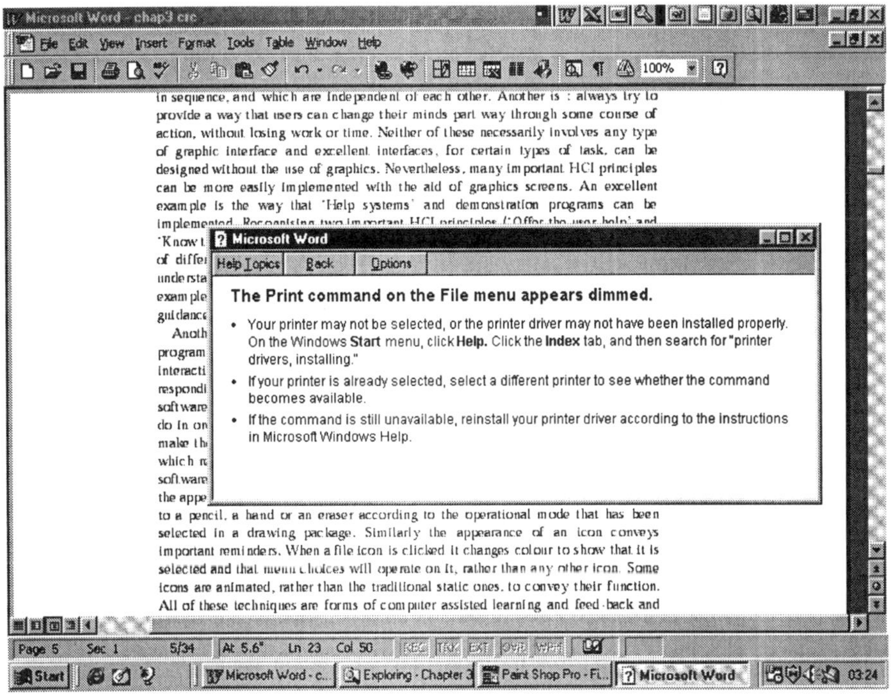

Fig. 3.3 A floating help window in Microsoft Word. Help can be viewed whilst working on the task

There are many other general principles which lie behind the design of a good HCI, some of which have nothing to do with graphics. An example is: always break down complex actions into a number of separate simpler ones which can be tackled in sequence, and which are independent of each other. Another is: always try to provide a way that users can change their minds part way through some course of action, without losing work or time. Neither of these necessarily involves any type of graphic interface and excellent interfaces, for certain types of task, can be designed without the use of graphics. Nevertheless, many important HCI principles can be more easily implemented with the aid of graphics screens. An excellent example is the way that 'Help systems' and demonstration programs can be implemented (see Fig. 3.3 for an example). Recognizing two important HCI principles ('Offer the user help' and 'Know the user') means that a variety of help must be provided, suitable to a range of different types of user and recognising that users learn and develop in their understanding, needing different help at different stages. Graphical systems can, for example, provide a wide range of 'pop-up' windows which offer explanation and guidance whilst the user can still see the original screen, to which this help refers.

Another use of graphics in this context is the provision of tutorials. These are programs which take the novice through all the main features of the package in an interactive manner – encouraging the learner to practice particular exercises and responding with appropriate comments. A third approach is that of demonstration software. This takes the form of a series of demonstrations of what the package can do in order to illustrate what is possible and to stimulate the user's imagination to make the best use of the software. A fourth example is the use of visual feed-back which reminds users of important facts about what is happening as they use the software. These often take the form of a change in the mouse cursor or a change in the appearance of an icon. The cursor might normally represent an arrow but change to a pencil, a hand or an eraser according to the operational mode that has been selected in a drawing package. Similarly the appearance of an icon conveys important reminders. When a file icon is clicked it changes colour to show that it is selected and that menu choices will operate on it, rather than any other icon. Some icons are animated, rather than the traditional static ones, to convey their function. All of these techniques are forms of computer assisted learning and feed-back and take advantage of graphics to make them more effective.

Another way that graphics can assist HCI is the use of windows – overlapping rectangles of information on the screen. Many human tasks involve 'multitasking' – doing two or more things at once. In the context of a traditional office this often means many documents strewn around a desk and the user glancing from one to the other. But computer monitors are small (compared with a desk) and of relatively low resolution. Until monitors are available which are desk-sized (if ever) another approach is necessary and one method is the use of overlapping windows. Multitasking, here, can mean simply being able to access more than one document – in different windows – but it can also mean running more than one application at a time. Each document or application runs in a different window and the windows can either overlap like pieces of paper placed on top of one another or be placed side by side (sometimes called tiles). Of course each window, because of its small size, will show only part of the output of the program which is associated with it and in some systems only one program can actually be running (performing some processing activity) at one time. This window is described as being active but it will be easy to change which window is active at any time. In other systems all the windows will be active by sharing the attention of the central processor in rapid rotation. In either case windows can usually be increased or decreased in size, moved around the screen and brought to the top of the 'pile' so that attention can be concentrated on one process at the expense of the others. This then provides a system equivalent to a number of pieces of paper being shuffled and read as required.

Another useful facility which is an improvement on the paper-based office is the ability to transfer information rapidly and easily from one source to another and this also can be made easy by the use of a graphic environment. Word-processors usually provide a copy/move facility in which blocks of text can be moved or copied from one location in the document to another. A graphics environment often offers a similar 'cut-and-paste' function which allows transfer of material from one application to another. This usually means specifying a rectangular area within one window (for example, some of the data in a spreadsheet) using a mouse and transferring it to an imaginary board (often called a clip-board) where it is held temporarily. This might be symbolized by moving a suitable icon to a part of the screen designated as the clip-board. The operation is termed 'cutting'. Then the information is transferred to another window, perhaps one running a word-processor and 'pasted' in to it, by moving the icon which represents it. This sort of technique has the effect of enabling users to create their own integrated software from a number of different applications and to visualize easily what is happening.

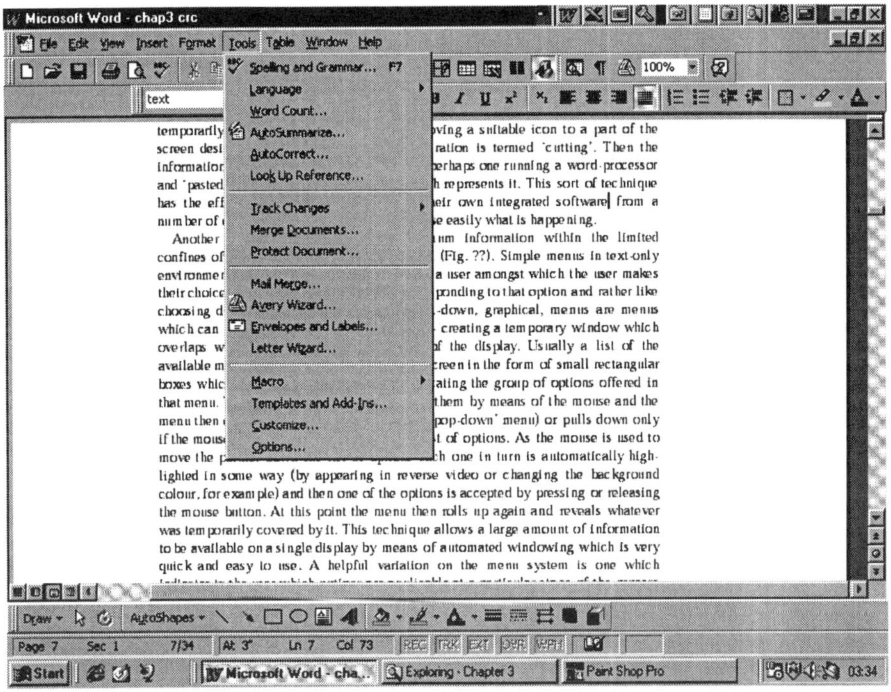

Fig. 3.4 A pull-down menu in Microsoft Word

Another method of displaying the maximum information within the limited confines of the display is the pull-down menu (Fig. 3.4). Simple menus in text-only environments were lists of options available to a user amongst which the user makes their choice, usually by typing a number corresponding to that option and rather like choosing dishes at a Chinese restaurant. Pull-down, graphical, menus are menus which can be pulled down like a roller blind – creating a temporary window which overlaps whatever is currently in that part of the display. Usually a list of the available menus is displayed at the top of the screen in the form of small rectangular boxes which each contain a suitable title indicating the group of options offered in that menu. The user moves a pointer to one of them by means of the mouse and the menu then either pulls down automatically (a 'pop-down' menu) or pulls down only if the mouse button is clicked, revealing the list of options. As the mouse is used to move the pointer down the list of options each one in turn is automatically high-lighted in some way (by appearing in reverse video or changing the background colour, for example) and then one of the options is accepted by pressing or releasing the mouse button. At this point the menu then rolls up again and reveals whatever was temporarily covered by it. This technique allows a large amount of information to be available on a single display by means of automated windowing which is very quick and easy to use. A helpful variation on the menu system is one which indicates to the user which options are applicable at a particular stage of the process or in the current mode of operation. This is done by displaying non-valid options on the menu in faint type. To emphasize the point further, that option will not respond to the mouse in the same way as the others (by changing colour, for example, as the cursor points to it). At a different stage, when that option is valid, it will be displayed in the normal way.

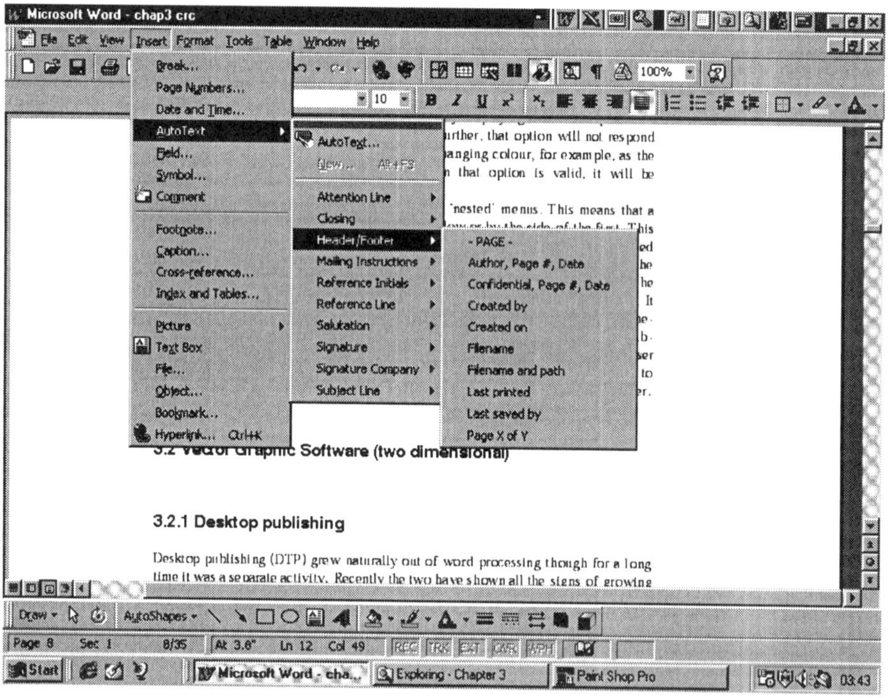

Fig. 3.5 A three-level menu in Microsoft Word

A further development of this is the system of 'nested' menus. This means that a choice on a menu gives rise to a further menu, below or by the side of the first. This in turn may give rise to a third. Fig. 3.5 shows an example of a three-level nested menu system. Sometimes the menus appear from left to right instead of the commonly used top-to-bottom system. This system makes it easy to visualize the tree-like structure of the system of choices which branch out, one from the other. It is possible to retrace one's steps up the tree by the use of a particular key which one-by-one rolls up the menus until all of them have disappeared or until a chosen sub-level has been reached. An example of another HCI principle ('Give the user control') which has been applied to menu systems is the facility to allow the user to 'tear-off' the menu panel and move it around the screen to a place that suits the user.

3.2 Vector Graphic Software (two dimensional)

3.2.1 Desktop publishing

Desktop publishing (DTP) grew naturally out of word processing though for a long time it was a separate activity. Recently the two have shown all the signs of growing back together again. The difference between basic word processing (WP) and DTP can be seen by considering the traditional function of the author of a printed document, as compared with the function of the printer. Before the advent of the desktop computer the author was responsible for producing a typescript – the process of assembling words in the right order. The printer then took those words and (perhaps with the aid of a designer or typographer) laid out the text in a particular manner, with or without appropriate illustrations, and printed them. The modern author does exactly what his predecessor did, but using a word processor, so that the words do not have to be re-typed by the printer. What DTP does is to automate most of the functions of the printer, using a desktop computer. Four developments made this possible: the desktop computer with a GUI, DTP software, the laser printer and the page-description language – the PDL (see Chapter 5 on scaleable fonts).

The importance of the laser printer was that a high-quality final product could be produced without the need for traditional typesetting processes (particularly the use of moveable type). The early laser printers, operating at 300 – 400 dots per inch (dpi) could not rival traditional printing processes but could produce results that were acceptable for many everyday purposes, and at a much lower price. The development of higher resolution laser printers and the digital type-setter (now called an image-setter) have since made it possible for work of almost any quality to be produced this way, though the term DTP, in some people's minds, is still associated with a poorer quality, amateur product. The importance of the PDL is discussed in Chapter 5.

The importance of the GUI lay in the fact that the function of DTP software is to lay out pre-prepared text and graphics and a GUI allows the user to see immediately an accurate representation of the final product. This 'what you see is what you get' (WYSIWYG) feature is vital to DTP though the slogan should be taken with a pinch of salt. 'What you see' on a 72 dpi screen can never be a wholly accurate representation of 'what you get' on a 300 – 1200 dpi (or better) printer. The slogan should, perhaps, be changed to WYSIANATTCMTWYG – 'what you see is as near as the technology can manage to what you get'. A necessary feature of a DTP package, therefore, is a zoom facility which displays a portion of the document at a larger size than normal so as to display it at something much closer to the resolution of the final printed product. Unfortunately only a small part of the document can be seen at any one time in this magnified mode. The reverse process – that of displaying a page or more with the individual characters, particularly the small ones, shown in very low resolution is called 'Greeking' (see Fig. 3.6). The purpose of this is to show the general effect of the page lay-out on a comparatively low resolution display, even though the smaller text may be unreadable and is only displayed as a series of grey bars or dots, representing the lines of text.

This idea that the software enables the user to lay out, electronically, the various items of text and graphics was an important aspect of the 'metaphor' of the first DTP program – Aldus PageMaker (now Adobe PageMaker). The screen is used to represent a 'paste-board' of the sort used by graphic designers – a large drawing board on which is placed a sheet of paper together with various items of text and graphics. These items can then be dragged onto the paper and re-arranged until a pleasing result is obtained. Each of the text and graphic items is contained in its own 'frame' – a rectangular boundary – as if it were on its own separate piece of paper, and these are then moved and pasted into position to form the final design. The two main features of DTP software, apart from the WYSIWYG aspect, are the fine control such software offers the page designer and the automation features which enable the speedier production of the final product.

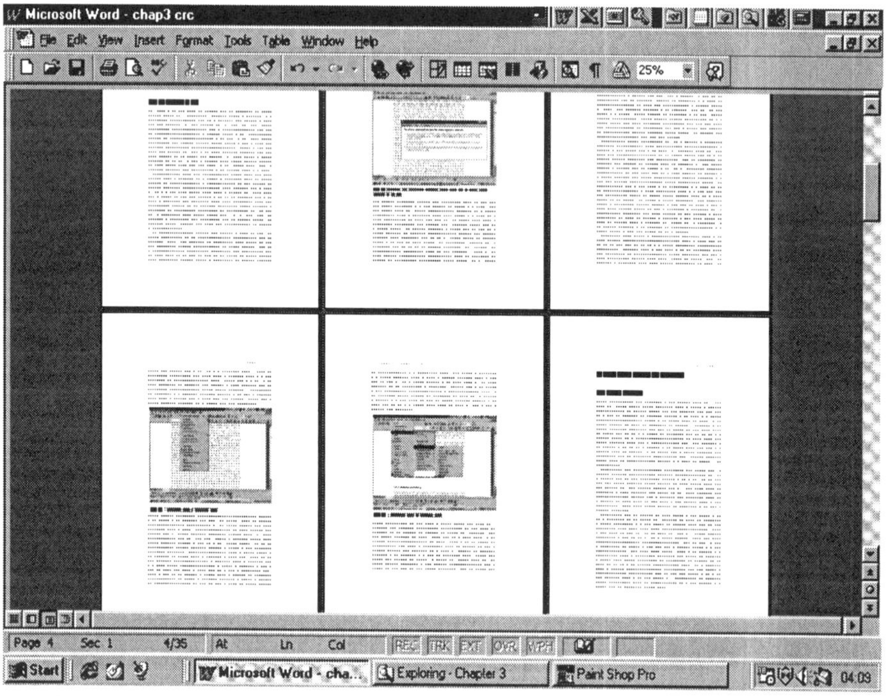

Fig. 3.6 *Greeking: the presence of lines of text is indicated but no attempt is made to display the individual characters*

Fine control over layout

Control over the layout of a page is provided by a number of features such as accurate rulers and guidelines to aid the placing of blocks of text and graphic frames but here we will look at the fine control offered for the precise specification of inter-line, inter-word and inter-character spacing both in general and when kerning and justification are used. The term 'kerning' is defined later in the section. We will begin with a discussion of proportional spacing. The traditional typewriter, by the nature of its design, uses a mono-spaced font (see Fig. 3.7). Each character and inter-word space occupies the same width on the paper because of the way that

Plate 1a *A bit-mapped image (provided with Adobe PhotoShop) at normal magnification*

Plate 1b *Part of Plate 1a, magnified 600% so that the individual pixels can be seen*

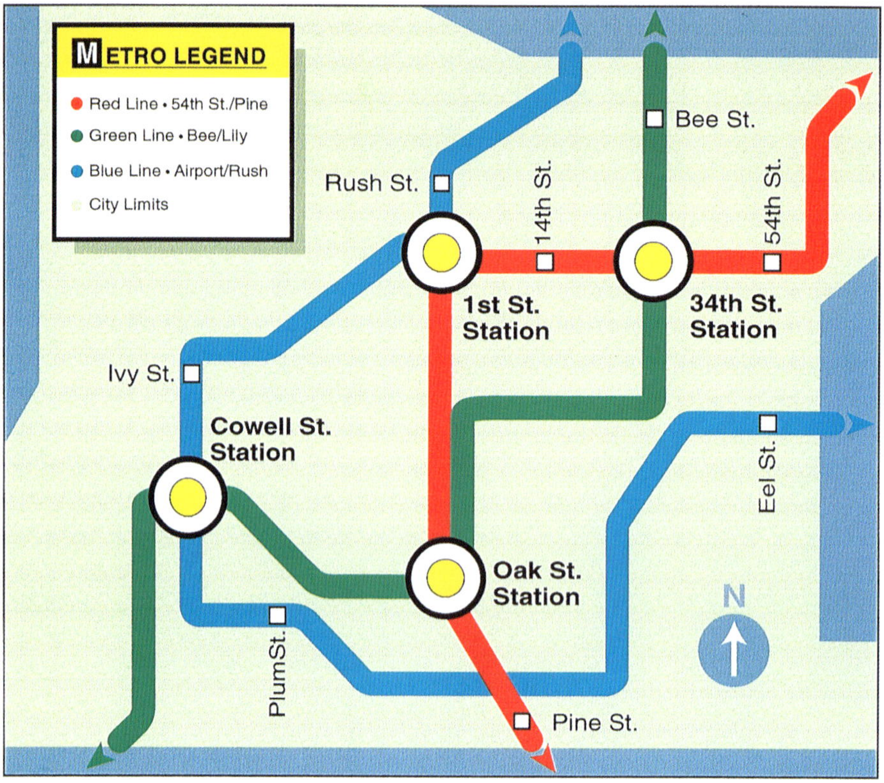

Plate 2a *A vector image (provided with Adobe Illustrator) at normal magnification*

Plate 2b *Part of Plate 2a, magnified 1200%*

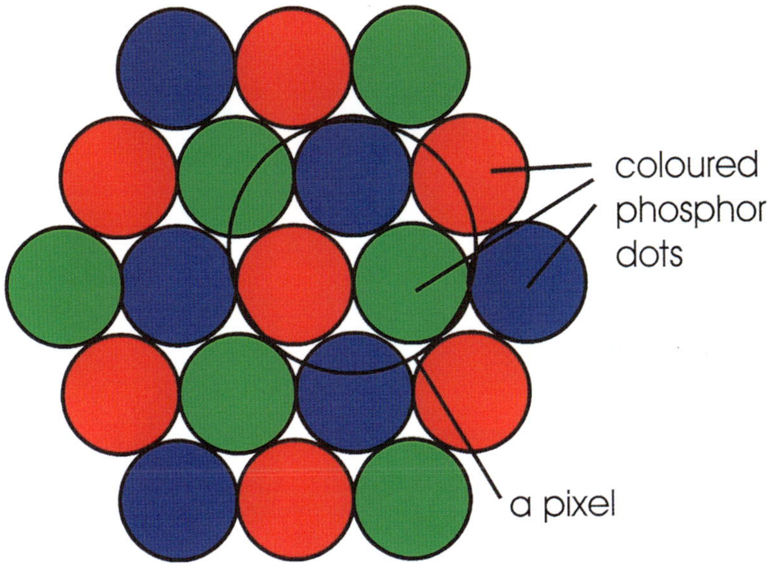

Plate 3a *Coloured phosphor dots arranged in a triangular format*

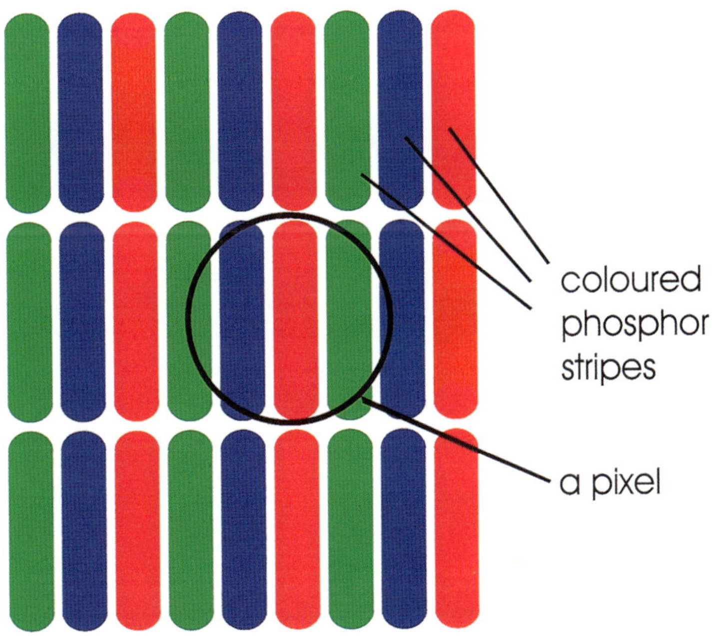

Plate 3b *Coloured phosphor stripes arranged in a linear format*

Plate 4 *A Graphical User Interface (GUI). This is Microsoft Windows-98*

Plate 5 *A rendered three-dimensional image (sample model provided with "POV-Ray for Windows")*

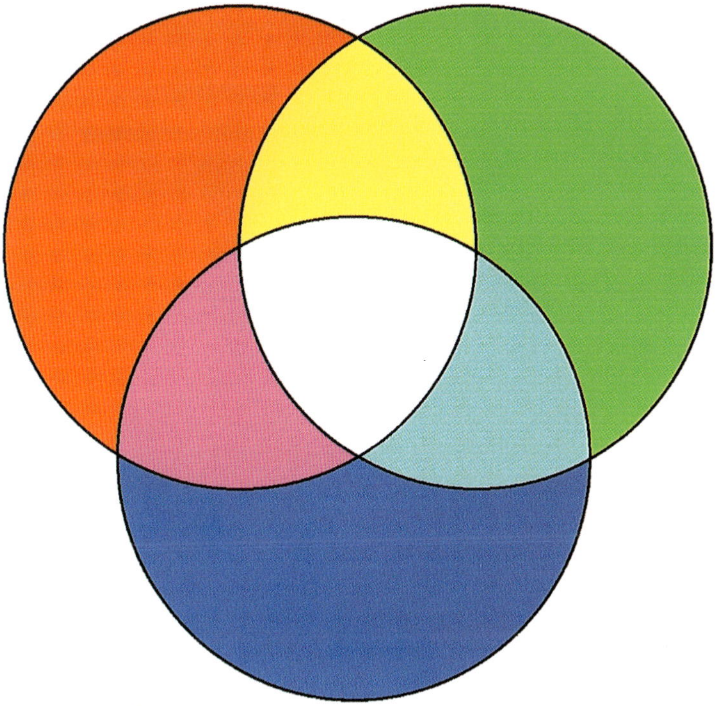

Plate 6a *Additive colour: red, green and blue combine to form yellow, magenta, cyan and white*

Plate 6b *Subtractive colour: magenta, yellow and cyan combine to form red, blue, green and black*

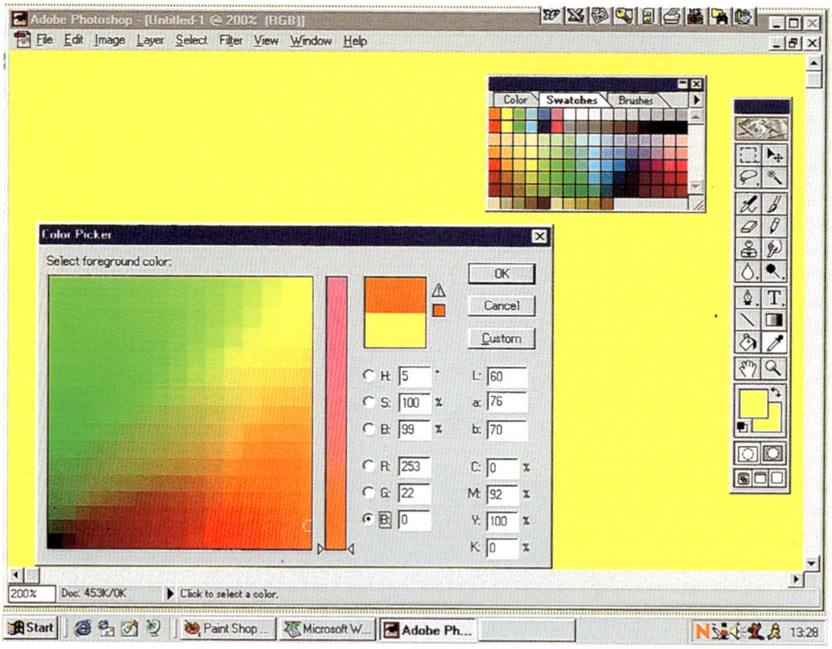

Plate 7 Defining new colours in the colour palette in Adobe PhotoShop

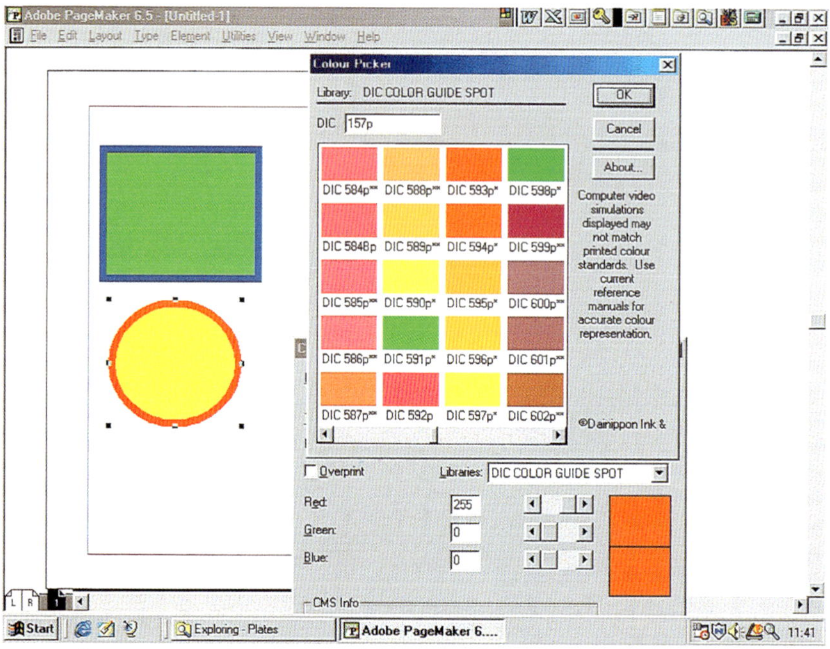

Plate 8 Choosing standard colours using colour swatches in Adobe PageMaker

Full colour image of fruit

Cyan components of the image

Magenta components of the image

Yellow components of the image

Plate 9 *Colour separation - in addition to the cyan, magenta and yellow components there is usually a fourth - black.*

Plate 10 *A magnified bit-mapped image of a rose using about 2000 different shades, together with a dithered version of the image using only 256 colours*

Plate 11 *A colour wheel. Each colour has a value of Hue 18 degrees different from the adjacent one, starting with red at the top (Hue = 0)*

characters are placed on the paper. High-quality printing, on the other hand uses proportional fonts – each letter occupies only a space that is appropriate to its shape, as chosen by the typographer who designed that font. An upper-case 'W' takes up much more room on the line than a lower-case 'i', for example. Spaces between characters in a word are determined by the small gap which is associated with each

Monospaced font : Wi

Proportional font : Wi

Fig. 3.7 *A typewriter-style mono-spaced font and a proportionally-spaced font*

character by its design. All these distances are fixed by the designer (unless the user chooses to increase or decrease them by some fixed percentage) until some over-riding design consideration, like justification is used. Right-justified text is text that is positioned so that the ends of all the lines match up to an imaginary vertical line (as in this book). A typewriter automatically produces left-justification but not right-justification; it leaves a ragged end to the lines because in most cases they contain a different number of characters and so will not line up. Simple right-justification on a WP can be done by adding extra character-sized blanks at arbitrary positions in the line (between words of course) but this can produce large glaring white spaces, as seen in many newspapers, particularly when narrow columns of text are used in combination with long words. A better approach is to use spaces between the words and between letters in words which are not of some standard fixed length but are calculated to suit that particular line of text. This involves a calculation based on the number of characters and spaces being used in that particular line so that the spaces between all the letters and all the words can be increased pro rata (in proportion).

WA WA

Fig. 3.8 *Kerning : the first pair of characters are set at a normal spacing; the second pair are much closer together*

A good typesetter will go one better by using his initiative to split some long words into two to avoid having to transfer a whole word on to the next line when it will not fit on the current line (a process which is called 'hyphenation'). This involves a judgement as to which words can be split in this way and where the split should occur. Basic WP software usually offers the facility of hyphenation but the operator normally has to decide, or at least confirm, whether a particular word should be split in this way, and if so, where. DTP software, on the other hand, usually offers some form of automatic hyphenation. This is based either on a set of rules (an algorithm) or by reference to a special dictionary which contains words in acceptable hyphenated forms or a combination of the two.

Kerning is the process of placing specific pairs of characters in positions which are appropriate to their individual shape. An 'o', for example, can nestle up in the space following a 'P' or 'W' and a 'W' which is followed by an 'A' can fit very closely because of their complementary shapes (Fig. 3.8). Basic WP software allowed the same space for all letters, if only because that is the way that characters were shown on the monitor in text-only displays. DTP software, however uses scaleable fonts which contain considerable amount of extra information about the shape and size of letters at different sizes and so kerning is a possibility. Automatic kerning is another of the facilities usually offered by DTP programs. These type of sophisticated controls could have been used in text-only computer displays but graphic displays offer the facility of allowing the user to see immediately the result of any change that is made and this makes all the difference.

Page-level layout

Another aspect of the control of layout, provided by DTP, is that of the way that material is placed in blocks to determine the overall impression of the page. Most page designs treat the page as if it were divided into a grid by means of columns and rows. The simplest example of a column layout can be seen in most newspapers but magazines, for example, will use a more sophisticated version of this design by using columns with different widths, by using separate blocks of text and images which over-ride the column structure and by varying the font. All of this requires aids to the placement of material and DTP software provides these in the form of rulers, non-printing guidelines, non-printing grids with 'snap' facilities and separate frames containing text and images. These are illustrated in the Fig. 3.9 and some are taken up again in the context of other graphics software.

The most important of these is the use of guidelines and frames. Normally text will 'flow' inside the limits set by the margins of the page but for text to be arranged in columns extra guidelines – column guides – are provided. All DTP software uses the concept of a 'frame' – a rectangular box which contains text or graphics. For the majority of the text the frame is set by the margins – as just described – but for more complicated page designs extra frames are required. When a frame is added on top of another frame – as with an illustration in the middle of a page – the main text can be made to flow round the second frame. Most software also has some system which allows text to flow round graphics or blocks of text which are not in a rectangular frame.

Automation

DTP software provides many features which will automate what would otherwise be time-consuming, repetitive tasks. One is the concept of a 'master page'. This is a page, on which can be placed repeating items like page numbers, headers and footers (headers and footers are repeating items – like chapter titles – placed at the head or foot of a page). Another valuable feature is the style or style sheet which is, in essence, a list of the characteristics of a block of text. Any block of text will have half a dozen characteristics which control its appearance – items like the named font, the font-size, the 'leading' (the inter-line spacing), the size of the indent on the first line, the alignment, whether or not it is hyphenated, and so on. Once chosen and applied to that block of text they can then be saved under a name – a style – and applied *en masse* to any other block of text. One final example of an automation

Fig. 3.9 *Rulers, frames and non-printing guidelines in Adobe PageMaker DTP software*

feature is the facility to create an index and a list of contents. For an index, for example, the author must specify which words (and which occurrences of that word) are to be included but the software will then identify all of those by page number and prepare an alphabetized listing along with the appropriate page numbers.

General features

The increasing power of the general purpose desktop computer has led to what some critics have termed 'software bloat' – the tendency for software companies to add ever-more features to their software with each succeeding version (a disease, some have called 'featuritis' – an ever-increasing list of features). One of the examples of this is that word processor software has gradually acquired many of the facilities once reserved for DTP software, and to some extent the reverse has happened also. Initially DTP software was for layout only and the text and the graphics would have been created using WP and graphics packages. Now DTP software often has both word processing and drawing capabilities. These tend to be limited, however –

particularly in the graphics features which are often restricted to the creation of straight lines and simple geometrical shapes, line and fill-patterns and colours.

An area of growing importance, however, is that of colour separation. The subject is treated in detail in Chapter 4 since it applies to many different types of graphics software but it relates to the way that desktop publishing can be used to produce professional results by accessing professional printing technology, via the image setter. Professional typographers and graphic artists will often do their work on desktop computers and will use standard laser printers to produce 'proofs' of their work but the final result will generally be produced as a photographic master on an image setter, the final printing being done using a *litho* printer (see the chapter on hardware). Colour work demands colour separations and modern DTP software is equipped with a range of facilities for the production of these separations, for the specification of the colours and for such processes as 'colour trapping' (discussed in Chapter 4).

3.2.2 Electronic publishing (CD-ROMs and the Internet)

In recent years more and more material has been published electronically rather than on paper. The two most important new media have been CD-ROM and the Internet. As a result modern versions of many DTP packages and word processors provide the facility to output files in the formats which have been developed specifically for these two media – particularly HTML (HyperText Markup Language) and PDF (Portable Document Format). At first sight that might seem all there is to say on the subject and for some documents that might be true; a document, once prepared, is simply output in the appropriate file format instead of being printed. To take full advantage of the new media however this is not likely to be satisfactory for both positive and negative reasons.

First the negative reasons. Computer screens are small and of low resolution compared with most forms of paper publication. Screens operate at about 70 – 80 dpi while even the poorest resolution output on printed paper, for example that from a cheap laser printer or an ink-jet printer, offers 300 dpi. In fact, most laser printers now operate at 600 dpi and more expensive ones at 1200 – 1600 dpi. Professional printing technologies use even higher resolution – the equivalent of 2,000 – 3,000 dpi. This means that there is no comparison between the amount of information – the detail that can be displayed – on a screen, compared with printed matter. Then there is the question of size. Even a 15 inch monitor is only a little larger than an A4 sheet of paper while many magazines are A4 or greater and can also make use of a 'double-spread' (two facing pages when open) which corresponds to A3.

Now the positive reasons; monitors are not inferior in every respect. They offer brighter, more vibrant colours than cheap colour printing and at no extra expense (except file size). They also offer movement, which brings us to the second area of interest – multimedia. Screens can display changing (apparently moving) images – either as digitized video or the various forms of 2-D and 3-D animation, scrolling, etc. Computers are no longer restricted to screens for their output either. High-quality sound is increasingly a standard provision. All these are extra facilities, available in electronic publication but not available with the printed page. Another feature of electronic publication is the use of hyper-links. These are built-in links between related material and they depend on the ability of the computer to make rapid jumps from one place in a database of information to another, and to maintain a list of all these jumps so that the user can go back quickly to any place on the route. Hyper-text is the name given to links between related items of text and is exactly the same, in principle, to the methods used in traditional printing where the author says 'for more information on this topic see page xx', or 'see Appendix C', or 'see *another author's* book', or provides details in a footnote. The power of hyper-text in electronic publishing is that it becomes practical to establish hundreds or even thousands of such links because the computer organizes the process so efficiently and quickly.

The hyper-text principle has also been extended to links to photographs, drawings, sounds, video, animations, tables of figures, maps etc. and the benefit to the user is that vast amounts of information can be made available – in such a way that the user can decide how much to access and in what order. Print publishing on the other hand is still, essentially, a linear process. The reader reads the material in the order dictated by the writer, starting at the beginning and going on to the end. Hyper-linked material has no unique beginning and no unique end.

All this means that electronic publishing, though having many obvious overlaps with paper publishing, is a very different medium needing different skills and different software. Table 3.1 provides a summary of some of the benefits of the two different approaches.

Table 3.1 A comparison of the advantages of paper versus electronic publishing

Paper publishing	Electronic publishing
High resolution; much more information per square inch; better quality typefaces and diagrams	Cheap to publish, to customers who already own a computer
Portability (no power supply needed) and compactness	High-quality colour at no extra expense (again, if a computer is already available)
Cheap (no need to spend > £1,000 on a computer)	Animated images and sound
Immediate 'view-ability' (no 'down-load' time)	Hyper-linking
	Instant distribution and up-dating (Internet)

New types of graphically-oriented software have been designed to produce electronic publications: web-publishing software; web-graphic design software; multimedia 'authoring' software; PDF publishing software. One of the potential problems in establishing new software products of this kind is that of the proliferation of standards. Two standards, already referred to, are the PDF format – established by Adobe through its 'Acrobat' suite of software. The other is the HTML format, now in the process of being extended to XML (Extensible ML), DHTML (Dynamic HTML) and VRML (Virtual Reality ML).

Acrobat and PDF files

The PDF file format is used mainly for producing CD-ROM editions of existing printed products like computer manuals and magazines. To help establish the PDF format, Adobe created viewer software (called Acrobat 'Viewer'), versions of which are available for all the major operating systems free of charge. PDF is, in fact, an

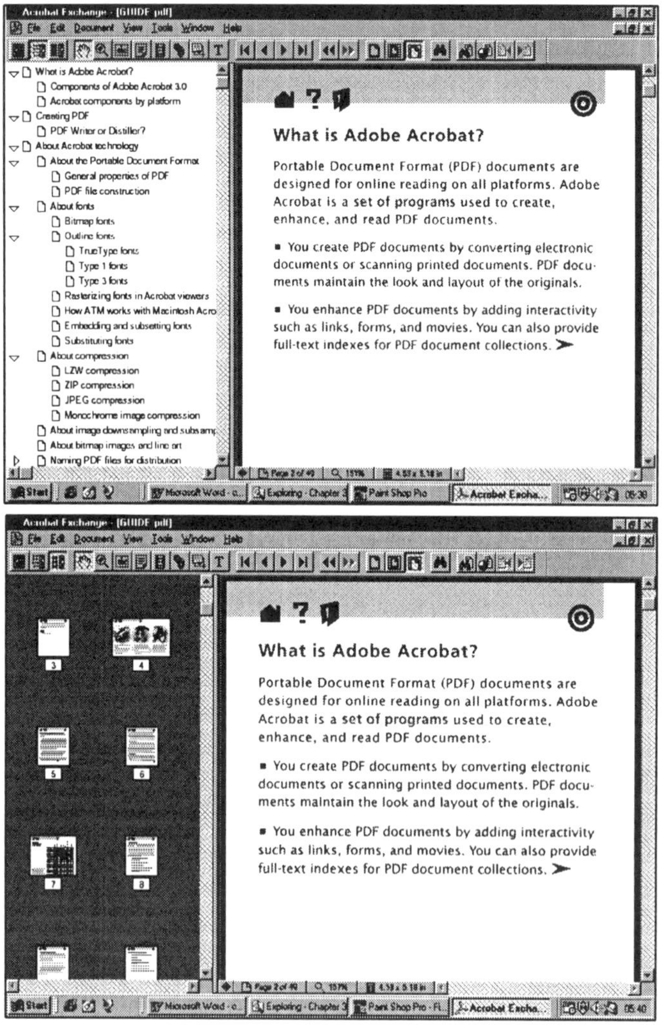

Fig. 3.10 *Adobe Acrobat screens. One shows a summary of the pages as 'Bookmarks'. The other summarizes them as 'Thumbnails'.*

extension of PostScript – Adobe's Page Description Language (PDL). Both PostScript and PDLs are discussed in more detail in Chapter 5. For simple documents, all that is needed to produce a PDF document is a special 'printer driver' that doesn't print – or at least, doesn't print on paper as one might expect but 'prints' to a file. The beauty of this approach is that, in principle, any software designed to produce text output – like a word processor – can be used to produce a

PDF document. Once the special printer driver software (Acrobat 'PDF Writer') has been installed as part of the operating system the user selects that driver at the output stage and 'prints' to a PDF file any document created in that software. In the case of more complicated documents containing embedded EPS graphics, for example, a two-stage process is needed. For the first stage a PostScript printer driver is used so that the document is converted into a PostScript file. A second piece of software (called Acrobat 'Distiller') is then used to convert this to a PDF file. Another special piece of software (called Acrobat 'Exchange') can then be used to enhance any PDF file by the addition of hyper-links, video and sound files and other ways of indexing and visualizing the contents of a PDF document (see Fig. 3.10). Another member of the Acrobat suite (Acrobat 'Capture') can be used to scan existing paper-based documentation, converting them into PDF files and automatically 'OCR-ing' them; OCR stands for Optical Character Recognition whereby the software recognizes the shape of individual characters in the bit-mapped scan and creates a text file instead of an image file.

The beauty of the PDF system is that, like PostScript itself, it is platform-independent and scaleable. What is seen on the screen is essentially an image of the printed page but it is not a bit-mapped image. This means that file sizes are reasonably small, text can be searched (as in a text file) and the images can be enlarged without loss of quality (at least – as far as the text is concerned).

HTML documents and editors

The HTML format was designed as a way of describing the appearance of a web page. Web viewers like 'Netscape' and Microsoft's 'Internet Explorer' are widely available either free or at a small charge and for exactly the same reason that PDF viewers are free – an attempt by software houses to establish their software as the dominant standard. HTML can also be thought of as a PDL (Page Description Language) which enables the user to specify what a Web page should look like and how it should link to other pages. HTML documents are simply text files that contain codes 'embedded' in the text. Here is a simple example, created using a modern word processor – by typing a few words, using two different fonts and two

Heading

This is a test file to see what HTML code looks like

Italic

Fig. 3.11 *A simple HTML document as seen using a Web-page viewer*

different sizes, some words being bold and some italic. This was then saved as an HTML file and the result examined in a text-editor to reveal the codes as well as the normal characters. The original file consisted of the three lines and looked like Fig. 3.11. The first line used the font 'Arial Black', bold, size 24 points. The second line used the font 'Times' – size 10 points. The third line used the same font and size as the second but the word was set in Italic. When viewed using a text editor the main body of the HTML file looked like this:

```
<B><FONT FACE="Arial Black" SIZE=6><P>Heading</P>
</B></FONT><FONT SIZE=2><P> </P>
<P>This is a test file to see what HTML code looks like</P>
</FONT><P> </P>
<I><P>Italic</P>
```

Without being any sort of expert at HTML code it is possible to see that the codes are separated from the text by the symbols '<' and '>' and to guess that the code <B> means *bold*, that <I> means *italic* and that <FONT FACE="Arial Black" SIZE=6> changes the font to *Arial Black* and a larger size.

It can be seen that, in principle, a Web page could be written using any text editor but the author would need to have a good understanding of all the embedded codes which are placed in the text to control the appearance and behaviour of the text and image blocks. Those who have acquired the expertise continue to work in this way but much of this is no longer necessary since special software (the equivalent of DTP software for Web pages) is available, which uses a graphic interface and generates the correct codes automatically. Good Web authoring software will, however, enable the user to see and edit the HTML code that is created so that special effects can be added to those created automatically.

3.2.3 Computer aided design (CAD)

CAD is a classic example of a graphic application which has grown up on large powerful computers and at one time it would have been considered quite impractical to do any serious work of this type on a desktop computer. It is true that much important CAD work is still done on graphic workstations but increasingly powerful applications are now also being run on ordinary desktop computers. One of the simplest types of computer-aided design is the preparation of 2-D plans – the sort of work done traditionally by draughtsmen on a drawing board with the aid of tee-squares and compasses (Fig. 3.12). This type of work can be done very rapidly with software which provides an electronic tee-square, 'rubber-banding', standardized parts and geometrical shapes, 'instancing', 'filleting', grids, layers and a library of standard shapes.

The electronic tee-square is a computer simulation of a pair of sliding horizontal and vertical rulers. It consists of a pair of lines at right-angles to each other and parallel with the sides of the display which are moved around the screen by mouse or stylus. The drawing of horizontal and perpendicular lines is automated by the user moving the lines until they are correctly positioned and then indicating how long the lines are to be. Appropriate lines are then drawn immediately on the screen. This, and other processes which involve positioning objects, are considerably aided by the use of a grid (already mentioned in the section on DTP). This is either a set of mutually-perpendicular lines drawn on the screen as an overlay, like graph paper, or a set of points corresponding to the intersections of such a grid. These act as reference lines or points to help the operator place objects correctly, a process which is further aided by 'snapping'. Snapping means that objects, when placed by the operator, automatically move to the nearest reference line or point, as if attracted by a magnet. They 'snap' into position. This means that the operator need only place objects close to the correct position, a process which is much quicker than exact positioning. The rest of the process is automatic. Grids can be made visible or invisible and in either case they do not become part of the final image. Snap can be switched off if positioning by hand, with the aid of the grid, is required.

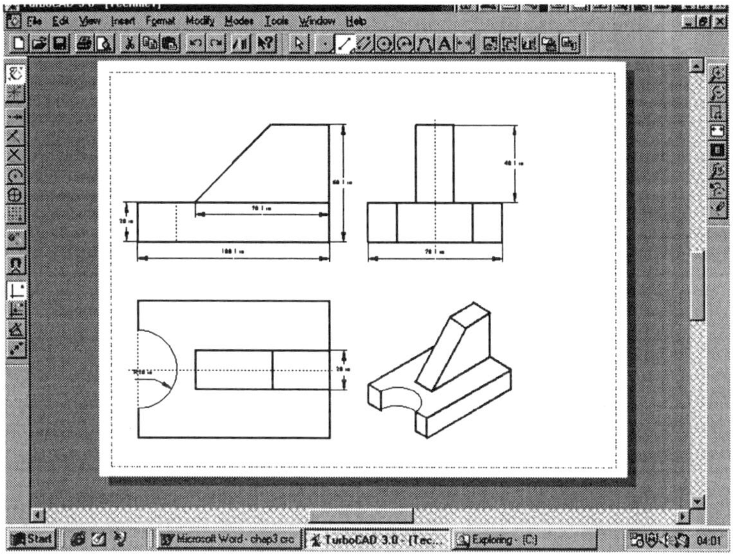

Fig. 3.12 *Screen shot taken from IMSI's 'TurboCAD' software*

Although the concept of a grid (and the associated idea of snapping) is commonly used on all vector-based software, CAD software has developed the idea much further. CAD drawings involve the creation of quitc complicated shapes which are built up from many individual components and it is important for the quality of the final product for these many joining operations to be done very precisely. CAD software therefore offers a whole variety of snapping options in which lines are snapped to other lines (rather than to points on a grid). Examples of this include 'intersection snapping' (drawing one line to snap to the intersection of two other lines), 'mid-point snapping' (drawing one line to snap to the mid-point of another line), 'end-point snapping' (drawing one line to snap to the end of another line) and 'tangent snapping' (drawing one line so that it makes a perfect tangent to a circle). There are many other possibilities. Another valuable aid to positioning is that of alignment. One object can be chosen as a reference object and other chosen objects then automatically aligned with it, as if they were being pushed up against an invisible reference line (either horizontal or vertical).

Rubber-banding is a technique for drawing other lines, usually those which are not horizontal or vertical. A cursor is moved to the position where the line is to start and that point is then fixed by a click of the mouse). The cursor is then moved away and the program draws and redraws continuously a straight line from the fixed position to any other position to which the cursor is moved. It is as if a rubber-band had one of its ends fixed so that when the other end is moved an elastic, straight line constantly joins the moving end to the fixed end. When the line is in the desired position the other end is fixed and a permanent straight line is left on the screen stretched between the two points of interest. The same principle is extended to the creation of rectangular boxes, circles and ellipses. In this case, once the fixed point has been designated, a rectangular 'bounding' frame of four moving lines joins it to the moving point, the points being at the diagonal corners of the frame. When the moving point is fixed either a rectangle or a circle/ellipse which fits into the rectangle is drawn – according to which command has been selected. What the rubber-band method does is to help the user visualize the size and position of an object whilst in the act of drawing it and to edit the size dynamically before being committed to it.

The ease of editing is one of the important attributes of any vector-based drawing package (the other being the high-quality of the final printed product). Each graphic component in a drawing is maintained as a separate item in a list kept by the computer so that at any time that element can be edited by the user without affecting any other element. This is usually done by the user's simply selecting the object and 'dragging' it into its new size, shape or position – or at least, that is how it appears to the user. In reality the computer removes that element from the drawing and substitutes a new version of it, using the same algorithm that was used to create the first one, but so quickly that it seems as if the original entity was being modified. The same basic technique can be used to provide an 'Undo' feature' which simply back-tracks by reversing the last operation and restoring the state that existed immediately beforehand. Exactly the same principle explains why objects can have their 'attributes' altered so easily. The attributes of an object are such qualities as the thickness of a line, the type of line (dotted or continuous, for example), the colour or the pattern of the filling of a bounded shape. And, finally, the same principle illuminates what is happening when a drawing is 'zoomed' – and also explains why this can be such a slow process in the case of a complicated drawing. Zooming, like all editing processes is actually a re-drawing process. When a single shape is edited the rest of the drawing may be left untouched but when a drawing is zoomed everything is re-drawn.

Another feature of CAD that has found place in other styles of graphic software is the use of 'layers'. A diagram is thought of as being drawn on a number of transparent sheets of paper (each one a separate layer). In an architectural plan, for example, the main structure of the building might be drawn on one layer, the electrical services on another, the central heating and water system on another and the fixed furniture on another. All of these can be superimposed if necessary to see all the information at a glance but to make a complicated picture easier to understand some of the layers can be removed, leaving only the ones that are of special interest at any one time.

In addition to these generalized drawing aids, standard shapes like hexagons (for bolt-heads) and electrical and other engineering symbols are available from a library of images, and can be placed and drawn at a chosen size, with a single command (see Fig. 3.13). 'Instancing' provides a means of repeating some part of the diagram without re-drawing. A portion of the plan is designated as an instance of something which is needed many times and the user then simply specifies where the copies are to be placed.

'Filletting' is the name given to the process of joining two straight lines (usually perpendicular to each other) with a curve to give a smooth transition where they meet. This represents the fact that, in most manufactured articles, corners of objects are smoothed over to give a curved edge rather than a sharp one (for both aesthetic and safety reasons). This can be done automatically in CAD software simply by specifying the radius of curvature to be used and then indicating which corners are to be treated. A similar feature is the automatic 'chamfer' – a corner is replaced, not with a part circle but with an oblique straight line. This is the equivalent of 'shaving off' a corner in a piece of woodwork and is done by the software once the distance from the corner is specified.

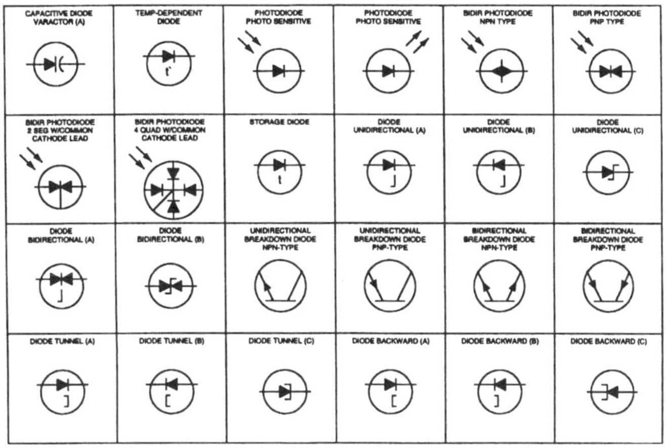

***Fig. 3.13** Part of a library of CAD symbols, provided with IMSI's 'Turbo-CAD' software*

A unique feature of CAD software is the provision for scale drawings. Most vector drawing packages are not concerned with the size of the object being drawn. In engineering and architectural drawing, however, the object is to create a representation of something that will be actually made and the sizes of the parts are important. For this reason CAD software provides a facility for specifying the scale to which the drawing will be made (for example, 1 : 100 or 10 mm represents 1 metre). Once specified the user can then draw shapes and enter their size in 'real world' units. This means that a wall could be drawn and set to be 20 metres long and the software will translate that into a line which is 200 mm long on the drawing. Of course the screen display will be able to work at many different values of magnification so there will not be any fixed relationship to the length on the screen but the length when printed will preserve the scale that has been chosen.

One final aid is the automatic production of witness and dimension lines. These are a system of arrows and numbers to indicate the length of parts of the drawing (the dimension lines), together with guide lines which are drawn from the end of the arrows to the edges of the parts being indicated (the witness lines). All the operator has to do is to choose the line on the drawing which needs the dimensions indicating and the software is able to do the rest since the length of the line on the screen is known and so is the scale to which the drawing is made. The operator can then move the dimension line to a suitable position.

3-D CAD

Everything which has been mentioned so far has been applied to 2-D drawings but the more powerful CAD packages can be used to design and represent 3-D objects. These are called sometimes called 'solid-modellers' because they create a complete and unambiguous description of a 3-D object in the computer and can display images with hidden lines removed and exterior surfaces shaded. Because of the wide-spread interest in 3-D modelling, which has now spread well beyond the boundaries of CAD, this subject is treated in a separate section.

3.2.4 Illustration (drawing) software

Though CAD software is associated with engineering design and other forms of technical drawing the facilities offered by such packages have proved useful in a wide variety of other applications. Illustration (or simply Drawing) software can be thought of as CAD software with a less specialized purpose. Like CAD software the shapes that are drawn are created and stored as vectors and so this type of software should be distinguished from 'Paint' software – described in a later section – which

Fig. 3.14 *A vector image, supplied with CorelDRAW, showing the use of shading in Illustration software to create more realistic images*

is used to create and modify bit-mapped images. The differences between CAD and Illustration software lie in emphasis and direction rather than principle. In both types of software the user can assemble and edit a range of line-based geometric shapes; objects can be separately selected, moved, distorted and re-sized; bounded shapes can be filled with colours and patterns; objects can be grouped and treated as single objects and a variety of positioning aids like grids and snapping are available. The differences lie in a number of enhancements required, and a number of specialist features not required, by the typical user who might be using the software to produce semi-technical illustrations but might equally be producing non-technical drawings for advertisements, leaflets and magazines. In general such applications require a larger range of fonts, more colour and colour-effects, a completely different library of ready-made drawings ('clip art') and a more sophisticated range of curves. The images that are to be produced by this type of drawing package are less severely functional and more aesthetically pleasing – more like 'art'.

Fig. 3.15 *Examples of decorative fonts*

The most obvious enhancements lie in the area of colour and shading; a much wider range of colours and shades are needed. Early CAD systems made little use of colour and, because pen-plotters were the standard output device, a handful of primary colours were all that was required. The output of illustration software – a more recent development – is produced on laser and inkjet printers and a wide range of colours, shades and colour gradations are desirable. Colour gradation (colour shading) consists of a series of adjacent coloured bands, each one slightly different from its neighbour, usually placed on a bounded shape and having a number of geometrical forms. These can be used for aesthetic effect but can also be used to create 3-D like images (see Fig. 3.14). Traditionally, artists have created an illusion of depth in their drawings by adding light and dark shading to the surfaces, copying the effects of lighting on different parts of the object. Drawing software allows users to create their own shading by specifying the two extremes that are required, the software then filling in all the intermediate values.

The greater range of curves (see also the chapter on algorithms) makes it possible to draw shapes other than those needed for manufactured objects, which are often of a simple form. The greater range of fonts is needed because it enables text to be used as a decoration and to suggest ideas about the context of the design (see some examples of decorative fonts in Fig. 3.15). Text can also be constrained to follow a curved line or fit inside an 'envelope' (see Fig. 3.16). A transitional effect, analogous to the colour shading, is one which will produce a simple form of 'morphing'. Morphing involves a gradual change from one image to another and drawing packages will usually allow this to be done with simple geometrical shapes. For example a star might be gradually changed into rosette. Whereas in true morphing software this transition will be displayed as a dynamic, cartoon-like process, in drawing software the aim is usually to display the transition as a series of images strung out along a curve in a single static image.

Because vector software maintains a list of each of the component parts of an image it is possible to control the relationships between these parts. A simple example of this is in the ability to bring any component to the front of another when they are overlapping. A more sophisticated application, however, lies in the use of Boolean combinations of objects. This principle will be described in more detail in the section on 3-D modelling software but here it can be illustrated with an example.

Fig. 3.16 *Text is distorted to fit inside an 'envelope' using Illustration software. In this case the result is to produce a perspective effect*

A designer might wish to create the effect of a window, through which another picture can be seen. This is trivial if the window is a simple rectangle but interesting effects can be created using other shapes as the window. In an advertisement, the name of the product – in large letters – can be splashed across the page and the letters themselves act as a window through which some idyllic scene is shown. Here the outline of the characters acts as a 'mask' – a controlling shape – and is overlaid on top of the scene. The relationship between the two images is determined by the rule: the inside of the letters is treated as being transparent, the outside as opaque. Other 'rules' for combining overlapping shapes could be semi-transparency. A shape acts as if it were made of coloured glass. Anything underneath it can be seen but its colours are modified by the colour of the overlying shape.

3.2.5 Business presentation software

This is another type of vector software with a very focussed application – the rapid production of 'presentations' (informative talks or short articles) which summarize as compactly as possible a set of ideas and/or data. The main features are: simple drawing facilities (like illustration software), clip-art, attractively presented, small quantities of text and graphs. The target user, unlike the user of presentation software or CAD, is not a designer and therefore it is important to be able to automate the production of an aesthetically-pleasing result. This is done by the provision of a wide range of 'templates'. A template, in the ordinary use of the term, is a pattern or guide that is used to help in the creation of some object – like a plastic sheet with the shape of letters of the alphabet cut in it which can be used to rapidly trace letters onto paper. In graphics software a template is a design which the user can quickly adapt to their own purposes. For example it could be a screen of 'dummy' text – perhaps a 'bullet' list – which users adapt by substituting their own text for the one provided. The point of the exercise is that a professional graphic designer is employed in creating the templates – in choosing suitable fonts and colours, perhaps with a patterned background – and so the user does not need any design skills to produce a professional looking result. The process is also a lot quicker for the user than creating the screen from scratch.

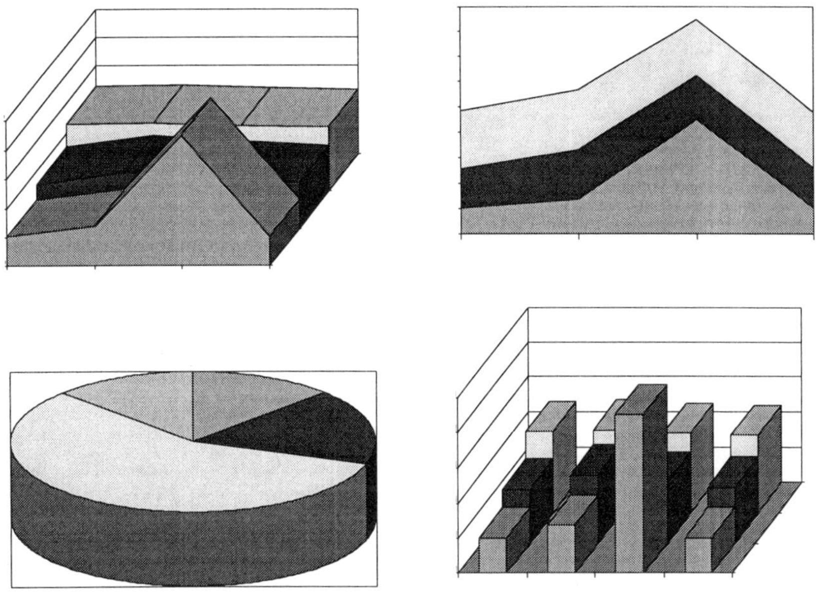

Fig. 3.17 The same set of data displayed in four different ways using Presentation software

The output of this type of software is often referred to as a 'slide' which emphasizes the fact that each image can be thought of as a photographic slide of the sort that is projected onto a screen during a talk. Because these slides are designed to be projected and read from a distance, rather than printed, the amount of information on each slide is severely limited and tends to consist of headlines, lists, diagrams or charts. A presentation consists of a series of slides, and in many cases the output may well be converted to real photographic slides, but alternatively it can be presented directly on a computer screen. The advantage of using a computer display is that the computer can be used to add dynamic effects. These can be in the form of transitions between slides or animation effects on the slide itself. Transition effects include screens which slide out of (and into) view from above or below or to the side, screens which gradually appear as if seen through a circular iris which grows in size and screens which disappear as if they had been gradually washed off by raindrops. A commonly used animation effect which is helpful in concentrating attention on items in a list is one in which those items slide onto the screen from the side one by one – like trains coming into a station on parallel tracks.

In addition to simple bullet-lists there are a variety of ways of presenting information including a wide range of graphs and charts (see Fig. 3.17). Great emphasis is placed on the use of colour and decorative fonts and in the variety of styles of graphs and charts. Line graphs are the traditional style of graph, plotted on a two-dimensional Cartesian system in which the data points may or may not be indicated by some symbol but are joined by straight lines. The scatter graph is a similar style of graph in which the data points are represented by symbols such as asterisks, small circles and triangles but are not joined up by lines. Line and scatter graphs present raw data without attempting to 'draw conclusions'. A trend graph, on the other hand, is designed to show the general tendency which lies behind the data. It presents the results of a simple statistical analysis of the data which is designed to discover the underlying trend – the general direction – of the events which give rise to the data. It is designed to ignore the accidental or unimportant fluctuations which affect all real-life measurements and to emphasize the underlying causes. In general, the resulting graph will be a straight line or simple curve rather than the zig-zag line which joins the data points in a line graph. In the bar chart the data are represented by the length of a series of rectangular bars – usually plotted vertically but sometimes horizontally. The bars can be plotted with or without separating spaces and are sometimes grouped together, two or three bars per group, to clarify some relationship between components of the data. This type of display is suitable for data which represent discrete events, such as the number of items sold by a shop each week, which are necessarily integers. Numbers which are continuously and smoothly varying, such as many of the quantities measured in scientific experiments are better represented on a line graph. In the pie chart the data are represented by slices of a 'pie', that is as sectors of a circle; for an example of a 3-D pie chart see Fig. 3.17. The relative sizes of the sectors indicate the relative proportions of the data rather then their absolute values, as the sectors normally add up to a complete circle. The pies can be wholly or partially 'exploded' which means that some or all of the sectors are removed a small way from the pie to draw attention to them. All these can be individually annotated, in addition to the automatic provision of suitable axes and labels. Text, clip art and charts can be grouped together and extra graphics drawn directly.

In addition to these standard graphs other features are sometimes available. Some genuinely offer extra information or alternative ways of viewing the data. Some are simply ways of making the display more striking or attractive. One is the facility to plot 3-D graphs but this term is rather ambiguous. It can mean nothing more than the use of bars which are represented as 3-D boxes rather than 2-D rectangles. In this case it is only a cosmetic device – designed to make the display more eye-catching – but adds no new information. A second possibility is that it means the use of 3-D boxes to represent data with three variables. This usually takes the form of a number of two-variable graphs or charts drawn one behind the other in a perspective or parallel projection (see the fourth chart in Fig. 3.17). For example the sales figures of a company in each month of the year might be required for three consecutive years. This could, of course, be displayed in a 2-D bar chart with the figures for each of the three years grouped together and plotted on one chart but a 3-D display would show the charts for each year one behind the other and viewed from some suitable position.

A third possibility involves the display of a smoothly varying 3-D function. This means that the data do not take the form of discrete figures which can be represented by a limited number of bars – as in the example of the sales figures – but rather they represent a smoothly varying quantity like measurements of air pressure in the atmosphere. A 2-D graph of this type of data is a smoothly varying curve; a 3-D representation is a 3-D surface and the creation of this type of display involves the use of hidden surface removal techniques as described in the chapter on algorithms.

This sort of facility is available in some mathematically-oriented graph drawing packages but not usually in the more routine business-oriented ones. A second sophistication that might be incorporated into graph-plotting software is the facility for curve-fitting. This has some similarities to the trend graphs described earlier. A curve-fitting routine attempts to discover a mathematical function that passes smoothly through the data points and so can in principle interpolate points (predict the values of extra points within the range of the plotted data) and extrapolate

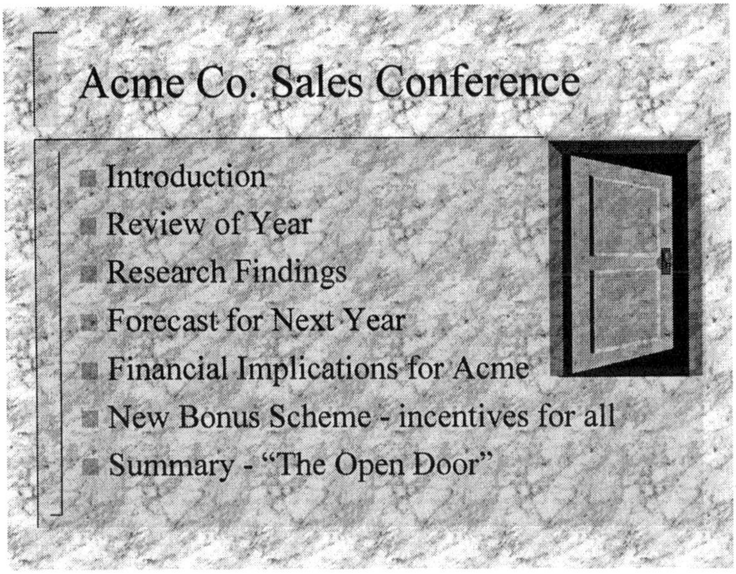

Fig. 3.18 *Presentation software enables the unskilled user to produce slick slides very quickly by the use of pre-prepared styles, fonts and clip-art*

(predict values outside that range). This is the sort of facility which is widely used in scientific work but can also be of use in the business context – usually in an attempt to make predictions about future trends in such quantities as the likely demand for products. It would be a suitable alternative to a trend graph if the data were known not to suffer from significant statistical fluctuations. Other extra facilities which might be available include graphs plotted on logarithmic scales (where the data covers a very wide range of different magnitudes) and multiple displays where more than one graph can be shown simultaneously in windows, sometimes overlapping.

The key word in this type of software is speed. It is no accident that advertisements for this type of product are often based on the scenario of 'how can I produce 20 slides that will impress the boss/client in only half an hour?'. The answer is that most presentations use a predictable range of slides – made from bullet lists, charts, graphs, tables, annotated diagrams – and all of these have been prepared already. Only the words/data need to be changed and that takes very little time. The process is not so much drawing and layout as substitution (see Fig. 3.18).

Drawing by Assembly

This realization that many users' needs can be predicted in advance has led to an interesting variation on the normal vector-based drawing package – one in which the user creates all images using editable clip-art. Because vector shapes can easily be edited, joined together, moved around, a great many needs for graphics can be satisfied by software in which nothing is drawn – everything is assembled. A simple example brings us back to where we started – CAD. An electronic engineer designs

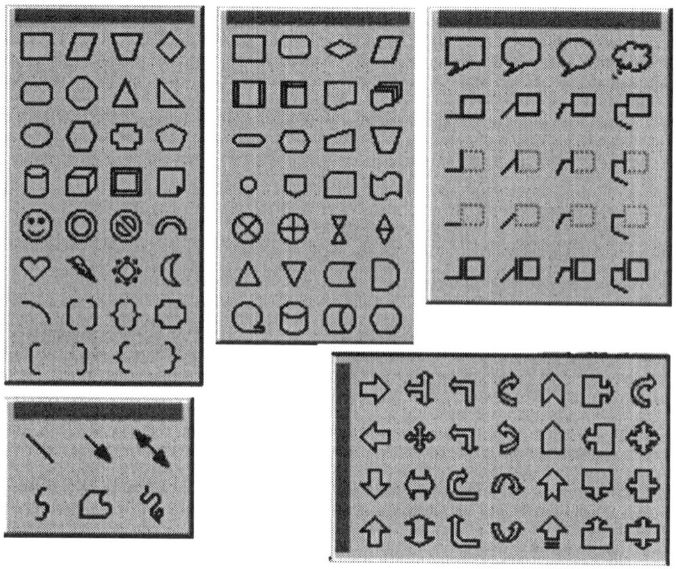

Fig. 3.19 *Editable shapes, from Microsoft Word, that can be assembled to produce flow charts and other diagrams*

electric circuits using a wide range of standard components, each of which has agreed symbols. Drawing a circuit is essentially a matter of assembling a particular set of components in a particular arrangement and connecting them up. Many other types of chart and diagram can be produced using the same principle (see Fig. 3.19). If a good range of standard symbols are available the user simply places them and connects them. A nice feature of this type of software is that the connections have the rubber-band properties already described. Once a pair of items are connected by lines, signifying electrical or other logical connections, those connections are correctly maintained even when the items are moved. This means that overall editing of the diagram, can be done – say, to fit in an extra component – without the need for tedious re-drawing of all the connecting lines. What this type of development recognizes is that general-purpose, do-anything software is fine for designers faced with many different sorts of tasks, but for many specialists software that does only one job, very efficiently, has a market also. Many users will happily trade freedom and creativity for speed and ease of use.

3.3 Bit-Mapped Software

The last six sections have been concerned with vector software – DTP and Electronic publishing where the vector shapes are scaleable fonts, and CAD and its offshoots (Illustration and Presentation software) where they are lines drawings. The next three types of software are concerned with the creation and editing of images that are stored as bit-maps. There are two reasons for storing images as bit-maps and

Fig. 3.20 *Corel 'PhotoPaint' – a bit-mapped painting package*

they are nicely illustrated by two, overlapping, categories of software – paint packages and photographic retouching software. In the first, the emphasis is on providing an electronic substitute for the traditional artist's medium of paint and pencil. Here images are stored as bit-maps because they are created, not by in-built algorithms, but by the artist, painting with a mouse or stylus. In the second, existing images, usually photographs are scanned (which inevitably produces a bit-map) and the software is then used to modify that image.

3.3.1 Paint packages

Painting packages are designed to be, to the artist, what CAD and Illustration software are to the engineer or designer. It enables the artist to draw free-hand, using a stylus or mouse in a wide variety of colours and special effects and to simulate non-digital forms of drawing and painting (Fig. 3.20). Because it is a digital simulation, such software can also automate the production of patterns and repetitive effects. Such software will contain standard drawing facilities like those in applications already described, such as pre-drawn geometrical shapes and a wide variety of fonts, so that at first glance it might be difficult to see any difference from vector-based software. Any such illusion can easily be dispelled however, by simply zooming in on an image using the 'magnifying glass' tool, when the individual pixels which make up the image will soon be revealed.

The special characteristics of this type of application centre around the simulation of different types of drawing and painting styles and the use of the computer to produce patterns and dynamic effects. Whereas CAD software must store the basic shapes as individual vectors, painting programs store images as pixel-based bit

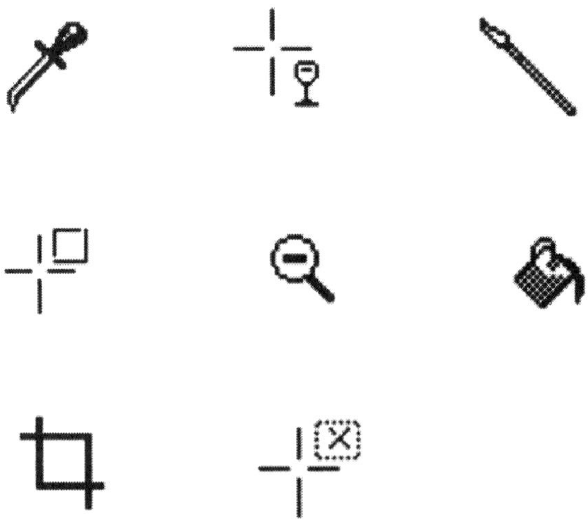

Fig. 3.21 Some examples of the special mouse cursors used in Corel 'PhotoPaint'

maps. Information is entered by a process of direct drawing onto the screen rather than by co-ordinates or measured lengths and angles. The over-riding philosophy of the paint program is to provide an interface which is as near as possible to the one with which the artist is familiar. The metaphor of the child's paint box to provide a palette is a good example. A colour is chosen from a palette by 'dipping' the brush into that colour, that is, touching the colour of choice with the mouse. The colour palette can be seen on the right-hand side of the screen dump in Fig. 3.20. This now becomes the colour which will appear when the artist draws. New palettes and new colours can be created and saved either by the normal technique (by altering the red, green and blue or the cyan, yellow and magenta primary components) or by a simulated mixing of colours, such as an artist would use. This means 'picking up' two colours (as an artist might) and placing them down side by side on the display where they then flow into each other to create a whole series of intermediate colours, one of which can then be picked up and added to the palette. There is an extended discussion of the specification of colour in Chapter 4.

Modern images can contain such a large range of colours that it can become difficult to identify the correct shade of colour required for a particular task. What is needed is some means of selecting a colour already in use on the screen. Here another metaphor comes in useful. The 'Eye-dropper' tool (its symbol can be seen on the top left of Fig. 3.21) is a tiny syringe. It acts as if a small quantity of paint could be sucked up from the painting and then, itself, used for painting.

Different thicknesses and shapes of drawing 'brush' or 'pencil' can be chosen and even different types of painting implement – a pencil, a paint brush, a palette knife, a spray-gun or air-brush, a charcoal stick. Each of these effects is simulated by the precise patterns of pixels which appear as the drawing is done and the chosen implement is often indicated to the user by the use of a range of drawing cursors such as a tiny icon. A typical selection can be seen in Fig. 3.21. Styles of painting and drawing depend not only on the chosen medium (such as paint or pencil) but also on the type of paper and some paintbrush software can simulate this variable as well. It is possible therefore to 'paint' in oils on canvas or in watercolour on suitable paper, for example. A third factor can also simulated to some extent – the actual painting style, or at least, the technical aspects of it. Some software will simulate the Pointillist style (the image being made up of dots of paint) or the Impressionist style – by deliberately softening the edges of shapes.

Another useful tool is the eraser. In vector software all the components of an image are geometrical shapes, each being held in a list, so that any shape can be selected, edited and deleted at will. In bit-mapped software the picture is simply a collection of pixels and so erasing parts of an image, like drawing itself, is done by the user, pixel by pixel with a simulated eraser. Because it is an electronic facility the normal characteristics of an eraser can be extended. An eraser can be used which will only erase one chosen colour – or will replace the foreground colour with the background colour – and this often makes the task much easier because parts of the image are much less likely to be erased accidentally. If they are, then a good 'Undo' facility is important. Undo simply reverses the last operation. This is achieved by keeping copies of previous versions of the whole image so that they can be restored if the last operation turns out to have been a mistake and a good implementation of this will store many previous images.

Various types of automatic repetition can be very productive. A simple example of this is the automation of repeated patterns of the sort that are used on wallpaper and fabrics like curtains. Once the basic unit of the pattern has been designed a single command (usually called 'Tiling') is all that is necessary to repeat it across the screen so that the overall effect can be seen immediately. Another useful facility in this context, is that of re-defining the palette so that the same pattern can be seen in many different colours without any further drawing being needed. Patterns can also be used in the flood-fill mode; instead of a boundary being filled with a solid block of colour it is filled with a pattern. A wall, for example, can be drawn by filling a suitable outline with a repeated brick pattern.

Another type of repetition involves the creation of an artist-designed brush (sometimes called a 'Clone' brush). In this context, the 'brush' is any pattern of pixels produced on the screen as the cursor is moved in drawing mode. The simplest brush is a circle or square such as would be produced by a pencil but the artist can designate any group of pixels as a brush. This means that a pattern of any desired complexity can be designated a brush and then 'drawn' with. As a result the pattern will be continuously repeated and superimposed, each one on the last, as the stylus is moved over the screen producing a sort of smeared-out effect. It is a variation on the instancing described in CAD systems but with the difference that copies of the image flow off the brush as it moves. When a single example of the brush is placed on the image this is called 'Stamping'.

Another useful effect is that of a type of pixel-based zoom as described at the beginning of this section. In bit-mapped software, zooming simply replaces each original pixel with an identical, but larger one so that the image occupies much more space and its structure becomes much clearer. Of course, very little new detail is revealed in this process, since the normal-sized pixels are almost visible to the unaided eye, but it does become much easier to see, and to make alterations, on a fine scale – even pixel-by-pixel if necessary. It is the equivalent of viewing the image through a magnifying glass but with the added advantage of being able to make changes to the image in a magnified form also. Fig. 3.22 shows part of the image seen already in Fig. 3.20. In one window the image is at the normal magnification; in the other it has been 'zoomed' ten-fold so that individual pixels can be easily distinguished.

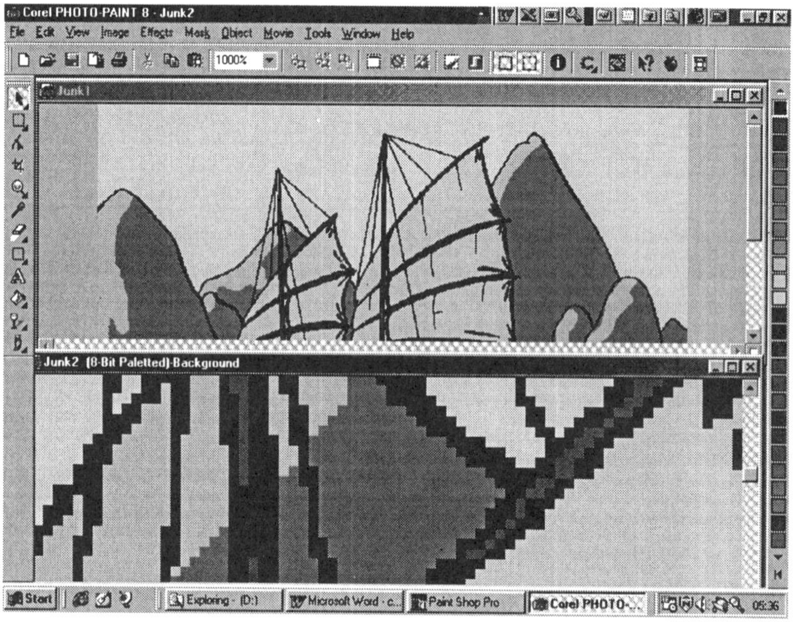

Fig. 3.22 The same image, in Corel 'PhotoPaint', one magnified by a factor of ten compared with the other

The power of a good paint system is also enhanced by the ability to cut and paste images or parts of images and to import into the design images created by other means – digitized photographs and video images, for example. All these functions enable the artist to create collages rapidly which can then be endlessly re-arranged and whose colours can be changed instantly until the desired effect is obtained. Paint systems usually provide the user with a storage area in which images can be placed until needed, then retrieved and brought back into the main picture as part of this cut-and-paste philosophy.

3.3.2 Photo-retouching software

The development of the document and film scanner and the digital camera (all described in the chapter on hardware) has led to a demand for software that can be used to enhance and 'improve' these digitized photographs. Some of the processes mimic those that have been used for many years by photographers in 're-touching' photographic images. For example in black and white pictures, blemishes (either of the subject of the photograph or introduced accidentally by the photographer) can be carefully removed from a negative using a brush and special dye. Sometimes faults are removed at the printing stage. All of these types of re-touching are trivially easy with digitized pictures since each pixel can be changed to whatever colour or shade is desired. One technique is to make a copy of a surrounding region in the picture (one without a blemish) making it into a brush and then painting over the blemish region with that brush. In Adobe PhotoShop (see Fig. 3.23) the tool for this is called a rubber-stamp.

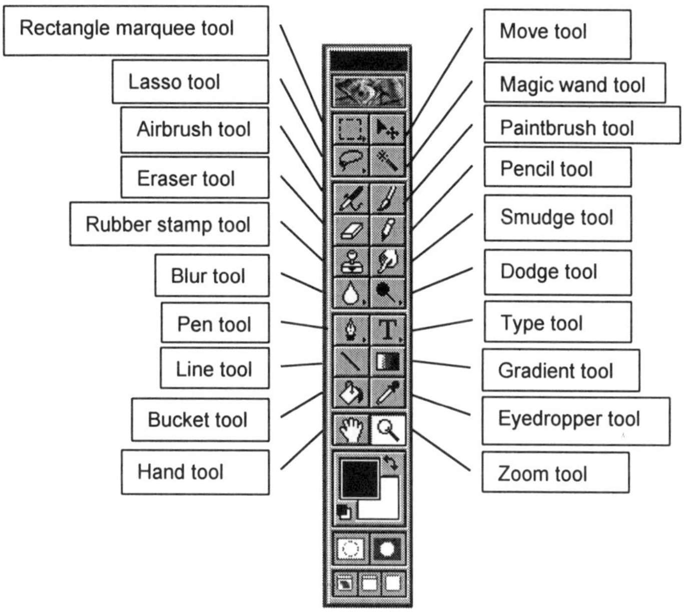

Fig. 3.23 *The Tool Bar from Adobe's 'PhotoShop' software, illustrating the range of image manipulation facilities*

Other facilities illustrated in Fig. 3.23 include a variety of drawing, writing and erasing tools (Pencil, Paintbrush, Airbrush, Line, Type, Bucket, Gradient, Eyedropper and Eraser), selection tools (Lasso and 'Magic wand') and editing tools (Dodge, Smudge and Blur). Eyedropper is a tool for selecting an existing colour from a picture so that it can be used as the drawing colour. Dodge is used for making an area of the image lighter (and takes its name from an equivalent technique used in traditional photography).

A more subtle defect in photographs can be the result of poor lighting conditions when the picture is taken or unsuitable processing, resulting in pictures which are too light, too dark or with the wrong contrast range (too little or too much variation in light and dark) and re-touching packages are provided with a range of facilities for tackling this type of problem. Use of these will mean that a picture taken in dull light with very little in the way of shadows, or a picture taken in very bright light with dark, harsh shadows can be re-balanced to produce a more pleasing effect.

Many facilities go beyond what would be possible in conventional photography. A properly focussed picture could be re-photographed using a soft-focus lens if such a result is needed but it is not easy to do the reverse – to change a badly-focussed image into a sharply-focused one. Both are possible with software enhancement. Some effects have no equivalent in traditional photography. Pictures can be 'pixellated' – have the size of their pixels enlarged to produce a 'blocky' effect. False colours can be introduced and separate images can be combined to produce composites. To achieve this last effect it is often necessary to be cut portions from an image and a so-called Magic Wand (see Fig. 3.23) is a very useful tool for this purpose. The wand selects a region of a picture based on the colour (usually a range of similar colours) so that a green apple, for example, could be isolated from the blue china bowl in which it sits. The apple can then be added to another picture in a wholly convincing way – particularly if the edges of the apple are 'softened' to disguise the clear-cut boundary that might otherwise make the inserted object stand out against its new background.

3.3.3 Animation software

A clear distinction needs to be made between 2-D and 3-D animation. 3-D animation requires vector type software which is an extension of CAD and is dealt with under 3-D modelling. 2-D animation, which is dealt with here, is usually done with a specialized type of painting software.

The creation of animated images follows the same pattern as that used in television, cine-photography and cartoons. A large number of separate images must be created in such a way that when they are shown in rapid succession they create the effect of smooth motion. Computers, for example, are increasingly being used to help create animated cartoons. Here the computer has two main functions – to separate the image into layers ('cels') and to interpolate images automatically. The first function is essentially similar to layers already described and used widely in CAD, drawing and paint software. The purpose, for animation, is to avoid re-drawing those elements of an image that remain the same from one frame to another. In traditional animation this is done using sheets of celluloid (cels). In the simplest case the background of the image is drawn on one cel and the foreground (the animated character) on another. The two cels are superimposed and one frame

Fig. 3.24 Three separate cels (foreground, mid-ground and background) are superimposed to form a composite image

of the cartoon photographed with a special cine camera. For the next frame, only the character on the front cel has to be drawn again (in its new position); the background cel can be re-used. Some scenes, ideally, should have many cels to maximize the efficiency of the process but there is a limit to the number of cels that can be used because of the small amount of light absorbed in each cel. When the cels (or layers) are created digitally in a computer there is no such limit. Fig. 3.24 shows three cels – foreground, mid-ground and background.

The second function is to automate the 'in-betweening' (or 'tweening') process. Traditionally, one artist draws the main characters and creates the important stages in the movement of that character but others are employed in drawing all the many in-between stages where less creative skill is required. The computer can now be used for much of this work. It can automatically create the large number of images that are needed because each small difference between one frame and another – say when the cartoon character raises his arm to throw a ball – is predictable, given a starting point and a finishing point. This process of filling in values between two known end-points is called interpolation and its success depends upon the condition that the intermediate values change smoothly, one from another.

3.3.4 Morphing

A different kind of interpolation is required for 'morphing' (a word based on the term metamorphosis). Here, what is changed is not the position of an essentially unvarying component of an image – say a car driving down a road or a man's leg moving as he walks. Morphing involves the shape of one object changing so that it seems to become a completely different object – say, a man changing into a lion. This is a more complicated type of interpolation and involves a great deal more intervention from the user of the software. In essence, two images are chosen – the start image and the end image – and the user must then identify a large number of pairs of points in these images. The user, for example, must designate a series of points that outline the mouth of the man and link them up with the same number of points that outline the mouth of the lion – point by point, in equivalent pairs. During the morphing process the computer then generates a set of intermediate values for each of these points in the image. They will be intermediate in both colour and position, given that the shape of a man's head is different from that of a lion's and the colours are also different. This produces a set of images and when they are displayed in rapid sequence they produce an animation and give the illusion of one object gradually changing into another. 3-D morphing uses a similar principle but must generate 3-D images with all the attendant extra complications that involves.

3.3.5 Multimedia software

This is a very diffuse collection of software types for the simple reason that the term itself is so ill-defined and the effects so widely disseminated. Early computers used text-only displays as the only medium of communication between the computer and the user. Later, crude graphics were added and elementary sound in the form of beeps and buzzes. Both of these (graphics and sound) have improved enormously in quality to the point that images approaching photographic quality and sounds of CD-quality are now commonplace. With the increased power of the computer to process and move data around and the increased storage capability, digitized video and other moving images can now be handled also. The result is the 'multimedia' computer and this wide range of visual and sound data is now increasingly incorporated into every type of software. All software categories are now potentially multimedia. Word processed documents can now contain video, sounds, animation and photographic images. In this setting the only software that can be particularly entitled multimedia is the category 'Multimedia Authoring'. These are packages that are specifically designed for use in creating multimedia products like CD-ROM encyclopaedias and training and educational material.

What distinguishes one multimedia authoring package from another is usually the metaphor used in assembling the various media components and the sophistication of the programming language. One package uses the metaphor of a film-studio where the media components such as text, images and sounds are termed 'the cast' and these are used to create a 'movie' by placing them on a time-line which determines when and how long they feature in the final product. Another metaphor is that of the flowchart. This can be a very easily understood way of illustrating the events that determine the way the final product operates and is particularly useful for training and educational software, in which the user answers questions or makes decisions which then trigger new processes.

The software already discussed in the electronic publishing section of this chapter can also be thought of as multimedia software and has much in common with multimedia authoring packages.

3.4 Three-Dimensional Modelling

Here we return to a form of vector software, but one that is very different from all of those discussed earlier in the chapter. 3-D Modelling involves specifying the positions in 3-D space of all the components of a solid object (either a real object or an imaginary one) and then constructing a 2-D image – one that can be displayed on a computer screen – that represents the view an observer would have of that object from some specified position (also in 3-D space). This is an extremely complicated process that requires a considerable amount of data processing, especially if a very realistic image is required. In fact, different applications require different degrees of realism in the image. Some only need wire-frame images – images in which the edges of the object are represented by lines, looking like a simple model made from wire. Others need the surfaces to be represented in some way and there are a variety of degrees of realism possible here; there is further discussion on these points in the chapter on algorithms.

As far as the user is concerned the big problem tends to be that of imagining the object when only 2-D views are available on the screen. Usually three or four different views of the object to be modelled are presented simultaneously (see Fig. 3.25 where three views are presented). The four commonest views are a view from above, a view from the side, a view from the front and one from a such a position that all the three previous aspects can be seen, at least partially, at the same time (an 'isometric' viewpoint).

The process of creating a 3-D model takes place in four distinct phases. The first consists of creating an unambiguous specification of the object; the software must have access to details of the positions, in 3-D space, of all the surfaces of the object.

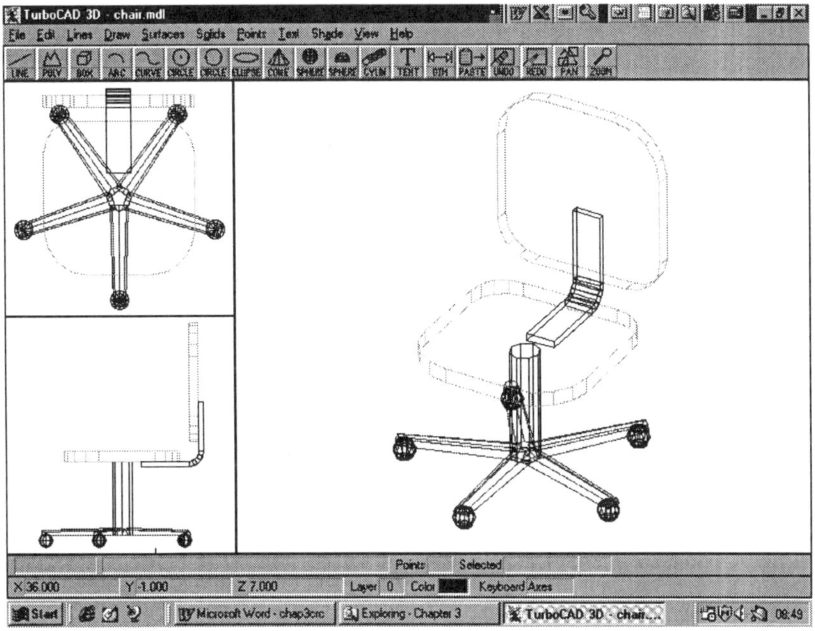

Fig. 3.25 A screen from IMSI's 'TurboCAD 3D' showing a wire-frame view of an office chair in three different views

Secondly, the software must calculate what that object will look like from a specified position in space. Initially this will take no account of the transparency – or otherwise – of those surfaces. All surfaces will be seen in such a view – usually a simple wire-frame view. Thirdly, the software must then identify all those surfaces (and parts of surfaces) that will not be seen by the viewer because they are obscured by intervening surfaces – a process called 'hidden-surface removal'. Lastly the surfaces must be represented in a realistic way. Each of these will be briefly reviewed. The algorithms that lie behind some of them are discussed in the appropriate chapter.

The objects themselves are mostly modelled, either by assembling pre-existing 3-D 'primitives' – basic geometric shapes like tubes, cylinders, spheres, pyramids and rectangular boxes that are provided with the software – or by extruding or rotating 2-D shapes (see Fig. 3.26). The process of combining these components together can be made very versatile by the use of Boolean combinations. This involves the use of logical combinations of those overlapping regions of two objects which must be imagined to be able to exist in the same region of space, like cartoon ghosts (see Fig. 3.27). Once every surface has been specified the computer uses three-dimensional geometry to calculate what each surface would look like to a viewer at a particular position in space. In essence, this amounts to drawing imaginary projection lines in space from all important points on the object towards the viewer – either with parallel projection lines or, better, with perspective lines. At the position of the viewer a viewing plane (corresponding to the screen of the computer) is created and the points of intersection of the projection lines with that plane produces a 2-D image of a 3-D object.

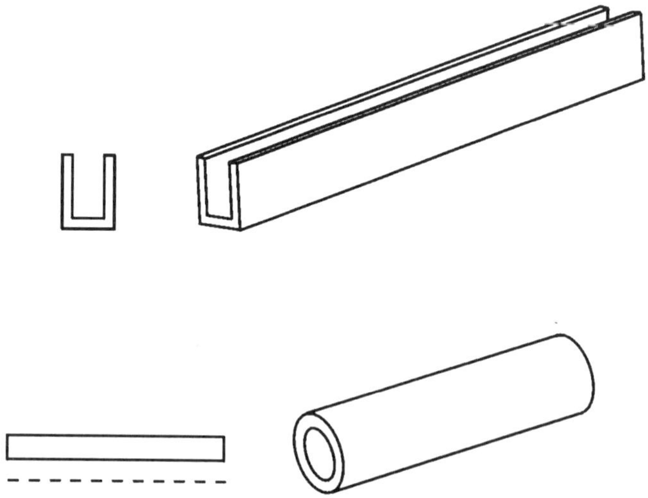

Fig. 3.26 *Two ways of creating 3-D shapes from 2-D shapes. The top shape is made by extruding. The bottom shape is made by rotation about the dotted axis*

The third process is to calculate which of the many parts of the object should not appear in the final image because their view is obstructed by other parts of the object. If the 3-D 'object' is, in fact, a group of objects then this process is more complicated because parts of one object may be obscured by parts of a completely different object. Because of the complexity of this process a number of different

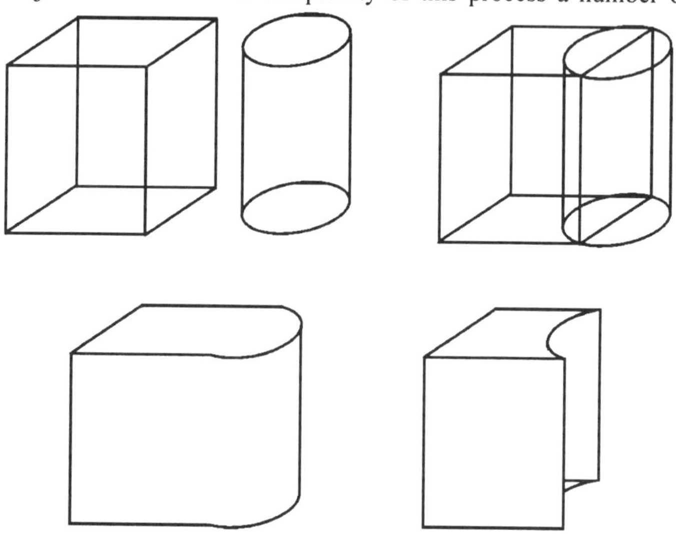

Fig. 3.27 *A cube and a cylinder are brought together and then combined in two ways: using the Boolean OR and using the Boolean subtraction*

algorithms have been devised; some are quicker than others because they take can advantage of inherent restrictions on the shape and position of the objects in the scene.

The final process is to reproduce the appearance of the surfaces themselves. The appearance of a surface is determined by many factors such as the type of surface (the colour, surface texture, transparency, for example), the illumination of the surface (the colour of the lighting, its distance and its type – highly directional or scattered, for example) and the effects of other objects which might throw shadows or scatter light onto it. The degree of realism of the final image will largely depend on the appearance of the surfaces of the object, given that its geometry has been modelled accurately (see Plate 5).

3.4.1 Virtual reality (VR)

VR is an extension of 3-D modelling in which the appearance of 3-D synthesized objects can be rapidly re-calculated in response to input from the viewer. The object is to give the impression that the viewer is actually inhabiting a synthetic world (one that only 'exists' in the computer). This requires that the computer be constantly fed information about the position in real space of the viewer – movement of the head and hands, for example – so that the user's view of the objects can be instantly re-calculated by the computer. This gives the impression that the viewer is moving in a real world since it 'responds' appropriately to any movements as the real world does. For a good sense of realism the computer must generate two slightly different images of the synthetic world – one for each eye – to produce a much stronger illusion of depth – and this requires special head-sets with two screens. The head-set can also be used to feed information back to the computer about the user's head movements. Some systems also monitor the user's hand movements by means of special gloves and even foot movements via a special tread-mill. The processing of all this data in real-time is an enormous challenge and it is extremely difficult to provide very realistic images under these conditions though flight-trainers for use by civilian and military pilots show what is possible.

The application of these systems includes games and leisure – where entertainment is the purpose – as well as a variety of training and educational purposes. Of all the many applications of computer graphics, this is the area that is best fitted to soak up almost any amount of processing power that can be thrown at it. The best quality systems are those where the number of variables can be restricted and are most easily predicted – such as a pilot learning to fly an aircraft into a particular airport. Here there are limits to the manoeuvres that are both physically possible and considered safe and comfortable for the passengers as well as limits to the detail that is expected of the images.

3.5 Graphics Utilities

Graphics utilities are software packages which are designed to solve one specific problem associated with the use of graphics software. They are therefore highly specialized applications that don't produce any obvious product, as all the other applications discussed in this chapter do, but are designed simply to make life easier for the user.

3.5.1 Graphics file conversion

Probably the most common and frustrating problem for graphics users is that caused by the proliferation of graphics file formats. This is so central to work in computer graphics that a whole chapter is devoted to a discussion of the topic and graphics file conversion software is discussed there.

3.5.2 Image archiving

A second problem – and one that is not unique to computer graphics – is that of knowing exactly what is in a file. Modern computers have hard disks measured in gigabytes and it is quite possible for a user to accumulate thousands of files, of many different sorts. At least modern operating systems allow the user to give a file a sensible name like 'letter to Mr Jones about his bill' instead of the 8.3 formula which tended to produce names like 'letjonbi.doc'. However, the best name in the world will not always remind the user of exactly what is in a file and it often becomes necessary to examine its contents, if only to eliminate it from a search. File viewer software is software that recognizes a wide variety of file types so that the viewer can easily examine the contents of text, spreadsheet and data-base files, for example, without having to run each separate piece of application software (or even to own a copy). Such software usually will cope with a range of graphics formats also so that it is almost as quick to look at the contents of a graphic file as it is to look at a text file. However, there is an even quicker method, though it necessarily uses up extra disk space. Archiving software will produce 'thumbnails' of a large number of images and keep them in a single file. A thumbnail is a small replica of an image which contains much less detail than the original but should be just detailed enough to for the user to recognize it. An array of these images is displayed on the screen looking very like the 'contact prints' that photographers produce for exactly the same purpose.

3.5.3 Screen grabbing

There are many occasions when a user would like to take a copy of whatever can be seen on the screen of a computer in order to print it or to incorporate it into a document. The production of a book like this is an obvious example, as is the production of advertising for computer software, reviews of software for magazines and the production of manuals for software. The process of taking an exact copy of a screen is called 'screen grabbing'. The software that does this must be run at the same time as the application that is to be 'grabbed' – and must, of course not produce any signs of its existence on the screen, or it will be counterproductive. Usually the grabbing process is activated by the use of a 'hot-key' – a key, or combination of keys, that trigger the software into taking a copy of the current image and putting it into memory or directly to a file. Microsoft 'Windows' has such a facility built in, triggered by the Print Screen (PrtScr) key. Good commercial alternatives usually offer other facilities to make the screen grabbing more versatile. Useful facilities are those such as the ability to grab the active window only, to grab a pull-down menu, to grab a mouse-cursor and to crop unwanted material from the image before saving it.

3.5.4 Font organization

Because of the widespread use of scaleable fonts, the subject of fonts has become important enough to warrant a chapter in this book to itself. One problem associated with the use of such fonts is the huge number of fonts that tend to accumulate on a computer, often without the intervention of the user. Many graphics application are provided with a collection of fonts that are copied onto the hard disk of the computer during the installation of the software – without giving the user any warning or option of refusing them. As a result 400 or 500 fonts might accumulate quietly over a few years, taking up a lot of disk space, and perhaps never being used. Font utilities can help this situation in a number of ways. The first facility that is helpful is one that makes it easy to view and print samples of the fonts so that a decision can be taken about which are to be kept and which deleted. The second is one that allows the user to group fonts of a similar type together so that a particular type of font can be more easily found. A final useful aid is to be able to 'switch' them off and on. A font that is switched off is not deleted from the disk but is treated by the operating system as if it was not there. This means that rarely-used fonts are removed from the list that is displayed within an application making it much easier to scroll down the list and select one that is really wanted.

Exercises for the Reader:

Note : To do exercises in this section the reader will need access to the different specialist types of application software covered in the chapter. In a surprising number of cases, however, there exists high-quality shareware packages which the reader can use for up to 30-days (for evaluation) and which can usually be bought for a very reasonable registration fee. In addition, some software companies give away full early versions of their products via computer magazine cover discs (usually with a special offer to upgrade to the latest version). In some cases limited versions of the current package are also given away as a form of advertising – 'try before you buy'. These are limited either in the sense that they will run for only 30 days (or for a fixed number of times) or in the sense that files cannot be saved or printed. Whatever the limitation, the reader can obtain valuable experience of what might be very expensive software for no initial cost. Finally most new computers come with bundled software and although this is usually limited to 'office' suites – a word processor, a spreadsheet and a database, for example – sometimes some form of graphics software is provided even if only in the form of built-in graphics facilities in the word processor.

Exercises are provided here for the types of software most easily obtained free. If the user has already purchased any speciality graphics software then the manual or help system is the best source of ideas for things to try.

Graphical Interfaces: if you have access to more than one GUI – e.g. two or more from the following list: Windows 2.0, Windows 3.0 or 3.1, Windows-95, Windows-98, X-Windows (used on Unix workstations), Macintosh OS, Amiga OS, Archimedes OS – study the similarities and differences. The similarities are obvious – menus, icons and windows. The differences lie in the way they are used. Look out for:

- pull-down and pop-down menus (one type has to be held down but flies back up without help; the other stays down, once clicked, but has to be cancelled after the user's action);
- the names given to the items (particularly the icons that represent the sub-directories);
- stylistic features – for example flat or bevelled icon buttons, items that change in some way when pointed to or pressed;
- the use of mouse cursors that vary according to the local environment;
- the scroll-bars. Do they disappear or change their appearance when there is nothing to scroll?
- does the length of the moveable bar on the scroll bar indicate anything?
- the icons themselves – can you guess what the icons represent or do they need some form of explanation?
- how are icons explained (pop-up messages when they are pointed to or permanent captions, for example?)
- are there alternative ways of doing the same thing (for example, icon buttons and menu items and keyboard shortcuts?). If so, is their any indication of this (for example, keyboard shortcuts or icon images displayed on the equivalent menu item?);
- is there complete consistency in the 'metaphor' – for example, if the user can delete a file by dragging its icon over a waste-basket, can printing be done by dragging an icon over a printer icon or E-mail be sent by dragging an icon over a posting-box icon?

There are many more similar points to be discovered by comparing different implementations of a GUI.

Desktop publishing: modern word processors contain many DTP features so most readers can attempt exercises in this category. Look at a magazine and try to identify all the features that define its design:

- the use of newspaper-style columns, drop-caps (large first letters at the beginning of a paragraph or articles),
- text that is aligned to left or right or centred,
- headlines that are force-justified (made to match at both ends even when that means using unusually large gaps between letters),
- unusual values of leading (line spacing),
- text flowing round pictures (including those that are not rectangular),
- a variety of fonts,
- bold and italic,
- text in coloured boxes,
- lines between columns,
- text flowing across columns.

Once you have identified all these features try to create a replica of one page. To do this you will have to work out how each of the identified features is achieved in your package. If a scanner is not available to scan the original images, use clip-art as a substitute. To reduce the labour of typing in the text, use an existing text-file for the body of the text but type in headlines. The key to the success of this enterprise (apart from the problem of finding identical or very similar fonts) is to be very systematic. Measure the page size, the margins, the space between columns, the positions of each block of text and each picture and use these measurements (with the ruler facility) to place items in a sensible order. Be prepared to print off a number of trial pages to check that the fonts, the line spacing, the indents etc. are looking right before committing a lot of effort to the details. This sort of exercise is an excellent way of getting to grip with the features of a DTP package as well as to alert yourself to all the features that make up a printed document.

Electronic Publishing: many modern word processors will export (and in some cases import) documents in HTML formats so many readers will be able to attempt something in this category also. Try creating documents in a word processor or DTP program and then exporting them as HTML files. Then, obtain a web browser (some are free and can be downloaded from the Internet or copied from a computer magazine cover disk). Use these to view the file you have created. If you have a copy of a dedicated package you can explore Web-page creation further. For example, 'Netscape Communicator' is distributed free to students and staff in educational institutions and to others on a 90-day trial basis. This software contains a web-browser so that HTML documents can be viewed but it also contains software for creating web documents. Learn about the basics of HTML tags by creating simple HTML documents and then looking at the tags in a text editor.

In the case of PDF documents you will need a copy of 'Adobe Acrobat Reader' which is distributed free and quite a lot can be learnt about the PDF format from looking at the On Line Guide provided with it. This is a simple manual provided in PDF format and illustrates the use of links, bookmarks and thumbnails as well as explaining how to use the viewing software. To go further, however, involves buying a full copy of the Adobe Acrobat suite which contains all the software needed to create PDF documents from existing documents, to incorporate sound and video files, to create hyper-links, thumbnails and bookmarks.

Computer Aided Design: in addition to shareware CAD packages there is now a wide range of cheap commercially produced CAD software (both 2-D and 3-D) designed for the home and small business user, any of which will enable the user to explore the main features of this type of software. Some of this software is designed for specialist use – for example laying out a garden or designing a kitchen. Many of these are simple 3-D packages. An interesting introductory exercise is to produce plans for a house. This involves careful measurements of all the dimensions, setting an appropriate scale, learning how to draw a variety of shapes and how to join them precisely using snapping, use of the grid, copying and editing and other basic CAD functions. If the software is 3-D CAD then it is possible to visualize the appearance of a house with an added extension or with a change in colour schemes or different furniture.

Illustration (drawing) software: an early version (version 3) of one of the leading packages for the PC (CorelDraw!) has been made available free via a number of computer magazines on CD-ROM so the reader could, in principle, get experience of vector drawing at no cost. Try creating line drawings of the sort used in text books – experimenting with creating geometrical shapes, assembling them into more complicated shapes, 'grouping' these components into a single object, altering line thicknesses, colours and fill patterns. Experiment with shading facilities to produce the appearance of 3-D objects like balls and boxes. Change characters into editable shapes and so produce new fonts. Fit characters into envelopes and along curved lines.

Paint packages and photo-retouching: a simple example of a paint package is supplied as an accessory with Microsoft Windows. In addition CorelDraw! (version 3) referred to above is, in fact a small suite of programs and includes a paint package (Photo-Paint). Finally, many document scanners and digital cameras are supplied with bundled software for re-touching digitized photographs so it should be possible for all readers, one way or another, to experiment with paint packages. The most important activity for beginners is to appreciate the difference between a bit-mapped image and a vector image. Many samples of both types of image are available as clip-art, distributed with other software – like word processors and graphics software of all types – and also with computer magazine cover disks. Obtain a BMP or other bit-mapped format file and then use the 'zoom' facility until the pixels are clearly seen. The same experiment, performed on a vector file with a vector-drawing package will reveal no pixels at all (though they are there of course!).

It can be an interesting experiment, if both types of drawing software are available, to start with the vector package (like CorelDraw!), use a sample vector file provided with it, and look at the image at a number of different zoom settings. In each case, 'screen-grab' a copy of the image (using the Print Screen key – as described earlier in the section on Graphics Utilities). This version of the image is, of course, a bit-mapped image and can be pasted directly into Windows 'Paint' (or 'Paint Brush', depending on the version of Windows being used). When this version is zoomed, the pixels soon become obvious whereas, what seems to be the identical image in the vector software, shows no pixels.

4

Colour and Grey Scales

4.1 Introduction

The earliest microcomputers were monochrome, text-only systems. The displays were limited to a set of pre-defined characters, based on the character-sets of the typical typewriter, supplemented with a few simple character-sized shapes which could be assembled together to produce a very crude 'graphic' display, such as a bar-chart or line graph (see Fig. 4.1). The two developments which heralded the beginning of modern computer graphics were the bit-mapped display and colour. In this chapter we are concerned with the second of these developments.

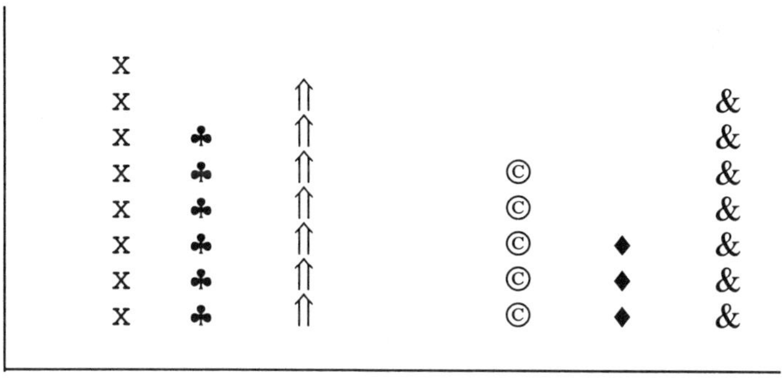

Fig. 4.1 *Simple bar-chart created using a text-only display*

First, it helps to be clear about the meaning of some of the terms – like 'colour' and 'monochrome'. As indicated in chapter 1, in normal speech we distinguish between a 'coloured photograph' and a 'black and white photograph' although most people would accept that black and white are both colours. This a legacy of the fact that in both photography and printing, black and white images were the accepted norm long before full coloured images became an everyday possibility. To avoid this confusion, black and white images are now often called 'monochrome' ('one colour') but this term can also be a little confusing. Strictly speaking, no image can be made from one colour; there must be a minimum of two. For example, in drawing, there is the colour of the pencil and the colour of the paper. Without the contrast between the two there can be no image. This distinction is sometimes reflected in the use of the terms 'foreground' colour and 'background' colour – or the drawing colour and the paper colour. The term monochrome makes more sense if we treat black and white as two extreme shades of the one colour. This use of the idea of shades of a colour is an important one, to which we will return.

The other area of confusion is the one already mentioned in Chapter 1 – that between the use of the term colour to distinguish named hues ('blue', as against 'red', for example) and its use to distinguish different versions of the 'same colour' ('dark red', as compared with 'light red', for example). In the context of drawn or printed monochrome images the term 'monochrome' might mean an image made from one foreground colour (usually black) and one background colour (usually white) or it might mean an image made from a variety of shades of one foreground colour (usually shades of grey). Any grey can thus be thought of as a mixture of black and white – these being treated as the extreme cases in a spectrum. In computing the first type of image is sometimes called 'line-art' and the second a 'grey-scale' image. The photographer's term for the latter is a 'half-tone'. It is clear that describing colours, even monochrome colours, can be complicated and involves more than one variable.

Most of our problems arise from the fact that colour is a physiological effect – a human sensation – caused by light striking the retina of the eye, the resultant changes being processed by the brain. This makes the recognition of colour a highly subjective process. When we try to make the process more objective using, for example, descriptions of colour that are made in terms of measured wavelengths we find ourselves in trouble because there is no simple relationship. It is true that it is possible to establish a general relationship between colour and wavelength but the eye, under certain circumstances, is perfectly capable of seeing colours that the scientist says are 'not there'. In fact there is a well-established field of study which straddles the borders between human physiology and psychology devoted to the subject of colour perception and so in a book of this sort only some of the main themes can be explored.

The earliest computer images were monochrome in the most literal sense that they were made up from one foreground colour (white) and one background colour (black). In printing, the background (paper) is naturally white and so printing inks are black. In computer displays the background is naturally black (when the electron beam is turned off and no light is emitted) and the foreground white (when the beam is turned on). In time, this was corrected by developing software which would display black characters on a white background so that the screen would look much more like the final printed product. The important point, however, is that the simplest displays used only one foreground colour. True grey-scale images – images with a variety of shades of grey intermediate between black and white – came later, along with the development of colour displays.

4.2 Colour

Colour displays, described in the chapter on hardware, use three primary coloured phosphors to produce a wide range of colours. In fact all colour systems – whether printing, photography, painting or television – use three (or more) primary colours to produce their effects. This stems from the fact that the eye itself has three different types of receptor, sensitive to three different wavelengths of light – red, green and blue. Early experiments with a prism showed that normal, white light (by which we usually mean sunlight) contains a mixture of wavelengths in its visible spectrum, ranging from red (long waves) to violet (short waves). When white light falls on the eye all three of the receptor types are stimulated – producing red, green and blue signals – and the brain experiences the sensation that we call white. When two or less of these types of receptor are stimulated, or when some receptors are stimulated more than others then we see other, intermediate colours. Although all colour technologies produce their effects by a mixture of primary colours, as in the eye, it is important to distinguish 'additive colour' mixing from 'subtractive colour' mixing.

When a colour television or computer monitor is in operation it generates light from three different types of glowing phosphor, the energy coming from the high-voltage electron beam which is absorbed in the phosphor dots. Intermediate colours are therefore created by the presence in the eye of more than one primary colour of

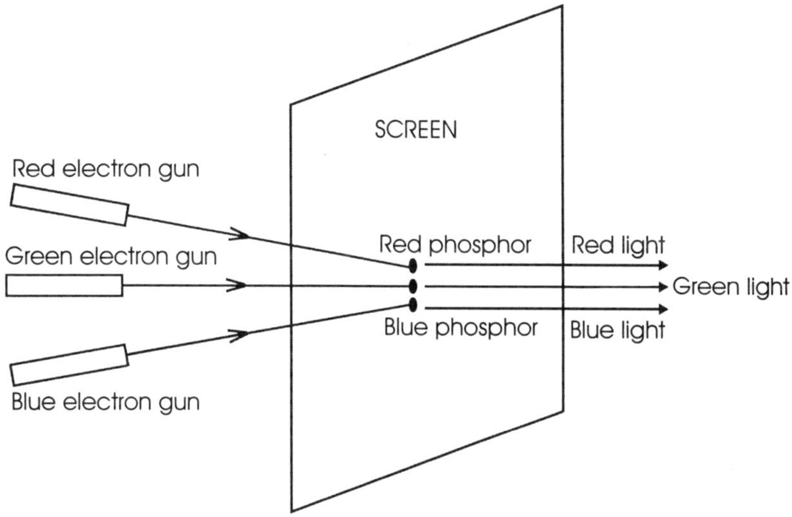

Fig. 4.2 *In a computer display, three identical electron guns fire electron beams into different types of phosphor producing light of three different colours (red, green and blue) by an emissive process*

light, stimulating the different receptors (see Fig. 4.2). This system is called an 'additive' or 'emissive' process because the image (the screen) actually emits light – of more than one colour – and the various wavelengths add together in the eye (see Plate 6a). Light is emitted and added together. Printed colour technology is quite different. Books do not emit light – they need the illumination of a good external, white, light source and the colours that enter the eye are created by a process of absorption (subtraction) in the printing inks. Thus, black ink is ink that has the property of absorbing all wavelengths of light equally so that when it is illuminated by white light, none of that light is reflected into the eye. Red ink has the property of absorbing all except the red wavelengths which are present in white light so that only red light enters the eye (see Fig. 4.3). Printing inks, therefore, subtract components of the, originally, white, light which illuminates them by a process of selective absorption. The process is called subtractive or absorptive because the function of the inks is to absorb coloured components – thus subtracting them from what was originally white light, light which contains all colours (see Plate 6b).

Colour displays and most colour printing techniques do have this in common, however, that both use tiny dots of colour to produce their effect. However, although a small region of a printed colour image is made from primary colours, in the form of tiny dots of printing ink, they require different colours from those used in display devices. They use the colours magenta, yellow and cyan. Magenta absorbs green light, yellow absorbs blue light and cyan or blue-green absorbs red light. Thus, if a green light is used to illuminate a red ink almost no light will be reflected and the eye will see a black area. The same effect is produced if all three primaries are mixed and viewed in white light. Since all major components of white light are absorbed the result is no light black. This contrasts with additive colour in computer monitors where mixing all three primaries produces white. The subtractive primary colours are sometimes called pigment primaries.

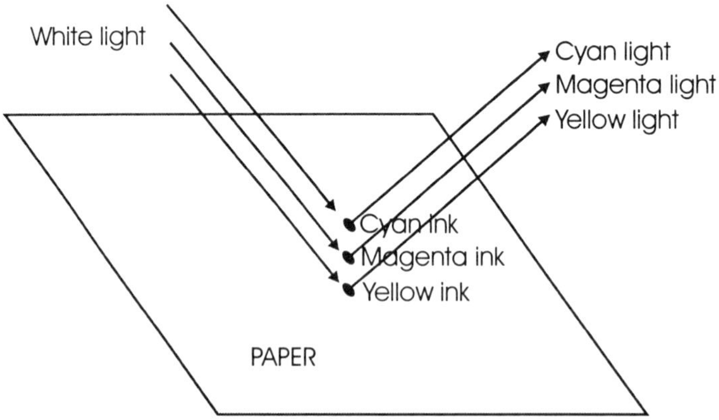

Fig. 4.3 *Printer's inks selectively absorb colour components from white light which contains all the colours of the rainbow*

It also follows from the general principles of absorption (subtractive) colour that the perceived colour of an ink depends not only on the characteristics of the ink itself but also on the type of illumination, since it works by selectively absorbing particular wavelengths from the light that illuminates it. An extreme example of this can be seen in the way that sodium (yellow) street lights make certain colours look black which would not be black in ordinary (sun) light. Subtler examples include the effect of fluorescent shop light on the colour of clothes, which look different under tungsten filament lamps, and different again in sunlight. The designers of artificial light sources do their best to create lamps that produce light with exactly the same spectral distribution as sunlight but most discriminating users would still claim that they can tell the difference. In any case sunlight is not always the same; the time of day, the direction of illumination, the location on the earth's surface, all have subtle, and not-so-subtle, effects on the quality of light, as artists have long recognized.

4.3 Colour Gamuts

The term 'colour gamut' or 'colour space' is one that indicates a full range of colours. The word gamut was originally used to refer to a range of musical notes. A colour gamut is often illustrated by means of a 2-dimensional or 3-dimensional diagram – see Fig. 4.4. This approach is expanded in a later section on colour models and this chart explained in more detail. It is important to realize at this stage that the colour gamut which corresponds to the visible spectrum (all the colours we can see – if we are not colour blind!) does not correspond exactly with the colour gamut of a printer or the colour gamut of a display. In general, printers and displays have a smaller gamut than the visible spectrum – we can see more colours than we can print or display on a screen. It also means that colours that can be displayed on a screen cannot necessarily be printed and vice versa (see Fig. 4.5).

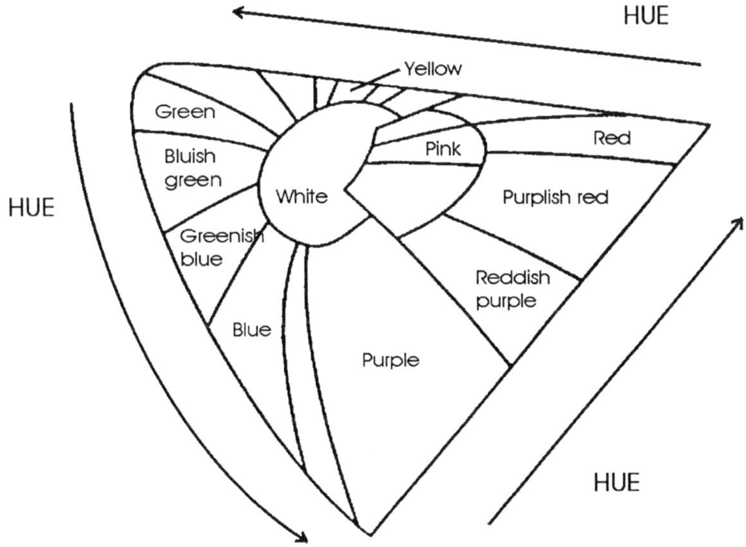

Fig. 4.4 *A CIE colour chart showing the full gamut of colours visible to the human eye*

4.4 Colour Displays

Since colour pictures are created by a mixture of primaries it follows that a coloured image stored in a computer will occupy more space in memory than a monochrome image. The simplest bit-mapped image, described in chapter 1, uses one-bit-per-pixel. This is capable only of coding for the simplest kind of monochrome image since a bit can exist in only two states. The two states are used to code for background colour and foreground colour. If 'real' colour is required then more than two bits are needed for each pixel. The earliest colour system used on IBM-PC compatibles was called the CGA (Colour Graphics Adapter) and offered only 4 colours. This implies a 2-bit-per-pixel system since two bits can store four different numbers (0 to 3 in decimal; 00 to 11 in binary). A better system was used in the BBC microcomputer. Here three bits were assigned to each pixel and each bit coded for one of the three primary colours (corresponding to the three electron guns in the CRT display). Table 1.1 (Chapter 1) shows how the eight colours (red, green, blue, cyan, magenta, yellow, black and white) arise. In the table 0s and 1s indicate whether the red, green and blue dots are 'off' or 'on' and the final column shows the colour generated.

Clearly the more colours that are used in the image, the more memory is needed to store that image – assuming that the same number of pixels is used. In early computers there was such a shortage of memory that the user often had to decide between the number of pixels and the number of colours to be used in any particular image. The computer's graphic system could be operated in a number of 'graphics modes'. Some modes had more colours but fewer pixels; others had fewer colours but more pixels. Even with modern graphics systems where the number of pixels and colours is far higher than was once possible there is still a range of graphics modes available and the higher resolution modes (the ones with the most pixels) will usually have fewer colours than the lower resolution modes.

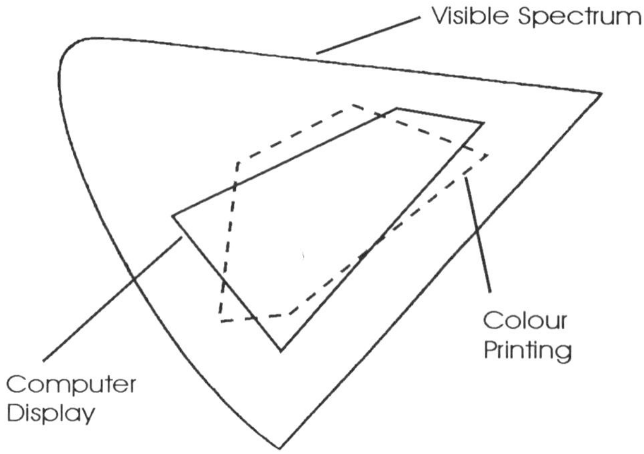

Fig. 4.5 A comparison between the colour gamuts of the human eye, the computer display and the colour printing process (CMYK process colours)

The question arises as to how these extra colours are actually produced and coded. These are, in fact, two completely different questions – one (producing the colours) relates to the hardware of the display system, the other (coding the colours) relates to the issue of how information about colour is stored in memory. In the example of the three-bit colour system given above, each bit in the refresh-buffer was coded for whether or not a particular electron gun in the CRT display was off or on. The implication was, that an electron gun could only be off or on, which was true of these early systems, and with such a restriction only eight combinations, and therefore, eight colours were possible. For more colours to be available, the guns need to be able to operate at different intensities – intermediate between fully off and full on. If, for example, the intensity of each of the three electron guns could be set to any one of four values (off, 1/3 on, 2/3 on and fully on, for example) then $4 \times 4 \times 4 = 64$ different colours could be created. In order to code for this greater number of colours more memory would need to be set aside – two bits per primary colour (per pixel) which is six-bits-per-pixel. In general, the formula which specifies how many colours can be coded by n bits per pixel is 2^n since each bit can be in one of two states and each bit is independent of every other. Thus if $n = 1$, $2^1 = 2$ colours can be coded. If $n = 2$ or 4 then 2^2 or $2^4 = 4$ or 16 colours can be coded. In the example, just worked out, of two bits per primary colour (six bits per pixel) $2^6 = 64$ colours are possible. Compare Table 4.1 with Table 1.1 (Chapter 1) which corresponded to the situation where each electron gun in the display could only have one of two states – off or on. Here each gun can exist in one of four states and the first four rows of the table correspond to those four states for the blue gun (the other two guns being off : 0 0). The second four rows correspond to those same four states for the blue gun but with the green gun in a state: 0 1. The complete table would have 64 rows, corresponding to 64 colours.

Table 4.1 *Truth table for a display where the red, green and blue guns can each be set to four different intensity levels*

Red		**Green**		**Blue**	
0	0	0	0	0	0
0	0	0	0	0	1
0	0	0	0	1	0
0	0	0	0	1	1
0	0	0	1	0	0
0	0	0	1	0	1
0	0	0	1	1	0
0	0	0	1	1	1
etc	etc	etc	etc	etc	etc

We began this discussion with the topic of grey-levels, a subject that was temporarily set aside while the question of colour displays and colour coding was tackled. It ought to be clear, now, that the subject of how grey-levels are displayed and coded relates directly to the questions of intensities, just discussed. With a colour monitor, white is achieved by setting all three guns to maximum intensity. Values of grey are achieved by setting the intensities of the guns to lower values, all three values being the same. In a monochrome monitor – with only one gun – grey levels are achieved by setting that one gun to values which are intermediate, between off and on.

4.5 Colour Palettes

At this stage it is worth considering the refresh-buffer requirements of modern colour systems. The super-VGA, for example, which is standard on PCs today, offers display resolutions in the range of 640 × 480 to 1280 × 1024 with the numbers of colours ranging from 16 to over 16 million. This means that the maximum number of pixels in such a system is 1.3 million (1280 × 1024) and the maximum number of bits per pixel would be 24 (2^{24} = 16,777,216). The refresh buffer would therefore need to be, in the extreme case, 3 × 1.3 = 3.9 million bytes. Until very recently, this would have been out of the question except for very expensive graphics workstations. In recent years, however, video cards have commonly been fitted with at least 4 Mbytes refresh buffers. This does not mean, however, that all graphic systems need such a large amount of memory. Most standard monitors cannot adequately cope with these extremely high values of resolution and many applications do not need millions of colours – more than the eye can detect. In many circumstances, then, a compromise system with fewer colours and less resolution is quite acceptable.

Many images need only a comparatively few colours, but those colours may be specific to that particular image – a different set from those required in another image. What is needed is a sub-set of colours, chosen from a larger range. This is called a 'palette'. The use of the term palette draws an analogy with the artist who mixes a limited selection of colours for a particular painting and keeps them on a small board, called a palette. By this means it is possible to keep the refresh buffer down to a reasonable size and to keep screen re-draw times more reasonable. An example will show the sort of memory saving which are possible. Suppose that the hardware is capable of producing 16.8 million colours – corresponding to 24-bit-per-pixel (three bytes) but that 256 colours are all that is required for a particular application. A palette of 256 colours needs only eight bits per pixel ($2^8 = 256$) not 24 bits, so the refresh buffer could be one third the size.

Table 4.2 *Colour Look-Up Table*

Colour code	**Red intensity**	**Green intensity**	**Blue intensity**	**Named colour**
0	0	0	0	Black
1	20	20	20	Dark grey
2	0	255	255	Cyan
3	255	0	255	Magenta
4	255	255	0	Yellow
5	255	0	0	Red
etc	etc	etc	etc	etc
250	255	125	25	Pink
251	150	15	140	Purple
252	0	145	100	Olive green
253	30	15	130	Violet
254	230	230	230	Pale grey
255	255	255	255	White

If colour palettes are to be used then there must be some method by which the programmer or user can specify which of the total of all available colours are to be included in a particular palette. The link between the two is achieved by the use of a colour Look-Up Table (Table 4.2). Instead of using the refresh buffer to store the intensity values of the three guns directly, it is used to store a 'colour code'. This is an arbitrary number – in the case of our example all the numbers between 0 and 255 (decimal). The function of the Colour Look-Up Table (CLUT) is to maintain a dictionary which shows what each code actually means, in terms of the actual intensity values on each gun. Each colour code in the table is cross-referenced to the three numbers which specify the intensities of the red, green and blue guns (and therefore the intensities of the phosphor dots in the display). The number of colour codes in a palette is restricted by the number of bits which are assigned, in the refresh buffer, to each pixel in the display. The total number of colours from which the choice is made, however, is only restricted by the number of intensity levels to which the three primary colours can be set, something that is determined by the hardware.

A computer need not be restricted to only one colour palette – in fact one of the major advantages of the system would be lost if it were. Every image can, in principle, have its own palette, saved with the image as part of the image file. See Plate 7 for a software implementation of a colour palette. If a photograph is scanned by a scanner capable of measuring 16.8 million colours it is likely to find only a few hundred, or a few thousand colours at most, in that one image. If the image is to be saved in a file which is restricted to, say 1024 colours, then a palette of that number of colours is created. If there are more than that number of colours recognized in the image then the 1024 most common colours will be placed in the file and any other colours will be changed to their nearest values in the palette. When a different photograph is scanned a different palette will be created. When the images are later displayed the palette is loaded along with the image information. The palette (the CLUT) then 'translates', for the benefit of the computer, how the colour codes are to be interpreted for that particular image. The effects of this can be seen when a series of digitized photographs, each with its own palette, are displayed one after the other. Since the palette information and the picture information are two separate parts of the file, one will be loaded before the other and this means that there will be a brief period when an image will be displayed with the wrong palette, producing a most disconcerting effect.

It seems reasonable to ask, at this stage, why it should be necessary to provide as many as 16.8 million colours. An image made from, say, one million pixels cannot contain more than one million colours – even if every pixel were a different colour, which is most unlikely. In any case the human eye cannot distinguish that number of colours. The truth is that 16.8 million colours is not necessary; a million or so would be quite enough, but it is convenient from a designer's point of view, to allocate one byte per primary colour, rather than, say, 6 or 7 bits because computers process data in byte-sized pieces. Most applications never need anything like one million colours at any one time – in any one image – but may need that sort of choice when constructing a palette for a particular image. Two examples will illustrate why. The first concerns art and design software. Here the number of colours in the palette may not need to be very large but the artist will wish to have complete freedom in choosing exactly what those colours should be. In other words, the user may want only a few shades of blue and pink, for example, but it is most important that they be exactly the right shades and this is why some paint packages offer a palette of only 256 colours chosen from 16.8 million. The other areas of application are 3-D modelling and digitized photographs. Here the important concept is that of intensity-values (or shades) of a particular colour to create realistic looking pictures (sometimes called 'photo-realism', meaning as realistic as a photograph). A green subject like the leaves on a tree or a field of grass, for example, realistically portrayed or photographed, might contain dozens, or even hundreds, of shades of green because of the varied light and shade effects and so a special palette with all these slightly different greens is needed. A 'standard' palette with only a few greens would be no good. The same principle, of course, applies to any other colour.

4.6 Colour Matching

Colour matching can be a problem for anyone involved in the production of coloured objects, whether they be magazines, clothes, wallpaper or cars. These problems are of two sorts – consistency and viewing conditions. The consistency problem is that when objects, like tins of paint or rolls of wallpaper, are mass-produced it is difficult to ensure that every batch has exactly the same colour as every other one. The human eye is capable of detecting very slight differences and manufacturers will sometimes guarantee colour consistency across only one production batch of paint or wallpaper, for example. The viewing problem is that different lighting conditions can have a big impact on the perceived colour of an object – as discussed earlier in the chapter. Both of these problems can affect the production of computer-generated printed colour images and an even bigger difficulty results from the differences between the additive and absorptive colour systems that are used – one in creating the images on a screen, the other in printing them on paper. There can be enormous differences between an image which is produced by emission, on a glowing computer screen, and the equivalent image on paper, viewed by absorption of the ambient light (the light which is present in the environment in which the picture is viewed).

A number of techniques have been devised to reduce these problems but there are two broadly-different approaches to this major question of colour mismatch between the screen and the printed product. In one, attempts are made to calibrate the output of screens so that the colours which they produce are standardized and match the equivalent colours produced by printers. In the other approach, it is accepted that this will never be totally satisfactory and efforts are therefore concentrated on controlling and visualizing the output of the printer, regardless of the screen image. The first approach involves calibrating the screen.

4.7 Calibration and Characterization

Computer screens, like television sets, are supplied with controls to alter the brightness and contrast of the picture. These are often altered by the user in order to produce a picture which satisfies some aesthetic sense or to make the picture easier to see under the prevailing lighting conditions. Whatever the reason for altering the controls the result is a non-standard and potentially variable quality of picture. One can hardly expect a colour printer to 'know' how a particular monitor was adjusted when the colours that were used in a particular image were chosen and it is not, therefore, surprising when the printed result looks nothing like the screen version. The same sort of consideration applies to the lighting conditions. A colour will look very different when viewed in a darkened room, as compared with its appearance when brightly lit by strong sunlight. In addition to all this and apart from any adjustments made by the user, the colour characteristics of screens can gradually change over a period of time as electronic components age and their characteristics subtly alter.

One way of dealing with these problems is to use a special piece of hardware – a colour calibrator – which is a type of spectrophotometer. This is a small light detector that is placed on the front of the screen, which measures the spectral properties of the light being produced by the screen (see Fig. 4.6). Using these measurements the display can then be adjusted to ensure that it is performing in the way that the manufacturers intended. This is done using a special piece of software that changes the values in the Look-Up Table which, in turn, changes the intensities on the red, green and blue guns so as to produce the correct colour. If this is used regularly – say, once a week – and if environmental conditions (the lighting, the colour of the walls, etc.) are kept constant the user can be sure that the screen is always producing consistent results. Calibration is essentially a process of putting the screen into a known, reproducible state by the use of objective measurements.

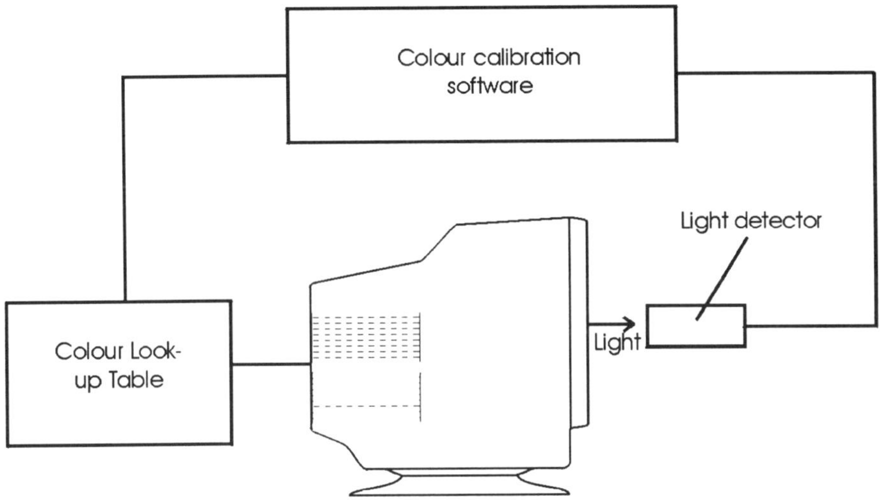

***Fig. 4.6** Colour calibration using a spectrophotometer*

Other devices, like colour scanners and colour printers will not be subject to the same variability from day to day and do not have the same controls that can be altered by the user, but there is still the problem of matching them to each other and to particular screens. The problem is not simply that printers as a whole will tend to produce different colours from those produced by screens but that different models of printers or scanners, from different manufacturers, will vary. There needs to be some way of specifying how any particular model of printer, scanner or screen performs. This is called characterization – specifying the exact characteristics of a device. Increasingly this being done by a system in which the manufacturers provide data about the colour characteristics of their products. This data is handled by special 'Colour Management Software' (or Colour Management System – CMS) which matches the output of a printer or a screen, say, to the input provided by a scanner. A summary of the colour characteristics of any particular device is called its 'profile' and the function of a CMS is to map the profile of one device to that of another so that the colour seen on a screen, for example, will be matched by that produced by the printer (see Fig. 4.7).

This type of specialized software was originally provided by a number of different manufacturers who each used their own way of specifying the characteristics of the devices; such software was offered as part of particular applications software, like painting packages or DTP software. In recent years colour management software has been built into the computer operating system and standard ways of characterizing devices have been proposed.

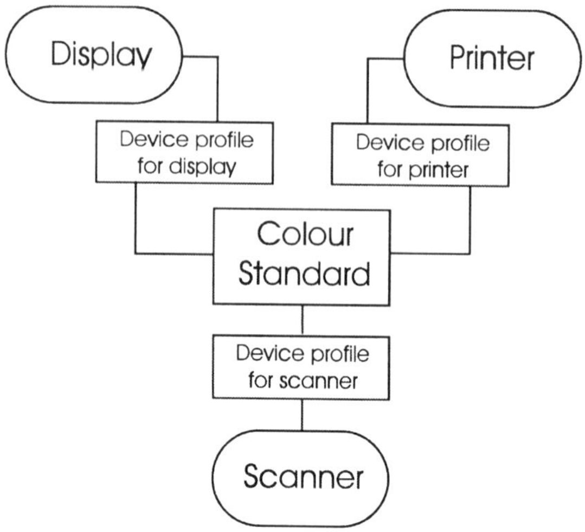

Fig. 4.7 *Using device profiles to match the colour characteristics of different graphics devices*

4.8 Colour Swatches

The second approach to the general problem of matching screen colour to printer colour is to bypass the problem altogether! If the screen colours are accepted as only an approximation to those that will be produced by the printer – and if the user is happy to do this – then all that is required is a way of seeing exactly what colours the printer can produce and to be able to choose and specify the ones required. This is done using the simple idea of swatches of coloured card. The term 'swatch' is usually used of samples of coloured cloth or fabric which can be used by a designer in choosing material when a larger sample is not available. The same principle is used in selling paint, though here the problem is that small samples of a colour can look very different from the same colour when it covers a large area like a wall. In the case of the printing industry, the printer manufacturers produce cards of printed colour samples so that when colours are chosen by a customer it is clear what the colour will look like when printed on particular types of paper or card. Of course it would be inconvenient if every printer had its own set of colours, as do paint manufacturers, and so a number of standard systems are used, such as 'Pantone', 'Munsell' or 'Trumatch' (all trade names). Once an agreed set of colours has been produced, and given suitable names or code numbers, then it becomes the responsibility of the printer manufacturers to make their printers in such a way that they will produce output just like the standard swatches (see Plate 8).

None of this guarantees, of course, that a computer screen will be able to mimic faithfully that colour – in fact this is unlikely if a CMS is not in use – but it should mean that the designer can tell, from a swatch, what a particular colour on the screen will translate into when printed. This system, in practice, requires that the user buy a set of colour swatches in order to choose the colours that are required for a particular design, and that the software manufacturers incorporate some of these standardized colour systems into their applications. The users can then use the chosen colours in their designs, see an approximation of what they will look like on the screen and know exactly what the outcome will look like, when printed – by looking at the swatches.

One final word on the subject of colour matching between screen and printer. One very simple and pragmatic way of dealing with the problem that requires no specialist equipment or software is called 'back-to-front colour matching'. It involves doing an early version of a design which uses all the colours which will be required in the final piece of work and then printing the result using whatever printing systems will be used for the final product. The print is then compared with the screen display and the screen adjusted, by eye, to match the print. If the colours on the print are very different from those intended it may be necessary to change the design colours and repeat the process. However, once the printer is producing colours that are acceptable the designer knows that the screen matches the final result simply because it has been adjusted to do just that, with that particular set of colours, if no other.

4.9 Colour Separation

All of the forgoing leads very naturally to the question – 'how exactly does a colour on a screen specify ('translate') to a colour produced by a printer?'. If a desktop printer like an inkjet is being used then the answer is that the colour signals from the computer are used to drive the three different colour processes in the printer without further intervention from the user. If professional printing processes are to be used then the answer lies in the process of 'colour separation' and this section is concerned with that case. It should be remembered that, as already described in chapter 1, there are two ways of mixing colours for the purpose of printing. Spot colours are colours which are pre-mixed before printing takes place and is used when only a small number of colours are needed. Process colours are those which are, in effect, mixed in the eye. The primaries are laid down on the paper in large numbers of tiny dots and the eye sees a composite effect, depending on the ratio of the primaries which are printed at any point on the paper. This method is used whenever a large number of colours are required.

The screen and the printer have this in common – that both use a minimum of three primary colours to produce their effects: red, green and blue in the case of a screen and cyan, magenta and yellow in the case of simple printing systems (with black added, usually, for reasons already explained). This means that, although the eye sees all three colours simultaneously, in order to produce the composite effects that we call colour vision, the hardware systems almost always deal with the primary colours separately. The screen receives three different image signals which drive three different electron guns, firing three different electrons beams at three different sets of fluorescent spots with the aid of the shadow mask. Printers often print the three (or more) different coloured spots in three separate operations, the paper passing through the printer at least three times. In professional-level printing systems this requires that, for each primary colour, a separate image is needed in preparing the master 'plates' (the originals from which the printing is done). Good quality graphics software is designed to produce these three or more separate images (called 'separations') from the image created on the screen. To obtain proper

Fig. 4.8 *Colour separations taken from an image supplied with Adobe 'PhotoShop'. Each image represents the intensity(printed in black) of the four component colours: cyan, magenta, yellow and black (clockwise, beginning at top left)*

matching it is necessary for the software to do this using a system like the Pantone system. What happens is that when a colour is chosen from a swatch card, the code or name is used to specify to the computer what that colour is and the software then attempts to produce on the screen the nearest possible match between the Pantone colour, based on cyan, magenta, yellow and black printing inks (CYMK), and the screen colour, based on red, green and blue phosphors (RGB). When the final image has been created the software then produces colour separations by outputting separate prints, each one corresponding to the amount of one of the primary CYMK printing colours. These are colour separations (see Fig. 4.8 and also Plate 9). The printer uses these separations to prepare the masters.

4.10 Colour Problems

This process of colour separation and colour printing might look simple in principle but there are practical problems. Some of them have been discussed in the chapter on hardware since they relate to hardware design and operation. Some are discussed here, briefly, because they have consequences for the design and use of colour software.

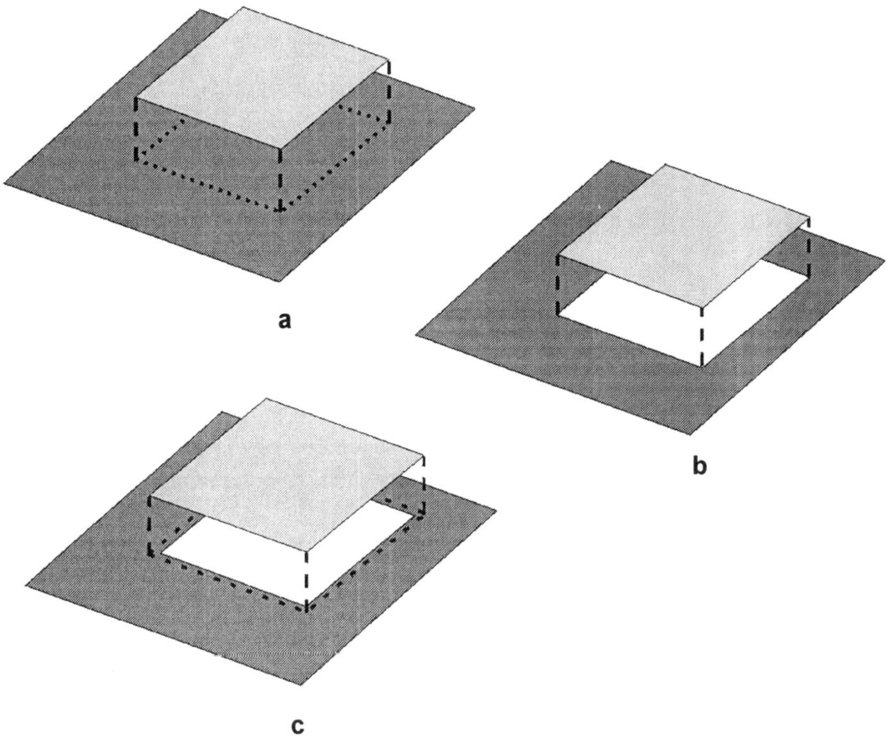

Fig. 4.9 *Overprinting (a), knockout (b) and trapping (c)*

When blocks of different colours overlap on a screen display the underlying colour is not displayed because the overlying colour has replaced the original colour in the screen buffer. In printing this effect is sometimes achieved by printing one colour on top of another (called 'overprinting' – see Fig. 4.9). This can, however, lead to problems when the two colours blend to form an undesirable result. The alternative is to create the colour separations in such a way that (in printing terminology) the top colour 'knocks out' the under colour. This means that the process of creating the colour separations ensures that a 'back' colour is removed whenever a 'front' colour is present in the same position – leaving a space – so only one colour is printed in that position (see Fig. 4.9). However, it is not always possible to ensure that the different primary colours line-up precisely during the printing process. Paper sometimes stretches or shifts slightly as it goes through the printer and the master plates themselves might be distorted or aligned incorrectly, even though 'registration' marks are normally printed on the separations to aid in setting up the printer properly. This problem of misregistration can lead to small gaps of unprinted paper appearing between blocks of colour (together with corresponding areas of paper with two ink colours). One solution is to deliberately 'overprint'. This means specifying a small overlap in adjacent blocks of colour – a process called 'trapping' – and good colour software will offer automatic (and manual) trapping.

Successful trapping requires a knowledge of what colour result will be produced when two other colours are printed on top of each other and sometimes the designer will by-pass the problem by redesigning an image so that trapping is not required. However, sometimes overprinting is used, not as a solution to a problem, but as a design feature to produce special effects. Usually this is done to produce a new colour or a shadow or silhouette effect

4.11 Dithering, Half-tones and Grey-scales

The subject of dithering was introduced very briefly in Chapter 1 and was mentioned again in Chapter 2 in order to explain how laser and other printers could produce grey-scales. It should have become clear in this chapter that a similar technique is used to produce process colours in printing. It is necessary to explore the topic in more detail because modern computer printers are increasingly encroaching on the territory once reserved for professional printing and the quality of printed grey-scale and colour images (particularly photographs) depends on an understanding of some of these details.

The most widely-used modern printing technology is the lithographic (or offset) printer which uses a flat, rather than a raised or engraved, surface (a 'plate') as the master. This type of printer is described in the chapter on hardware. One of the advantages of this technology is that these plates can be created photographically from any suitable source. Line-art (monochrome) images can simply be photographed and typescript created digitally using a typesetter. Photographs, and other similar illustrations, are another matter, however, because they are 'continuous-tone' images (they contain many grey-levels) and must be converted to 'half-tone' images. A half-tone image is one in which the original variations of light and dark have been replaced by patterns of dots of varying size. The normal printing technique for doing this involves photographing the original image through a mesh-like transparent screen. This produces a series of spots on the final image, in such a way that dark regions in the original image produce large spots in the final photograph and light regions produce small spots. The general effect can be seen very easily, with the aid of a magnifying glass, in any photograph printed in a newspaper – where the spots are particularly large – but the same principle holds true in higher-quality printing where the spots are much smaller. The average size of the spots depends on how closely packed together are the lines in the screen. The 'screen frequency' (the number of screen lines per inch) varies from about 70 lines per inch (lpi) in newspapers to 200 – 300 lpi in high-quality printed books. The smaller the dots, of course, the higher the quality of the final image.

The similarity with dithering is obvious. The difference lies in the fact that desktop computer printers tend to place equal-sized dots on the paper whereas photographic half-toning produces dots of different sizes; in some cases the dots are large enough to overlap each other. However, the development in recent years of laser printers which can produce dots of different size is obscuring this difference. Computer printers lay down their dots in horizontal rows because of the way that the paper is fed through the printer but the photographic screens used in traditional half-toning are usually arranged at an angle (normally 45 degrees for monochrome images) because this way the lines of dots are less obvious to the eye, which is less distracted by lines in this orientation. Coloured images are created by a separation process – already described – and it is normal to use different screen angles for each of the separate colour screened images, for similar reasons.

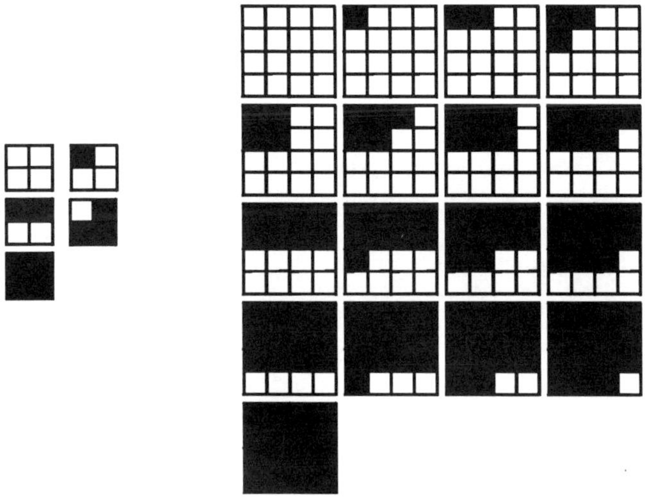

Fig. 4.10 Two examples of dithering – one based on a 4-dot unit, the other on a 16-dot unit

One of the obvious advantages of traditional photographic screening over simple computer-printer dithering lies in the density of the dots. Because most computer printers use fixed-size dots, the smallest picture detail in a grey-scale image (so far called a pixel) will always be much larger than a dot. It becomes necessary at this point to distinguish two different ways of describing a pixel or dot. The term could apply to the smallest dot which a particular printer or display is capable of producing – the minimum sized graphic unit from which all images are created. Or it could refer to the smallest unit of spatial information. Some authors use the terms 'printer dot' and 'half-tone dot'. This is another way of describing the situation. Fig. 4.10 shows two examples of dither 'cells' (or half-tone cells). The black squares are printer dots. The rectangular grids (partially filled with printer dots) are half-tone dots. A cell is therefore a collection of printer dots; the cell acts as a basic pixel – a unit of spatial detail or picture detail.

If a cell contains only a maximum of four printer-dots then it can display only five grey-levels because the total number of dots that can be 'turned on' varies from 0 to 4 (see Fig. 4.10). If a cell contains 16 dots then it is capable of displaying 17 grey-levels because the total number of dots that can be 'turned on' varies from 0 to 16. If more grey-levels are required then more dots are needed per cell; for example 25 dots will provide for 26 grey-levels. If the dots are of a fixed size, however, such a cell will inevitably be larger and there will be fewer pixels in the image. This means that there must be a trade-off between numbers of grey-levels and detail in the image. Photographically-produced screened half-tones, however, produce dots of variable size so that dots and pixels are essentially the same. Plate 10 shows colour dithering as used in a display device rather than a printer.

Colour images are produced by litho printers in exactly the same as monochrome except that four or more colour separations are produced. Different screen angles are used for the four separations so that distracting patterns of dots are not created. When done correctly the dots form a symmetrical pattern called a 'rosette'.

4.12 Colour Models

It has been seen that screens use emissive colours, specified used red, green and blue primaries (the RGB system) and that printers use absorptive colours, cyan, magenta, yellow and black (the CMYK system). It should not be thought, however, that these are the only ways of accurately specifying a colour. There are, in fact, many ways of doing this and good graphics software will offer a number of methods to the user.

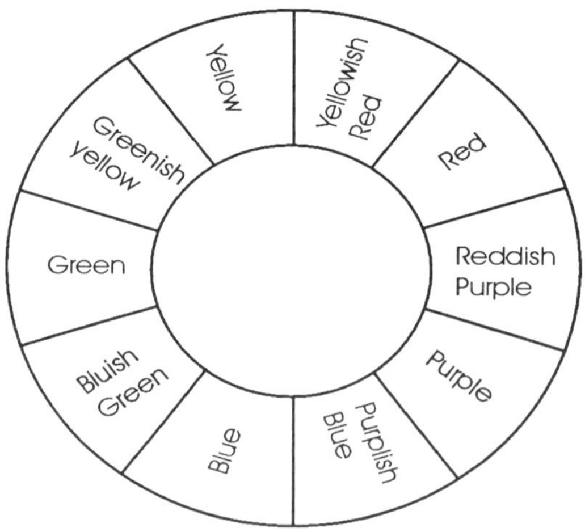

Fig. 4.11 *A colour wheel*

The RGB and CMYK systems have the advantage that they reflect the technology that is used to produce the final product but they don't match the way that we think about colours.

Most people think of colour in terms of the named colours like pink and orange and purple and not in terms of the primaries which have to be mixed to produce them. We identify a particular colour with the nearest named colour and then modify our description in terms of whether it is 'strong' or 'pale', light or dark, mixed with some other colour, etc. and end up with descriptions like 'a purplish blue', 'blood red' or 'pale pink'. This, more natural, approach has been the basis of a number of systems of specifying colours, usually involving colour models. Colour models are systems which help the user to visualize three variables which have been chosen to specify a colour. They usually involve some sort of two- or three-dimensional diagram which illustrates the effect of changing one of more of these variables. One of the earliest was devised by Isaac Newton, who did important experiments which showed that white light could be broken down into the colours of the spectrum and then re-constituted to produce white light again. He suggested that the colours of the spectrum be arranged around the edge of a circle (a colour 'wheel') so that the red and blue extremes joined (see Fig. 4.11, and also Plate 11 for another format). At the centre of the circle was white, the additive mixture of them all. This type of model has two dimensions or variables – the 'hue' (the recognizable colour) which is drawn round the edge of the wheel – and the degree of mixture which is shown across the diameter of the wheel, with a total mixture at the centre. One of the results of this approach is that many, later, models use the units of degrees – there being 360 degrees in a complete circle – to designate a hue.

It is instructive to use a piece of graphics software which incorporates a number of colour models in order to compare the way that a particular colour is described in the two systems we have already met (RGB and CMYK). Graphics packages which allow the user to create colours usually use the metaphor of three slider bars so that the colour components can be altered and the results immediately displayed. Others allow percentage or other values of the colour components to be typed in. Most also allow a direct choice from some form of two-dimensional colour space (see Plate 7). In this example the RGB and CMYK models are compared with the HLS model, which is described below. Here we consider only one variable – 'Hue'. Table 4.3 shows how the six colours – red, green, blue, cyan, magenta and yellow are measured in the three systems.

Table 4.3 *A comparison of three colour models*

Colour	**RGB Model**			**CMYK Model**			**HLS Model**
	Red %	Green %	Blue %	Cyan %	Magenta %	Yellow %	Hue degrees
Red	100	0	0	0	100	100	0
Yellow	100	100	0	0	0	100	60
Green	0	100	0	100	0	100	120
Cyan	0	100	100	100	0	0	180
Blue	0	0	100	100	100	0	240
Magenta	100	0	100	0	100	0	300

It can be seen that, whereas the RGB and CMYK models consider the basic colour to be formed by the mixing of three primaries, the HLS model considers colour ('hue') to be determined by position on a 360 degree circle which corresponds to the natural spectrum of colours (see the colour wheel in Plate 11). There are a number of colour models which use hue as the basic variable. Two widely used models are the HLS – 'Hue, Luminance (or Lightness) and Saturation' and the HSV – 'Hue, Saturation, and Value'. We have already seen that the term hue corresponds to the everyday term colour. The meaning of the term Saturation is often equated with the idea of the strength, or purity, of the colour. Terms expressing similar ideas include 'intensity', 'chroma', 'purity' and 'vividness'. When artists' paints are mixed the final results are determined not only by the ratios of the primaries used (determining the hue) but also by the use of black and white pigment (oil paints) or dilution with water (water paints). The saturation of a colour corresponds to the amount of colour pigment that is used as compared with a neutral colour like grey which dilutes or reduces the strength of the pigment. With no dilution (100% Saturation) the colour is 'strongest'. With 0% Saturation there is no 'colour' at all – simply a grey. So if a colour like red is chosen (100% red, 0% green and 0% blue on the RGB model), this will be 0% hue (see top line of Table 4.3), 50% lightness and 100% saturation on the HLS model. If the saturation is varied the two limits are 100% for strongest red and 0% for no red (grey).

If the lightness is varied, on the other hand the result can be compared with the 'grey-level' variable (as applied to colour scales). If an electric light is attached to a dimmer control its brightness can be turned up or down and, if the light source is a white one, the effect produced is of a series of shades of grey. If the light source is

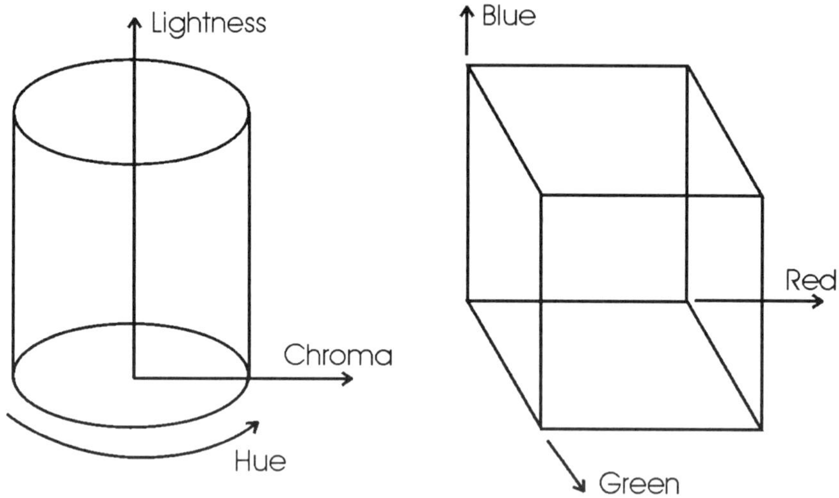

Fig. 4.12 Two different types of 3-D colour model, the cylinder and the cube

coloured the equivalent variation is the one described as the Lightness. The two limits of this variable are white (100%) and black (0%). Other names for this variable then are 'brightness' and 'amplitude'. A very similar system to the HLS model is the HSV colour model – based on similar variables called hue, saturation, and value.

The type of model described so far is primarily designed to help the user visualize the differences between colours in terms of three independent variables. For these systems to be useful in characterizing systems it is necessary to try to assign numerical values to these variables. Munsell and Ostwald did a series of experiments at the turn of the century which involved showing people small samples of closely related colours to determine the smallest noticeable differences. This type of work made it possible to describe the relationship between the three variables quantitatively. As a result 3-dimensional colour models can be constructed, the shape of which demonstrate important facts about human perception of colour. The two commonest types of 3-D shape are the cube and the cylinder. The cube uses a rectangular co-ordinate system and the cylinder a polar co-ordinate system to relate the three colour variables (see Fig. 4.12). The exact shape of the models depends on the relationships among the variables contained in those models and the way that the model chooses to express those relationships. For example, in the CIE (Commission Internationale d'Eclairange) model the solid cylinder becomes a series of parallel

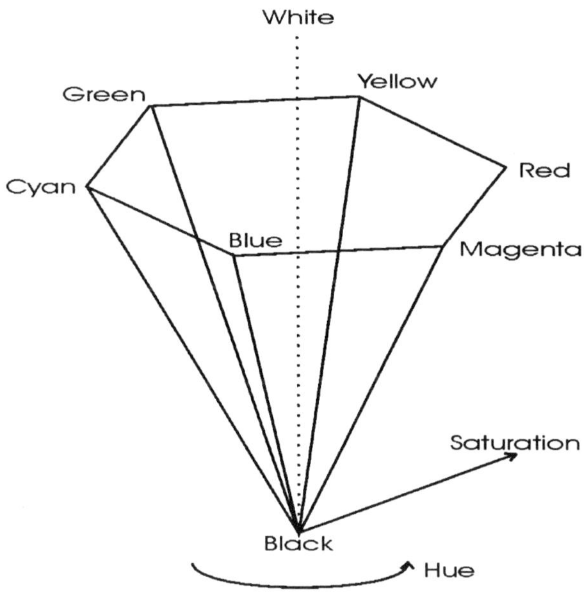

Fig. 4.13 *A 3-D colour model for HSV (Hue-Saturation Value)*

circular discs arranged along a central axis – effectively a series of cross-sections through the theoretical cylinder so that the variation colours can be illustrated. The long axis represents the brightness variable, the rotation round the discs, the hue and the radial variations, the saturation. However, the cylinder is not a cylinder – the discs reduce in radius towards the two ends of the axis. This represents the fact that the eye is much less sensitive to small differences at low and high values of brightness.

The CIE have adopted a widely used, and simpler variant of this model which uses only two variables and ignores variations in brightness. This leads to a 2-D model looking like a triangle with two of the sides meeting at a curve rather than a point (see Figs. 4.4 and 4.5, earlier in the chapter, where the basic shape was used to illustrate colour gamuts). When the HSV system is expressed as a 3-D model the result is a hexagonal, cone-like shape (see Fig. 4.13).

Exercises for the Reader:

(1) Obtain a paint brochure with printed samples of paint colours from a DIY shop. Show it to a number of friends and ask them to name as many colours as

possible – without letting them see the names given by the manufacturer. Observe: (a) how many unique names they use for these colours (e.g. red, purple, mauve etc.); (b) the extent to which they have to use compound names (eg. a 'pinkish-purple'); (c) the extent to which there is agreement about the colours. Do they all give the same name to a particular colour? Do you come across anyone who is clearly colour-blind?

(2) Look at the screen of a colour TV and a computer monitor (switched on, in both cases) with a magnifying glass. You should be able to see the coloured phosphor dots and to be able to work out how the appearance at a normal viewing distance depends on the intensity of these dots. If you have access to a number of TVs and monitors you should be able to see differences in the size of the dots and the shapes. Look again at the chapter on hardware if you have forgotten why there are these differences.

(3) Use the colour facilities of a graphics package to familiarize yourself with the differences between absorptive and emissive colours. Any good graphics package – like a DTP, drawing or painting package – will allow the user to create or edit colours by altering their RGB and CMY components – usually by means of a slider-bar model. Use this to look at the emissive and absorptive primaries – RGB and CMY – and switch between the two systems to see how a colour is described. For example, how is cyan described in the RGB system? How is blue described in the CMY system ? What about white and black in both systems? If other systems like the HLS or HSV are used, compare the way that any particular colour is described in these systems also.

(4) Explore the way that objects seem to change their colour under different illumination conditions. Look at a variety of coloured objects in sodium (yellow) street lighting or in the light of coloured domestic light bulbs. Obtain some coloured celluloid or other coloured semi-transparent material to use as light filters (for example some sweet wrappings and other packaging materials). Use them to make your own coloured light sources and study the effect of coloured light on the perceived colour of an object.

(5) Find out why all objects seem to lose their colour at night (when the light levels are very low compared with daylight).

(6) Try to discover if the human eye is equally sensitive to the three primary colours.

(7) Look at the handbook of the display card in your computer and find out how many different modes it can use. How many pixels and how many colours does each mode have and how do they relate to the amount of memory supplied with the card ?

(8) If you have access to a good graphics package that will print colour separations, then create an image that has a variety of colours in it and print the four colour separations on a monochrome printer. Compare the separations with either the original, displayed on the monitor or with a coloured print obtained with a desktop colour printer.

5

Fonts, Typefaces and Printing

5.1 Introduction

Until recently the worlds of amateur and professional printing were clearly separated. Amateur 'printing' meant the typewriter and the early forms of word processing, using dot-matrix or daisy-wheel printers. Professional printing meant the old-style hand-set moveable-type or the 'hot-metal' printers used in the newspaper industry. The innovation that changed all this was the laser printer. Although the first laser printers, which operated at 300 – 400 dots per inch, could not compete in quality with traditional printing technology they constituted a big move in that direction and an enormous improvement on impact dot matrix printers and typewriters. Modern laser printers (operating at 600 – 1600 dpi) and image setters which provide even higher resolution, together with the gradual move to litho printing have now bridged the gap between the worlds of amateur and professional printing. Typesetting can now be done digitally on a desktop computer and the laser printer or image-setter provides the photographic master for the litho printer. This blurring of the lines between the worlds of the amateur and the professional has led to a corresponding rise in the importance of digital fonts and it is important to understand something of the jargon and the technology associated with them.

5.2 Mono-Spaced Fonts

The terms 'font' (or 'fount') and 'typeface' are often confused but both have the general meaning of 'printed characters, in one particular style' and the more subtle distinctions should become clear later. Many terms used in this chapter, including 'font' and 'typeface', derive from the printing industry but most users of computers are not professional typographers or print workers and are more familiar with the traditional typewriter, from which the earliest computer printers were derived.

These used what are called, 'mono-spaced' fonts – that is, fonts in which each character has been designed to have the same width as every other (see Fig. 3.7, Chapter 3). Another name for them is 'fixed pitch' and the size of the fonts can be specified in terms of the number of characters per inch. The traditional typewriter placed the characters at equal distances from each other, used the same size of space between words and the same space between lines of text. All of this followed from the basic design of the machine. In a typewriter the characters imprint on the paper in a fixed position and so the paper must be moved between letters and between lines. These movements between letters are fixed, regardless of what character is to be printed, and so each of those characters must occupy the same space on the paper. This led to the design of special mono-spaced character sets in which a letter like 'i', which is normally very narrow, is artificially widened with the addition of 'serifs' (see Fig. 5.1). Serifs are short decorative items (sometimes called hooks or barbs) at the end of one of the lines which makes up the character. Wide letters like 'w', on the other hand, are made narrower than usual. This process of reducing all letters to the same width has two effects. It makes the text take up more space than it would otherwise, because the reduced width of the wider letters is more than compensated by the extra width of the narrower ones. It also leads to text which is harder to read.

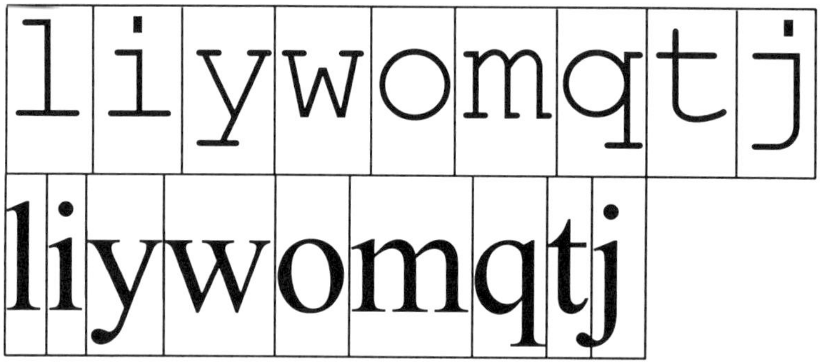

Fig. 5.1 *Two fonts. The mono-spaced (Courier, at the top) uses characters of equal width; they fit into equal sized boxes. The proportionally-spaced (Times) uses characters with very different widths which even overlap in the case of the last two characters*

Similar fonts were used in impact dot-matrix printers where the printer head was moved by fixed amounts between letters, but the advent of the laser printer changed all that. Laser printers are sometimes called page printers because, unlike the dot-matrix printer, a whole page of characters is created in memory before being transferred to the paper. Characters are not laid down one at a time and since each letter is made up from large numbers of tiny dots, they can have any shape, and be placed in any position that is required. Fonts designed for modern printers, therefore, are said to be proportionally spaced, which means that the space occupied by characters is proportional to the width of those characters. Because they are formed at much higher resolution than a dot-matrix printer they can also take on much more subtle shapes. Notice how all the characters in the Courier font in Fig. 5.1 are made from lines of equal width, whereas the characters in the Times font are made from lines with varying width.

5.3 Fonts and Typefaces

Traditional typefaces have always offered a certain amount of variation in the appearance of printed characters (see Fig. 5.2). In principle, each character can be produced in the 'normal' form – sometimes called 'Roman', in 'bold' and in 'italic' and, of course, in a variety of sizes. Other variations that might be available include varying degrees of boldness (or 'blackness') – usually called the weight of the type (light and heavy versions) – and varying widths ('condensed' – narrower – and wider versions) – see Fig. 5.3. It might seem obvious that once a standard character has been designed all the other variations could be derived very simply by a process

Roman **Bold**
Italic ***Bold-Italic***

Fig. 5.2 *The four basic variations: normal (Roman), Bold, Italic and Bold-Italic*

of scaling it up and down (to get the other sizes), thickening or thinning the strokes (to get bolder or thinner variations) and leaning it over (to get the italic). In fact, however, when typographers design these variations they often introduce subtle changes to the proportions of component parts of a character. For example, when a character like 'i' is reduced in size it may be necessary to increase the thickness of the vertical stroke in proportion to its height (as compared with the proportions at a larger size) to ensure that it does not get so thin that it cannot be printed or seen properly. It might also be made slightly wider overall. The reverse may be true if the character is enlarged considerably, to prevent it looking too thick.

Goudy Sans Light
Goudy Sans Medium
Goudy Sans Black
LATIN EXTRA CONDENSED
LATIN

Fig. 5.3 *Two types of variation in fonts: lighter and heavier versions (Goudy) and extra condensed and wider versions (Latin)*

Because of these variations in a character – bold, thin, italic etc. – a named set of characters like 'Times' or 'Helvetica' is really a family of characters, with many possible variations. The term font (or fount) is used to refer to all the characters available in a particular typeface, style, size and weight. This means that 'Helvetica 12 point bold' would be considered one font (the term 'point' is a measurement of size). 'Helvetica 16 point italic' would be another font. The term typeface, on the other hand, is a much broader term, referring to the overall design itself – in this case 'Helvetica'. Font names, like Helvetica, are trade-marked, but similar (virtually identical) fonts can be bought from other suppliers as long as the trade-marked name is not used. Often a similar, or related, name is used, e.g. 'Switzerland' instead of 'Helvetica', 'Ambo' instead of 'Bembo', 'Modern' instead of 'Futura', 'Palladia' instead of 'Palatino' and 'Zurich Calligraphic' instead of 'Zapf Chancery'. The word 'fount' derives from the same source as the word 'foundry' and refers to a process of making something from molten metal, as the traditional type was made.

5.4 Classification of Typefaces

Typefaces can be grouped together into a number of broad categories. One distinction has already been mentioned – those with and without serifs. Traditional typefaces have always had serifs but many more modern designs are much plainer

A sans serif font

A serif font

***Fig. 5.4**: Serif fonts have tiny end-strokes; sans-serif fonts are much plainer*

and are called 'sans-serifs' (meaning 'without serifs') – see Fig. 5.4. These are simpler not only because of the lack of serifs but also because the strokes are usually of uniform thickness whereas serif typefaces often use strokes which vary with the direction of the stroke – as in the case of traditional handwritten text where the metal nib of a pen produces different widths of stroke according to the direction in which the pen is moved.

Another way of distinguishing typefaces is into those which are suitable for use as 'body text' and those which are more decorative. The former are typefaces that are suitable for large bodies of text of normal size, such as the text in this book. The latter are more suitable for small amounts of (usually large) text to be used in headlines. These are sometimes called 'display' or 'decorative' (see Fig. 3.15 in Chapter 3). A third category is that of speciality typefaces like Greek or Hebrew characters and symbols (see Fig. 5.5). A fourth is that of Script fonts – designed to look like handwriting (see Fig. 5.5 also).

ϒ≤⁄∞ƒ↔≥∝≠≈⊕∅⊆®⇔©

This looks like handwriting

***Fig. 5.5** Two special fonts: symbols and script*

5.5 Specifying the Size

The term 'point' was introduced in the last section as a measurement of the size of a typeface. This, together with the 'pica' is a traditional printers' unit, the values of which are given in Table 5.1.

Table 5.1 *The relationship between inches, picas and points*

Inch	Pica	Point
1	6	72

The pica is a large unit, used to specify such quantities as the margins of a page or the length of a line. The point is a unit more suitable for specifying the size of characters. 12 points (or 1 pica), for example, is 1/6 inch and this is about the height of a character in a typewriter font and so is a suitable size also for printed body-text. Values between 9 and 12 points are usually used; this book is set in Times New Roman 10 point. 12 point text produces about ten letters per inch of line, since the width of characters is less than their height. The size of mono-spaced fonts are often quoted in characters per inch, since they have a uniform width, but this obviously is not suitable for proportionately-spaced fonts. Special typography rulers are manufactured so that typefaces can be measured in points and picas but this is not as easy as it looks because it is not immediately obvious how to measure the height of a letter. Some letters (like 'o') are much shorter than others (like 'h'). Some letters have tails ('descenders') that drop below the line. The size of a font, therefore, is measured from the bottom of a letter with a descender to the top of a letter with an

Fig. 5.6 *Measuring the size of type: the top two lines can be used to measure the size of the font. The distance between the second and the third lines is the line – spacing – the 'leading'*

'ascender' (see Fig. 5.6). When the Apple Macintosh was designed with desktop publishing in mind the specification of the display was set at 72 pixels per inch (monochrome screen) so that there would be a simple correspondence between screen pixels and the printers' unit of measurement – the point.

5.6 Bit-Mapped and Scaleable Fonts

It has been stated already in Chapter 1 that early microcomputers did not use bit-mapped screens. In part, this was due to the memory requirements of such display systems. Even the earliest and simplest bit-mapped graphics display that was used on the IBM-PC had a resolution of 640 by 200 pixels (two colours, one-bit-per

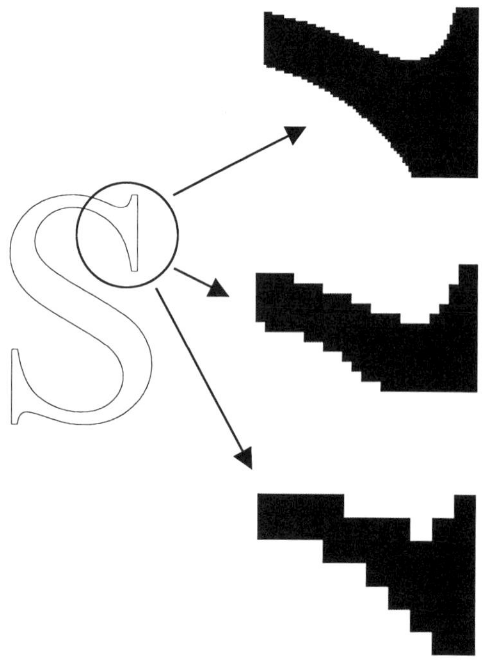

Fig. 5.7 *The shape of the character (S) is stored as a vector but bit-maps are generated for display or printing, using the size and numbers of bits appropriate to any particular device. Three different values of resolution are illustrated.*

pixel), which required a minimum of 640 × 200 / 8 = 16,000 bytes, and many early microcomputers only had a total of 4 or 8 K of memory for all purposes – operating system, applications software, data and screen display. The compromise that was used was a 'text-only' or 'character-mapped' display. The shapes of all the permitted characters were stored (as bit-maps) in a separate ROM and each character was given a code (the ASCII code). The memory set aside for the display, therefore, only had to store a one-byte ASCII code for each character on the screen (perhaps 2000 characters at most) – needing 2,000 bytes, not 16,000. This system, of course, would only work with mono-spaced fonts (each character taking up the same space on the screen) and could only provide one font (the 'system' font). This system is discussed in more detail in the chapter on algorithms.

When bit-mapped systems became available it then became possible to create WYSIWYG displays – but they still used bit-mapped fonts. The difference was that a wider variety of fonts was created – both for the printers and for the screen displays. Bit-mapping, where every pixel was under direct control, also meant proportionately-spaced fonts became a practical proposition. There were two problems, however, with this system. One was that every font – each size and each type (bold, italic, bold-italic etc) – needed its own set of printer bit-maps, which took up large amounts of disc space. The other was that separate screen fonts were needed – one for each printer font – but mapped at about 70 dpi instead of, say, 300 dpi or more for a laser printer. A true WYSIWYG system needed a better approach to the whole question of fonts, and a scaleable font system, pioneered by Adobe and called 'PostScript', was the answer. In a scaleable font system the basic shape of every typeface is specified only once as a mathematically specified vector 'outline', and individual fonts – at a particular size, boldness etc. – are created as bit-maps when they are required. In Fig. 5.7 the outline shape of the letter 'S' has been used to create three bit-maps : one suitable for a high-resolution printer (at, say, 600 dpi), one for a low-resolution printer (100 dpi) and one for screen display (60 dpi). This system provides a classical 'trade-off': a saving in memory but an increase in computer processing since every font has to be created, as a bit map, whenever it is required.

5.7 PostScript and PDLs

The PostScript system was the first commercially available scaleable font system and has therefore become an industry standard even though rival systems are now available. PostScript, however, is more than a font system. It is a programming language in its own right, though a rather specialized type of language – often referred to as a 'Page Description Language' (PDL). This means that it is possible to write a computer program that describes every detail of a printed page, including the appearance of any text, but also any graphics which includes geometrical shapes, line types, pattern fills and colours. Because PostScript is a computer language it needs to be 'translated'. Any high-level language is written as a series of 'statements' or commands and before these can have any effect they must be translated into a much larger number of machine-level instructions which have 'meaning' to the computer's central processor – that is, are part of the processor's 'instruction set'. Depending on whether the translation is done for the whole of the program before being implemented by the computer, or is done a line at a time (in 'real time') as it is being operated upon, this process is called 'compiling' or 'interpreting'. The software that does this process is called a 'compiler' or an 'interpreter', respectively. PostScript is interpreted and the normal method is to supply the interpreter as part of the printer – making it a 'PostScript printer'. This means that a PostScript printer is itself a specialized computer with its own microprocessor, its own memory and its own ROM (containing the copy of the interpreter program). Very few users wish to write their own PostScript programs and so desktop publishing or word processing applications software will contain suitable PostScript software, capable of taking the description of the page created in the software and then creating a PostScript file – a PostScript program – which is a text file that is then sent to the printer. The printer interprets the program (i.e. runs the program) and this produces a bit-mapped image which the printer can output as hard-copy. Fig. 5.8 shows this process in outline. The design of the page which has been created on a computer is turned into a PostScript file by the application software. This text file is interpreted by the PostScript language (probably in a ROM chip in the printer) and the bit-mapped image so created sent to the printer hardware. This sounds like a complicated process but it has the supreme virtue of 'hardware-independence'. The fonts, and any other geometrical shapes, are stored in the PostScript program as generalized mathematical descriptions and are converted into bit-maps only within the printer. This means that the final output is optimized for

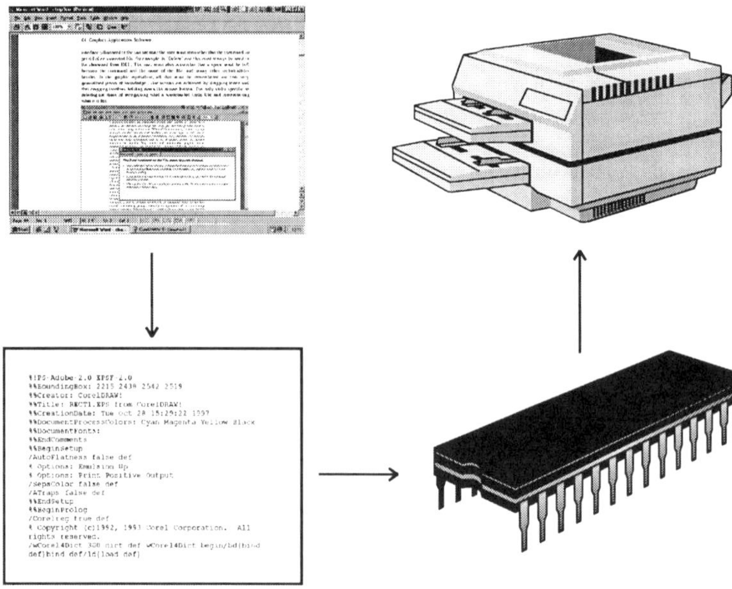

Fig. 5.8 *The PostScript process : the page is converted into a text file using the PostScript PDL which is then raster-converted into a bit map and printed*

the particular printer (or any other output device, in principle). A 300-dpi printer creates and prints a bit-mapped image at 300 dpi. A 1200 dpi laser printer creates and prints a 1200 dpi bit-map. A high-quality digital typesetter working at 2,540 dpi creates and prints at 2,540 dpi. The image in each case will be the same within the limits imposed by the resolution of the device – only the quality will be different. This means that 'proofs' of an image can be produced using a cheap laser printer and the user knows that when the same PostScript file is sent to an expensive typesetter the result will look just the same, except for the higher quality that will result from using 70 times as many (much smaller) dots.

The only disadvantage of the PostScript system lies in the need for special PostScript printers because they are inevitably more expensive. Part of the extra cost lies in the fees which must be paid on each printer for licensing the PostScript interpreter. The other cost lies in the need for memory, though any good modern printer needs memory – at least sufficient to hold a copy of one or more pages of output to ensure that the computer is not tied up during the much slower process of printing. A laser printer, however, being a page-printer, needs enough memory to hold a bit-map of the whole page since the whole page must be rasterized (converted into a raster-based bit-mapped form) before printing can begin. The processor that does that is called a 'raster image processor' (RIP).

However, if cost is an important issue there is no reason why the interpretation of the PostScript program need be performed in the printer and so other PostScript interpreters have been written (sometimes called PostScript 'clones') which can be run by the computer, which then sends the final bit-mapped image to the printer. This has the advantage that any printer can be used but it might be a slower process since all the processing must be done by the computer's central processor. Clone PostScript interpreters have largely disappeared because of the development of TrueType (see next section) and ATM (next paragraph). They still have a use where someone, who does not own a PostScript printer, wishes to send a PostScript file to a bureau for printing and needs to see a proof copy first.

One of the drawbacks of PostScript is that it is a PDL ('Page Description Language') and not a 'Screen Description Language'. In order to see the output on a screen users had initially to use pre-build sets of bit-mapped screen fonts – one for each size that was required. Adobe, therefore, created a piece of software called Adobe Type Manager (ATM) which was designed to help the user install and remove fonts and also to rasterize Postscript Type 1 fonts (the most commonly used) on-the-fly for display on the screen. It does this, not by rasterising the outline description of the font (as it does for printing), but by using a limited number of bit-mapped fonts supplied with the software. Where the user chooses to use a font size that is not supplied, ATM creates one 'to order'. These two types of information are stored in two different types of font files. On a Windows system, for example, a PFB file contains the outlines of the font and a PFM file contains the 'metrics' (such information as character widths, kerning pair data and a bit-mapped screen font). On a Mac system there will be a number of bit-mapped files, for different screen sizes, but ATM can produce any size required from one of them and so other sizes can be deleted to save disk space. ATM also allows non-PostScript printers to print Type 1 fonts.

PostScript is the system most widely used in the printing industry. It provides the most fonts (more than 20,000), which are of the highest quality fonts. Some fonts are supplied with Postscript printers – Courier, Helvetica, Times, Avant Garde, Bookman, New Century Schoolbook, Palatino and Zapf Chancery – amounting to 35 fonts when the bold, italic and narrow versions are taken into account. Any others must be purchased from 'type-foundries'.

5.8 TrueType

A similar approach is used in one of PostScript's main commercial rivals – 'TrueType'. This was developed by Apple and licensed by Microsoft and has been supplied with Microsoft Windows (since version 3.1) and with the Macintosh operating system since System 7. Because TrueType is supplied with the computer's system software and not with the printer, scaleable fonts can be used with any printer. All the processing is done by the computer using a rasterizer supplied with the operating system and a bit-map is then downloaded to the printer. It also contains its own screen-font manager. In many ways this is a system designed for the ordinary user. It provides many of the advantages of a scalable font system at a low cost. Of course, because the processing cannot be downloaded to a secondary processor in the printer, there is a price to be paid in terms of printing speed but when laser printers were expensive items this was a price many users were prepared to pay. There are many high-quality TrueType fonts now available (though not as many as PostScript) and there are also a large number of, in many cases, lower-quality, public domain TrueType fonts.

Fig. 5.9 *A smoothly-curved character like 'S' does not match the rectangular grid of pixels*

Both PostScript and TrueType are designed to produce scalable fonts and both use a system called 'hinting' or 'instructing' to cope with some of the problems, already discussed, of scaling a wide range of character sizes from a single definition. Hinting is mainly concerned with the problems of small characters. In addition to the problems found with traditional printing technology, where small characters have to be thickened and widened a little to retain their readability, digital typography poses special additional problems. These arise because of the difficulty of mapping a smoothly curving shape onto a rectangular grid of pixels (see Fig. 5.9). Compromises have to be made with any size of character and digital versions of a typeface may be changed slightly so that the shapes match more closely with the grid. Small characters may need a more radical re-design because, at that scale, there are so few pixels for the designer to play with. Making these sort of changes when a character is rasterized is what 'hinting' is all about. Hinting is usually applied to typefaces below 12 point for 300 dpi printers and 18 point on VGA screens. Printer hints are not needed for high-resolution printers (600 dpi and above)

There is a difference between the way that PostScript and TrueType apply hinting. TrueType embeds the hinting instructions into the typefaces themselves – which tends to make the font files larger than PostScript files. Modern versions of TrueType, for example, embed bit-mapped versions of small characters into the outline font file. PostScript files, on the other hand, contain only the minimum information, about which strokes in a character need hinting, and the actual hinting process is performed by ATM. This has meant that improvements to the hinting process have been applied to all PostScript typefaces when newer and better versions of ATM have been developed.

TrueType fonts require only one file per font (the TTF file) although Windows 3.1 will create much smaller FOT files – one for each font – as a pointer to the location of the font data.

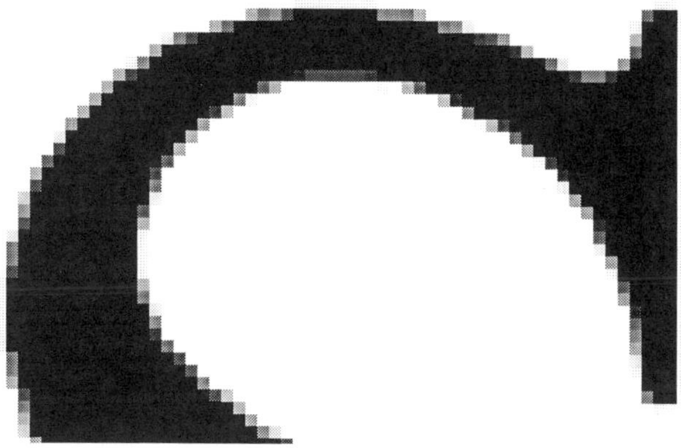

Fig. 5.10 *Anti-aliasing used to give a smoother edge to a letter 'S'*

With larger characters the problem is more likely to be that screen fonts show jagged edges where there should be a smooth curve. TrueType can cope with this by the use of anti-aliasing (sometimes called font smoothing). This involves the use of pixels in one of three different grey levels, in addition to black, so that steps in the edge of a character can be given a smoother appearance (see Fig. 5.10 and also Fig. 1.9, Chapter 1). The particular shade of grey that is used depends on how what proportion of a pixel should have been occupied with black. Font smoothing is available for Windows-95.

The major difference between the PostScript and TrueType systems is that TrueType is only concerned with the display and printing of fonts whereas PostScript is a general-purpose PDL and handles a wide range of graphic functions. PostScript, for example, is used to specify vector graphic images as Encapsulated PostScript (EPS) – see the chapter on graphics files.

5.9 Other PDLs

There are two main alternatives to PostScript and TrueType – both created by well–established companies involved in the manufacture of printers. One is Hewlett Packard's 'Printer Control Language' (PCL) and the other, Agfa Compugraphic's 'Intellifont'. PCL was originally a system designed for dot-matrix printers which were controlled by 'Escape-codes'. These were codes sent by the computer and distinguished from character codes by the associated use of the Escape-key. Since these printers created basic mono-spaced characters one at a time, the codes effectively switched the printer into and out of modes – like bold or italic. After a bold code the printer would print every character in bold until a 'cancel' code was sent. However, PCL has been upgraded over the years into a fully-fledged PDL with outline font support and the Hewlett Packard vector graphics language used on its pen-plotters. It is sufficiently well established to be provided on a wide range of printers, not only those made by Hewlett Packard, and can be faster than PostScript.

Microsoft Windows uses a graphical device interface (GDI) which is capable of driving a printer. The purpose of this was to simplify the relationship between the application and the printer. Before Windows, when PC software ran under DOS, each application – say a word processor or DTP program – needed to provide a printer driver for each popular make of printer. By specifying the GDI as part of the operating system each Windows application need ensure only that it created output that matched the specification of the GDI. Similarly each printer manufacturer need provide only one printer driver – for Windows. One spin-off of this situation is that it is possible to make laser printers which are designed to print output only from the Windows GDI. The main advantage of this approach is that the printer can be made more cheaply than an ordinary laser printer since the rasterization is done in the computer not the printer. The disadvantages are that such a printer can operate only under Windows and the process can in some cases be slowed down if the computer is rather low-powered since the processing cannot be off-loaded to the printer. On the other hand time is saved because one stage of the normal process – converting from the GDI specification of the file to one suitable for the printer, via the printer driver, is omitted. Another advantage is that the printer can become faster when the computer is up-graded to one with a faster processor or more memory. The equivalent piece of software to Windows GDI in the Mac is called QuickDraw.

5.10 Font Handling

Scalable fonts can be stored in the computer (as in the TrueType system) but it is often better, from the point of view of speed, to store the fonts in the printer. A basic set can be stored in ROM in the printer (called resident fonts) but with 20,000 or more fonts available there has to be a way that users can add a selection of other fonts that they have bought. One method is to add extra ROM chips to the printer. Some printers accept font cartridges – which are small plastic boxes containing the fonts on a chip. Some printers can be fitted with their own hard-disk drives and fonts which have been bought on floppy disks or CD-ROMs loaded onto the drive. Fonts supplied as software are usually termed 'soft fonts' (compared to 'hard fonts' supplied in ROM). When fonts are supplied on CD-ROMs they are often supplied as a set of thousands, protected by a set of codes. When a particular font is needed the code number is made available by the supplier on payment of a fee and the font can then be 'unlocked' and downloaded from the disk.

The Mac operating system will recognize if a chosen font is not available in the printer but is on the hard-disk of the computer and will automatically download it to the printer. Sometimes the chosen font is not available on either the printer or the computer and another one must be used instead. Some systems have a 'font substitution' facility which chooses a font of a similar type. The user usually has the choice of whether to accept the proposed substitution or choose another. One of the problems associated with font substitution is that seemingly identical fonts from different foundries can be significantly different in fine details like width and though not obvious to the eye these differences can make huge differences to the appearance of a printed page. Slight differences in the width of characters will cause more, or fewer, of them to fill a line and the consequent 'text re-flow' can cause havoc to a carefully designed page.

Exercises for the Reader:

(1) Using a word processor or DTP program, create a line of text, make a duplicate copy of it and then put one line into a mono-spaced font like Courier and the other into a proportionally-spaced font like Times – in the same size. Look carefully at the characters and the spaces between words and notice how much more space is taken up by the mono-spaced font. This can be most clearly seen by enlarging the display using the zoom facility. Estimate how much more space is taken up by the first font by setting a long paragraph, first in one font and then in the other, and counting how many lines are needed in each case. Which of the two do you find easier to read?

(2) Look at a list of font files on your computer. In Windows 3.1 they are stored in the Windows/System directory. In Windows-95 they are in the Windows/Fonts directory. Most of them will probably have the extension .ttf (TrueType). Notice that some common fonts have four files. For example the font called 'Arial' has files called arial.ttf, arialbd.ttf, ariali.ttf and arialbi.ttf. These correspond to Arial Roman (the normal font), Arial Bold, Arial Italic and Arial Bold/Italic. Other fonts, however, only have one file. Does this mean that this type of font cannot be displayed in bold or italic? Find out by choosing such a font and, using a word processor, create some text in that font. Show that text in this type of font can in fact be boldened and italicized and then try to explain what is happening. Why create four separate font files for some typefaces when they don't seem to be necessary in practice ?

(3) Create some text in your word processor or DTP package in a large size – for example, 72 point (1 inch high). View it at high magnification (at a zoom value of between 200% and 500%) with the ruler facility displayed. It should be possible to measure the font size (the height) using the on-screen ruler. If necessary, draw two horizontal lines using the line-drawing facility and move these lines carefully into position so that one matches the bottom of a descender and the other the top of an ascender. These lines can help in doing the measurements when they are continued to the edge of the screen where the ruler is. Some rulers can have the zero-value reset by the user and if this is possible then re-set the zero to coincide with the top or bottom of a character. Some rulers have the option of allowing the user to choose the units used (inches, picas or points, for example) and if this is available change the units and measure the font using different units. Now select the line of text so that it is displayed in reverse video (white characters on a black background). Notice that the black rectangle so created is higher than the character height; it includes

the line spacing – the 'leading'. Try to measure this and then check with the default value as specified by the word processor. Find out how to change the line spacing and make it larger or smaller, observing the result and checking the measured value. What proportion is the default leading for a standard font (like Times 10 point) as a percentage? Is this *proportion* (not its absolute value) maintained for very large font sizes or does it vary with size?

(4) Investigate a bit-mapped font. The easiest way to do this is to use the system font in DOS mode (in a PC). Open a DOS window, type some text and then 'grab' the window using the Alt and Print Screen (PrtSc) keys simultaneously. This grabs a copy of the active window into the clipboard portion of memory. Then run the paint program that is provided with Windows and paste the contents of the clipboard into it (Ctrl-V) or Edit/Paste. Enlarge the image with the zoom facility and switch on the grid if it is not already on. It should be possible to see each individual pixel clearly. How many pixels are used per character? Using the zoom facility shows very clearly what happens when bit-mapped fonts are enlarged in contrast to what happens when TrueType, scaleable, fonts are made larger – last section.

(5) Investigate a PostScript file. You can do this only if: (a) you have a PostScript printer attached to your computer, or (b) are willing to pretend you have a PostScript printer attached to your computer (by installing a PostScript printer driver using the Windows installation disks) or (c) you have a graphics package which will save images as EPS (Encapsulated PostScript) files. If you are using either of the first two methods, create a text file in your word processor and then 'print to a file'. This will create a PostScript file. If you are using method (c) just save a graphic as an EPS file. Now open the file in a word processor. You will see that it is a text file and that you can recognize some of the words in it and possibly even guess what some of them do. To get any further you will have to consult a book on the PostScript language. The important point is to recognize that a PostScript file is a text file because it is a computer program, not a graphics file.

(6) Investigate the shape of characters from a scaleable font. This needs a vector drawing package – like CorelDRAW or Adobe Illustrator – which has the facility to convert characters into a graphic object (that is, a normal editable shape, like any other shape that can be drawn in that software). This type of facility will have a name like 'Convert to Curves' (Corel) or 'Create Outlines' (Illustrator). Simply type a character, using the text facility, and then convert it to a set of curves. It should now be possible to see the control points (described in Chapter 7 – the section on curves) and the levers which can be used alter the slope of the curve as it passes through those points. This usually involves a special pen-tool which can be used to add extra control points or delete or change the position of existing points. It can also be used to alter the slope of the curves. This facility allows you to see very clearly the way that scaleable fonts are defined and also allows you to change the shape of individual characters.

6

Graphics Files

6.1 Introduction

All applications software – word-processors, spread-sheets, databases, for example – generate files which are stored in a proprietary format, but no category of computer software seems to have spawned so many different formats as graphics software. The word-processor I am using to type these words offers a choice of 26 different formats in which to save the file but in reality most of these are variations of a very few basic types. For example, seven of them are associated with one word-processor package, the differences being those between the current and older versions, versions for the PC and the Mac, versions for DOS and Windows. In fact only four completely different proprietary formats are covered and these will probably cover 95% of user's needs. The same is true of database and spreadsheet files; three or four standard formats are all that are commonly used. A recent reference book on graphics file formats, on the other hand, gives detailed information on over 80 different types. Even this number does not give a true indication of the number of formats in use because many formats exist in more than one version. Why are there so many?

There are a number of reasons for the proliferation of graphics file formats. One very simple one is that there are two completely different types of graphic file – bit-mapped (or raster) and vector, and most file formats are designed for one or the other – though some can be used to store either type. The second reason is that early graphics files were monochrome (1-bit-per-pixel) and with the development of colour displays, extensions had to be made to these formats to cater for the extra data involved. This has led, for example, to a number of different versions of the widely used PCX file format, covering monochrome, 4-bit, 8-bit and 24-bit colour images. Early graphics systems had fixed colour palettes while later systems offered user-definable palettes and, again, graphics file formats had to be modified to store this extra information. The final, and most important, reason lies in the effect of competition in producing rival proprietary formats. This in turn led to attempts to reduce the problems so caused by the introduction of non-proprietary formats to act as intermediates, for conversion purposes, or as an attempt to create agreed standards. This might not seem to be enough reason why graphics packages should have spawned so many formats – as compared with, say, wordprocessors – but in addition there are many different types of graphics software: for painting and for vector drawing, for computer-aided design and for business presentations, for animation and for 3-D modelling, for digitising video and for multimedia presentations. In most cases the software developer who produced the first successful example of a particular graphics application created a file format that became an industry standard but that hasn't stopped other producers trying to create alternative standards.

A common feature of graphics files is that the data is usually compressed. Graphic data occupies a lot of space and so is it sensible to try to find ways of reducing the amount of memory needed when it is stored as a file. This not only reduces the space occupied on storage disks but also speeds up the rate at which it can be written to and from the disk.

It can be instructive to do a few simple experiments with appropriate calculations to explore this issue of file size – as applied to bit-mapped images. The principles of how to calculate the amount of memory needed to store an image in the refresh buffer have already been introduced in Chapters 1 and 2. For example a VGA image of 640 by 480 pixels in, say, 256 colours needs 640 × 480 × 8 bits = 2,457,600 bits, since 8 bits are needed to store 256 colours. This corresponds to 307,200 bytes (300 K) since no form of compression is used in the refresh buffer. When such an image is saved, however, a much smaller file often results. This can be seen by experiment. If the PrintScreen key is pressed on a PC, a copy of the current screen image is temporarily stored in the 'Clipboard'. This can then be viewed using the Clipboard Viewer (provided with 'Windows' software) and saved as a CLP (Clipboard) file. Using suitable graphics application software or file conversion software, other versions of the file can then be saved using a variety of formats. It is interesting to look at the results of such an experiment (see Table 6.1). A 640 × 480 (256 colour) image was saved in six formats: CLP, GIF, BMP (2 versions), PCX and JPEG. The file sizes are shown in the table. The terms GIF, BMP, PCX and JPEG are short-forms for four very common file formats – 'Graphics Interchange Format' (GIF), 'Windows Bit-Map' (BMP), PC Paintbrush (PCX) and 'Joint Photographic Experts Group' (JPEG). More details of these and of other graphic formats can be found in a table at the end of this chapter.

Table 6.1 *A comparison of the file sizes when an image is saved in six different file formats*

File type	File size
GIF	59 K
JPEG	87 K
PCX	142 K
BMP (RLE)	144 K
BMP (RGB)	302 K
CLP	603 K

The most striking result of this simple experiment is the discovery of how much variation there is in the file size. The size ranges from 59 K to over 600 K, a factor of more than 10. In fact one file (the CLP) seems to be twice as big as our calculated value for the uncompressed data. The 'Windows Bitmap' file – BMP (RGB encoded version) – is about the expected size for an uncompressed file. The BMP (RLE encoded) is about half that size – as is the PCX file. The JPEG and GIF files are about 3.5 and five times smaller, respectively. Whatever the explanation might be, it is clear that different file formats are using different methods of storing the data and that some are managing to store the information in a much more efficient way than others. The following sections introduce the important principles behind these various methods, as applied to bit-mapped images like those used in the above example. We begin with an explanation of compression – storing data in a form which takes up significantly less space than it does in its unprocessed form.

6.2 Pixel Packing

As we will see, pixel packing is not a compression technique in the normally understood meaning of that term but it does raise an interesting point concerning the way that graphics data should be stored. In the discussion on the mapping of screen pixels into the refresh buffer, it has been assumed that each pixel will be mapped by one or more bits. For example, a pixel that can be in one of 16 colours will need

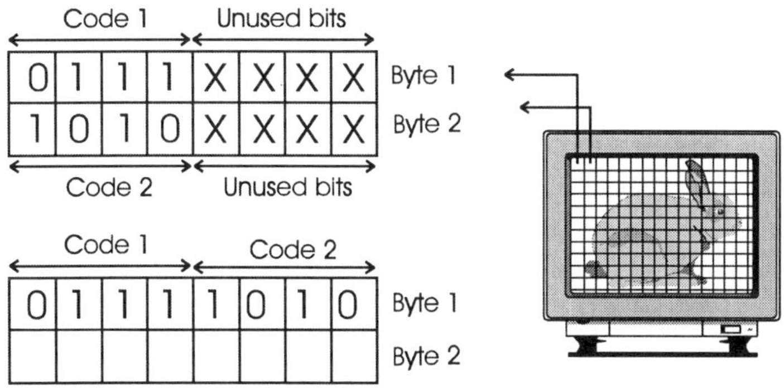

Fig. 6.1 *Two different ways of storing colour codes*

four bits to store one of the 16 possible colour codes (0 – 15, decimal). Computers, however, address memory in bytes rather than bits and so the easiest, and quickest way to store the codes for a 4-bit-per-pixel system would be to use one byte for each colour code, even though only four bits in the byte would be storing any useful information (top two bytes in Fig. 6.1). This, of course, means that half the memory would be wasted. An alternative is to pack two pixels into each byte (bottom byte in Fig. 6.1). Indeed, in all the calculations so far in this book it has been assumed that something like this will be done. If it is, then the file is said to be pixel-packed, and no memory is wasted, but it must realized that the price to be paid for this is the extra processing needed to combine two 4-bit digits into one byte, in the process of saving the file, and the reverse when the file is read back into memory. This will inevitably increase the time needed for these operations. Pixel packing, then, is not so much a compression technique as a more efficient but slower, way of storing uncompressed information.

This second factor – speed of processing – implies that simple calculations of file sizes, even for uncompressed files, which are based only on the number of pixels and number of colours, may not always produce the correct answers. Modern computers use 32 and 64-bit processors, rather than the early 8- and 16-bit chips, and handle data in 'words' (multiples of bytes). This suggests one possible explanation for the rather surprising fact that the CLP file, in the example above, occupied twice the space expected. It might be that this format was designed for speed in transferring data from one application to another, rather than compactness, and saves data in 2-byte words so that one byte in two is 'wasted'. Simple experiments on CLP files, as described a little later in the chapter, seem to bear this out but for the moment this can only be a strong likelihood since the author of a standard reference book on file formats confesses that the coding of the data in CLP files is 'unknown to me' despite considerable efforts to establish such information. The author of another reference book on file formats points out that it is impossible to persuade some companies to divulge the specification of their file formats – which makes it difficult, if not impossible, for programmers to produce software to read or write in these formats. This is, perhaps, the reason that virtually no graphics application software will actually read or write to the CLP format, not even the applications produced by the company that is the author of the CLP format (Microsoft).

The speed factor also gives us a clue as to why some file formats occupy more space than others. There are a variety of compression techniques and some are more efficient than others – as measured by the size of the final file. If they all involved the same amount of processing then it would seem that the less efficient ones would be ignored in favour of the more efficient ones, but in practice the more efficient ones usually involve more calculations and are therefore slower. This is an example of a classic trade-off: 'speed-versus-size' and explains why a variety of compression techniques are used. The user can choose whether efficiency of memory-use or speed is more important.

Another factor that has been ignored, so far, is the type of image. The simple experiment described above was one done on one image but it cannot be assumed that the same results would be obtained with a completely different image. Some compression methods might be better than others at certain types of image – and this does, in fact, turn out to be the case.

6.3 Run-Length Encoding (RLE)

One of the file types used in the above example was a BMP (RLE encoded) which was about half the size of the other BMP file (the RGB encoded version). The latter was about the expected size for uncompressed file but the 'Run-Length Encoded' version about half that size. Run-length encoding is a very simple but effective way of compressing data which is based on the observation that many bit-mapped files contain large numbers of consecutive pixels which have the same colour (and therefore the same colour code). For example, a scanned photograph of a landscape might have a large section of sky at the top of the picture which consisted of hundreds of blue pixels. In a normal, non-compressed, file this would be represented by the colour code for blue repeated many times. In run length encoding the computer counts how many repetitions of that code exist in, say, one scan line (a 'run' of repeating code) and simply stores one copy of the code together with a record of the number of repetitions. Thus, for example in a 256 colour system where each code is assigned one byte, 100 consecutive repetitions of a colour code which would normally occupy 100 bytes could be replaced by 2 bytes – one for the number 100 and one for the colour code. It is the difference between recording 'blue' 'blue' 'blue'... and so on, 100 times, as compared with recording the equivalent of '100 copies of blue'. In the simple example shown in Fig. 6.2, two rows of nine, blue, pixels and one row of nine, pink, pixels can be coded as 27 codes or as six : blue code – 9 – blue code – 9 – pink code – 9. An extension of this approach is called 'Vertical Replication'. If two consecutive scan lines are identical then this system uses a similar method to RLE to record that fact.

It can be seen that RLE is a very simple system that will be quick to implement but its efficiency will depend on how much repetition exists in the image. Some simple images that have large areas of one colour will compress very well. The example of the scanned photograph with lots of sky, however, may not compress as efficiently as expected because a blue sky might contain many different shades of blue – each with a different code. In the extreme case, if there were many changes of colour from pixel to pixel the 'compression' might even produce a larger file. For example, a 640-pixel scan line in which every pixel had a different colour from its neighbour would occupy twice the space when 'compressed' as when uncompressed because

Blue	Blue	Blue	Blue	Blue	Blue	Blue	Blue	Blue
Blue	Blue	Blue	Blue	Blue	Blue	Blue	Blue	Blue
Pink	Pink	Pink	Pink	Pink	Pink	Pink	Pink	Pink

Colour of pixels

10	10	10	10	10	10	10	10	10
10	10	10	10	10	10	10	10	10
8	8	8	8	8	8	8	8	8

Colour codes for those pixels

10	9	10	9	8	9			

RLE encoded colour codes

Fig. 6.2 *Run-Length Encoding*

each pixel would need two bytes – one for the colour code and one to store the number of consecutive pixels in that colour (the number 1 in each case). Of course this is an extreme example; almost all images contain significant numbers of consecutive pixels which have the same colour code but it does explain why some images will compress more efficiently than others using the RLE technique. We shouldn't, therefore, expect that two different images that have the same number of pixels and the same number of colours will necessarily have the same file size when stored in compressed form.

6.4 Huffman and CCITT Compression

The CCITT is an international standards committee that has developed a number of compression techniques, some of which are based on a method developed by David Huffman. As an example of the principles involved, one of the simplest of these techniques (developed for fax machines and early document scanners) is described here. This technique is particularly suited to bi-level images (images which are only either black or white at any point). It uses a 'dictionary' system, which means that strings of original data are replaced with smaller ones, obtained from a dictionary. A dictionary, in this context, is more like a two-column table, or a list of synonyms, than a real dictionary. Every 'word' has another word listed alongside it. For this reason the dictionary is sometimes called a 'translation table' or a 'string table'. The process is like one in which a book, which has been written using very long words, is shortened by the simple process of substituting for each long word a much shorter word which has been obtained from the dictionary. Using that same dictionary the process can be reversed at any time to re-create the original, longer book.

In this case the dictionary was created by analysing a large number of typical images (black and white documents containing text in a variety of languages and typical examples of line-art) to find out which are the most commonly occurring sequences of pixels. These are then given short codes. Less commonly occurring sequences are given the longer codes. This method obviously has something in common with RLE encoding in that strings of pixels are replaced by shorter codes. One important difference is that in RLE encoding a string of original data always consists of repetitions of the same colour whereas in the CCITT method a data string will often contain a mixture of colours (or black and white combinations in the case of bi-level images). It is defined as a commonly occurring string of values rather than as a string of identical values. The other difference lies in the use of arbitrary codes rather than the simple sequence of the colour code and the number of pixels in the string. The principle of using the shorter codes for commonly-occurring strings is one which was adopted a long time ago in the design of the Morse-code where common letters like 'e' are coded with a single 'dot' and the longer sequence codes like 'dash-dash-dot' are reserved for uncommon letters like 'Z'. Because the 'dictionary' is pre-defined it does not have to be stored as part of the image; it is provided as part of the compression software.

6.5 LZW (Lempel–Ziv–Welch) Compression

This is a compression technique associated with Abraham Lempel, Jacob Ziv and Terry Welch. It is also a dictionary-based technique but it differs from the ones described above in that the software builds up its own dictionary during the compression process, basing this on a small built-in table of values. This means that it creates a dictionary that is appropriate to that particular image – rather than relying on a pre-determined dictionary based on a statistical sample of images. Because of this feature of the algorithm it is not necessary to keep a copy of the final dictionary in order to reverse the process. The decoder works in a similar way, again building up a dictionary based on the same initial table. The two advantages of this approach are the suitability of the dictionary to the image (already mentioned) and the saving in space that comes from not having to store the dictionary, either with the image or with the coding software.

The LZW technique is not a single algorithm since a number of variations and improvements have been patented and used in commercial software. One consequence of this is that the GIF format, for example, which is widely used on the Internet, contains a patented LZW algorithm and royalties must be paid for its use. As a result a replacement file format for use on the Internet, designed to replace GIF and called PNG (Portable Network Graphics), has been developed and the format is publicly available, without royalty payments.

Like a number of compression algorithms, LZW compression is not restricted to the compression of images and is the basis of a number of widely used applications. This is the subject of a section later in the chapter

6.6 File Headers

After an excursion into compression methods we now return to the subject of how graphic files are constructed. The experiment in calculating file sizes threw up an interesting question – why was the uncompressed BMP file a little larger than the calculated size (2 K, in fact)? There are two reasons. One is that the disk operating system allocates space to files in units of a minimum size (called 'clusters'). On the hard disk used for this experiment the cluster size was 1 K so that if the raw picture data occupied exactly 300 K, as calculated, any extra information required by the file would take the file size over this value. In this case this extra information need only be a little more than 1 K to explain why the file was 302 K; inevitably some of that extra 2 K is 'wasted'. The question naturally arises – what might this mysterious 'extra information' be that is needed to construct a graphics file? The answer is that even an uncompressed bit-mapped file consists of more than a simple string of colour codes. Before the computer can display such an image it needs to know how to interpret this data and this information is stored in the file 'header' – a section of code added to the beginning of the image data.

A typical file header consists of a number of separate pieces of information. One piece of information must be a 'file identifier' – a code number that specifies which file format is being used. It is this that tells the computer whether the image has been stored as a BMP, a PCX, a TIFF etc. Another piece of information specifies which version of that format is being used since many formats have undergone revisions and improvements over the years. Sometimes the earliest version of a format was designed for black and white images only. Later this would have been revised for colour, but perhaps only 16 or 256 colours. Later versions might have allowed for individual images to have a unique colour palette. As a result, a file format type might have five different versions (like PCX for example) or even more. Other important pieces of information relate to the image itself – how many pixels wide and how many long – since the one-dimensional string of colour codes in the file must be translated into a two-dimensional image and it is important to know where each scan-line begins and ends. It is also important to know how many colours are used since some formats allow for images to be stored, for example, using 4-bits per pixel, 8-bits or 24-bits. If four bits are used per pixel (and it is pixel-packed) then half a byte refers to one pixel and the other half to the next. If eight bits are used per pixel then the whole byte refers to one pixel. If 24 bits are used then three consecutive bytes refer to one pixel.

Other important pieces of information specify what colour palette has been used and which compression method has been used (if any). Some formats allow compression to be used but do not require it (hence the two versions of BMP used in the earlier experiment; one uncompressed and labelled RGB, the other compressed using an RLE method). A typical graphics file for a bit-mapped format, then looks like this :

File Header

- Image type ID
- Version number
- Length of header
- Length of the file
- Image width
- Image height
- Number of bits-per-pixel
- Number of colours

Image date

- Palette
- Colour codes

6.7 Exploring a Bit-Mapped Graphics File

Another simple experiment can be used to explore these ideas. If an image is created in a paint package and then saved, the image file can then be examined using a suitable text editor to see what is stored in each byte of the file. {The term 'suitable text editor' means the sort of editor that programmers use, which can display the contents of a file in characters – usually in hexadecimal as well as ASCII symbols. There are many such Windows-based editors available as shareware. A text-based equivalent called DEBUG is also distributed with Microsoft DOS.} In this experiment the image was 60 pixels wide and 40 pixels high and consisted of vertical stripes of red, white and blue, each stripe being four pixels wide (see Fig. 6.3).

First, to see how such an image is stored in the computer's refresh buffer it can be saved as a RAW file. This is the only type of graphics file that does not employ any sort of compression and does not have a file header. It is simply a copy of the raw data stored in the computer's memory. In this case the file consists of a string of colour codes looking like Table 6.2.

Table 6.2 *Colour codes in a RAW data file*

Address	0 1	2 3	4 5	6 7	8 9	A B	C D	E F
0000	09 09	09 09	0F 0F	0F 0F	0C 0C	0C 0C	09 09	09 09
0010	0F 0F	0F 0F	0C 0C	0C 0C	09 09	09 09	0F 0F	0F 0F
0020	0C 0C	0C 0C	09 09	09 09	0F 0F	0F 0F	0C 0C	0C 0C
0030	09 09	09 09	0F 0F	0F 0F	0C 0C	0C 0C	09 09	09 09

This type of table is explained in a little more detail in the next example but for the moment it can be seen that in the main body of the table the codes 9, F and C are repeated over and over again (they are written as 09, 0F and 0C). These are hexadecimal numbers and are the equivalent of 9, 15 and 12 in decimal. In this file they are the colour codes for red, white and blue respectively. Since each stripe is four pixels wide then each code is repeated four times – once for each pixel. The total number of codes (and therefore the total number of bytes) is 60 x 40 = 2400. It should be appreciated that because of the absence of a file header it is impossible to

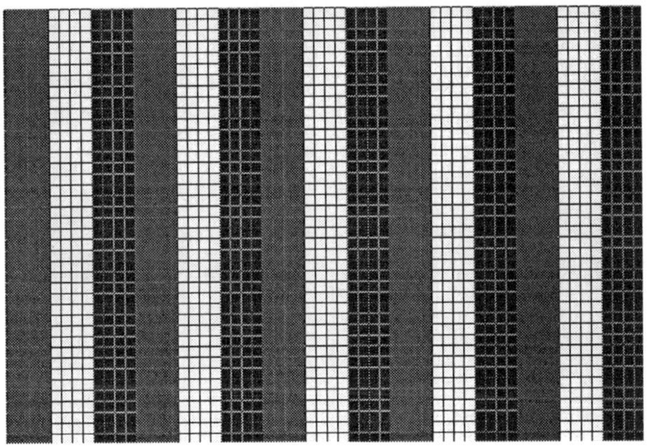

Fig. 6.3 *Test picture made up of a repeating pattern of red, white and blue vertical stripes, each four pixels wide*

re-construct an image from a RAW file unless the user knows how many pixels there are in each line of the image. This is exactly the sort of information that is stored in the header of other file types. Now, the same image is saved as an uncompressed BMP file and then looks like Table 6.3.

To analyse this table in detail needs a few more explanations. First, all the entries are in hexadecimal which is a number system which has a base of 16, instead of 10, and which uses the usual numerical symbols 1–9 and the 6 extra alphabetical symbols A to F. For convenience Table 6.4 provides the conversions from decimal to hex. In Table 6.3, for ease of reading, each cell represents two bytes = one 'word'. Each piece of information stored in the header of a BMP file uses at least one word.

Table 6.3 *Contents of an uncompressed BMP file*

Address	0 1	2 3	4 5	6 7	8 9	A B	C D	E F
0000	42 4D	76 05	00 00	00 00	00 00	76 00	00 00	28 00
0010	00 00	3C 00	00 00	28 00	00 00	01 00	04 00	00 00
0020	00 00	00 05	00 00	CE 0E	00 00	D8 0E	00 00	10 00
0030	00 00	10 00	00 00	00 00	00 00	00 00	80 00	00 80
0040	00 00	00 80	80 00	80 00	00 00	80 00	80 00	80 80
0050	00 00	C0 C0	C0 00	80 80	80 00	00 00	FF 00	00 FF
0060	00 00	00 FF	FF 00	FF 00	00 00	FF 00	FF 00	FF FF
0070	00 00	FF FF	FF 00	99 99	FF FF	CC CC	99 99	FF FF
0080	CC CC	99 99	FF FF	CC CC	99 99	FF FF	CC CC	99 99
		and	so	on	Until :			
0570	FF FF	CC CC	00 00					

Secondly, in reading the data in a word, the first byte (meaning the most significant byte) is to the right and the second byte (the less significant) is to the left. This is the opposite of our normal convention where the digits to the left are of higher value than those to the right. Thus the first word of data must be read as 4D 42 not 42 4D.

Finally the first column in the table represents the first address in the row (again, in hex). Since there are 16 bytes per row the address of the first byte in the second row is therefore 0010h = 0016d. [The abbreviations h and d are used for hex and decimal; note that d for decimal should not be confused with D, a hex 'number'.]

Table 6.4 *Decimal to Hexadecimal conversion*

Dec	Hex	Dec	Hex	Dec	Hex	Dec	Hex
0	0	4	4	8	8	12	C
1	1	5	5	9	9	13	D
2	2	6	6	10	A	14	E
3	3	7	7	11	B	15	F

The explanation of Table 6.3, then, is as follows:

Line 1:

Bytes 0000–0001 (one word)
The file ID. File IDs are assigned by the originator of the format. For BMP files the ID is 42 4D. These hex numbers are 66d and 77d which are the ASCII codes for B and M ('Bit Map').

Bytes 0002–0005 (two words)
The size of the file in bytes; = 00000576h = 1398d. The file actually occupies 2 K on disk because of the 1 K cluster rule explained earlier.

Bytes 0006–0009 (two words)
These are 'reserved' (not currently used) and set to zero.

Bytes 000A–000D (two words)
The 'image data offset' – that is, the length in bytes from the beginning of the file to the point where the image data begins = 00000076h = 118d. This shows that the image begins at address 0076h (see later).

Bytes 000E–000F (one word)
The header size in bytes = 0028h = 40d. This also identifies, indirectly, the version of BMP being used since different versions have different header sizes. It is Windows 3.x in this case. After the first 40 bytes the image information follows (the palette and the actual colour codes).

Line 2:

Bytes 0010–0013 (two words)
The image width (in pixels) = 003Ch = 60 pixels wide.

Bytes 0014–0017 (two words)
The image height (in pixels) = 0028h = 40 pixels high.

Bytes 0018–001B (two words)
The number of image 'planes' = 0001h = 1d. The concept of an image plane is discussed in the next chapter.

Bytes 001C–001D (one word)
The number of bits-per-pixel = 0004h = 4d; this corresponds to a 16 colour palette.

Bytes 001E–0021 (two words) {carries over onto Line 3}
The compression method. Possible values = 0,1 or 2. Here = 00000000h = 0d (no compression).

Line 3:

Bytes 0022–0025 (two words)
The size of the compressed data; does not apply in this case.

Bytes 0026–0029 (two words)
Horizontal resolution (in pixels per metre) – used in printing; the figure corresponds to about 96 pixels per inch.

Bytes 002A–002D (two words)
Vertical resolution (in pixels per metre) – used in printing; as above.

Bytes 002E–0031 (two words) {carries over onto Line 4}
The maximum number of colours that can be used in this image = 00000010h = 16d (16 colours).

Line 4:

Bytes 0032–0035 (two words)
Number of important colours used in the palette = 00000010h = 16d; used when displaying the image on hardware which cannot reproduce all the colours actually recorded in the image.

Lines 4–8:

Bytes 0036–0075 (31 words)
The palette.

Line 8 and onward (not all lines are shown):

Bytes 0076–0575
The actual colour codes.

In this case, the image contains 60 × 40 = 2,400 pixels, and uses 4-bits-per-pixel. Therefore each byte contains the codes for 2 pixels. The repeating code sequence is: 9999 FFFF CCCC, corresponding to the codes for 4 pixels in red, 4 pixels in white and 4 pixels in blue (the codes are 9, 15 and 12 in decimal). This should mean that the image would need only 2,400/2 = 1,200 bytes but the area actually used is larger: 575h – 76h + 1h = 500h = 1,280d. The extra 80 bytes are used to record the ends of the scan lines (40 lines, 2 bytes for each 'end-of-line-marker' which is 00 00). Although not shown in this abbreviated table the first marker can be found at address 0094–0095h (148–149d) which is 30 bytes beyond the start point (0076h = 118d). Since each byte stores the codes for two pixels this corresponds to 60 pixels, the length of one line.

6.8 Compressed Files

It is instructive to do the same experiment but, this time, to save the file as a BMP (RLE) – that is, compressed with Run-Length Encoding. To see the sort of savings that can be achieved by RLE the image is rotated through 90 degrees before saving so that the stripes now run horizontally. This produces long runs of the same coloured pixels. The table of hex values looks like this:

Table 6.5 *Contents of an RLE-compressed BMP file*

Address	0 1	2 3	4 5	6 7	8 9	A B	C D	E F
0000	42 4D	66 01	00 00	00 00	00 00	76 00	00 00	28 00
0010	00 00	28 00	00 00	3C 00	00 00	01 00	04 00	02 00
0020	00 00	F0 00	00 00	CE 0E	00 00	D8 0E	00 00	10 00
0030	00 00	10 00	00 00	00 00	00 00	00 00	80 00	00 80
0040	00 00	00 80	80 00	80 00	00 00	80 00	80 00	80 80
0050	00 00	C0 C0	C0 00	80 80	80 00	00 00	FF 00	00 FF
0060	00 00	00 FF	FF 00	FF 00	00 00	FF 00	FF 00	FF FF
0070	00 00	FF FF	FF 00	28 CC	00 00	28 CC	00 00	28 CC
0080	00 00	28 CC	00 00	28 FF	00 00	28 FF	00 00	28 FF
0090	00 00	28 FF	00 00	28 99	00 00	28 99	00 00	28 99
		and	so	on	until :			
0160	00 00	28 99	00 01					

The main differences in the file are as follows :
Bytes 0002–0005
The size of the file in bytes = 00000166h = 358d. This is four times smaller than the uncompressed version though the file actually occupies 1 K on disk (half the size) because 1 K is the minimum cluster size.

Bytes 0010–0013 and 0014–0017
The image width and height (in pixels) are reversed because the image has been rotated.

Fig. 6.4 *The pattern of stripes turned through 90 degrees (detail)*

Bytes 001E–0021
The compression method. This now = 00000002h = 2d. There are two forms of RLE compression available. Here, 4-bit RLE is being used, that is RLE for BMP files using 4-bit-per-pixel; a code of 1 would indicate 8-bit RLE.

Bytes 0022–0025 (two words)
The size of the compressed data = 000000F0h = 240d. The picture data (excluding the palette data) occupies 240 bytes instead of 1280 bytes. Note that the compression of the picture data (over five times) is better than that suggested by the reduction in the file size since the file also contains the header and the palette data which are not compressed. This means that a larger, similar, picture will seem to have an even better compression ratio because a higher proportion of the file will be pixel data.

Bytes 0076–0115
The colour codes in RLE format. The repeating pattern is 28 CC (4 times), 28 FF (4 times) and 28 99 (4 times). 28h = 40d, which means that there are 40 consecutive identical colours codes, making one complete line of the picture, this being repeated for the next three lines since each stripe is four pixels deep. This is then repeated for the two other coloured stripes and then the whole pattern recurs. CC, FF and 99 are the colour codes for blue, white and red (12d, 15d and 9d respectively). The colour codes seem to be in the wrong order because the stripes are red, white and blue (top to bottom) but the coding of the pixels is recorded from the bottom upwards (as seen on the screen).

Again, 0000 occurs every 40 pixels as an 'end of line' marker and 0001 is the 'end of image' marker.

6.9 Vector and Metafile Formats

It has been seen that bit-mapped graphics files consist of a string of data corresponding to the colour codes of all the pixels in the image – probably compressed – with a header at the front to enable the computer software to interpret this string of numbers. Vector formats, by their nature, have a completely different format. One

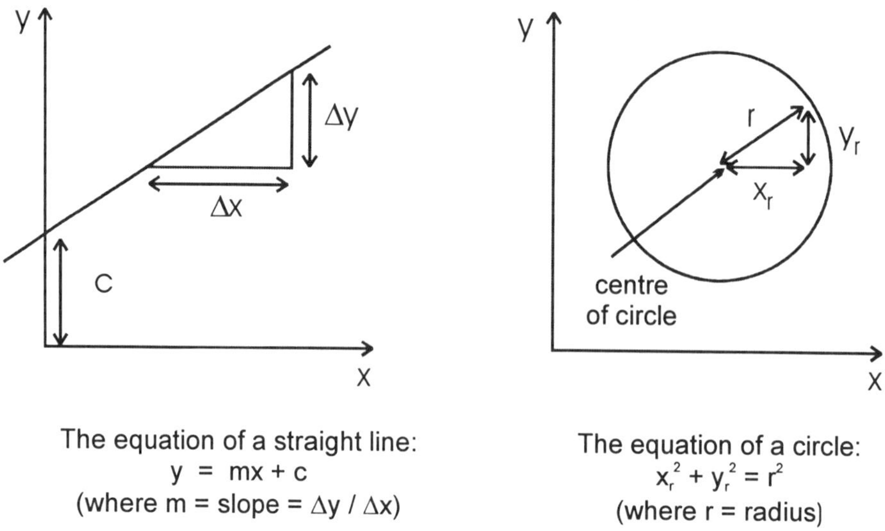

Fig. 6.5 Basic geometrical shapes like straight lines and circles can be specified by means of their equations

major difference is that the component parts of a vector image are treated as separate objects. A vector image is assembled from a set of graphics 'primitives' – geometrical shapes like circles and straight lines – and these objects are stored as discrete items in the file. This is sometimes very obvious when a complex vector image is being loaded from a disk; the computer display can be seen to be building the image up, on screen, one item at a time. Some components can be seen to be drawn 'on top' of others, just as they were created in the original drawing package. If there are a large number of components this process might take some time. In contrast, a bit-mapped image, however it might have been created, when saved, is simply a series of pixels set out in a rectangular raster of scan-lines. It is created on screen one scan-line at a time, starting at the top of the screen and working down gradually to the bottom. If objects have been drawn on top of other objects in the original drawing process the ones 'underneath' are lost as the newly drawn pixels obliterate the older ones. The file does not store any sort of 'history' as to how the image was created.

The second difference is that each of these component objects is stored as a mathematical equation which defines its shape (see Fig. 6.5) – together with a list of its 'attributes' – its particular features, such as the colour or thickness of a line or the colour and pattern which is used to fill a closed shape (see Fig. 6.6). The file is a sort of recipe which tells the computer how to draw an image. This means that the data section of the file contains many different types of information. Instead of a list of colour codes – one for each pixel – there are codes which specify which geometrical object is to be drawn, codes to specify where it is to be drawn (for example the position of the centre, for a circle), codes to specify its size (for example, the radius of a circle), codes to specify the line-thickness, codes to specify how it is to be filled, and so on. A vector file still needs a header, as in a bit-mapped file, to specify such matters as the type of file, the version, the starting point of the image data and whether or not it has been compressed.

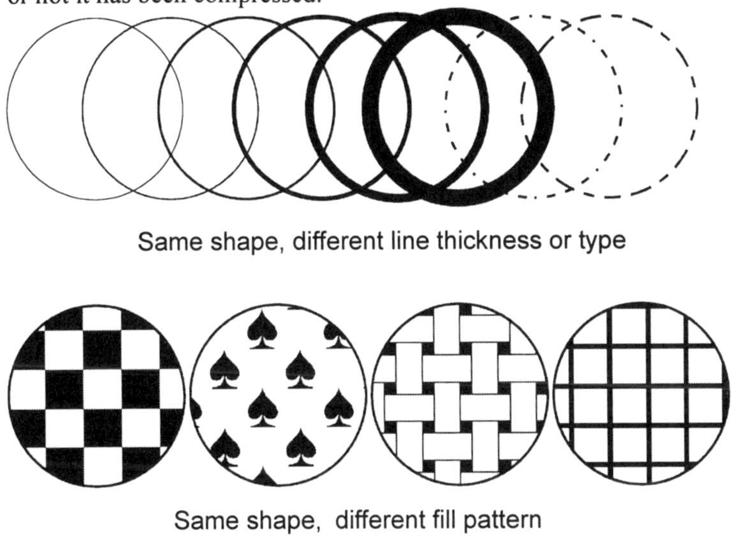

Fig. 6.6 *Some attributes of a shape – line thickness, line type and fill pattern. Other attributes include colour*

A third type of graphic file – the metafile – should be mentioned here, because a metafile is a file which can store both bit-mapped and vector data. In practice it tends to be used for the storing of vector information only – or for vector files that might have some bit-mapped data added. Four well-known cxamples are the Word-Perfect (WPG), the Computer Graphics Metafile (CGM), the Mac PICT and the Windows Metafile (WMF) formats. The file structure of the last example (WMF) is given below:

Header

- Type of metafile (whether stored in memory or on disk)
- Size of header
- Version of Windows
- Size of metafile
- Number of objects in the file
- Maximum record size
- Number of parameters (not used – set to zero)

Data Records

- Record 1
- Record 2
- Record 3
- etc

Each record contains:
- Size of record
- Record type
- Parameters
- End of record marker

It can be seen that the header contains information similar to that stored in the header of a bit-mapped file. The data, however, consists of a separate record for each object that makes up the image. The form of a record is simple: the length of the record (so that it is possible to determine where each one ends and the next begins), the type of record and the parameters associated with that record. The record type identifies what sort of 'instruction' is being given to the computer.

Examples of this include:
- Arc (draw an arc),
- Ellipse (draw an ellipse),
- Rectangle (draw a rectangle) and
- SetBkColour (set the background colour)

Each of these instructions needs extra information in order to be implemented and these extra pieces of information are called the parameters. For example, Arc would need the parameters that defined where the centre of the arc is to be, what the radius is and at what angles the arc is to stop and start. SetBkColour, on the other hand would only need one parameter – the colour code.

In order for an image to be created on the screen the computer must 'know' how actually to draw these shapes. In the case of the Windows operating system this information is contained in the Windows GDI (Graphic Device Interface). This is a set of 'functions' – software sub-routines – which are part of Windows and contain the details of how each shape is drawn. One of these functions is called BitBlt and this is can be used to cater for any bit-mapped images that might be part of the metafile.

6.10 Encapsulated PostScript (EPS) Files

EPS is an interesting example of a vector file format. PostScript, as described in Chapter 5, is a PDL (Page Description Language) which has sophisticated font-handling capabilities, but the line description functions can be used to create a graphics file. Unlike other vector files the EPS file takes the form of a computer program – just like normal PostScript output to a printer. If a simple graphic, drawn in a vector drawing package, is saved as a EPS file and that file then examined in a text editor the result is something like this:

```
%!PS-Adobe-2.0 EPSF-2.0
%%BoundingBox: 2215 2438 2542 2519
%%Creator: CorelDRAW!
%%Title: RECT1.EPS from CorelDRAW!
%%CreationDate: Tue Oct 28 15:29:22 1997
```

```
%%DocumentProcessColors: Cyan Magenta Yellow Black
%%DocumentFonts:
%%EndComments
%%BeginSetup
/AutoFlatness false def
% Options: Emulsion Up
% Options: Print Positive Output
/SepsColor false def
/ATraps false def
%%EndSetup
%%BeginProlog
/Corelreg true def
% Copyright (c)1992, 1993 Corel Corporation. All rights reserved.
/wCorel4Dict 300 dict def wCorel4Dict begin/bd{bind def}bind def/ld{load def}
```

It should be noted that this is only the opening section of the file, but it can be seen that this is clearly a fragment of a computer program. In fact the graphic specified by this file was created in CorelDRAW, as can be seen by the last few lines of this fragment. One of the differences between a 'normal' PostScript file – one that is used to produce printed output from a word processor, for example – and an EPS file is that an encapsulated file is confined to describing a single page. The second line of the printed fragment defines the 'bounding box' which limits the size of the image. It is possible to do a simple experiment to demonstrate how the graphic is actually stored. If a very simple shape is drawn – here it was a rectangle – and the end of the file is examined in a text editor it is possible to find the five lines that actually specify the dimensions of the rectangle. They are not shown in the printed fragment but they look like the following set of 10 numbers:

2220.98	2514.60
2537.42	2514.60
2537.42	2443.32
2220.98	2443.32
2220.98	2514.60

These are sets of x and y co-ordinates for the four corners of the rectangle and specify the four strokes that must be drawn to draw the four sides (see Fig. 6.7). Thus the lines represent:

x_1, y_1 = the first corner

x_2, y_2 = the second corner

x_3, y_3 = the third corner

x_4, y_4 = the fourth corner

x_1, y_1 = the first corner, again

and the length of the sides can be calculated from pairs of consecutive lines:

$$x_2 - x_1 = 2537.42 - 2220.98 = 316.44$$
$$y_2 - y_3 = 2514.60 - 2443.32 = 71.28$$
$$x_3 - x_4 = 2537.42 - 2220.98 = 316.44$$
$$y_1 - y_4 = 2514.60 - 2443.32 = 71.28$$

This portion of the program, therefore, is simply a set of instructions to draw the rectangle which are just like the ones that might drive a pen-plotter: draw a line from x_1, y_1 to x_2, y_2; draw a line from x_2, y_2 to x_3, y_3 etc.

An unusual feature of EPS files is that they can be saved with a bit-mapped version of the image (called a 'preview' image and often taking the form of a TIFF file). This enables an EPS image to be seen on a screen, despite the fact that the display screen is not a PostScript device. Of course the quality of this preview image will not compare with the quality of the final printed image – it is the equivalent of a bit-mapped screen font – but it does enable the user to visualize the final version.

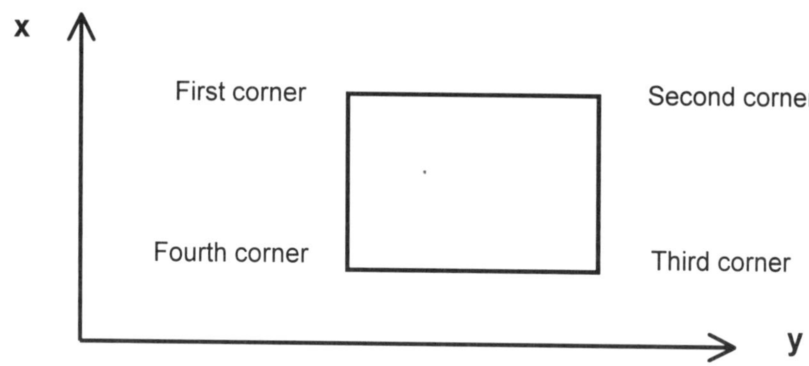

Fig. 6.7 *The four corners of the rectangle, in the order specified in the EPS file*

6.11 Lossy Compression

Most graphics file formats involve compressing the image to reduce the storage space associated with the file and it has been taken for granted in the discussion so far that the original data that constituted the image can be recovered at any time by reversing the compression process. This is sometimes called 'loss-less' compression to indicate that nothing is lost in the process of compression. There are, however, compression techniques that are called 'lossy' techniques because data is actually lost in the process of compression. It might be wondered why it should be considered acceptable or even advantageous to 'throw away' information. The advantage of a lossy technique is that the compression can be made more efficient; the final file can be made smaller than by a loss-less method.

The reason that this is acceptable in many cases is that not all image data is actually required in some applications. These are usually situations where the eye is not capable of detecting some of the image data that is stored in a graphics file and so there is no reason for retaining it. The two standard compression algorithms that are based on this philosophy are called JPEG and MPEG. JPEG (Joint Photographic

Fig. 6.8 *Loss of quality in lossy compression. An image has been saved using loss-less compression (on the left) and then using lossy compression (on the right)*

Experts Group) compression is most suitable for scanned photographs where there are usually a large number of colours, often involving many shades of the same colour. This is a type of image that does not compress very well using the sort of compression algorithms discussed earlier in the chapter because they are based on the assumption that there will be a significant amount of repetition from one pixel to another. In any case, many early bit-mapped formats did not support more than 256 colours (8-bit colour) and the development of modern display systems, larger memories and faster processors has led to a demand for what is sometimes called 'true-colour' (24-bit colour) images and file formats to support them.

Now, the eye is less sensitive to small changes in colour than it is to small changes in grey-level. JPEG compression therefore involves converting the image to a YUV format. This is the type of format used in broadcasting TV images where the Y component represents the luminance (brightness) and U and V components represent the chrominance (colour) parts of the image. The advantage of this is that it now becomes possible to store the colour information in less detail than the brightness information. For example, the colour information of every other pixel may be thrown away but the brightness variations are retained. This means that every alternate pixel is treated as if it had the same colour as the previous pixel. A second stage of the process detects how frequently pixel colour and grey-level values are changing across a block of 8 by 8 pixels so that the rapidly changing components can be discarded but the more gradual changes retained. The final stage uses Huffman encoding to compress the image further, but without loss of information. By this means printed images with 300 dpi resolution can be compressed to up to 25:1 with little noticeable loss of quality. With screen images of lower resolution (70–80 dpi) the equivalent figure is 15:1. Fig. 6.8 shows a simple experiment in which a high-quality photograph (1,000 × 670 pixels and 16.8 million colours) has been saved, first as a BMP file (RBG encoded – that is, without compression) and then as a JPEG file. The original file occupied 1,968 K bytes and the compressed file (compressed at 90:1) was only 23 K bytes. The illustration shows that there is a definite loss of quality (both images have been magnified by a factor of 6 to make this easier to see) but even at this very high compression ratio the result is still fairly acceptable and the file is 85 times smaller. If a smaller compression ratio was used the quality would be significantly better.

The second lossy algorithm, MPEG (Motion Picture Experts Group), is applied to moving images like digitized video. MPEG is different from JPEG for two reasons. One is that moving images often incorporate a sound track and so sound compression is needed. Secondly, changing images offer new ways of reducing data. One simple but important factor is that consecutive images in a video will contain a lot of material in common. If a car is seen to be moving along a road everything in the image may stay the same for many consecutive frames – except for the position of the car itself. Much of the background will remain unchanged from frame to frame and is therefore said to be 'redundant' (not needed because it has already been recorded in an earlier frame). Another factor is that when the eye is looking at a series of rapidly updated images it fails to spot small imperfections in any individual image because they are so soon replaced by the next. This effect can be seen clearly when individual frames from a TV broadcast are examined using a video recorder in 'freeze' mode. They can be seen to be of a much poorer quality than expected, as judged by the usual viewing mode.

With loss-less compression, where there is a choice as to the degree of compression achieved, the 'trade-off' is between the amount of compression and the speed of compression (and decompression). With lossy compression there is a different trade-off, between the amount of compression and the amount of data lost (and therefore the quality of the image when it is recovered).

6.12 Fractal Compression

The term fractal is the name coined by a mathematician Benoit Mandelbrot for a class of mathematical functions that have fascinating properties – particularly when viewed as images. The best known is the 'Mandelbrot set' but many others exist. The Mandelbrot set can be generated either as the full set (as in the first image in Fig. 6.9) or in varying degrees of detail – as if magnified – though in practice a new set of calculations is required to produce each image. The surprising thing is that the same basic shape repeats itself over and over again as the magnification increases and it was realized that, in this way, fractals mimic many natural shapes. For example, a satellite view of the coastline of a country shows a characteristic shape of inlets, bays and promontories which is repeated over and over again – in smaller scale –as the view zooms in. This phenomenon in which the same pattern seems to be repeated at different scales has been called 'self similarity'. It means, for example, that a close-up photograph of small broken rocks might be indistinguishable from a much more distant picture of a rocky cliff.

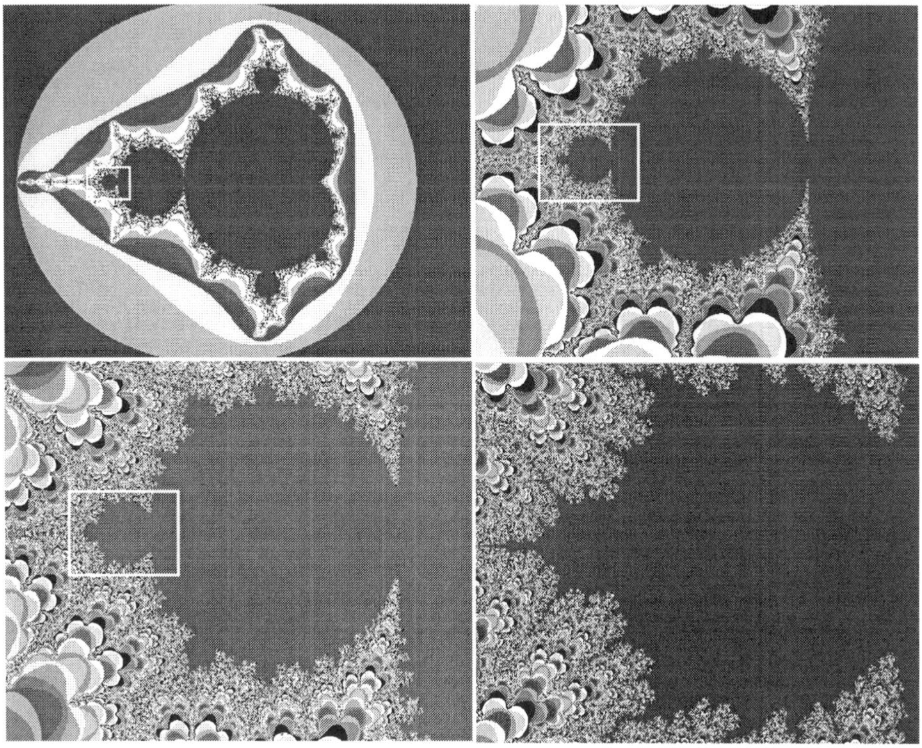

Fig. 6.9 The Mandelbrot set: the first picture (top left) shows the full set. Each subsequent picture (left to right, top to bottom) is an enlarged portion of the previous one (see white rectangles)

The same sort of effect is often seen in biological organisms – like trees which show the same basic pattern of branching at many different levels. The whole tree has its major branches, but similar-shaped minor branches grow out of major branches, and twigs grow out of minor branches and, in some cases, even the leaves have a similar structure.

This observation has led to the development of methods of computer simulation of the shapes of natural objects (see the section on 3-D modelling) but another mathematician suggested that the reverse ought also to be true. It should be possible to take pictures of natural objects and detect the fractal mathematics underlying those shapes and so store the information in a highly compressed form.

Fractal compression, like JPEG and MPEG techniques, is a lossy method but has the advantage over them that the degradation in the quality of the image at higher compression ratios is less obvious. It differs from them also in that it is an asymmetric technique. Because of the huge amount of mathematical processes involved in finding formulae which describe the underlying patterns in the original image the compression process can take a long time. On the other hand, the decompression process can be very fast. For example an experiment, in which an image was compressed and then decompressed, first using JPEG and then using fractal methods, produced the following figures: the JPEG process took 41 seconds (in both directions); the fractal process took 8 minutes to compress but only 7 seconds to decompress. This means that fractal methods can be ideal for archived images (for example in a CD-ROM encyclopaedia) where they are compressed only once by the publisher but decompressed many times – whenever the user wishes to see the image. Here the asymmetry is actually an advantage since the fast stage is the one which is performed many times by a user (with a relatively low-level computer) whereas the slow stage is performed only once by the provider who can afford to increase the compression speed by the use of a very powerful computer equipped with special hardware designed for fractal compression.

6.13 Stand-alone Compression Software

Although the principles of file compression are not unique to graphics files, the sheer size of graphics and video files makes all aspects of compression of particular interest to practitioners in the field of computer graphics. Compression software comes in many forms. There is, firstly, the software which users do not even realize they are using – those discussed so far, in fact – because they are built into graphics application software like drawing or painting packages. These automatically compress and decompress graphics data as they save, load, import and export files in PCX, WMF, CGM, BMP etc. formats.

Secondly there is software that is sold as stand-alone data compression software which can be used to compress any data, not just graphics files, but which must be consciously and deliberately used – it is not a hidden process. Some excellent examples of this type are distributed as 'Shareware', to be paid for and registered if used regularly but easily obtainable for evaluation. This type of software usually uses variations on the LZW compression techniques which have been described already and is capable of compressing graphics files even further. For example a simple experiment was done with a bit-mapped file which consisted of 642 by 543 pixels. It was created in a graphics package which provided a palette of 256 colours though this particular image was created using only 8 colours. The result was that, though it occupied $642 \times 543 \times 1 = 340$ K bytes in memory, it reduced down to only 31 K bytes when saved as an RLE encoded BMP file. This degree of compression is not surprising because with only 8 colours being used there are long strings of pixels with the same colour. However when this image was further compressed using a well known compression package it occupied only 11 Kbytes – a further saving of 67%. An obvious question is: Why was this degree of compression not achieved when is was saved as a BMP file, since RLE encoding is a compression technique? The simple answer is that the algorithm used in the special compression software is more efficient (in terms of the degree of compression) than the one used in the BMP file format and is probably patented and so not available to be incorporated into the BMP format. Another answer is that good compression software usually offers a number of options to the user. The more efficient ones take longer to compress the file than the less efficient ones and the less efficient ones are faster; the user can choose. In a file format like BMP the emphasis tends to be on speed since the user may not even realize that any compression is happening.

A third type of file compression is sometimes called 'on-the-fly' compression. This is a system in which all the files on a storage disk are compressed into a single file so as make more effective use of the disk. The software is often sold under a slogan like 'double your disk space'. Like the compression algorithms used in graphics file formats, the user does not need to know they are using compression methods. When a file is required it is automatically decompressed, and when saved, automatically compressed again 'on the fly' (that is with little or no delay, and only when required).

6.14 File-Type Conversion

There are so many different types of graphics files that it is inevitable that problems will arise because the user will find that the file is of the 'wrong' type. For example, an image is to be incorporated into a document in a word processor or desktop publishing package but the software only accepts BMP or PCX files and the image happens to be a TIFF or GIF. Software designers try to reduce this problem as much as possible by building in format converters into their products. For example, the word processor I am using to write this book will accept 16 different graphics file

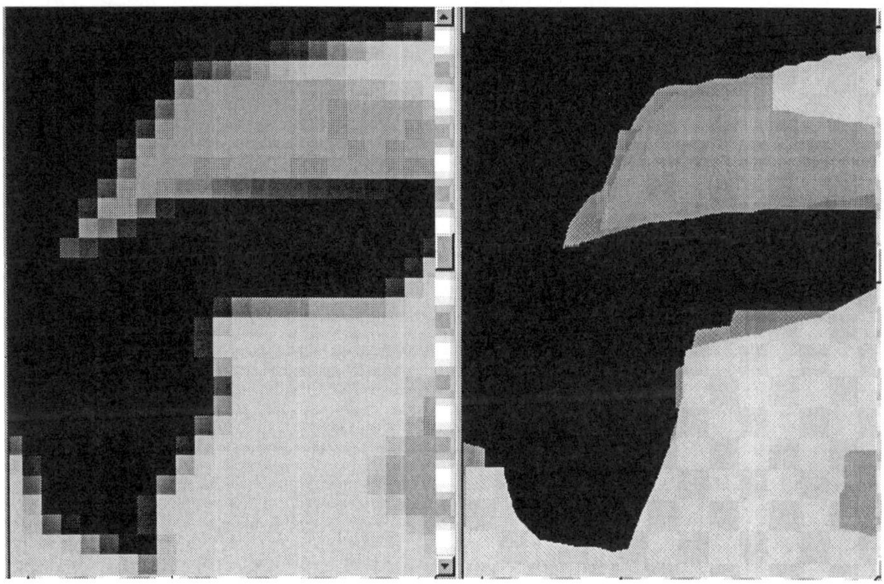

Fig. 6.10 Detail from a bit-mapped image (left) which has then been traced to produce a vector image

formats. This facility is sometimes called an 'import' facility and it implies that, whatever format the software uses as its standard one for handling graphics, it can convert many other formats to that standard. There is a limit, however, to what is practical and this means there is a market for specialized utility software which is designed to convert a wide range of formats, one to the other. Such a package might handle up to 60 different formats and if it were capable of converting any one format into any other this would involve $60 \times 59 = 3540$ different conversion algorithms; the general formula is n × (n–1) where n is the number of formats. In practice it is much more sensible to use one format as a 'half-way-house' and write conversion algorithms into and out of that. If CGM, for example, was chosen as the intermediary format then 60 programs would be written to convert any format to CGM and an equal number to convert CGM to any format = 120 conversions in all, instead of 3540. All conversions involve two stages and might take twice as long as a single purpose-built conversion but the process becomes a much more practical proposition.

This type of software may offer facilities for both bit-mapped and vector images but will probably only convert bit-mapped files to other bit-mapped files and vector files to other vector files or metafiles. In principle, it is not a problem to convert a vector format to a bit-mapped format, at the resolution of the screen display. This is essentially the same process as 'grabbing' a screen display – taking a copy of whatever is on the screen and saving it as a file. If a vector file was used to create the screen display and it is then saved as a bit-mapped file then a conversion from vector to bitmap has taken place. Of course a great deal of information will probably be lost in the process since a vector file can store all manner of information that might not be displayed in any one screen view but that is inevitable in this type of conversion.Conversion in the other direction – bitmap to vector – is a much more difficult process but special software does exist to perform it. This type of 'tracing' software must perform the same type of task as when a child traces an image like a photograph. Using a transparent overlay – like tracing paper – the child draws lines around the important components of the image to produce a line-image which contains copies of all the important shapes which were in the original. A bit-mapped image, like a photograph, will contain many grey-levels or colours and the person (or computer) that produces a trace must therefore identify those boundaries between different colours or grey-levels which are important to the image. Tracing software does this and then fits a mathematical curve to those boundaries. Sometimes a significant amount of human intervention is needed at this stage to choose which of the various lines which have been created are really important, since too many curves are sometimes created and the image needs to be simplified by deleting some of them. Only the human brain can decide which of them are wanted. In the same way human intervention is sometimes needed to decide how complicated these curves need to be. They frequently need to be simplified – which sometimes means re-tracing the original image using a different set of parameters and sometimes involves an editing process using a vector drawing package.

6.15 Summary of Common File Types

Finally, from the dozens of graphics file formats which exist, 21 commonly used examples have been chosen for brief comment:

Format	Type	Comments
Adobe PhotoShop (PSD)	Bitmap	One of the many formats associated with a leading software application – in this case, a photographic retouching package.

AutoCad (DXF)	Vector	Associated with the leading CAD package; widely used for exchanging CAD and other vector files.
AutoDesk Animator (FLI)	Bitmap	Used for storing animated images.
Computer Graphics Metafile (CGM)	Metafile	Developed by two standards organizations as a platform-independent interchange format.
Encapsulated PostScript (EPS)	Metafile	Encoded in a subset of the PostScript 'Page Description Language'.
Fax	Bitmap	There are many fax formats (more than 20) but they are very similar, RLE encoded systems like PCX and TIFF.
Graphics Interchange Format (GIF)	Bitmap	Designed by CompuServe Inc. for the storage and transfer of multiple bitmaps over the Internet. Uses LZW compression.
JPEG	Bitmap	Strictly speaking a method of lossy compression standardized by the Joint Photographic Experts Group but now associated with a file interchange format also.
Kodak Photo CD	Bitmap	A system for storing scanned images in a number of different resolutions (usually 6) from 64 × 96 pixels ('postage stamp') to 2048 × 3072 pixels ('professional').
Lotus PIC	Vector	Devised to store graphs generated by the spreadsheet program Lotus 1-2-3.
Macintosh Paint	Bitmap	The first bitmap format devised for Apple Macs (and therefore monochrome only).
Macintosh PICT	Metafile	Associated with the 'QuickDraw' drawing tools supplied with the Macintosh.
Microsoft Windows Bitmap (BMP)	Bitmap	Associated with Microsoft 'Windows' graphic interface and so in wide use.
Microsoft Windows Metafile (WMF)	Metafile	Used for vector images in 'Windows'.
MPEG	Video/ Audio	Used for storing compressed video & audio data to a standard set by the Motion Picture Experts Group.
PCX	Bitmap	One of the earliest, and most widely used bitmap formats; associated with ZSoft's 'PC Paintbrush' program.
QuickTime	Video/ Audio	Devised for storing compressed video & audio data on the Apple Mac but also used for 'Windows'.

Targa Image File (TGA)	Bitmap	An example of a format devised by a hardware company; Targa make a line of graphics adapters.
Tag Image File Format (TIFF)	Bitmap	Devised by Aldus Corp. for monochrome images created by scanners and DTP programs; now incorporates colour.
WordPerfect Graphics Metafile (WPG)	Metafile	Devised by the WordPerfect Corp. for its word processing and graphics software

In summary, the table illustrates:

- how much overlap there is in graphics file formats – there are many formats which do the same thing
- the different origins of formats – some devised by software companies, some (fewer) by hardware companies, some by service companies and others by standards organizations
- the relevance of the platform – some are found on only one hardware platform (e.g. Macintosh) while others span a number of platforms
- the importance of colour – some handle only monochrome images, others colour, others only a few colours, others moving images.

The table does not attempt to show any detail but it should be realized that there are some very important features which might not be realized at first – such as the fact that some formats will only handle 256 colours while others can store 'true-colour' images (16.8 million colours).

Exercises for the Reader:

(1) Look at all the computer software you have access to and identify what graphics file formats it can handle. The software need not be 'graphic software' like a painting package; modern word processors and spreadsheets will import graphics files. To identify the types of files a package can deal with you will have to find the facility for 'importing' or 'inserting' graphics and then look at the dialogue box that it displays which enables you to choose the file. There will usually be a 'filter' that can be set to particular file types. Alternatively the manual or help system should list the types that it can handle. Sometimes a package will be able to import more types than it can export (or vice versa).

(2) Do your own experiments on bit-mapped graphic images – of the type described at the start of the chapter. Save an image in as many different versions as you can and record the file size. To do this you will need either:

- a file-conversion utility or
- a graphics package that has a range of 'export' or 'save-as' facilities.

In the absence of both of these it might be possible to use a number of different non-graphics packages of the sort that can incorporate graphics.

(3) To understand the results, repeat the experiment with different types of image. The images can be created by you in a graphics package or you can use clip-art, but you should be able to see very real differences in the file size according to the following factors:
   - the number of colours (both the theoretical maximum that the format supports and the number actually used);
   - the number of pixels;
   - the type of image – photographs as compared with simple stylized images with many consecutive pixels having the same colour;
   - the file format.

(4) This and the next exercise need a simple text viewer of the sort described earlier in the chapter – one that will display each byte in the file as a hexadecimal number. There are a number of shareware editors of this sort that are distributed on the CD-ROMs attached to computer magazines or can be downloaded from the Internet. There is also a copy of DEBUG supplied with Microsoft DOS. If you can find a graphics package that will save images in RAW format create a fairly simple image, save it as a RAW file and then see if you can see the connection between the bytes in the file and the coloured pixels on the screen. An alternative, for programmers, would be to 'look directly' at the contents of the display buffer with the aid of a simple piece of code (for example in BASIC, the PEEK statement can be used to display the contents of any byte of memory). You will need to know the memory location of the beginning of the refresh buffer to do this. For those with less technical or programming knowledge, some utility software will display the contents of memory locations.

(5) Now save some files in BMP format (with and without RLE compression if possible) and use the information given in the chapter to explore how the file headers and the data section of the file relate to the images. Use a simple image (at least to begin with) to make it easier to unravel the information.

(6) Draw a very simple shape in a vector drawing package, save it as an EPS file, and try to work out how the final lines of the file relate to your image.

(7) Save a bit-mapped image in both a loss-less format (like BMP or PCX) and then in a lossy format (like a JPEG). Carefully examine the same magnified area in each file, displayed in a paint package and try to identify the differences. What has been lost in the lossy file and how much saving in file size has been achieved?

(8) Try compressing (further) a series of file types using general-purpose compression software like PKZip or WinZip. How much more saving is achieved and how long did it take ? Are there examples where the 'compressed' file is actually bigger?

7

Graphics Algorithms

7.1 Introduction

Chapter 1 contains a general description of the principles used in storing images, in coded form, in the refresh-buffer of a raster scan display system. There has, however, been no discussion so far of the process by which the coding is actually done. Take, for example, the simple case of a monochrome display of a straight line, created in a vector-based drawing package. It should be clear that each pixel on the screen will have a corresponding bit set in the refresh-buffer. It should also be clear that the position of the line has been defined in the application software by the x and y co-ordinates of the two ends of that line. What is not clear is how these two are connected. How, given the co-ordinates of the end points, does the software calculate which pixels should be set to the foreground colour and which bits in the refresh buffer will therefore be assigned the appropriate colour code (Fig. 7.1)?

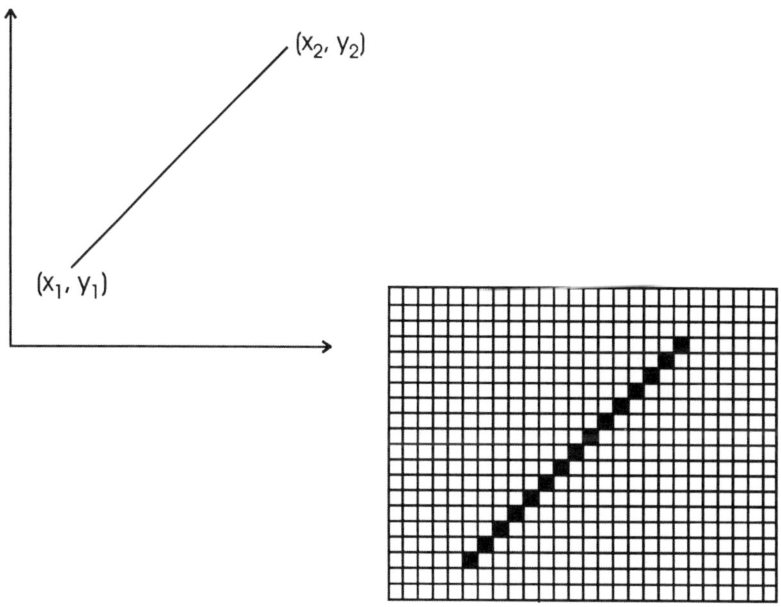

***Fig. 7.1** How does the computer translate a straight line, defined in terms of co-ordinates, into a series of pixels ?*

First we must establish that there are two different types of question to be answered here. One concerns activities that are common to all graphics applications. Consider, for an example, the case of an existing image – say a colour photograph – which is scanned using a document scanner. Once the data is acquired it can be taken for granted that systems software exists that will store the data in a file on a magnetic disk, say, and similarly there must be some standard way that the same data can be copied into the refresh-buffer such that the image will appear correctly on the screen. However, suppose that the image, having been displayed, is to be changed in order to 'sharpen' it. This requires specialist algorithms available only in photo-retouching software. The first type of algorithm is a basic one which relates to all images and is best handled by standard systems software; the second type of algorithm is highly application-dependent. This chapter is concerned with both, but with an emphasis on the second type of algorithm. However, since there are many different types of graphic software and many different ways that graphic shapes can be created and manipulated, only a selection of these can be discussed. The important point is to start thinking in terms of algorithms – a logical sequence of steps that will produce the desired result. First things first, however. How is information concerning text and graphics actually stored in the refresh buffer?

7.2 Systems-Level Algorithms

7.2.1 Colour codes and the refresh-buffer

This discussion is based around the standard S-VGA graphics adapter used in the PC, but similar considerations will, of course, apply in other adapters and other computers. The first thing to realize is that a graphics adapter can operate in many different modes – some of them only of historical interest and included only for reasons of backwards-compatibility – so that old software can still be used. S-VGA has 28 modes – 23 are bit-mapped graphics modes and 5 are text-only modes. The graphics modes cover a range of different resolutions – 320 × 200, 640 × 400, 640 × 480, 800 × 600, 1024 × 768, 1080 × 1024 and 1280 × 1024 pixels – each of which may offer a number of different colour palettes, from 2 to 16.8 million. In general, the higher the resolution the smaller the number of colours, the exact number depending on the amount of video memory fitted.

The second important point is to understand how the data stored in the refresh buffer (the colour codes) relate to the colour of the pixels on the screen. In early monochrome, two-colour (one bit-per-pixel) systems this was simple. Each bit in the refresh buffer could be on or off and the electron gun in the CRT could also be either on or off and so there was a simple correspondence between software and hardware: bit on/pixel on, bit off/pixel off. This simplicity continued with early colour systems also. An eight colour (three bits-per-pixel) system used each bit to code the state of each of the three electron guns – red, green and blue (again, either on or off, for each gun).

Life became more complicated, however, when CRTs were introduced with electron guns that could be set to intermediate intensities – somewhere between on and off. This meant that a much wider range of coloured shades could be generated but in many cases there was no longer any obvious relationship between the state of the bits in the refresh buffer and the state of the electron guns in the CRT. There are exceptions to this rule, of course. For example, if three bytes are assigned to each pixel and each of the electron guns can be set to 256 different intensity levels, then one byte (which can exist in 256 binary states) can be assigned to each primary colour (each electron gun) and every state of that byte corresponds to one of the 256 possible intensity states of that gun. Where there is no simple relationship like this, however, the data in the refresh buffer can be thought of as a series of arbitrary colour codes. The device that is used to connect these codes to the state of the hardware is the CLUT (Colour Look-Up Table) or LUT – already introduced in Chapter 4.

In considering the S-VGA graphics adapter we will consider seven different colour options. The simplest, the two-colour mode, has been discussed already. It would require only one bit per pixel and should have no need for a CLUT (see Fig. 7.2). Although two-colour systems were common in the early graphics systems, where memory was at a premium, they are no longer necessary since any modern graphics adapter will have sufficient refresh-buffer to offer at least 16 colours even in its highest resolution mode, and considerably more in the lower-resolution modes. This doesn't mean that modern computers cannot run software written for the early two-colour systems, only that they are able to display more; at least 14 colours will be 'wasted'.

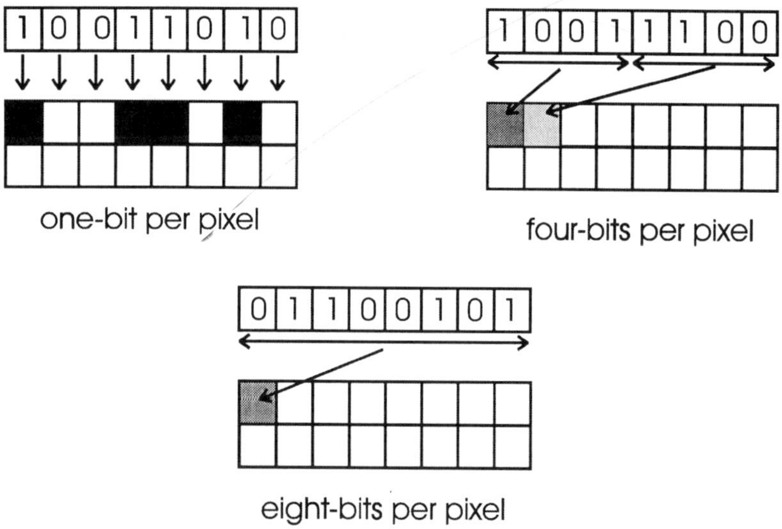

Fig. 7.2 One-bit per pixel systems can only display two colours. Four-bit and eight-bit systems can display 16 and 256 colours respectively

The next two common modes are the 16 colour mode which uses four bits per pixel and the 256 colour mode (eight-bits per pixel). In the first, each byte in the refresh-buffer stores the colour codes for two adjacent pixels and in the second, each byte stores the code for only one pixel (see Fig. 7.2). In both cases the digital colour codes must be converted into analogue red, green and blue intensity signals by a DAC (Digital to Analogue Converter). Modern graphics adapters use three eight-bit DACs, each one capable of outputting 256 different intensity levels to one of the CRT guns and, therefore, of producing 16.8 million colours in total. In lower-colour modes, like these two, the CLUT is needed to define the restricted palette of colours actually available. The CLUT is a specialized type of memory chip (or part of a chip) which when addressed by data from the refresh buffer outputs a three-byte (24-bit) word which is fed to the three DACs. This means that, for example, a 256-colour code (with eight-bits per pixel) can be used to generate a 24-bit signal suitable to a hardware system capable of displaying 16.8 million colours (see Fig. 7.3). Which 16 (or 256) colours are actually generated depends on the contents of the CLUT – and these can be changed at any time to produce a different palette.

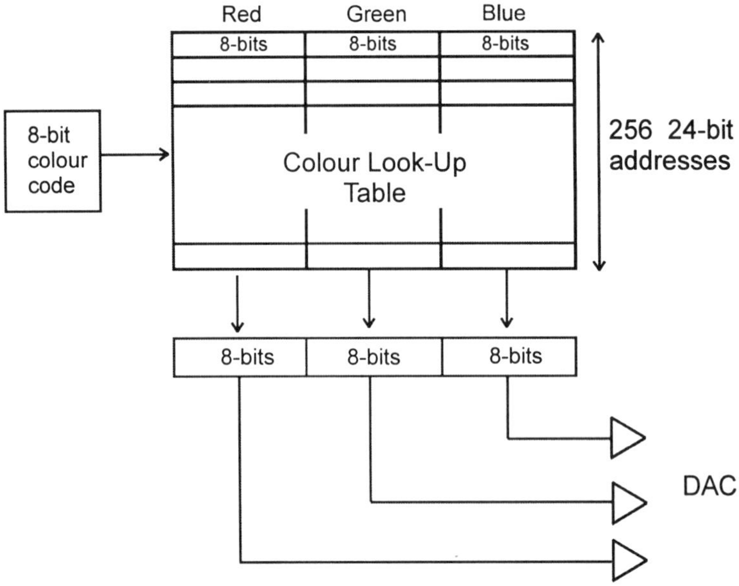

Fig. 7.3 *An eight-bit colour code is used as an address for a 24-bit word which generates three separate analogue colour signals (using three DACs)*

The next three modes are, the 32,768 colour (15-bits per pixel) mode, the 65,536 colour (16-bits per pixel mode) and the 16.8 million (24-bits per pixel) mode. In the first two – sometimes referred to as 'high-colour' – two bytes are reserved for each pixel, one bit being unused in the case of the 15-bit mode. In the third – sometimes called 'true-colour' – three bytes are reserved for each pixel. It should be clear that the third mode does not need a CLUT since the three bytes can be used to drive the DACs directly. In fact the 15-bit and 16-bit modes also bypass the CLUT. In the 15-bit system, each primary colour in each pixel has five bits assigned to it and these are used to drive the high-order values of the DAC. This means that the lowest three bits of the DAC are not used at all and therefore the very darkest intensity values of each primary colour are unused in the display. The 16-bit system is similar except that green is assigned six bits instead of five, on the principle that the eye is most sensitive to green.

It might seem that 24-bit colour (16.8 million colours) should be enough, since the eye cannot detect that number of different shades but, in fact, 32-bit colour systems are becoming common. Sometimes the extra byte is used for extra colours (as with professional-level scanners – see the chapter on hardware). Sometimes the extra byte is used for other types of information, and this will be discussed later.

7.2.2 Bit planes and colour depth

It should be clear from the above discussion that though images are stored in the refresh buffer in digital form they must be converted into analogue form before they are fed to the CRT display – that, of course, is the function of the DACs. It follows therefore that in a full colour system one third of the data in the refresh buffer must be linked to one DAC (say the red one), one third to another (the green), one third to another (the blue). For this reason it is helpful to think of the refresh buffer as being divided into separate zones or planes ('bit planes'). For example, in a one-bit-per-pixel system the bits are thought of as all lying in one plane. In a two-bit-per-pixel system they can be thought of as being in two planes – like two monochrome refresh buffers. In a three-bit system they are in three planes – one for each primary colour. One way of visualizing this last system is to imagine the three planes as if they were like pages of a book, or better, like transparent sheets of film. One sheet of film has all the red portions of the image, the second sheet has all the green portions and the third has all the blue. If they are overlaid so that the points on each film that correspond to the same part of the image match up, then the complete colour image is obtained (Fig. 7.4). Of course, when more than three bits are used per pixel then two or more planes can be used to store each of the red, green or blue portions of an image and more than one plane will feed a single DAC. One term that arises from this way of organizing data is that of colour 'depth'. A three-bit-per-pixel system is said to have a colour depth of three – it has three bit-planes.

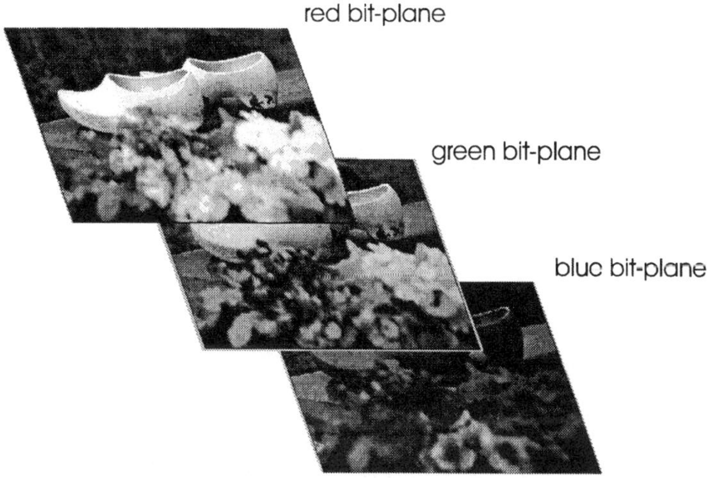

Fig. 7.4 *A picture divided into three bit-planes. One contains all the red components, one contains the green and one the blue*

One of the advantages of organizing the data in bit-planes lies in the way that images can be manipulated by changing the values in the look-up-tables rather than by changing the data itself. Suppose one bit-plane stored an image of blue text characters and the others stored the rest of the image. It would then be possible to make the text flash on and off simply by re-setting the value in the CLUT which corresponded to that shade of blue. The contents of one address in the CLUT are used to 'interpret' the meaning of one colour code and, by changing that one value, all instances of the colour are re-defined – in this case as visible or invisible – without changing all the bits in the buffer that actually describe the text itself. This sort of effect is discussed later in the section on animation.

7.2.3 Text-only modes

It might seem surprising that there are text-only modes in the modern graphics adapter. In fact the reasons are largely historical – mostly to maintain backwards compatibility – but it should not be forgotten that computers are still used for non-graphical purposes. Some users are content to use a non-graphical interface (like Microsoft DOS) and want to continue to use DOS-based software, which has still been sold until very recently. For these purposes a text-only mode is fine and has the advantage that it can run satisfactorily on the lowest-specification computer. 'Text-only' is not in fact the best name for these modes. It would be more accurate to call them 'byte-mapped' display systems (as compared with 'bit-mapped') in which graphics are restricted to a limited range of pre-formed shapes, each of which consists of a standard-sized rectangle made of many pixels. For most users these pre-formed shapes are characters from the 'system font' provided with the computer, stored in a ROM. Each alphanumeric character (alphabetic or numeric character), has its bit-pattern recorded in ROM. They are displayed either by the use of the keyboard or by means of a programming language statement that issues the appropriate one byte code (normally the ASCII code).

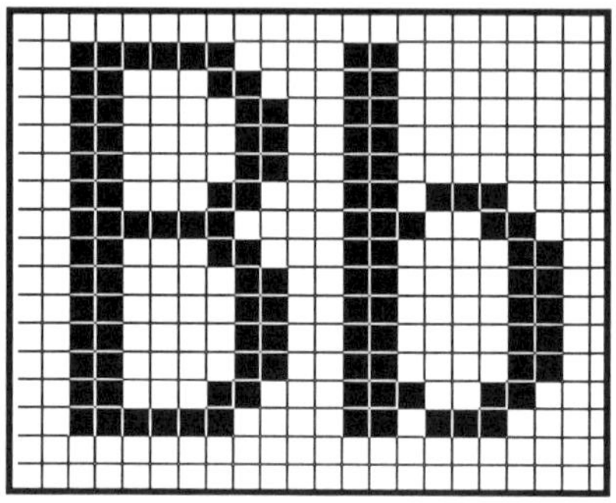

Fig. 7.5 *Two characters from the bit-mapped system font*

The important distinction, then, is that in graphics modes each screen pixel is under separate control and has one or more bits assigned to its colour code, but in text-only mode rectangular groups of pixels (the characters) are pre-defined and assigned a one-byte code. The reasons for the use of text modes in early systems lay in the efficient use of memory. Consider the example where each character occupies a block of 9 × 14 pixels (see Fig. 7.5) and the screen can fit 80 characters to a row and 25 rows to a screen. This, in fact corresponds to an early system called 'Hercules', after the manufacturer who created the standard, and used a screen with 720 × 350 pixels. A bit-mapped screen, even monochrome like the Hercules system, needed 720 × 350 / 8 = 31,500 bytes (one-bit-per-pixel). The text only system (one byte per character) needed only 80 × 25 = 2,000 bytes. This huge saving in memory was paid for by the comparative inflexibility of the system. The only shapes allowed are those that are pre-defined in the ROM, are constructed of blocks of 9 × 14 pixels and are placed in positions defined by a grid of 80 columns and 25 rows.

However, the one-byte per character system does allow for 256 different graphic shapes and only a small proportion are taken up by alphanumerics. The rest can be any useful shape – playing card symbols, small quarter-character-sized blocks, printer's marks and accented letters, for example. The smaller, quarter-sized blocks can be used for simple graphics if enough shapes are available. It is not enough to have the obvious minimum – four, corresponding to a 'mini-block' in each corner of the standard rectangle. It is also necessary to have all possible combinations of two

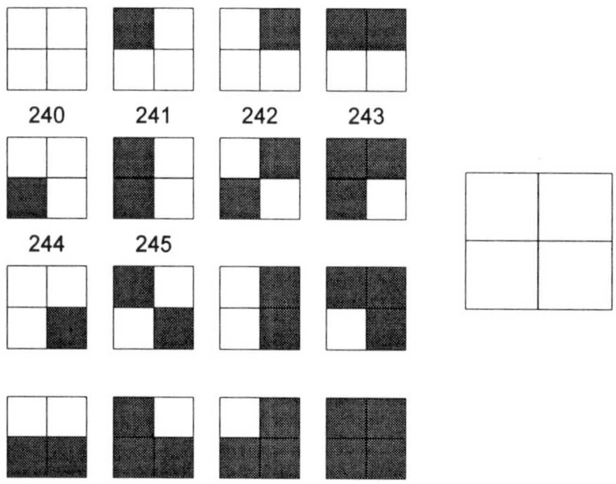

or three mini-blocks as well. In total $2^4 = 16$ characters was needed to cover all possibilities (see Fig. 7.6). With these, a crude graphics system became available with an effective resolution of 160 × 50 (80 × 2 and 25 × 2). Some ingenuity is needed to use these shapes. The reason for this is that the mini-blocks are not independent entities. Suppose that, at some stage of a graph plotting exercise, for example, the top-left-hand mini-block at a particular character position had been displayed using its appropriate code, 241 (Fig. 7.6). It now becomes necessary to switch on the bottom-right mini-block at that same character space. This creates a problem because if the code corresponding to a bottom-right-hand block, 248, is sent to the appropriate byte in the refresh buffer it would displace the code currently stored there, causing the top-left-hand block to disappear from the display. Only one code at a time can be stored in the byte corresponding to one character space. What is needed is a system, such that on every occasion that a new mini-block is to be added to the display, the code, if any, already stored in the byte that coded for that position be examined – so that it is possible to work out which new symbol would represent a combination of the existing symbol and the one to be added.

Table 7.1 *Binary codes for two symbols are combined using the Boolean OR*

Code for existing symbol	11110001	(decimal 241)
Code for new symbol	11111000	(decimal 248)
Code for resultant symbol	11111001	(decimal 249)

This is actually easier than it might appear – by making use of the Boolean logic operation OR. The numbers allocated to the symbols are chosen in such a way that when the code for the new symbol is OR-ed with the code for the symbol already present the result is the code for the symbol which combines the previous two. Careful examination of the binary version of the codes for the symbols in Table 7.1 shows how this is possible. To take the example considered above: the code for a top-left block is 241 (binary 11110001) and the code for a bottom-right block is 248 (binary 11111000). The result of a logical OR operation between these two is binary 11111001 (decimal 249), which is the code for the correct composite symbol. Fig. 7.6 and Table 7.2 show how this system works. Each of the four mini-blocks has assigned to it a different binary digit to code whether it is off (zero) or on (one). Only four are needed, the least-significant bits, so the most-significant four bits are all set to 1. Thus, bit 0 codes for the top-left, bit 1 for the top-right, bit 2 for the bottom-left and bit 3 for the bottom-right. Use of the OR operation ensures that when symbols are added, all the bits which are set in the two component symbols remain set in the composite symbol. The PC text-mode does not have mini-blocks, as described here, but does have a wide variety of graphic symbols including Greek letters and other accented letters. The Teletext system (described below) is a good example of one using mini-blocks to provide simple graphics.

Table 7.2 *How the mini-blocks are coded*

How used	Not used	Not used	Not used	Not used	Bottom right	Bottom left	Top right	Top left
Decimal	128	64	32	16	8	4	2	1
Binary	1	1	1	1				

If a colour text-only system is required then, as with true-graphics, more memory is usually required. Each character is assigned two bytes – one for the character code and one for the colour (or 'attribute') code. This might be expected to provide 256 different colours – and in a sense it does – but when the colour code must apply to the whole of the character the details are different. In a bit-mapped system the colour code applies to the individual pixel but in a byte-mapped system the code applies to the whole character which has two quite different elements – the foreground and the background. The foreground consists of all the pixels that constitute the shape of the character; the background corresponds to all the others. Table 7.3 shows how the colour code byte in the PC text-only system is used.

Table 7.3 *How colours are coded using the attribute byte*

Bit number	7	6	5	4	3	2	1	0
Colour	Flashing	Red	Green	Blue	Intensity	Red	Green	Blue
	Foreground	Background			Foreground			

The background is assigned three bits (one for red, one for green and one for blue) which means that the background can be one of eight colours. The foreground similarly can have one of eight colours (three bits) but a fourth bit is assigned to the foreground to determine the intensity of those colours so that in fact 16 shades are available (for example, blue and pale blue). The last bit is used to determine if the character is steady or flashing ('blinking'). Using this table it can be seen that the colour code for, say, a red character against a green background (no reduction in intensity and no flashing) must be: 00100100 (binary) = 32 + 4 = 36 (decimal).

It is very easy, and quite instructive, to explore this text-based display mode in the PC using the programming language BASIC (see the next chapter for more on graphics programming). Fortunately a version of BASIC is provided with Microsoft Windows. This is called QBASIC and is found in the DOS sub-directory. It is a DOS-based program and so a full-screen DOS window should be opened – or the computer set to run in DOS mode, which can be done in both Windows 3.1 and in Windows 95/98. There are two reasons for choosing to use BASIC for these experiments. One is that QBASIC is provided with Microsoft Windows at no extra cost so everyone with a PC is likely to have a copy. Second, QBASIC provides two useful statements: POKE and PEEK. POKE can be used to put colour codes into the refresh buffer to see what effect this has on the display. PEEK can be used to do the reverse – to examine the contents of the refresh buffer to see which codes are producing any particular effect that can be seen on the screen. Finally, the mainly blank DOS screen is ideal for seeing which pixels are 'lit-up' when a particular code is applied.

To do these simple experiments it is necessary to know the starting address of the refresh buffer. For the text-only mode this is B800 (in hex). The following simple QBASIC program will illustrate the way to explore text mode:

```
SCREEN 0             ' select the text-only mode
CLS                  ' clear the screen
DEF SEG = &HB800     ' set the starting address for the video buffer
POKE 0, 65           ' 0 = address of first byte in video buffer; 65 = ASCII
                     ' code for A
POKE 1, 1            ' 1 = address of first attribute byte; 1 = code for blue
                     ' foreground
```

Line 1 selects the text-only mode.
Line 2 uses CLS to clear the screen so that there is no confusion about what the effect of the rest of the program has on the display.
Line 3 defines which block (segment) of the memory is to be used by the POKE statements. The symbols &H establish that the address is specified in hex. Once a DEF SEG (Define Segment) statement is used in this way all addresses used by the POKE statement are relative to that starting address, not absolute addresses.
Lines 4 and 5 use POKE statements which take the form: POKE *address*, *code*.

In this example the fourth line pokes the ASCII code for the letter capital A (65) into the first byte in the refresh buffer – corresponding to the first position on the screen – the top-left corner. The next line pokes an attribute code into the attribute byte associated with that character. It should be remembered when doing these experiments that each character has two bytes – the first for the character code and the second for the colour code. Check with the table of the attribute bits to see why 1 (which is in decimal) in the attribute byte produces a blue letter against a black background. Changing this value will produce other colour combinations. Changing the data value that is poked into the address changes the character that is displayed; refer to an ASCII table to see the correspondence between codes and characters. Changing the address itself (to any other valid even number) changes the position on the screen where the character is displayed. The valid numbers are those in the range which corresponds to 24 lines of 80 characters each. 80 characters require 160 bytes so the maximum number of bytes is $160 \times 24 = 3840$ and the range of addresses is 0 – 3839.

7.2.4 Teletext

In addition to the use of text-only modes for running DOS programmes a similar system is used in Teletext broadcasts (Ceefax and Oracle in the UK). This has the general features already described, together with facilities for double-height text, flashing symbols and mini-blocks which are one-sixth the size of the standard character. The Teletext system, however, uses a different method of changing the colour of the characters from the one described in the previous section. The display system uses only one byte in the refresh-buffer, per character, in order to make the most economical use of the spare broadcasting capacity which Teletext facilities depend on. It uses these bytes to store not only character codes but also attribute codes. An attribute code in this case is a code which specifies the colour, height and other characteristics of the displayed symbols. An individual byte, of course, can only store one code.

T	h	e		N	e	w	s		F	o	r

84	104	101	132	78	101	119	115	32	70	111	114

Fig. 7.7 *The use of embedded codes in Teletext. The code 132 changes the colour of the text which follows to red*

The character codes are used in the normal way. The attribute code, however, has the effect of switching on (or off) the colour characteristics of all the characters that follow it in any one line – very like control codes sent to a text-only printer. It can be thought of as an invisible embedded control code (Fig. 7.7). They are invisible, for obvious reasons – they do not produce a readable character at that point on the screen. They are embedded in the sense that they occupy a byte in the middle of the text – and so cause a blank character-sized space in the display. This means that they must be fitted into natural spaces between words or other symbols (acting as spaces in fact) or used only at the beginning of lines. If two attributes are to be changed then two bytes will be needed and two blank spaces will result. The system clearly has the drawback that colour or other attributes cannot be changed in the middle of a word, without creating an unwanted blank space. It means, though, that colour and other attribute information need not be associated with the storage of each individual character and only half the memory space is required – the same as for a monochrome system. Once an attribute has been changed it stays changed for all the characters in that line but must be reset at the beginning of the next line.

Code = 190 +

1	2
4	8
16	32

Fig. 7.8 *Coding Teletext mini-blocks*

The mini-blocks in the Teletext system are one-sixth the size of a complete character, which gives better spatial resolution than the one-quarter size blocks described in the previous section. The size is ultimately restricted by memory considerations. This will be apparent if it is recalled that the programmer needs to be able to call upon a full set of character-sized symbols which contain all possible combinations of mini-blocks. In the case of quarter-sized mini-blocks this needs 16 characters but in the case of one-sixth sized mini-blocks this involves 2^6= 64 characters. Any attempt to create a system with smaller mini-blocks (e.g. one-eighth sized) would need even more character codes(2^8=256) and would be too much for a system which assigns only one byte to code for all available characters. The coding for the Teletext system is similar to that already described, except that six bits are needed to code for the 6 mini-blocks. The numbers 1, 2, 4, 8, 16 and 32 are assigned to the six individual mini-blocks and the codes for the 58 other combinations are obtained simply by adding up the codes of those blocks which are to be switched on (Fig. 7.8). Exactly the same method can be used for predicting the code for mini-block characters in the system described earlier if due account is taken for the offset in the number system; the codes begin at 240 and so 240 must be added to the values obtained by adding up the 1, 2, 4 and 8 values of the individual mini-blocks (Fig. 7.6). Teletext symbols begin at an offset of 190.

7.2.5 Bit-mapped modes

Unlike the text-only modes, the bit-mapped modes provide total control over every pixel on the screen by assigning each of them one or more bits in the refresh-buffer. The simple experiment described earlier, using QBASIC, can be extended to look at the way that these modes work. The difference is that instead of choosing SCREEN 0, the sample programs below use SCREEN 1 and SCREEN 2. These correspond to the modes offered in the very first graphics system available in the PC – the Colour

Graphics Adapter (CGA). This system looks archaic to modern eyes (it is) but it has the two advantages of being very simple, and of using relatively large pixels which are easier to see. SCREEN 1 corresponds to a 640 × 200 two-colour mode (black and white) and SCREEN 2 corresponds to a 320 × 200 pixel four-colour mode.

Here is the simplest program to switch on one pixel in the high-resolution mode :

```
SCREEN 2            ' select the two colour bit-mapped mode
CLS                 ' clear the screen
DEF SEG = &HB800    ' set starting address for video buffer
POKE 0, 1           ' 0 = address of first byte in video buffer; 1 pixel
                    ' switched on
```

Line 1 is different from the previous program; it switches on the two colour bit-mapped mode.
Lines 2 & 3 are the same as before.
Line 4 could be identical to that in the previous program but would, of course, have a totally different effect. A code of 65, instead of displaying the letter A, would switch on a series of pixels in a horizontal line. For simplicity we begin, however, by poking the value 1 rather than 65 into the first byte and the result is to switch on one pixel (white, in a two-colour mode) at the top left of the screen. This matches the text-only result where addressing also began at the top left. This mode uses one-bit-per-pixel so a 0 in any bit results in a black pixel and a 1 results in a white pixel. Each byte codes for a total of eight pixels so that the code 1 (decimal), which corresponds to 00000001 (binary), switches seven pixels off (black) and one on (white).

Note: with monitors which are not of the highest quality the pixels in the corners are more likely to show colour fringing, which is more noticeable when single pixels are turned on against a black background. If an address around 4040 is used instead, this will place the pixel in the middle of the screen and reduce fringing effects. This is quite important when we turn to colours other than black and white and the remaining programs will use this address (or an equivalent one when the mode is changed).

When only one pixel is switched on it is not easy to see which pixel, out of the eight possible ones, it actually is. If the program is extended by adding a loop, however, so that all the pixels are turned on and off in sequence, it becomes possible to see how the pixels are spatially ordered:

```
SCREEN 2
CLS
DEF SEG = &HB800
FOR N = 0 to 255
POKE 4040, N
SLEEP 1
NEXT N
```

The POKE statement is placed inside a loop and the value of N used as the data to be poked into the first byte in the buffer. The SLEEP statement (line 6) suspends the cycle for one second each time the loop is executed; otherwise the whole sequence, on a modern computer, would be over in a tiny fraction of a second. This programme will take 256 seconds (over 4 minutes) to run – with every possible combination of the eight bits – so it is probably better to reduce the cycle to N = 1 TO 30 (half a minute). This is enough to see the important point of the exercise, which is that as the data value increases the pixels build up from right to left. This means that the mapping must be as in Table 7.4.

Table 7.4 *How the bits relate to the pixels in a 1-bit-per-pixel mode*

Bits	7	6	5	4	3	2	1	0
Pixels	Left end							Right end

To predict the way that the pixels light up and switch off it is necessary to write out a truth table, looking like Table 7.5.

Table 7.5 *A truth table for three pixels, corresponding to the least significant three bits in a byte*

Pixel 2	Pixel 1	Pixel 0
0	0	0
0	0	1
0	1	0
0	1	1
1	0	0
1	0	1
1	1	0
1	1	1

This table represents the first eight cycles in the loop and each 0 corresponds to a pixel that is off (black) and each 1 to a pixel that is on (white).

In general, to set any one bit without affecting the others we must POKE *address*, 2^n where *address* is the byte address (the address of the byte) and n = the number of the bit, from 0 to 7. Thus the first bit is set with POKE *address*, 1 (since $2^0 = 1$) ; the second with POKE *address*, 2 (since $2^1 = 2$) ; the third with POKE *address*, 4 (since $2^2 = 4$) ; the fourth with POKE *address*, 8 (since $2^3 = 8$), and so on.

It is clear that any programmer wishing to write graphics software by accessing the refresh buffer directly will need to know a lot of fiddly details since common sense would not necessarily have predicted that the switching of the pixels would be from right to left, in any one byte, when the switching of the bytes themselves is left to right (as in the text-only mode). In reality, most programmers are able to use high-level languages which take care of these details automatically. Only the programmers who write the high-level language compilers need to worry about such things.

If the program is modified to use SCREEN 1 (the four-colour mode) then the coding of colour can be revealed using a similar program. It can probably be guessed, at this stage, that this mode will allocate 2 bits to every pixel in the following way :

Bit 7	Bit 6	Bit 5	Bit 4	Bit 3	Bit 2	Bit 1	Bit 0
Pixel 3		Pixel 2		Pixel 1		Pixel 0	

If so, the first four lines in Table 7.5 will correspond to the four colours available in Pixel 0 (with all other pixels switched to their first colour – black). The second four lines will correspond to a second cycle of those same four colours in Pixel 0, this time with Pixel 1 switched to its second colour. If the truth table were continued for another cycle of four values then the same thing would occur but with the second pixel switched to its third colour.

The following program confirms this for two cycles :

```
SCREEN 1              ' select four-colour bit-mapped mode
CLS
DEF SEG = &HB800
FOR N = 0 to 7        ' cycle through first 8 combinations in the truth table
POKE 4040, N
SLEEP 1
NEXT N
```

7.3 Application-Dependent Algorithms

So far we have considered only the most basic algorithms which place text characters and colour codes in the refresh-buffer. Now we must move on to a higher-level which, for example, takes vector-descriptions of graphic objects and establish where on the screen the corresponding pixels ought to be. This process is called scan-conversion or rasterization. The use of the word conversion draws our attention to the fact that though vector descriptions of graphic shapes come more naturally to us – and this is the way they are usually specified by the user – the raster scan display needs a bit-mapped equivalent of these shapes and therefore algorithms must be devised to do the conversion from one description to the other. These algorithms could be incorporated into the applications software but the most fundamental ones are normally implemented in the operating system – to be called by any program which needs them. For the fastest response times they can be implemented in specialist firmware in graphics chips.

7.3.1 Displaying a point

The position of a point is usually specified with reference to a Cartesian co-ordinate system – the origin of the co-ordinate system normally being placed at the bottom-left corner of the graph (see Fig. 7.1). Some programming languages use the top-left corner of the screen for the origin of the graphics co-ordinate system to keep in line with the text co-ordinates; text of course begins in the top left of the screen. One part of the algorithm therefore might have to convert from one system to another by subtracting all the y co-ordinate values (the vertical measurements) from a number which is equivalent to the height of the display, in pixels.

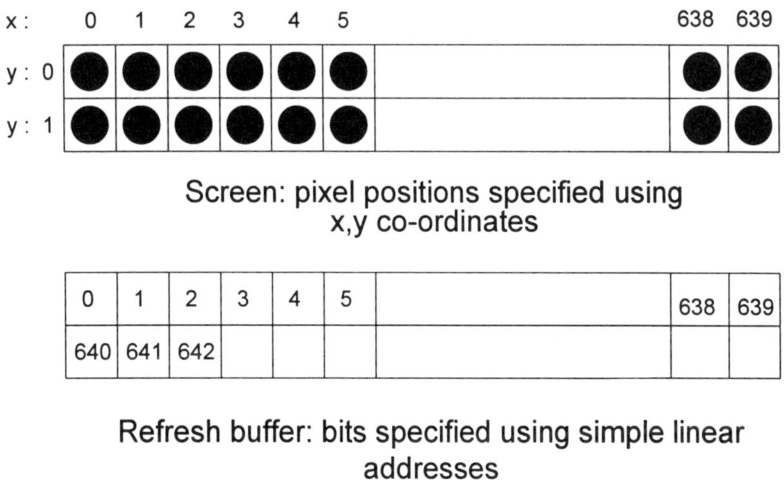

Fig. 7.9 *The simplest way of calculating the address of the bit in the refresh buffer that corresponds to a particular pixel in the display*

For simplicity consider a one-bit per pixel system. Let the refresh buffer begin at address 0 and, for the moment, treat the refresh buffer as if each bit had its own address, these addresses reading from left to right across the scan lines. Of course, memory is addressed in bytes and we now know that bits within bytes are addressed from right to left, but we can, initially, assign our own addressing system at the bit level and then convert back to the conventional system later. We will assume that the display allows 640 pixels per row (from position x = 0 to x = 639) and 200 pixels per column (from y = 0 to y = 199), as in the CGA system we have been using. We will also work with the origin of the co-ordinates at the top of the screen.

A pixel at the x = 0, y = 0 position (the origin of the co-ordinate system) corresponds to a bit switched on at bit-address 0; a pixel at position x = 1, y = 0 (the next one to the right) corresponds to address 0 + 1; and so on (Fig. 7.9 shows the first two rows). The last pixel in the top row corresponds to address 0 + 639. The first pixel in the second row (x = 0, y = 1) must correspond to address 0 + 640. From these and similar examples we can see that the general algorithm for finding the memory location for any pixel in any row involves

- adding to the start address (0, in this case) a number equal to (the number of filled rows) × (the number of pixels per row)
- adding to that, a number corresponding to the position of the relevant pixel in that final, partially filled, row.

(We can generalize this for a system which begins with the address N by simply substituting N for the initial 0.) Thus, in this case, for co-ordinate x, y, the address =

0 + (y × 640) + x . Where, say, x = 2 and y = 2 then the address = 0 + (2 × 640) + 2 = 0 + 1282. It should be noticed that this formula works only if the co-ordinate system treats the first values in both x and y as being zero. If the first values in x and y are 1 then a small adjustment must be made to the formula : substitute x – 1 and y – 1 for the values of x and y. Having established the principle it is now possible to make the necessary corrections and additions.

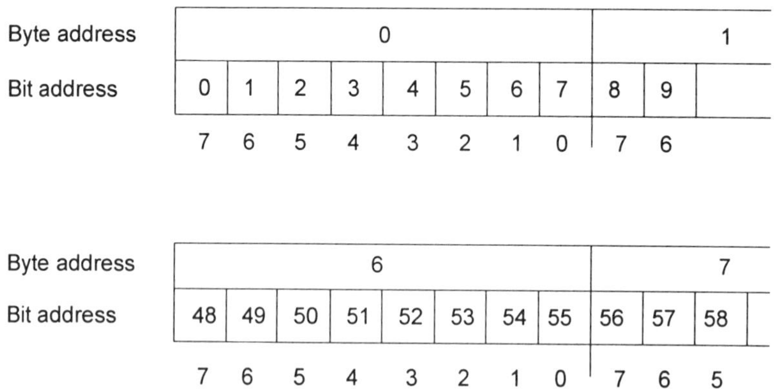

***Fig.** 7.10 Calculating which byte a bit is in, starting from a 'bit-address'*

First, to deal with the problem of byte-addressing already raised. Since eight bits constitute a byte then the address generated by the above formula must be divided by eight to give the address of the byte in which the particular bit is located. It is convenient to ignore the start address (0 or N) for the purposes of this calculation. N is effectively an offset address in bytes specifying where in the memory map of the computer the refresh-buffer begins. Because it is in bytes it makes our calculations less complicated if we drop it while we convert our bit-address into a byte-address and then add it back at the end of our calculations. In any case, in the BASIC programs we have been looking at, we have made N the offset address by setting:

DEF SEG = N

and have been able to forget about it for the rest of the program. We must also now take account of the reverse ordering of the bits (they are conventionally labelled right-to-left and we have been treating them as reading left-to-right).

If the bit-address is exactly divisible by 8 then the number obtained by dividing the bit-address by 8 is the byte-address and the bit of interest is the first bit in the byte when numbered left-to-right. See the top half of Fig. 7.10 for the simplest case – where the bit-address = 8. This means it is the so-called 'most-significant bit' in the byte (i.e. bit 7, when numbered right-to-left and starting with a zero). In the more general case the division is not exact and produces a remainder. Suppose the bit-address is 58. The division of 58 by 8 produces 7 with a remainder of 2. The number 7 indicates the byte-address; the remainder (2) indicates that the bit is the third in that byte (reading from the left) – see the bottom half of Fig. 7.10. This means it must be bit number 5, when measured from the right and starting with zero.

In a good modern BASIC or in Pascal the two numbers used above can be obtained directly by using DIV and MOD operators. DIV is an integer division operator which is used to divide two integers and generate an integer solution – that is, it ignores any remainder. MOD is complementary – it does the same thing but generates only the remainder. (Note that in Microsoft QBASIC and Visual BASIC the symbol for DIV is \ which should not be confused with the symbol for normal division, /).

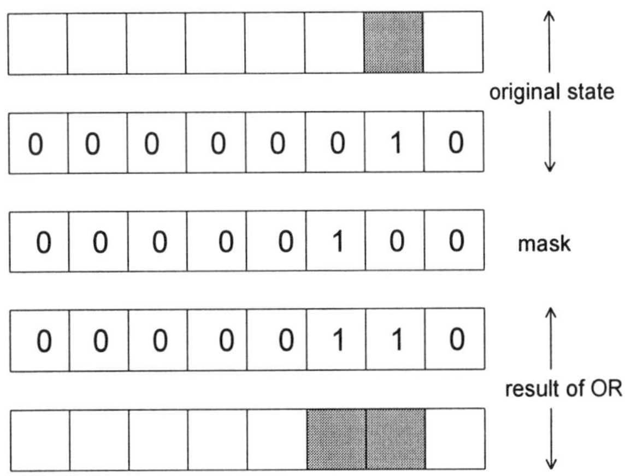

Fig. 7.11 *Using a mask and the logical OR operation to change individual bits*

There is one more complication. If we wish to experiment with this algorithm using the POKE statement, as before, we must note that simple data transfer statements like POKE do not work at the bit-level either. When a number is stored in the refresh buffer by poking a byte the operation potentially changes all the bits in that byte. Any number which might be stored in that location before the operation is lost. For example, suppose that a particular byte in the refresh-buffer has its second least significant bit 'set' signifying that a particular pixel on the screen is on (top two lines of Fig. 7.11). In numerical terms the byte stores the number 2 (decimal) which corresponds to 00000010 in binary (see second line of Fig. 7.11). It is now required to set the next most significant bit in order to switch on the next pixel. This could be done by storing the number 4 (00000100 in binary) in that byte but that would switch off the first pixel. What we really want is to have both pixels on – the equivalent to storing the number 6 (= 00000110 in binary). In order to alter one pixel of a display without changing other pixels unintentionally it is therefore necessary to use some method of changing one specified bit within a memory location without altering other bits within the same byte, and for this a simple 'store' or POKE-type of operation on its own is clearly not suitable. It can however be done by using the logical operation OR between the original state of the byte and a suitable mask – exactly the same method as described earlier in an earlier section for switching on mini-blocks.

The original state of the byte contains a number of set bits (coded 1) none of which must be changed by the operation. A mask is another byte which contains only one bit set – in the appropriate position – all other bits being reset to zero. OR operations between the zeroes in the mask and either zeroes or ones in the equivalent positions in the original byte leaves those bits unchanged. The only change which occurs, results from the OR operation between the only bit in the mask which is set and the corresponding re-set bit in the memory location. This then is the only bit whose state is changed.

It should be possible on the basis of this discussion to write a program which will accept x and y co-ordinates and using a POKE-type statement switch on any pixel on the screen without affecting any other – at least for a one-bit per pixel display. The following portions of the program are written for the two-colour CGA mode:

```
INPUT x                     'input x co-ordinate
INPUT y                     'input y co-ordinate
LET PD = (y*640) + x        'PD = the pixel displacement
LET NB = PD \ 8             'NB = number of complete bytes
LET NP = PD MOD 8           'NP = number of bits (pixels) remaining
```

This portion of the program calculates the number of pixels – and therefore the number of bits – from the starting address and then uses this value (called PD) to calculate how many complete bytes (NB) and how many bits (and therefore pixels) are remaining (NP) – if any. The number NB corresponds to the byte *address*; NP provides all that is needed to calculate which number should be poked at that address to set the correct bit :

```
POKE NB, 2 ^ (7 – NP)
```

Note: The symbol ^ in BASIC indicates that a number is raised to a power (called exponentiation); so x ^ y in BASIC is the same as x^y in normal algebra.

This line pokes the correct value into the byte after allowing for the reverse-order of the bit-addressing and the 'first' bit corresponding to zero. Thus, if the remainder is 2, as in the example discussed earlier (see Fig. 7.10) then (7 – NP) = 5 and the POKE command will switch on the third bit from the left with POKE *address,* 32 (since 2^5 = 32 = 00100000 in binary). When the number divides exactly then (7 – NP) = 7 – 0 = 7 and 2^7 = 128 = 10000000 in binary and the most significant bit is set.

The final refinement is to use the OR operation to ensure that no existing data in the refresh-buffer is overwritten. This means that the POKE statement printed above must be modified. Suppose that the existing contents of the *address* were already 8 (this corresponds to the 4th bit from the right being set).

Bit	7	6	5	4	3	2	1	0
Decimal value	128	65	32	16	8	4	2	1
					x			

The 'x' signifies that the corresponding bit is set.

Without altering the 4th bit from the right, we wish to set the 2nd bit:

Bit	7	6	5	4	3	2	1	0
Decimal value	128	65	32	16	8	4	2	1
							x	

We must use the form:

POKE *byte address*, ((PEEK *byte address)* OR *value*)

Where *value* is the data we wish to add to the byte without disturbing the current data. In this case (PEEK *byte address*) will return the value 8 and so POKE (8 OR 2) will result in a final value of 10 which is POKED back into the *byte address*:

Bit	7	6	5	4	3	2	1	0
Decimal value	128	65	32	16	8	4	2	1
					x		x	

It can also be expressed using the binary form:

Existing value	0	0	0	0	0	0	1	0
New value	0	0	0	0	1	0	0	0
Result (OR)	0	0	0	0	1	0	1	0

Thus the POKE statement becomes :

POKE ((PEEK NB) OR NB), 2 ^ (7 – NP)

7.3.2 Modes with more than two colours

To do the same thing for a two-or-more bits per pixel system is not much more difficult. Care must be taken to allow for the fact that a group of bits, not one bit, now codes for one pixel. Thus if it is a two-bit-per-pixel display, then one byte codes for only four pixels, not eight and therefore the bit address must be calculated on that basis. Thus using the figures applied to the previous case, position 0,0 on the screen is coded by bits N and N + 1; position 1,0 is coded by bits N + 2 and N + 3; and so on.

If it is desired to ignore the colour aspect of the problem, then simply treat the sets of bits in the same way that the single bits are treated (as just described) and then alter only the same bit for each set (e.g. the first bit of the pair each time). This means that the same colour is switched on for each pixel.

One final point should be made concerning the efficiency of our algorithm. In a high level language the method specified above uses multiply and divide operations. When implemented in the instruction set of the microprocessor the whole process can be made much quicker by using logical left and right shifts. These are simple operations in which the binary digits in a register are moved or shifted along to the left or right. One such move has the effect of producing a multiplication or division (depending on the direction of shift) by two – in exactly the same way that moving the decimal point one position in a base-ten number multiplies or divides it by ten.

These sort of exercises can be very illuminating about the way that information is stored in a refresh buffer and shows what is involved in even the simplest raster scan-conversion but fortunately for normal high-level language programming the routines for efficient point-plotting statements are built into the computer system and we are not called upon to master these sort of details in our programming. From now on we will use the point-plot statement provided in BASIC (PSET) and no longer POKE values directly into the refresh buffer. This means that there is less advantage in using QBASIC and DOS. Some of the remaining algorithms can therefore be tried in Visual BASIC or Pascal or any other high-level programming language, either in DOS or in Windows.

7.3.3 Drawing a straight line

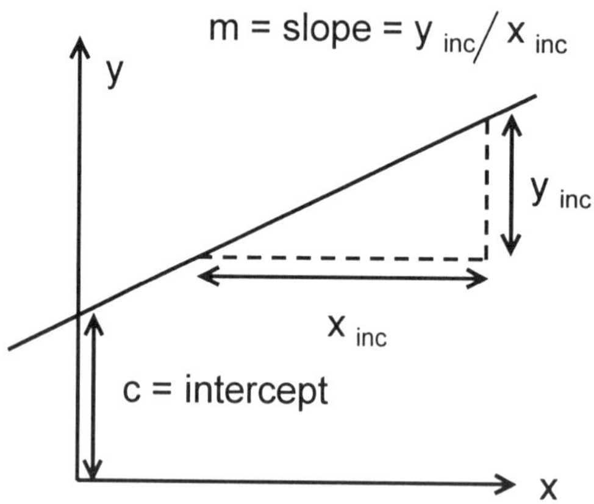

Fig. 7.12 *The equation of a straight line*

Given a statement to plot points it should easy to draw a straight line – or any other shape whose equation is known. In the case of the straight line the equation is:

$$y = m\,x + c$$

The term m signifies the slope of the line (defined as y_{inc} / x_{inc} where these correspond to small incremental values of y and x) and c the intercept of the line with the y axis (Fig. 7.12). Both m and c are constants which can easily be calculated from the initial and final co-ordinates of the line (for details see later). The line can then be drawn by means of a simple loop in which one of the variables, say x, is incremented and for each value of x the value of y is calculated from the equation and the point plotted using the plot-point statement.

However, before treating the general case of a straight line from and to any point on the display let us look at the particular case of horizontal and vertical straight lines. In the case of a one-bit-per-pixel mode, a horizontal line can be drawn simply by setting a number of adjacent bits. The bit corresponding to the first point in the line must be identified using a method similar to that described earlier. Then all that is necessary is to set that bit together with a number of adjacent bits, the number corresponding to the number of pixels in the line.

Drawing a vertical line involves a slightly more complicated version of this method because each pixel on a vertical line is on a different scan-line of the display. Thus if the display uses 640 pixels per line, the adjacent pixels of a vertical line will be 640 bits apart. The algorithm is therefore essentially the same except that instead of setting bits immediately adjacent to the first bit it is necessary to set bits with regular intervals (of 640 in this case).

In the general case, the equation of the straight line is needed. The first part of the program must calculate values of the constants *m* (slope) and *c* (intercept) from values of the endpoints of the line or from any other point known to be on the line, such as: (x_1, y_1) and (x_2, y_2). So, using the equation of a straight line:

$$y_1 = m\,x_1 + c \tag{7.1}$$

$$y_2 = m\,x_2 + c \tag{7.2}$$

therefore

$$m = (y_2 - y_1) / (x_2 - x_1) \tag{7.3}$$

Equation 7.3 is obtained by subtracting equation 7.1 from equation 7.2 and dividing throughout by $(x_2 - x_1)$. We can also show that:

$$c = (x_2 y_1 - x_1 y_2) / (x_2 - x_1) \tag{7.4}$$

Equation 7.4 is obtained by substituting equation 7.3 into equation 7.1 to eliminate the constant *m*.

The algorithm then is:

a. input values of x_1, y_1 and x_2, y_2 (usually the end-points)
b. calculate values of *m* and *c* (as above) which are then stored
c. plot the first point (x_1, y_1) using the plot-point statement
d. using a program loop, starting with the value of $x_1 + 1$ and incrementing x by 1 until the value of x_2 is reached, calculate the appropriate values of y, using the equation $y = m\,x + c$ together with the stored values of *m* and *c*, rounding the y values to integers and plotting with the plot-point statement.

In this example the program loop involved incrementing x but it should be realized that this is only appropriate for lines where the slope *m* is less than 1 (corresponding to an angle of 45 degrees). In plotting a line of steeper slope it would be better to increment y so that there is one pixel for every value of y (Fig. 7.13), otherwise the line will consist of fewer pixels than it might, which will degrade the quality of the line unnecessarily.

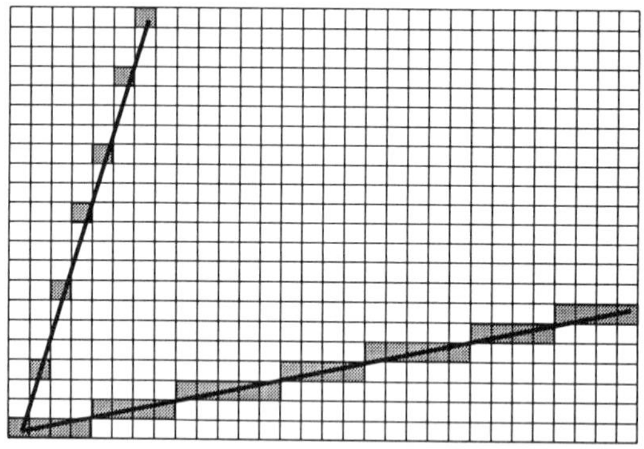

incrementing x

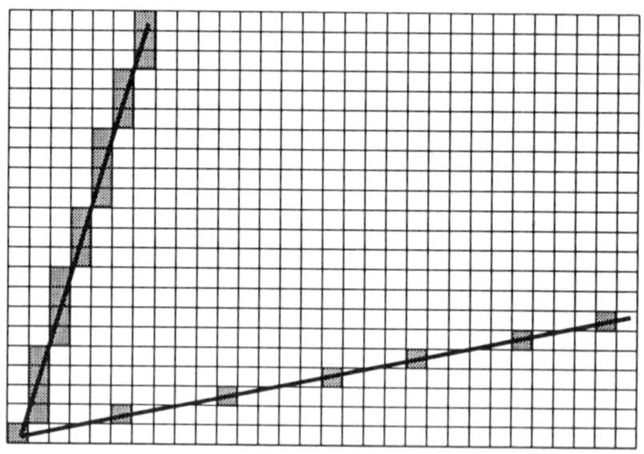

incrementing y

Fig. 7.13 *Two lines drawn, first by incrementing the x values and then by incrementing the y values*

This is an easily understood way of drawing a straight line but the inefficiency of this method will be apparent when it is realized how many floating point calculations and rounding operations are required. Though the values of x and y, needed for the plotting of each point, are integers the constants *m* and *c* are real numbers and the arithmetic involved in calculating each value of y involves:

a. a multiplication between a real number and an integer (*m* x)
b. an addition of two real numbers (*m* x + c)
c. a rounding of the result to obtain an integer value of y.

Plotting a straight line need not be such a lengthy and computationally – intensive process once it is realized that it is not necessary to calculate or make use of the constant c . The reason for this is that once the first point is plotted, using the given values of x_1 and y_1 (one of the endpoints), there is no need to calculate the absolute position in space of the other points – only their positions relative to that first point. The significance of the constant *c* is that it fixes the absolute position of the line in space; the constant *m* then fixes the slope of the line. All that is necessary, once the first point has been plotted, is to calculate the change in x and y values from one point to the next using *m* . This calculation is made much easier when it is realized that the change in one of these, say x, is always unity because of the nature of the incrementing process (a repeated addition or subtraction in value by a fixed amount). This incrementation is a by-product of the raster-scan system and the grid structure of pixels. The principle is simply illustrated by referring back to Fig. 7.12. This example is for a line of slope 1 or less, so x is the variable to be incremented.

The equation of a straight line is used in the form of equation 7.3 (see above) which omits the constant *c* :

$$y_2 - y_1 = m\,(x_2 - x_1)$$

The values x_1, y_1 and x_2, y_2 correspond to the end-points of the line. The quantity y2 – y_1 therefore is equal to the difference in y values between the end and beginning of the line; similarly for $x_2 - x_1$. The same equation, however, applies equally well to any part of the line, such as x_{inc} and y_{inc} (Fig. 7.12) and even the shortest distance – the distance between two adjacent pixels, and so from the diagram:

$$\Delta y = m\,(\Delta x)$$

where the symbol, Δ, the Greek letter delta, indicates a change in the value of the variable which follows it (in this case the change between one pixel and the next).

Thus, once the first point has been plotted, the next point is located using the simple equation :

$$\Delta y = m \quad \text{because, of course, } \Delta x = 1$$

thus :

(the new value of y) = (the old value of y) + m

For the purpose of plotting the point, the value of y must be rounded to the nearest integer but the calculation of each new point is reduced to the simple process of repeated additions of two real numbers, followed by a rounding to obtain the integer value of y.

This process can be coded in a high level language (the subscripts and italics have been omitted in the BASIC program) :

```
INPUT x1                          ' these 4 lines input the end-points of the line
INPUT y1
INPUT x2
INPUT y2
```

```
LET m =  (y2–y1)/(x2–x1)          ' calculate the slope m (also = Δy)
LET total = y1              ' total stores the un-rounded, accumulated value of y
SCREEN 2                          ' two-colour mode
CLS                               ' clear the screen
PSET (x1,y1)                ' plot the first point using the PSET statement
FOR x = x1+1 to x2          ' use loop to increment values of x from 2nd point on
LET total = total +m        ' calculate new value of total using m – Δy
LET ynew = INT(total + 0.5)       ' round value of total to nearest integer
PSET (x, ynew)                    ' plot each new point in turn
NEXT x
```

This exercise reveals an important point concerning the rounding process necessary before plotting. Rounding the values of y (in this case) before plotting is a necessary approximation – part of the raster display method – but it is vital that the calculation of the position of the next point should be based on the accurate value of the position of the previous point not on the rounded (and therefore inaccurate) value. If this is not done then errors can accumulate by adding one approximate value to another. It is important, then, that one of two approaches should be used: either, maintain a running total of the y values (made by adding up the un-rounded values of y) so that each point can be based on an accurate base or, refer all calculations back to the start point. This latter method is not recommended because it means that we must first add $1 \times m$, then $2 \times m$, then $3 \times m$ etc. to the starting value of y and so introduce an undesired extra multiplication into the process. In summary the algorithm is:

a. input values of x_1, y_1 and x_2, y_2
b. calculate value of $m = \Delta$
c. create a running-total variable called *total* ; set it initially to y_1
d. create a variable called *y-new* (for the rounded value of y)
e. plot the first point x_1, y_1
f. add *m* to *total* to create a new value of *total*
g. round value of total and place in *y-new*
h. plot next point using *y-new and* incremented value of x
i. loop back to f, incrementing x by 1 each time
j. continue till x_2 is reached

This is a rather clumsy program. In practice the variables *total* and *y-new* can be condensed into a single variable because point-plotting statements normally accept real numbers and automatically do the necessary rounding, but using two variables initially may make the process clearer.

The process can be made even more efficient by capitalising on the fact that in a raster-scan display there are a very limited number of pre-determined places where points can be plotted. J.E. Bresenham devised an algorithm which simply chooses whether to plot each point in one of two possible positions, on the basis of the position of the previous point together with an easily calculated 'error' term. It is a much more efficient method because the decision is based on simple addition and subtraction and only uses integers. The principle of the algorithm is illustrated in Fig. 7.14.

Suppose that the first point in the line is at x_i, y_i , and that the line has a slope whose value is positive and less than 1, which means that the line is to be plotted by incrementing x. The next point to be plotted can be in only one of two positions: at x_{i+1}, y_i , which is the next point along to the right (the value of y being unchanged) or at x_{i+1}, y_{i+1} which is the position diagonal to the first point (the value of y being incremented by one). The decision must be made by comparing these two options with the 'true' line, that is the ideal line which would be plotted if there were no restrictions on the positions of pixels. The distances of the two possible positions from the ideal position are labelled d_1 and d_2 and so the decision becomes that of calculating whether d_1 is greater than d_2 .

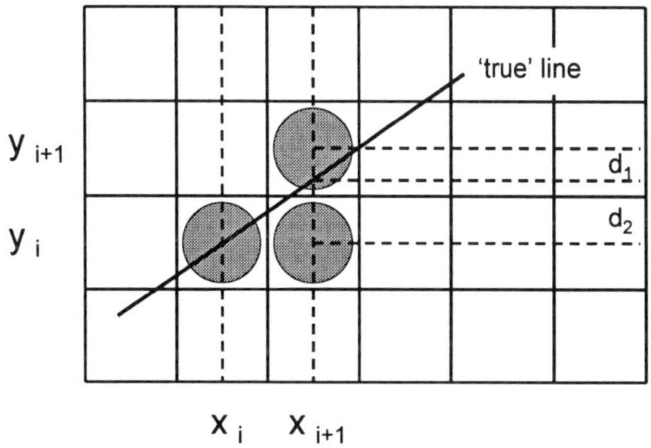

***Fig. 7.14** Bresenham's algorithm for a straight line*

Bresenham designated the difference between these two terms ($d_1 - d_2$) the 'error term' which makes the decision depend on whether $d_1 - d_2$ is positive or negative. He derived algebraically an expression for the error term in terms of Δx and Δy, the changes in x and y. He was able to show that this term changed from one point to the next by one of two increments. One possible increment is $2\ \Delta y$ and the other is $2\ \Delta y - \Delta x$. Which change in the error term is appropriate depends on whether its value is negative or positive at that point. Thus the algorithm is:

a. input endpoints of line : x_1, y_1 and x_2, y_2
b. calculate $\Delta x = x_2 - x_1$ and $\Delta y = y_2 - y_1$
c. calculate two values of change in error term :
    $E_1 = 2\ \Delta y$
    $E_2 = 2\ \Delta y - \Delta x$
d. plot first point (x_1, y_1)
e. initial value of error term $E = E_2$
f. loop (incrementing x); at each position:
    if E = positive: y becomes y + 1 ; E becomes $E + E_2$
    if E = negative: y is unchanged; E becomes $E + E_1$
g. then plot new point

The beauty of the method is that the two values of the change in the error term are efficiently calculated by integer subtractions and a multiplication by 2 (achieved by a simple shift in the binary digits). After that, each re-calculation of the error term is done by binary addition and the decision about where to plot depends only on a check as to whether the error term is positive or not. Only integers are used throughout; no rounding is required. In modern graphics systems this algorithm is implemented in hardware for maximum speed of plotting. Readers who would like to follow the method in more detail – in particular the proof – are advised to consult one of the many algorithm-oriented books on computer graphics.

7.3.4 Drawing filled polygons

With an efficient algorithm for drawing straight lines, drawing empty polygons should be no trouble. An interesting side-line to this is, however, the question of how to draw filled polygons (polygons whose interior is filled with a block of colour to look like a solid shape, or with a fill-pattern).

Fig. 7.15 Drawing a filled rectangle

The simplest case is the rectangle. A filled rectangle whose sides are vertical can be created by continuously drawing horizontal scan lines between the limits set by the maximum and minimum values of x (x_2 and x_1) and continuing to draw all possible lines between the maximum and minimum values of y (y_2 and y_1) – Fig. 7.15. Other shapes are more difficult. A rectangle which is not oriented in such a convenient way can, however, be treated as a pair of right-angled triangles attached along their hypotenuses. Two similar triangles which are not right-angled will make a parallelogram. Two or more non-similar triangles can be used to create a wide range of non-regular polygons. A large number of small angled triangles can even be arranged to make a circle or a segment of a circle. Thus, the facility to produce a filled triangle is the most useful single method and if this is the only one available it can be used to produce many other shapes. The approach to doing this is called the Scan Line method and can be generalized to create many simple geometric shapes. Here, a version of this method is described – applied to an irregular five-sided polygon.

If a simple, solid block-filled polygon is required then, rather than first drawing the boundary and then filling in all the space inside the boundary, it is simpler to bypass the first stage and just draw a series of scan lines designed to begin and end in the appropriate places (as in the case of the filled horizontal rectangle). These places are those points on the end of the scan lines which coincide with the boundary lines. It is therefore necessary to establish for each scan line where these two points are. Fig. 7.16 illustrates the principle. Compare the points where two consecutive scan lines, labelled 1 and 2, cross the straight boundary lines of a polygon. The y values for both ends of line 2 will be 1 less than those of line 1 (assuming each scan line corresponds to one line of pixels). The x values of the end points of line 2 will relate to the x values of the ends of line 1 by the slopes of the two lines. The principle is the same as that described in the discussion of straight-

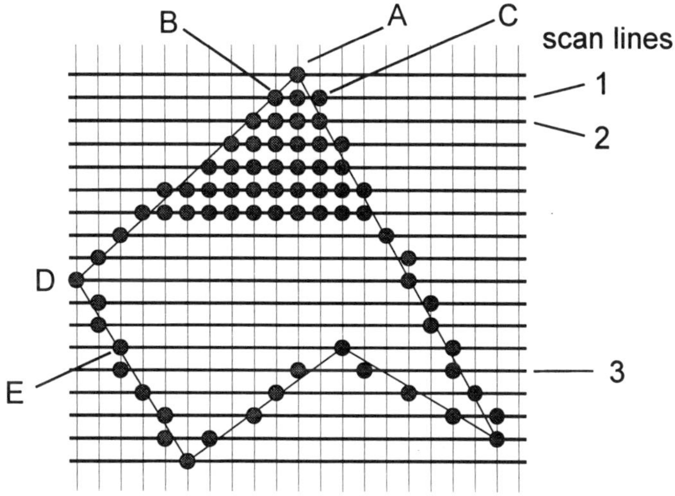

Fig. 7.16 Drawing a filled polygon

line algorithms. The only difference in this case is that here we are incrementing y values and so x changes by $1/m$; in the previous discussion, x was being incremented and y changed by m. Thus, if the value of slope (m) is calculated for each polygon boundary line, it is easy to establish the intersection points with one particular scan line from a knowledge of the equivalent points on the previous line. Then, all that is needed is to fill in all the intervening pixels on each scan line – between the two extremes; the first seven scan lines in Fig. 7.16 are shown filled in.

For this method to be implemented properly it is necessary to know where to begin and also which lines of the polygon are 'active' – that is, those which cross the particular scan line and must be considered at that stage of the scanning process. This is particularly necessary with a complicated shape where more than two lines may be active – see line 3. This information is obtained from a list of all lines making up the polygon which is sorted in order of the 'highest' vertices (i.e. those vertices with the smallest y values – nearest the top of the display). From this it is possible to calculate where to start. This must be on the scan-line immediately below the line containing the highest vertex. From this list of lines it is also possible to establish which lines are active – a list which must be updated at the beginning of each scan-line.

In the case illustrated, the first stage of the algorithm establishes which two of the 5 lines are initially active – that is, meet at the highest vertex (A). The slopes of these two lines are then calculated. Using the incrementation method described for the straight-line algorithm the two points B and C are then established; these are the intersection points of those two lines with the next scan line. All the pixels between (and including) those points are set to the fill colour. If the boundary is to have a different colour from the fill then a small addition to the algorithm sets the extreme pixels to the boundary colour and the rest to the fill colour. This method is then

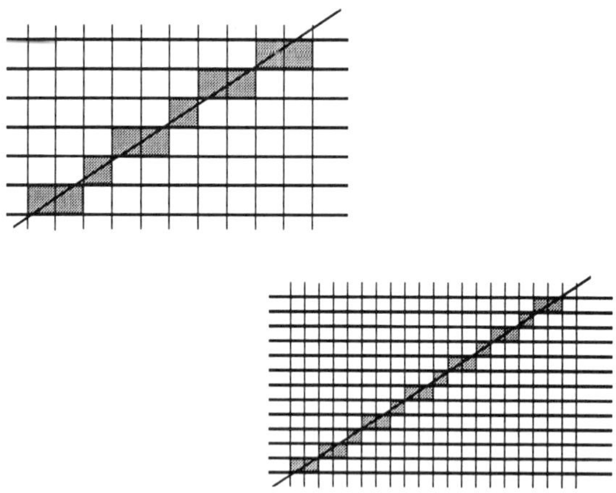

***Fig.** 7.17 The problem of aliasing decreases when smaller pixels are used*

repeated for increments of y = 1 (i.e. the next scan line down), each time checking to see if any other lines have end points on that scan-line. When such a condition is met (point D) it becomes necessary to drop one line from the list of active lines and add the new one (with its calculated value of slope). In some cases (the case of re-entrant shapes for example) a point is reached where there are four active lines in the list (point E in the diagram). Here it becomes necessary to treat them as two separate pairs of lines – as if they were two different polygons but the basic principle of the algorithm remains the same.

7.3.5 Anti-aliasing

Before leaving the subject of the straight line behind, attention should be drawn to a fundamental problem of all raster systems – the problem of aliasing, already referred to in Chapter 5. Fig. 7.16 in the previous section shows the ideal boundary lines of the polygon (as also used in the discussion of Bresenham's algorithm) as well as the actual pixels used to represent those lines. The raster method restricts the possibility of placing pixels to a limited number of positions on a rectangular grid but most lines, of course, do not fit into this straightjacket. The only obvious exceptions are horizontal lines, vertical lines and lines at 45 degrees. The result of this effect (called aliasing) is a jagged line (a line with steps). As display and printing systems have increased in resolution the effect has become less of a problem because there are more (and of course smaller) pixels to play with and these can therefore be placed nearer to the ideal position (see Fig. 7.17). The problem can however be made less obvious still by the use of grey-level pixels placed in appropriate positions (see Fig. 5.10, for example, in Chapter 5). This is called anti-aliasing. To see how this can be done, look at Fig. 7.18. One algorithm treats each 'real' pixel as if it were made up from a number of smaller sub-pixels (16 in this case). Two pixels with the same value of x are considered in the diagram. A count is made to see, in each case, how many sub-pixels are crossed by the ideal line; these are marked in

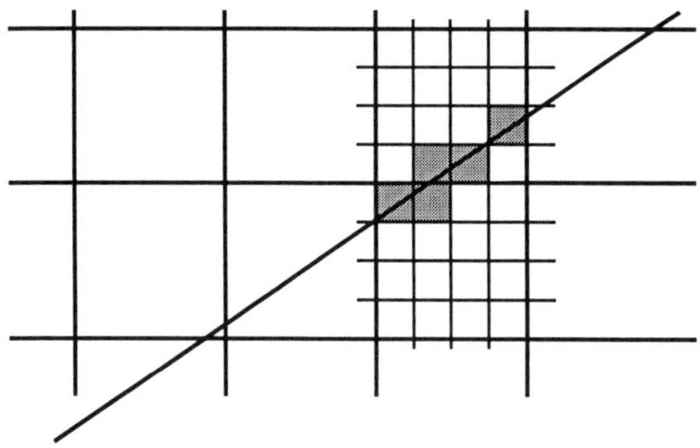

Fig. 7.18 Calculating the grey-levels in an anti-aliasing algorithm

grey in the diagram. Once the count has been done these two pixels are displayed using grey-levels. The more 'active' sub-pixels that are found within a pixel, the darker the grey-level that is used. In this case, where 16 sub-pixels are used per real pixel, the maximum number that could be touched by a straight line is four, and this would be black. In this example, there are three sub-pixels in the upper pixel and two in the lower that are touched by the ideal line. Similar techniques can also be applied to circles and to curves generally.

7.3.6 Drawing circles

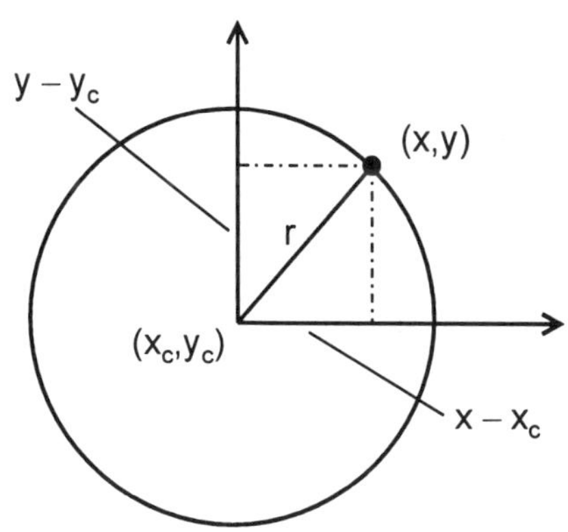

Fig. 7.19 The equation of a circle

Fig. 7.19 shows a circle, centre x_c, y_c and radius r. The position of any point on the circle can be discovered using the properties of a right-angled triangle:

$$(x - x_c)^2 + (y - y_c)^2 = r^2$$

Thus if values of x are incremented between the limits of x – r to x + r, values of y can be calculated in each case and a circle plotted in a similar manner to the first method described for plotting a straight line. This will be even slower than the

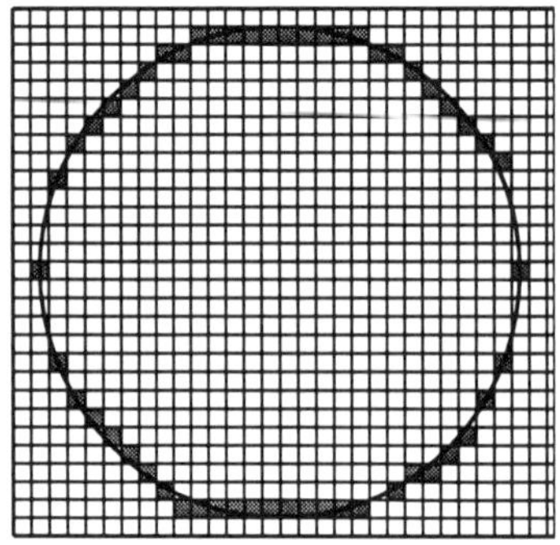

***Fig. 7.20** The problems of drawing a circle using a rectangular grid*

equivalent straight-line method, however, because it involves calculating squares and square-roots. The other problem is that the spacing of the plotted pixels will be very uneven; they will be very close together in some parts of the circle and far apart in others if all the points are plotted incrementing either x or y (see Fig. 7.20 where x has been incremented). This is because the slope of a circular line varies from a value of zero at the top to infinity at the sides whereas the spacing of the pixels in the x direction is constant. This problem is the inevitable result of using a rectangular co-ordinate system to draw a circular object. The problem can be reduced by plotting part of the circle incrementing the x values and part of it incrementing the y values, but a more appropriate answer is to use polar co-ordinates in which an angle is incremented rather than x or y as in rectangular co-ordinates. In practice, points are usually plotted using a rectangular co-ordinate system and so although the position of each point is calculated in polar co-ordinates it must then be converted to rectangular co-ordinates for plotting. There is no escaping the fact that a raster-scan display is based on a rectangular grid of points. Fig. 7.21 shows a circle, centre x_c, y_c whose defining equations are:

$$x = x_c + r \cos \phi \quad \text{and} \quad y = y_c + r \sin \phi$$

By incrementing ϕ a more even spacing of pixels is achieved but this produces the extra complication of the use of trigonometric functions (sine and cosine) which is not a recommended method for speeding up calculations!

The process can be speeded up, however, by taking note of the symmetry of a circle. Each quarter of a circle is a mirror-image of the quarter of the one below or above it. Equally, it is a mirror-image of the one to its left or right. This means that only the positions of the pixels in one quarter of a circle need be calculated from first principles – the others can be deduced from them. In practice, it is easier even than that because each quarter can be thought of a being made from two eighths – each a mirror-image of the other. As a result, only one eighth of the circle need be calculated and the other seven-eighths deduced. However, none of this overcomes the fundamental speed objections satisfactorily and the complete answer lies in an extension of Bresenham's straight-line algorithm. Again, the interested reader should consult a specialist text on graphics algorithms to know more.

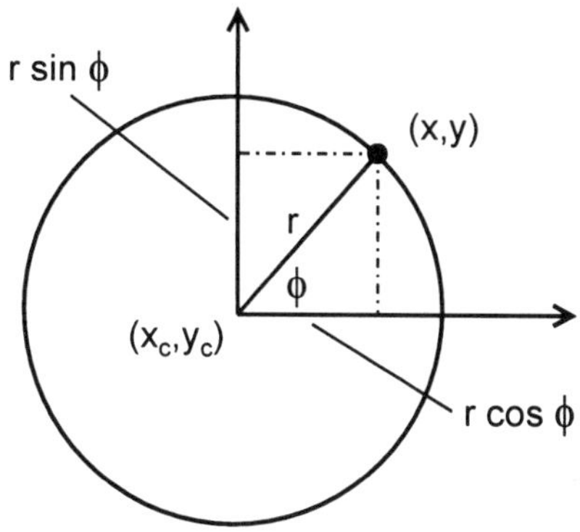

***Fig.** 7.21 Drawing a circle using polar co-ordinates*

7.3.7 Curves

So far all the algorithms discussed have been based on plotting points, drawing straight lines and, the simplest and most symmetrical form of curve – the circle. These algorithms have been based on the appropriate equations and this principle could clearly be extended to other curves which can be characterized by simple equations – the sine curve, the parabola and the hyperbola, for example. What many situations require, however, is a much less symmetrical type of curve – a smooth version of a generalized, hand-drawn curve of any shape. This type of curve is usually specified by a mathematical equation called a polynomial which is an equation of the type :

$$Y = a_0 + a_1 x + a_2 x^2 + a_3 x^3 + \ldots$$

(where a_0, a_1, a_2, a_3 ... etc are constants)

In other words, it consists of a series of terms, added together, each term involving a different constant and a different power of x. Specific cases of the polynomial are the *quadratic polynomial* where the greatest power is two and a *cubic polynomial* where the greatest power is three.

In general a curve is specified by defining a number of points in space through which the curve will pass – these are called control points (see Fig. 7.22) – and arranging for a series of subsidiary curves to pass smoothly through these points, each of them described by a cubic polynomial, with four appropriate constants. These subsidiary curves cannot be chosen independently of each other because they must blend smoothly into each other at the control points. Of course, more than one curve can still be fitted smoothly through a specified set of control points. In Fig. 7.22 the control points are represented by tiny hollow squares (one at each end and one near the middle of the curve). There is more than one solution to such a set of conditions since the curves can pass through the various points with a variety of different slopes. This means that a huge variety of curves can be created with only a few control points. In graphics application software the exact shape of the curve as it passes through a control point can be controlled using the 'levers' provided with each point. Such a curve is called a spline, a name that derives from the flexible wooden strips used to draw smooth curves before the days of computer graphics.

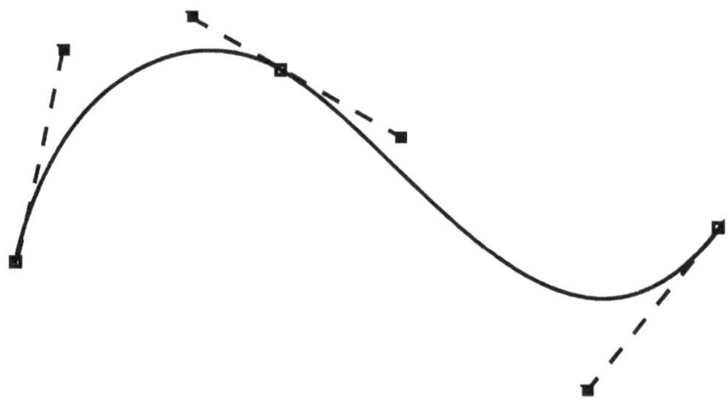

***Fig.** 7.22 A smooth curve whose shape can be altered using 'levers' and control points*

The two commonest forms of cubic spline curve are the Bezier curve and the B-spline. Both of these can be used in the context of two-dimensional graphics and also three-dimensional graphics, where, for example, non-uniform rational B-splines (NURBs) have an important role. A proper definition of the differences between these and the many other types of splines would involve a mathematical discussion that is beyond the scope of this book but the subject is well covered in many text books on computer graphics. They are mentioned here only because the reader is likely to find such terms used in manuals for graphics software and in help systems and should have some idea what they refer to.

7.3.8 Flood-filling an empty shape

With one exception, the algorithms discussed so far are concerned with the simplest level of graphic activity – that of drawing points and lines. The exception was the method for drawing a polygon that is filled with a single colour. It often happens, however, that a user will create a shape using drawing software and then decide at a later time to fill the shape with a colour or a pattern. The boundary might have a very irregular shape, drawn free-hand perhaps and with no recognizable geometry, and yet most bit-mapped graphics packages are provided with a tool which will achieve this result – known as flood-filling. All the user has to do, apart from choosing the fill colour, is to indicate any point inside the shape. This is how it works.

Starting from the point which is known to be inside the boundary to be filled (for example the point marked 'X' in Fig. 7.23), the algorithm examines the pixel on, say, the right, to establish from the refresh-buffer whether this is a point that should be changed – or not. This can be done in one of two ways. In the first, the colour code of the pixel is compared with the colour code of the boundary line of the shape to be filled. If it is different, then it is re-set to the fill colour; if the same, the boundary has been reached. The second approach compares the colour code of the original pixel with the colour code of the current background colour. If it is the same then it is changed to the chosen fill colour; if not then the boundary, or another object, has been reached. Using either of these methods, a repeated process of

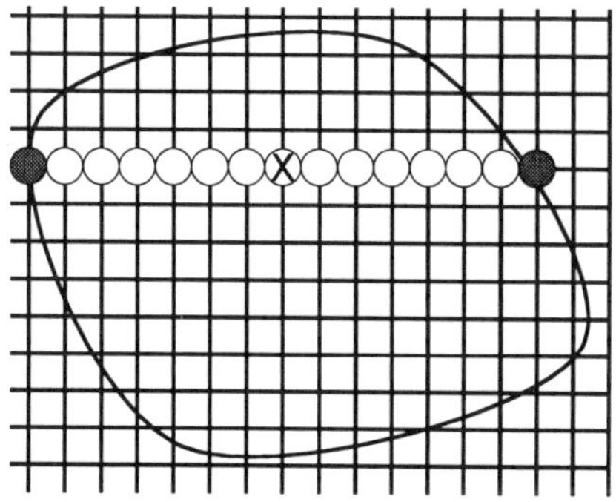

Fig. 7.23 Flood-filling an irregular shape

changing pixel colours and incrementing the x co-ordinate (i.e. moving along the scan line) is performed, until the boundary is reached. When that happens, the pixel is left unchanged and a similar process is set in motion, this time starting from the original pixel but working in the opposite direction.

When the whole scan line has been filled, the y co-ordinate is decremented (i.e. the algorithm gets to work on the next scan line) and that line filled in the same way. This process of filling lines is continued until all the lines below the original pixel and inside the boundary are filled. At that stage it is necessary to return to a pixel immediately above the first and repeat the process but this time working upwards until the top boundary is reached.

The reader can examine the principles of the flood fill in more detail by writing a program to do it using PEEK and POKE in BASIC. The simplest way of doing this is to use a graphic statement to draw a boundary shape, like a circle, as the first line in the program. Provide the program with a point known to be within this shape. Use three colours – say white for the boundary (the circle), black for the background and red for the fill colour. To make the POKE and PEEK operations as simple as possible it is advisable to use a one-byte-per pixel mode (i.e. a 256-colour mode). Otherwise, the program will have to extract from the data value obtained with each PEEK statement the colour code for one particular pixel and will also have to write back (using POKE) the new pixel value without disturbing existing values which relate to other pixels. This assumes that we are using a mode with fewer than 256 colours where one byte codes for more than one pixel. Similar but simpler problems exist if more than one byte codes for one pixel. All these problems can be solved but it is better to be less ambitious in the first attempt! The algorithm will look like this:

- draw the circle (or other shape)
- provide an internal starting point in the form of x, y co-ordinates
- PEEK the colour code at the starting point
- compare this with the code for white (or other boundary colour)

- if it is not white, then POKE the code for red (the fill colour)
- increment the x value (i.e. move one pixel to the right) and repeat the process until the new pixel is discovered to be white already (the boundary has been reached)
- then: do not change its colour code but return to the pixel which is one to the left of the starting pixel (it is clearly important to have kept a record of this value!)
- repeat the steps from line 3 but this time decrement the x value (i.e. move to the left)
- when the left boundary is reached, go to a pixel immediately below the starting point (i.e. with a y value changed by 1)
- repeat all the steps needed to complete another scan line, then:
- repeat for all the scan lines below the starting point, then:
- repeat for all the scan lines above the starting point.

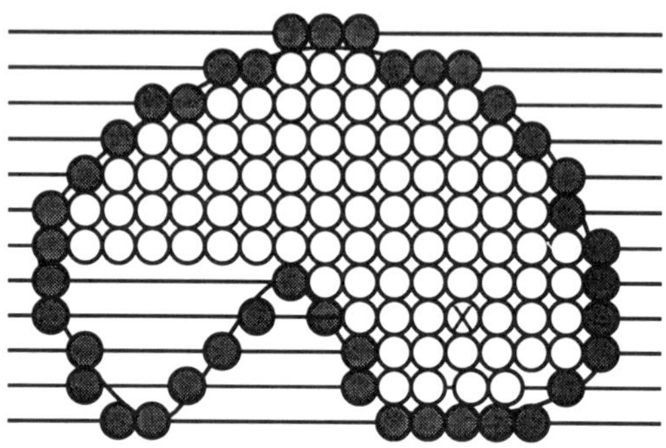

Fig. 7.24 *Problems flood-filling a re-entrant shape*

This technique enables irregular shapes to be filled but cannot cope with re-entrant shapes. Here, part of the shape, for example the bottom-left lobe of the shape in Fig. 7.24, has been missed. In these cases the regions which have been missed must be filled separately by a repeat process, starting from a newly designated interior pixel.

Another problem is that if the boundaries are not drawn properly and do not meet, even if only one pixel is missing, the colour might 'leak out' and fill the background outside the boundary.

The technique is usually called a flood-fill because the colour behaves like water, flooding flat ground until a boundary or wall is met. An alternative name is 'seed-fill' because a seed is planted in the area of interest, which then grows to fill that area.

7.3.9 Simple animation

Animation implies creating the illusion of a changing image by the simple expedient of presenting a series of different, static images, very rapidly, one after the other. There are a number of basic techniques for doing this. One consists simply of creating the first image, displaying it for a short time, clearing the screen with a *clear-screen* command, then creating the next, and so on. This method has two disadvantages. First it is slow because the whole of the image must be built up each time from a blank screen. Secondly the clear-screen command can produce a distracting, 'blinking' or flashing effect which spoils the apparently smooth change which is desired.

A better method involves selectively changing only those parts of the image which need to be changed. In principle, this can be done very easily by selectively redrawing the 'moving' parts of an image in the background colour (so that they disappear) and then redrawing them a second time, in a different position, in the foreground colour. This is obviously quicker than the first method because only parts of the image are deleted and redrawn. This type of activity is made much easier if different parts of the image can be stored in different sets of bit-planes. In an earlier discussion on the number of bits-per-pixel it was stated that 24-bits-per-pixel were quite enough because they provided for 16.8 million colours which is more than the human eye can detect. And yet some systems provide for even more bits-per-pixel (32, for example). The explanation is that the extra bits are not used to provide for even more colours. Some can be used as a 'z-buffer' – used in creating 3-D images and discussed later. Another use can be for animation.

One possibility is to store one image in the animated sequence in one set of bit-planes and the next image in another set. Under software control only one set of planes is used to feed the display at any one time – the other is 'in reserve' – but the two roles can be switched very rapidly. This means that while one image is being displayed, the other is being created. Only when the creation of this second image is complete is the current image switched off and the new image displayed. The process is then repeated by building up the third image in the first set of planes while the second image is being displayed. This means that any intermediate processes associated with the creation of an image are not seen – only the final result, when it is ready.

Another approach is to store one part of an image – the part that is changing – in one set of bit-planes and use the other planes to store the unchanging, background portion. A simple example might be the mouse cursor which is constantly being moved across the screen. Another might be the pop-up menus which act as an overlay, temporarily obscuring the screen. The bit-pattern of the cursor or menu is stored in a bit-plane (the overlay plane) which contains no other graphics. The normal screen display is in a second plane (or set of planes). The two are combined together in such a way that the objects in the overlay plane are always displayed in preference to objects in the equivalent position in the underlying plane but that other parts of the overlay are effectively transparent.

The advantage of this approach can be seen clearly by comparing it with the alternative approach – one where all parts of the image are stored in the same portion of the refresh buffer. Consider the case of a pull-down menu. The information about what the menu looks like is stored in the application software. When the user clicks the menu header this information is copied and superimposed on part of the screen. This is fine until the menu is released and disappears from the screen – leaving a rectangular hole in the image! How is the portion of the display that was overwritten by the menu to be restored? Clearly it is necessary, prior to displaying the menu, to store a copy of that information in memory, so that it can be restored after the menu is removed. It can be seen that whatever technique is used, it is essential to have a copy of such information somewhere so as to keep the whole of the image intact after overlays have been removed. Using two separate images – one for the intact screen and one for the menu – and producing a composite for display purposes, is obviously a good solution.

7.3.10 Logical colour operations

One of the basic problems of animation is how to create the effect of one object moving in front of another or, for that matter, behind another. The difficulty is that when the object has moved on, it is necessary to redraw those parts of the background which were temporarily obscured (and therefore lost) and there are a number of ways of tackling this problem. Two approaches have been described above; a third method involves the careful choice of colour codes and the use of logical combinations of them in such a way that the background colours are automatically restored.

Fig. 7.26 *Three elements of an animated scene: fore-ground (the car), mid-ground (the house) and back-ground (the city)*

This simple technique can be tried by the reader. First, however, it is important to see the problem that can be associated with the first method described earlier – that of making the moving object disappear by re-drawing it in the background colour. This works easily only if there is a single uniform background colour. Problems arise when the object is moving 'in-front of' or 'behind' objects other than the background. To distinguish the different backgrounds it is helpful to label one – that which is furthest away from the viewer – as the true background, and the other – the nearer one – as the 'mid-ground' (Fig. 7.26). The programmer may wish a moving object to pass in front of both or to pass in front of the background but behind the mid-ground. In either case we are dealing with a minimum of three colours. This problem could be overcome by the programmer taking care to ensure that the background (or mid-ground) colour used for the re-drawing process is changed as the object passes from one to the other but this is difficult, particularly when the object is in the process of passing from one background colour to another and is half-on-one and half-on-the-other. It would be preferable if this problem could be avoided altogether by some technique which will automatically re-draw back- (and mid-) grounds in the appropriate colour. This can in fact be done by a careful use of logical colour operations and colour re-definition.

Consider Fig. 7.26 again. It represents a blue car travelling either in front of, or behind, a red house, all on a green-field background (together with the skyline building which do not feature in this example). In our program we will use very simplified versions of these objects – coloured blocks to represent the car, the house and the green field – in order to demonstrate the principle. The basic technique of drawing, deleting and then re-drawing is done not in the normal way but by using the logical operation XOR (exclusive-OR). XOR is in fact used both for the drawing and the deleting stages. For example, if the shape of the blue car is first drawn using XOR onto the green background, then using the colour codes 0 for green and 1 for blue, this is equivalent to the binary operation 01 XOR 00 = 01 (see table).

Colour Code (binary)	Colour
00	Green
01	Blue
XOR	
01	Blue

This result corresponds to the blue car overwriting the green.

For the deleting operation we simply repeat the process: we draw the blue car using XOR on top of itself.

Colour Code (binary)	Colour
01	Blue
01	Blue
XOR	
00	Green

This corresponds to 01 XOR 01 = 00 which restores the green again.

Finally a new version of the car is now drawn in a different position.

To extend the process to crossing in front of a red house involves using colour code 2 for red but re-defining colour code 3 to be blue also (instead of whatever colour it normally codes for). In other words, two different colour codes – 1 and 3 – will now produce the colour blue. Thus when the blue car begins to move across the red house, part of it overlaps with green and part with red. Drawing the first part (blue on green) will produce the same results as before. In the case of the second part (blue on red) the drawing operation corresponds to 01 XOR 10 = 11 (which is 3 in decimal and therefore draws blue, as a result of our colour re-definition).

Colour Code (binary)	Colour
01	Blue
10	Red
XOR	
11	Blue

The deleting operation will of course still restore green to the section of car overlapping the green background, exactly as before. The deleting of the second half however corresponds to 01 XOR 11 = 10 which corresponds to red, so the red house is restored.

Colour Code (binary)	Colour
01	Blue
11	Blue
XOR	
10	Red

It is important to realize that in this last table the first blue (code: 01) corresponds to the car which is being drawn and the second blue (code: 11) corresponds to the car which is being drawn on.

To make the red house into mid-ground and enable the car to go behind it, instead of in front, all that is necessary is to re-define colour-code 3 to correspond to red instead of blue. Thus the drawing operation where the car overlaps the house becomes: 01 XOR 10 = 11 (as before) but now colour code 3 produces red instead of blue and that part of the car disappears behind the house. The deleting operation produces red again, as before. It will be evident that in this example we are using four colour codes but only three colours. Careful consideration will show that the fourth code is being used for those pixels which represent the car when it is behind (or in front of) the house, i.e. where the background and mid-ground overlap. It is this provision which enables us to provide the automatic restoration of mid-ground colour as well as the background colour.

For those wishing to try this technique a simple program looks like this in QBASIC:

```
SCREEN 7                          ' a graphics mode
PALETTE 0, 2                      ' re-define palette; code 0 = green
PALETTE 1, 1                      ' code 1 = blue
PALETTE 2, 4                      ' code 2 = red
PALETTE 3, 1                      ' code 3 = blue, also
DIM car (2500)                    ' an array is created to store the 'car'
LINE (10, 10)–(30, 30), 1, BF     ' draw blue car (a simple box shape)
GET (10, 10)–(30, 30), car        ' get car into array
CLS                               ' clear the screen
LINE (80, 60)–(150, 110), 2, BF   ' draw red 'house' (another box)
FOR n = 40 TO 150 STEP 10         ' move car across house using PUT
PUT (n, 80), car, XOR
SLEEP 1                           ' slow down the steps
```

```
PUT (n, 80), car, XOR          ' delete the car, ready for new position
NEXT n
```

This example employs the PUT statement which can be used with Boolean logical operations between the drawing colour and the existing screen colour. The LINE statement, normally used to draw straight lines will draw and fill rectangles with the addition of the B & F options.

An extension of this technique of re-defining colour codes so that a colour has more than one code can be applied to a method of animation which uses two colours only, in the extreme case – and in general uses a much smaller number than the maximum that are available. The principle of the two-colour version is that initially all available colour codes are re-defined to represent the chosen background colour. Separate frames of the animation sequence are then drawn – each using a different colour code and in such a way that there is no overlap between them. For the sake of example let us take the case of an eight-colour mode. Each colour code is redefined to correspond to black and the background is black. At this stage nothing is visible; the frames are 'there' but nothing can be seen because they are being displayed in black. To create the animation, each colour code is in turn re-defined to be another colour (say white) and then defined as black again to make it disappear before the next frame takes its turn. Thus if the animation is done in two colours only, as many frames can be simultaneously stored, revealed and hidden again, as there are colour codes available in that mode. For an increase in colours a smaller number of frames must be accepted. This is yet another example of the 'trade-offs' which exist in graphic systems between different types of information.

7.3.11 Sprites and Bit-Block Transfers (bit-BLT)

Moving graphic entities across the display, as described in the preceding section, is such an important feature of graphics programming that special facilities are provided in graphics languages to make the process easier. At the simplest level this might just be the facility to create a graphics object (like the car in the example above) and to be able to manipulate it as a single object. An example of this sort of facility was introduced under the discussion of text characters. Here, non-standard characters can be defined, assigned a code number and treated in the same way as the normal set of alphanumeric characters. The object does not have to be an alphanumeric character, however. Any character-sized collection of pixels can be defined as a graphic object. If the desired object is larger than a character then it becomes necessary to use two or more definitions, each with its own code, and to manipulate them together.

A convenient facility that automates this type of process is the 'sprite'. A sprite is a user-defined graphic object which may be larger than a normal character – up to some limiting size, probably the equivalent to about four or six characters. Once defined, sprites can be treated as single entities. They can be moved about the screen, passing in front of or behind other sprites or stationary graphic objects. The computer hardware automatically copes with the processes described in the last section, such as drawing the sprite in a new position as it moves, deleting it in its old position, restoring the background colour after deletion and detecting collisions.

Such a system requires that each sprite can be assigned a priority which determines which one obscures the other when they overlap.

A more powerful technique, which has some similarities with the sprite, is the bit-BLT operation. BLT is a short form of Boundary Block Transfer and has come to be pronounced as 'blit'. A hardware device which implements it is called a blitter. Early implementations of blitters were in software such as the GET and PUT statements in QBASIC (used above) but greater speed is now achieved through the use of dedicated chips. The basic BLT operation copies the bits in (usually) a refresh-buffer that represent a rectangular area of pixels on the screen into another area of memory (again, usually in the refresh-buffer). In its simplest form it therefore produces a rapid movement of any rectangular region of an image to any other part of the display. In this form it has two advantages over a sprite. It has an unrestricted size; the rectangle can be as large as the screen if required. Secondly the boundaries of the rectangle can be made anywhere in the bit-map (hence the name bit-BLT). In a one-bit-per-pixel display, where one byte codes for eight pixels, it is permissible to copy any rectangle even when that involves only some of the bits in a particular byte being 'moved'. The hardware masks out those bits which are to remain unchanged by the operation. Even in this basic form it is valuable operation.

In addition to its obvious use for moving graphic entities around the screen – like the sprite – it can be used for such activities as scrolling the screen by copying it to a new position, up or down or left or right. It can also be used to copy the bit-maps of characters from a buffer to the screen and for 'kerning' which is a form of fine adjustment in positioning text characters used in publishing. In modern implementations of bit-BLT this basic copying operation is supplemented by a wide range of other functions, which make the facility an even more powerful tool. For example, it is possible to use logical operations between the source rectangle and the destination rectangle so as to make the object pass in front of and behind other objects. It is also possible in some implementations to perform other manipulations such as rotation of the rectangle before copying to its destination.

7.4 Image Processing

All the algorithms described so far are of a geometrical nature – methods of creating a variety of geometric shapes, filling them, moving them – and this type of operation is clearly important for most drawing software. They are essentially vector operations being concerned with line-drawings. There are many operations, however, which apply to bit-mapped images, like scanned photographs. The last part of the 2-D section of this chapter is devoted to this area.

First, it is necessary to be clear that many of the algorithms discussed so far can be applied to both vector software and to bit-mapped software. All drawing packages, for example, offer facilities for drawing straight lines, circles and rectangles. The important difference lies in what can be done with a shape, once drawn. In a vector package a shape can be edited at any stage of the process because information about each shape is stored in a list. An image consists of a list of shapes and that means that a shape can be removed or re-drawn with different parameters. This process does not affect any other part of the image because objects that were underneath that shape (and so were unseen) can also be re-drawn and therefore revealed again when the uppermost shape is removed or changed. For this reason, such software usually has a 'send to front' and 'send-to-back' feature, which can be used to change the relative status of any two objects at any time – which is above and which beneath (see Fig. 7.27).

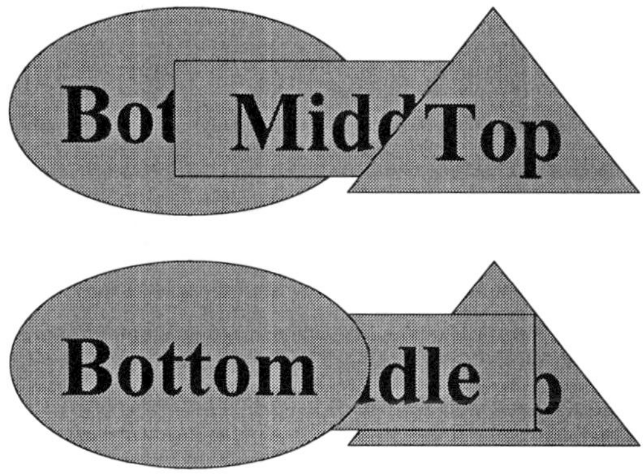

Fig. *7.27 Objects created in vector drawing packages can be re-drawn in any convenient order*

In a bit-mapped package, by way of contrast, a shape once drawn, over-writes any shape beneath. Its pixels take the place of those that were there before the drawing operation and no record of the previous state is maintained. The only exception to this is that good paint packages will keep two copies of the whole image – a 'before' and an 'after' – which gives the user an Undo facility. After a change is made to the image the previous version can be restored if the change is considered unsatisfactory. Usually only one Undo is allowed but with sufficient memory (or with a system of keeping copies on disk) multiple levels of Undo can be provided. It should be clear, however, that this is not the same as the process described for vector software. It is unselective – the whole image is stored – and therefore it does not provide for any editing of details – only a backtracking process.

Because a bit-mapped image contains within itself no history of how the pixels came to be the way that they are, the processing that can be performed is of a very different type. One example has been described already – flood-filling. This involves a process in which pixels are systematically examined and their colour codes compared with neighbouring pixels and then changed (or not) according to a chosen criterion. This general approach can have many uses, one example being the 'magic wand' tool described in the chapter on Applications Software. This selects an object in a digitized photograph (usually) so that it can be removed or moved or have its colour changed. The software recognizes the object using the principle that there will be a sudden change in colour at the boundary of the object (see Fig. 7.28). The user specifies where the object is by clicking on it and the software then uses an algorithm very like that for flood-filling for examining the colour codes of adjacent pixels until it finds the boundary on each scan-line where the colour suddenly changes. The important difference here is that in the flood-filling algorithm the boundary is drawn in a single colour and the criterion is very simple. In a digitized photograph there will be a variety of shades of the colour within the object and a variety of shades of a different colour in the surroundings. The criterion is not that there will be a simple change from, say, red to blue, but that there will be a change from some shade of red to some shade of blue. The algorithm must detect a range of shades that the user would consider to be one colour. This 'latitude' or 'tolerance' will also vary from one case to another and so the user must be able to alter it to suit the case.

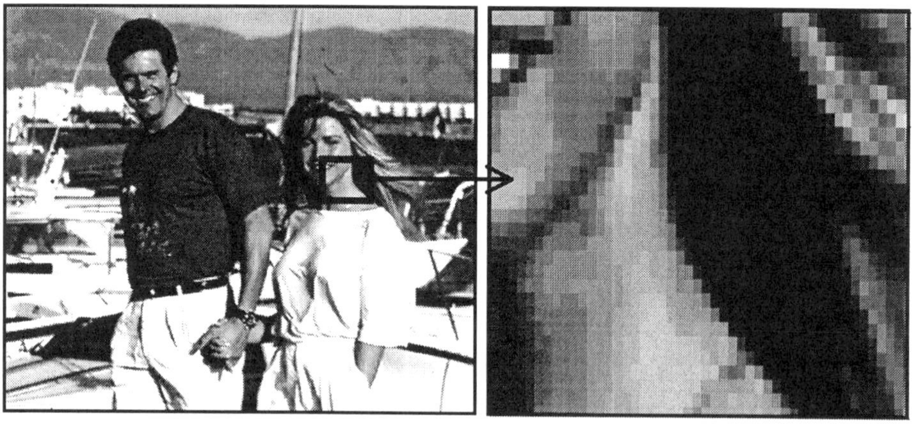

Fig. 7.28 *The 'Magic wand' tool detects the edges of objects by the change in colour of grey-level*

This ability to detect the edges of an object by a change in colour values can be used in other algorithms – such as those to sharpen and blur images. Many photo-retouching techniques mimic real-life photographic effects and these two simulate the result of taking a photograph – either through a properly-focussed lens or through one that is out of focus (or a 'soft-focus' lens). In both cases it is a case of finding the edges of objects (and parts of objects) in the image and then either enhancing or reducing the sharpness of that edge. This involves altering the rate at which a colour value changes with distance (see Fig. 7.29). In a well-focussed image the boundaries are clear and 'sharp' – there is a rapid change in grey or colour value at the edge of the object. In an out-of-focus image the reverse is true; the grey or colour values change gradually. In algorithms to sharpen or blur the software detects these changes that occur across boundaries and either make the graph steeper or less steep.

7.4.1 Other image processing algorithms

Modern photo-retouching packages compete with each other in their efforts to add methods of processing images – with dozens of 'filters' being available. Here it is possible to describe only a few:

Brightness and Contrast correction: many photographs are either over-exposed (too bright) or under-exposed (too dark), have too large a variation between the brightest and darkest regions (the contrast is too high) or have too little variation (contrast too low). All these defects can be reduced by changing the brightness values of pixels relative to each other – either globally (throughout the image) or in selected brightness bands (corresponding roughly to the shadow regions, the brightly-lit regions or the middle-tone regions of the image). A more subtle change can be introduced by changing the 'gamma' value of the image. In image technology the term gamma is used to describe the contrast of an image – in particular it is the slope

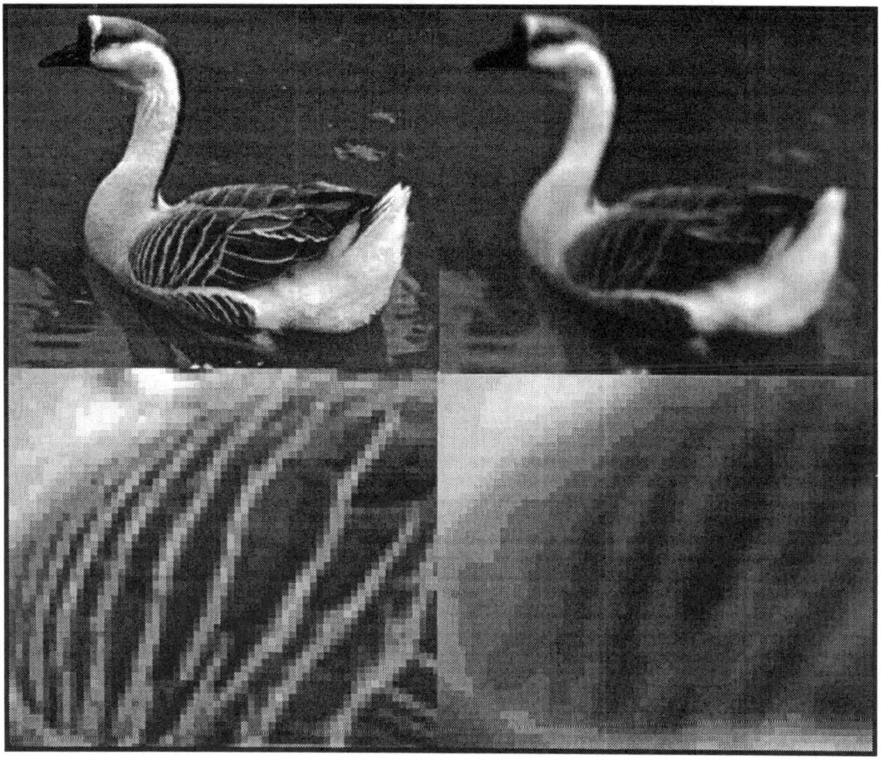

Fig. 7.29 *A well-focussed original photograph and the same image after blurring. The second set of images shows a detail taken from the wing. The result : fewer grey-levels are used in the blurred image*

of a graph which relates the input to the output functions. For example, in a traditional photograph, it relates the image density to the logarithm of the light exposure. In a computer image the corresponding graph relates the colour code for a pixel (the brightness, say, for a grey-level image) to the amount of light produced by the phosphor on the CRT tube. The simplest relationship would be that described by a graph that is a straight line – a linear relationship – but phosphors don't behave in a linear manner and this affects the contrast of the final image. Gamma correction is a technique to alter the shape of the graph (see Fig. 7.30) which will enhance the contrast in the darker regions and reduce it in the brighter (or vice versa). This sort of image processing is necessary to ensure that images displayed on a particular technology (a screen, for example, or a printer) look right, but can also be used to 'improve' or change images also.

Histograms: a histogram is a type of graph and in this context it refers to a graph which shows how the brightness of parts of an image relates to the proportion of that image which has that brightness (see Fig. 7.31). It shows if a lot of the image is very bright or very dark, for example. A histogram of an image can be one that describes the overall brightness or it can take the form of three separate graphs – one for each of the primary colours. A study of an image's histogram can help in a decision as to what changes might be made to improve its appearance.

Fig. 7.30 *Linear and non-linear characteristic curves which show the relationship between input (colour code or grey-level, and pixel brightness)*

Colour balance: one change that might be made, based on an examination of an image's histogram, is to its colour balance. For example, the colour balance of an old image might have changed with time as some of the colour components have faded more than others. Colour balance adjustments allow the user to enhance the red, green or blue components of an image selectively.

Image Editing: there is a collection of techniques that are designed to change an image in order to remove imperfections. These might have been introduced in the photographic process (for example, a scratch on the negative) or they might have

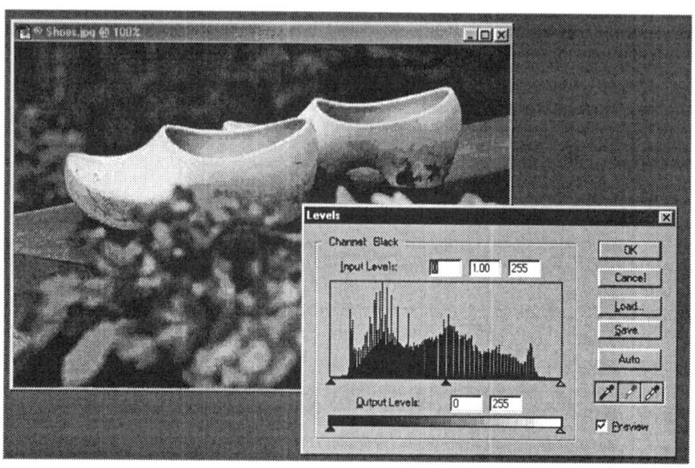

Fig. 7.31 *A screen taken from Adobe 'PhotoShop' showing a sample image together with its histogram (what proportion of the pixels have any particular brightness)*

been a part of the object being photographed (a bruise on an apple, stray hairs in a portrait). These can be removed by digitally 'painting them out' by changing the colour values of the appropriate pixels in a highly enlarged view. Because the colour values which are to be introduced are not uniform it is usually necessary to do this painting with a digital 'brush' that has been copied from another region of the image. For example, if a spot is to be removed from the face of a fashion model, a copy of a small region of skin from an adjacent area of the face is used to over-paint the spot, so ensuring that a realistic range of skin-tones are used, not a single colour value. Some image editing goes much further than that of removing 'imperfections'. Objects (a whole person or a car, for example) might be removed from an image and extra background added to fill in the space. Objects from a completely different image might be added. This usually requires careful editing of the boundary of the cut-out which tends to look too clean-cut and special processes are available to blend the boundary region to make it look more natural.

Artistic effects: while many image correction techniques are designed to correct for imperfections in the original image – to make it more like 'reality' – many more are designed to allow the user to make images look less realistic – for artistic and aesthetic reasons. One will distort an image so that it looks as if it is spinning round, one will add 'noise' so that it looks very grainy, one places boundaries round regions of one particular colour so that the image looks like a stained-glass window and there are literally dozens more.

7.5 Three-Dimensional Graphics

7.5.1 Introduction

To be strictly correct we would have to say that all computer graphic images are two-dimensional. All the images that a computer can produce, via a monitor, a plotter or a printer are displayed or recorded on a two-dimensional screen or sheet of paper. What is understood by the term three-dimensional graphics ('three-dimensional' will be shortened to '3-D' for the rest of this chapter) is that attempts are made to create the illusion of a third dimension – depth. It is as well to make this simple distinction at this stage because it is one that does not apply in the same way to other visual media. For example, in television and in photography generally it is just as easy to produce images of 3-D objects as 2-D objects. The camera lens automatically produces a 2-D representation of an object whether that object is a flat piece of paper or a house. But in computer graphics, where images are being created synthetically, a whole variety of techniques have had to be specially developed in order to produce the illusion of realistic 3-D objects and this makes it a much more complicated process to produce 3-D graphics. In some respects there is a parallel here with the development of painting and drawing techniques. Over a period of many centuries artists have developed means of creating more life-like pictures by the use of perspective, shadows and lighting effects and the development of pigments and painting techniques. In this last section of the chapter a review is presented of the main methods used in computer graphics to produce similar results

– many of them being mathematical representations of the techniques used in fine art.

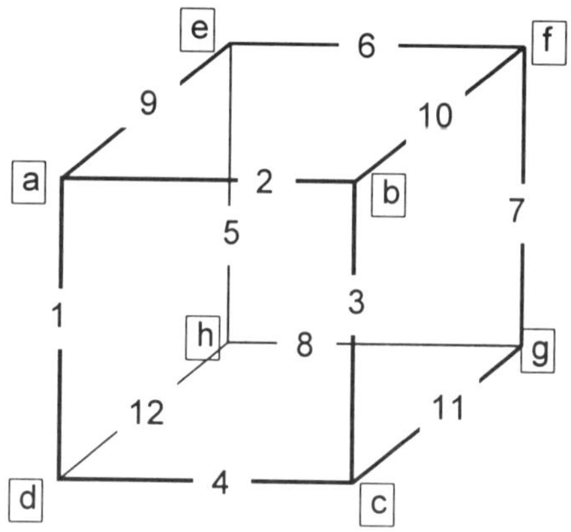

Fig. 7.32 The edges and vertices of a cube

An artist, painting a picture uses a number of techniques to produce the impression of 3-D and the sense of depth as the third dimension. The five main methods are size, detail, perspective, overlap and shading. First, the apparent size of an object gives a vital clue to its distance from the observer (as long as the observer knows what size it 'really is'). A tiny elephant must be a long way away because we know that elephants are large. Many reports of UFOs suffer from this effect because the UFO is of unknown size. A small object travelling close to the observer is seen as a large object, travelling very fast at a great distance. Secondly, the amount of detail that can be seen is a function of its distance: you can see that there is an advertisement on a distant bus but you can't read it till it gets closer. Thirdly perspective, which is but a specialized aspect of the first point and will be dealt with in more detail later. Fourthly, objects that are in the same general direction of view overlap – the further one being obscured in part by the nearer. Lastly the shading effects and the shadows produced by directional lighting give vital clues as to position and orientation in 3-D space.

There are four main stages involved when a computer is used to simulate these effects: specifying the shape of the 3-D objects, generating a 2-D view of the objects, establishing what parts of the objects can actually be seen and, finally, representing the surfaces of the objects in a realistic manner:

7.5.2 Specifying a 3-D object

An artist will draw an object from memory or from observation but a computer needs facts and figures. The 3-D shape of an object must be specified using measurements in 3-D space – which requires the use of three co-ordinates. Using such a system the position in space of any point can be recorded by three numbers (x, y and z). Using such a system the eight corners of a cube, for example, could be recorded but at a later stage it will be necessary to know where the faces of the cube are and for this, an equation – the equation of a flat surface (a plane) will be used. Fortunately this is very simple – it is an extension of the equation of a straight line, extended into the third dimension – see section 7.5.4.

It is one thing to have all the data available but it is another thing to be able to be able to use it efficiently and so some system of organizing it is needed. In general the co-ordinates of the corners (the vertices) of the planes are not in themselves enough information to model an object. We also need to know how these vertices are connected to form the plane edges. One way of doing this is to produce three lists. The first contains the co-ordinates of all the vertices (the corners of the cube, in this case). This is the lowest level of information – information about the position of points in space – and consists of values of x, y and z for each vertex. Each point is given a label for the purpose of cross-referencing it from the other lists. The second list contains information about all the lines (edges) in the model. This is clearly needed because there are many different ways of connecting points together and only some of them are correct for any particular solid. Each line also has a label. The stored information in this list consists simply of a list of labels, one for each line, together in each case with the labels of the two end points of that line. The third list contains information about the planes (surfaces) in the model. Again, each plane has its label together with the labels which identify the lines which define the edges of that plane, all of which are in the second list. Thus for the cube in Fig. 7.32 there are eight vertices labelled a to h (in rectangular boxes in the Figure), twelve edges labelled 1 to 12 and six faces labelled I to N (not shown, to avoid the confusion of too many labels).

Table 7.6 *Relating faces, edges and vertices in a cube*

Faces	Edges	Vertices
I : 1, 2, 3, 4	1 : a, d	a (x_1, y_1, z_1)
J : 3, 10, 7, 11	2 : a, b	b (x_2, y_2, z_2)
K : 7, 6, 5, 8	3 : b, c	c (x_3, y_3, z_3)
L : 5, 9, 1, 12	4 : d, c	d (x_4, y_4, z_4)
M : 9, 6, 10, 2	5 : e, h	e (x_5, y_5, z_5)
N : 12, 4, 11, 8	6 : f, e	f (x_6, y_6, z_6)
	7 : f, g	g (x_7, y_7, z_7)
	8 : h, g	h (x_8, y_8, z_8)
	9 : a, e	
	10 : f, b	
	11 : c, g	
	12 : h, d	

By the use of these tables all the planes which make up an object can be treated in a systematic manner. For each face, the appropriate edges can be identified and, in turn, for each edge the corresponding co-ordinates of the vertices obtained. For example, the face labelled K can be seen to have boundaries defined by the lines labelled 7, 6, 5 and 8. The end points of these lines can be discovered from the next list (they are f, g; f, e; e, h; h, g). The positions in space of these points can now be obtained from the last list.

By this means it is possible to systematically identify three vertices for each of the planes which make up an object and then calculate values for the three constants which establish a general equation for each plane. It should be noted at this point that the equation of a plane actually defines an infinite plane – it extends indefinitely in all directions. Information about the position of the edges is always needed to specify a real, finite plane.

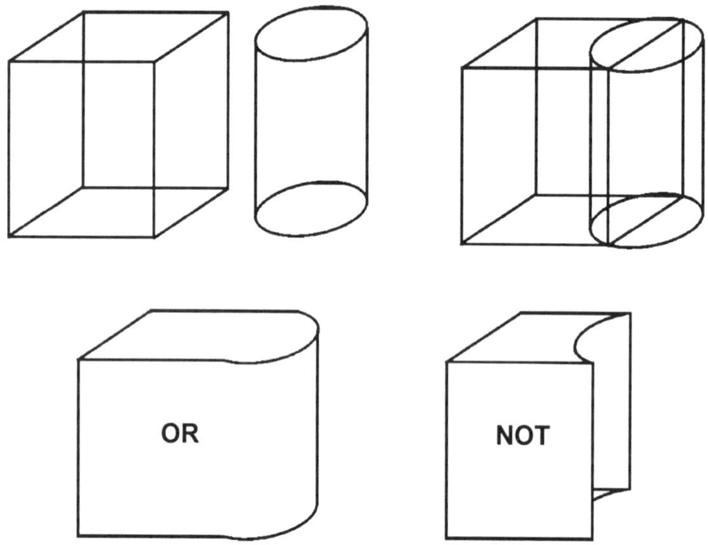

Fig. 7.33 Combining 3-D graphics primitives using Boolean logic

Of course, not all objects are made from planes, like a cube, and other equations must be used to specify spheres, cylinders, cones, and other shapes. The equations of most of these basic shapes are usually provided as part of 3-D graphics software so that composites can be assembled from these 'primitives' in just the same way that 2-D software provides facilities for 2-D primitives – like straight lines, circles, rectangles and polygons. An extremely valuable technique that is commonly available is that of assembling primitives using 3-D Boolean operations. To visualize this process it is necessary to imagine bringing two solid shapes into some desired relationship in space. In assembling these primitives into a composite they are treated as if they could pass freely through each other like cartoon ghosts. In Fig. 7.33 a cube and a cylinder are brought together (first three shapes). The Boolean operation then determines which parts of the two component objects remain in the new composite object. An AND operation, for example, leaves only those parts which are common to both of the original objects. An OR operation leaves those parts which existed in either. A subtraction (NOT) leaves those parts that exist in one but not the other. These last two cases are shown in Fig. 7.33. In this last case (the NOT) the one object can be thought of as a cutter – removing its shape from the other.

An alternative approach to the creation of 3-D models, usually used as a complement to the first, where suitable, is to use *rotation* or *extrusion* (see Fig. 3.26 in Chapter 3). These methods are appropriate to the creation of shapes which have rotational or linear symmetry. First a 2-D cross-section of the object is created using the methods described earlier in this section. A 3-D object is then created by either rotating this shape around an axis of symmetry (in 3-D space) or by extruding it into the third dimension like icing sugar being extruded from a nozzle.

7.5.3 Generating a 2-D view of that object

It has been said that computer-generated images, even those of 3-D objects, must ultimately take the form of a 2-D image that can be displayed on a screen or printed on a flat piece of paper. This is the second stage and is done by a process called projection. Mathematical equations are used to trace a series of straight lines, in 3-D space, from each important feature of the specified object, to a plane (the viewing plane). The simplest way of doing this is to use projection lines that are parallel to each, producing images like the diagrams drawn by architects of buildings (plan views and 'elevations'). In Fig. 7.34 a simple cube (shown with one surface shaded) is the 3-D object and two sets of parallel lines have been drawn, to the right and

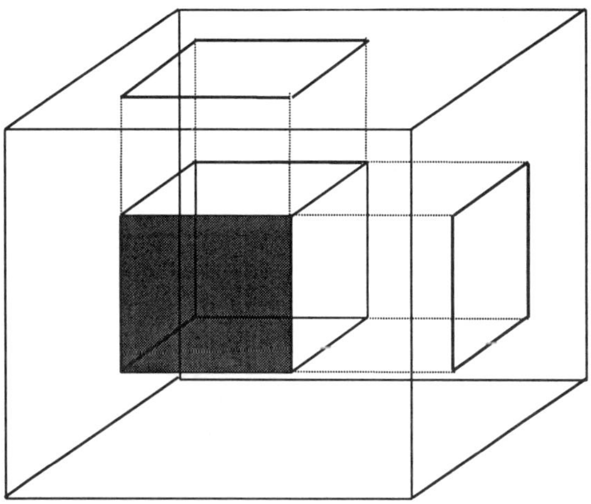

Fig. 7.34 *Parallel projections of a cube onto two viewing surfaces*

upwards. The standard views are from above, from the side and from the front – called orthographic projections, which means projections in three mutually perpendicular directions. This type of projection is ideal for engineering and architectural applications because it preserves the relative proportions of all the component parts and ensures that meaningful scale measurements can be made on the diagrams. A fourth viewing plane that is often used, enables the viewer to see three sides of the object in one view. This called an isometric projection and is best imagined as the view which is obtained when looking towards the 'origin' of the axes (the zero point), from a point equidistant from each of the axes. This is the one used in drawing Fig. 7.34.

Greater realism, and a more convincing sense of depth, is obtained, however, if the projection lines are not parallel but are drawn as if they would meet at some distant point – the 'vanishing point'. This is a perspective view (see Fig. 7.35). This projection inevitably involves more calculations and will take longer. As a rule, the more realistic the final image, the more calculations and the longer it will take. For this reason it is generally best for the user to be content with simple, outline representations of an object while making the many adjustments to the shape of objects, angle and distance of view and lighting – in order to get rapid feedback.

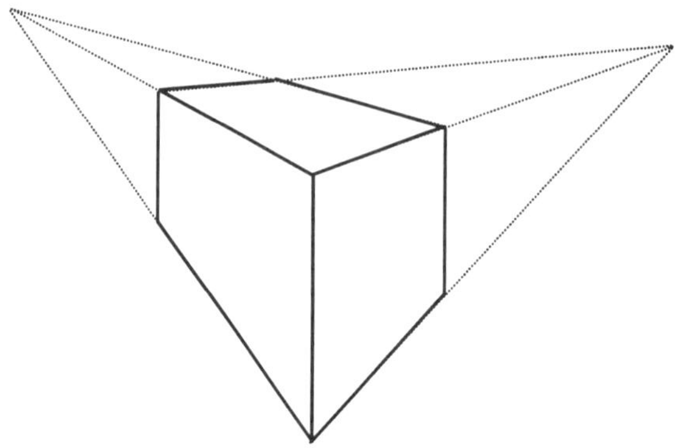

***Fig.** 7.35 A 3-D rectangular box drawn using perspective projection*

When all these changes have been made, then is the time to create more realistic images. As an example of this principle, most 3-D software is designed to produce a number of styles of image – including 'wire-frame' images which can be generated very rapidly and will still give a good impression of the shape of an object. Wire-frame images are simple line drawing in which only the edges of the surfaces are drawn but no attempt is made to represent the surfaces themselves. For example, a cube or rectangular box is drawn using 12 lines – four for the front, four for the back and four to join the front to the back. The lines represent the absolute minimum of information needed to define the shape of the object.

7.5.4 Hidden-line and hidden-surface removal

In a basic wire-frame image all edges are shown whether or not they would be visible in real life – the surfaces of the object are treated as if they were transparent. This can create ambiguities even in the simplest shapes and is the basis of a well-known optical illusion. When looking at the left-hand cube in Fig. 7.36, sometimes the eye sees one surface as in front and at others sees a different one as in front, and it is notoriously difficult at times to persuade the brain to see it a different way from the one which is currently dominant (see the other two version of the cube which have been given depth 'cues' – thicker lines in front and a grey front surface). According to which way we interpret the image we seem sometimes to be looking from below the cube and sometimes from above it. To improve the illusion of 3-D it is necessary to remove from the image all those parts that would not be seen in a real, solid, opaque object in order to obtain one or other of the two possibilities. When this is done with a wire-frame image it is called hidden-line removal. When it is applied to a more realistic image, in which surfaces are represented, it is called hidden-surface removal.

This technique is an important stage towards more realistic images but there are occasions when it is helpful not to remove the unseen lines or at least not to remove them completely, so as to create a transparent model and to see that which is normally unseen. In this case it is still necessary to identify the hidden lines but having done so, to draw them at a lower intensity to that which is used for the lines

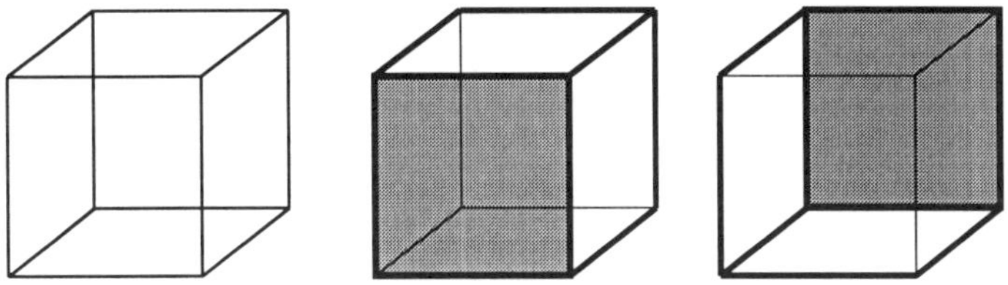

Fig. 7.36 *Difficulties in 'seeing' a wire-frame cube*

which are normally seen in an opaque object. The purpose of this is to assist in what is called depth-cueing. This term means the provision of 'cues' or aids to our knowledge of the depth of a particular part of an object – in other words to make it clear which parts of the object are in front and which behind to avoid visual ambiguities about depth. This gives the illusion of an object made from material which is transparent but which absorbs a small fraction of the light passing through its surfaces, so making the back surfaces of the object look dimmer than the front surfaces. This type of illustration has the same function as those demonstration models of machinery or car engines in which the outer casings really are made from transparent plastic to show the inner workings.

There are a number of different approaches to hidden-surface removal but most of them involve the equation of a plane, which can be thought of as a simple extension of the well-known equation of a straight line, already given earlier in the chapter as:

$$y = mx + c$$

where the two constants *m* and *c* specify its slope and its absolute position in space. An alternative way of writing this equation is:

$$Ax + By = C$$

At first sight this seems to imply the need for three constants instead of two, but a little re-arrangement of the second equation yields the form:

$$By = -Ax + C$$

or

$$y = (-A/B)x + (C/B)$$

In this form it can be seen that the equation confirms the fact that only two constants are needed to specify a line in 2-D space: (– A/B) and (C/B) because the ratio of two constants is itself a constant. In this case:

$$(-A/B) = m \qquad \text{and} \qquad (C/B) = c$$

To obtain the equation of the plane we have only to extend the equation for a straight line to the third dimension by adding a third term:

$$Ax + By + Cz = D$$

The same general considerations about the minimum number of constants apply to this, i.e. that only three constants are needed to specify a unique plane:

$$x + (B/A)y + (C/A)z = (D/A)$$

$$\text{or} \quad x + Ey + Fz = G$$

The way in which this equation can be used is this. To specify any plane for the benefit of the calculations needed in 3-D graphics the values of the three constants E, F and G are needed. These must be calculated from any three sets of co-ordinates of points in that plane. Suppose those co-ordinates are:

$$(x_1, y_1, z_1)$$
$$(x_2, y_2, z_2)$$
$$(x_3, y_3, z_3)$$

The three equations can be written:

$$x_1 + Ey_1 + Fz_1 = G$$
$$x_2 + Ey_2 + Fz_2 = G$$
$$x_3 + Ey_3 + Fz_3 = G$$

With three equations it is possible to discover the values of the three unknown constants E, F and G. The obvious three points to use for this process are three of the vertices of the plane which is of interest, though any points in the plane will do as long as they are not on the same straight line. Usually the basic data supplied to the program take the form of the co-ordinates of the vertices of the planes which make up the object being modelled. Once we have the values of the planar constants E, F and G we have a general equation which describes that particular plane. The value of having this equation will become clear in the next three sections which look at three different approaches to hidden-surface removal.

Painter's algorithm

This method mimics the technique often used by painters, who first paint the background of the picture, then paint, on top of that, objects which are in the mid-ground of the picture, and then on top of both, objects which are in the foreground. Each new layer of paint obscures the layer beneath and so surfaces or objects which should not be seen are literally hidden by the objects in front. This approach, of course, implies a knowledge of the relative depth in space (z values) of objects or surfaces so that they can be painted in the right order but given that information it is a simple process in a raster-scan refreshed display to lay down blocks of pixels 'on top' of the background images. What really happens of course is that the new set of intensity or colour values of a near object replace those current values which are stored in the refresh-buffer and correspond to a back object.

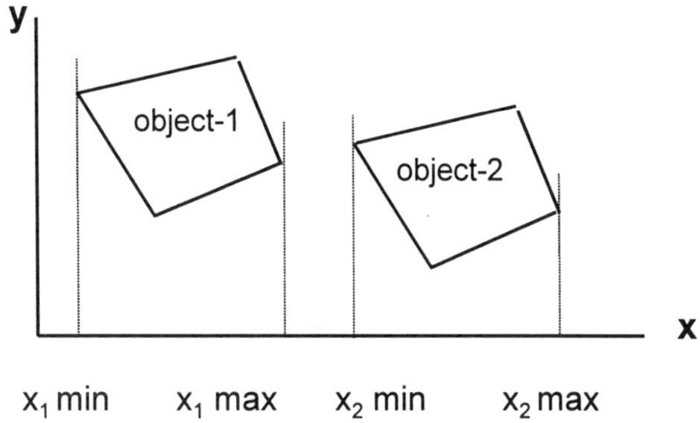

Fig. 7.37 Do two objects overlap in the x-direction?

The heart of the algorithm, therefore, is the process of sorting the objects and surfaces before displaying them in decreasing order of z values, later (nearer) surfaces replacing earlier ones where they overlap. Of course a solid object does not have a single, unique z-value and so in the simplest cases the ordering process involves comparing the maximum z-value of one object with the minimum z-value of another. In practice, not all objects have to be compared with all others. Some objects do not overlap at all with others in the chosen view and so it doesn't matter what their z-values are; they can be 'painted' in any order. These cases are discovered by comparing the maximum x-value of one object with the minimum x-value of another. Even if there is overlap in the x-direction it will still not matter as long as there is no overlap in the y-direction. In Fig. 7.37 a check is being made for overlap in the x-direction. Is x_2 *min* smaller than x_1 *max*? If so, there is overlap. Two objects only have to pass one of these tests to prove that they do not overlap from the observer's point of view.

This technique is particularly appropriate to certain types of 3-D situation where the objects have simple geometrical shapes and are placed in regular arrays. Examples in the professional context include software to help the design of seating arrangements in a new aeroplane or underground train or the positioning of machinery in a factory. Other examples in the home market are 3-D software packages sold for landscaping a garden or designing the layout of a kitchen. The algorithm can actually be seen in action as the computer draws objects one by one, on top of each other, beginning at the back and gradually working its way forward.

The scan-line method

This method is based on the principles of the scan-line area-fill algorithm described earlier in the chapter and so a brief resume of that approach may be helpful. Area-filling requires that all the pixels on a scan line within a polygon be changed to a required colour and so the points where those scan-lines intersect the polygon boundaries must be found. This is done using the equations of the two active straight lines which mark the edges of the polygon.

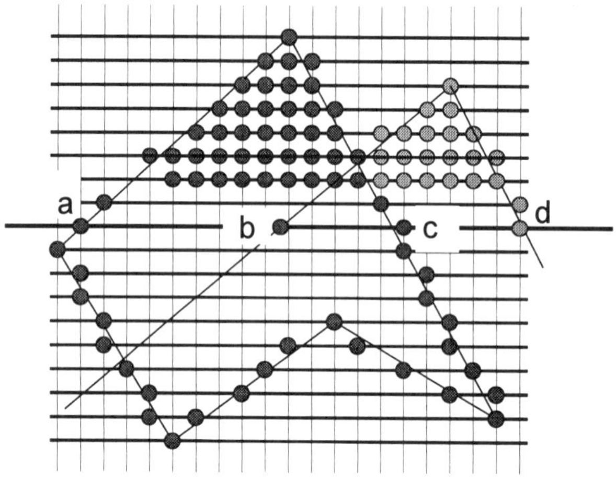

Fig. 7.38 *The scan-line algorithm*

In the 3-D scan-line method all the surfaces which are competing for display on a particular scan-line are examined together. In other words the algorithm concentrates on one scan line at a time, comparing all the surfaces in turn to see if they are in-front or behind. This means that for each scan-line a list of 'active' surfaces must be compiled from the total list of surfaces which comprise the various objects. Having done this the equations of the edges of those surfaces are now used in the same way that they are in the area-fill technique – they are used to determine the intersections of all the active edges with that scan line (a, b, c, d in Fig. 7.38). Then, starting with the intersection of the first surface (point a), the intensity values of all that surface's pixels on that scan-line are sent to the refresh-buffer until the edge of a second surface is met (point b). This signals the beginning of an overlap region and so when this happens a decision must be made as to which of the two surfaces is nearer the viewer. This is done using the equation of the two planes to calculate z values. The appropriate intensity values for whichever surface is uppermost are then sent to the refresh-buffer until another edge is met, implying either the end of one surface (point c) or a conflict with a third surface. This is repeated until all the active surfaces on that scan-line have been treated. The whole process is then repeated for all scan lines.

The advantage of this approach is that although z values have to be calculated, it is not necessary to calculate them for all points on each surface – only for those points where there is overlap. This approach is easily adapted to either surface removal or line removal. In surface removal each pixel is examined in regions of overlap. In line removal only edge pixels are examined in order to determine which of the two edge lines should be displayed.

Depth-buffer or z-buffer method

This method takes its name from the use of a special duplicate refresh-buffer – a depth buffer or z-buffer. Unlike the true refresh buffer, which contains intensity or colour values, this contains values of z (depth) for each pixel on the screen. The principle of the algorithm is that where two surfaces are competing for our attention it is necessary to compare points on the two surfaces, which have the same values of x and y, and then find the z or depth value for those two points. The point which has the lower z value (assuming that z is measured from the observer) is the one which will be seen. The other is obscured.

Initially all values in the z-buffer are set to the maximum depth of the image. The refresh buffer contains intensity or colour values corresponding to the background of the image. Each plane in the list of all the surfaces that make up the various objects is then examined in turn, and for every plane the following process is used. The plane is treated systematically, every pixel in each scan-line being examined, and from the x and y values of that pixel, and the equation of that plane, the z value is calculated. This is then compared with the value of z currently stored in the appropriate location in the z-buffer. If it has a smaller value than the one already there, then this means that this point is nearer to the viewer than the point currently stored. When this happens the new value of z replaces the previous one in the z-buffer and at the same time the equivalent intensity or colour value for that part of the plane is placed in the appropriate location in the refresh-buffer.

For the first plane which is examined it is inevitable that every point in the plane will be found to be nearer to the observer than the maximum z value of the image and so it will be displayed (all its intensity values will be entered into the refresh-buffer). As other planes are examined though, some points will be found to be nearer the observer and their z-values will be placed in the z-buffer and their intensity values placed in the refresh buffer. This process is repeated for each surface which makes up the object and when the process is complete the refresh-buffer contains the intensity values of all the points which are nearest the viewer.

In this method, the order in which the various surfaces are examined doesn't matter but it does require a large amount of processing and it does require spare memory for the z-buffer. In the early days of computers both processing power and memory were in short supply and only advanced computers like specialized workstations could be used for this approach. Now, any computer could be used though complicated images might take a long time. However, the algorithms, implemented in hardware, are becoming available at low cost in special 3-D video cards so that even in standard PCs these processes are becoming faster.

7.5.5 Representing surfaces

So far, the discussion of 3-D representation has been largely limited to wire-frame models with only a brief reference to the representation of surfaces. In the discussion of hidden-line removal mention was made of surfaces which can be represented as solid blocks of colour by area-filling of the wire-frame surface outline and some simple geometrical solids can be made to look quite realistic by this means. In general though to achieve a significant improvement in the realism of an image it is necessary to use shading and shadowing methods. These are based on the recognition that much of our sense of shape and depth comes from the fact that objects are almost always illuminated in an uneven fashion and the subsequent variation in reflected light intensity across the surfaces of the object, together with

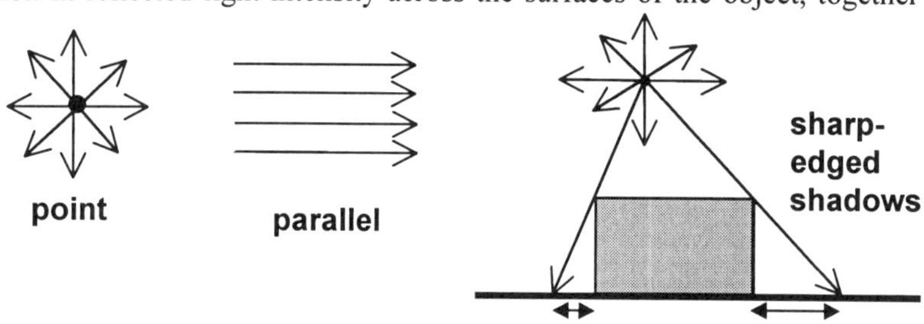

Fig. 7.39 *Point sources and parallel sources cast sharp shadows*

the shadows it throws, are the clues we use in assessing 3-D shape. In fact our knowledge of where one surface ends and another begins – for example at the edge of a cube – derives largely from the illumination which makes one surface more brightly lit than the other. Artists use this technique of shading to considerable effect but they are usually drawing 'from life', that is, by direct observation. Computer software must reproduce these effects by calculation, using the laws of physics to simulate the behaviour of light as it is reflected, refracted, scattered and absorbed by different types of surfaces under a variety of lighting conditions.

Light sources

The simplest type of lighting is that from a single 'point-source'. As the name implies this means a light source which is sufficiently small to be treated as a point, having no effective area – at least from the distance of the object. This approximation is valid for sources like a conventional filament-lamp which is only a few inches in diameter, for surfaces at a reasonable distance, but it is also valid for large light sources which are at a considerable distance – such as the sun. What matters is not the absolute size of the source but the angle that it makes ('subtends') when looked at from the point of interest (Fig. 7.39). The geometry of the light rays is very simple. Light rays from a point source travel in straight lines and so diverge away from the source. At a sufficiently large distance they behave as parallel rays but close to the source they are angled to each other.

To calculate the illumination caused by such a source on any particular surface it is necessary to establish the angle the surface makes with the direction of the light rays. A surface at right-angles to the light rays receives the greatest illumination; the light is spread over a small area. At any other angle the intensity of illumination is less; it is spread over a larger area. In fact it drops off as the angle changes in a well established manner (proportional to the cosine of the angle between the light rays and the perpendicular to the surface – called Lambert's Law).

An important, second, variable is the distance the light is from the source. The closer to the light the greater the illumination. The intensity of light on a near surface is large because it is spread over a small area; that on a far surface being spread over a larger area. This is described by the inverse square law which relates the intensity to the inverse of the square of the distance from the source.

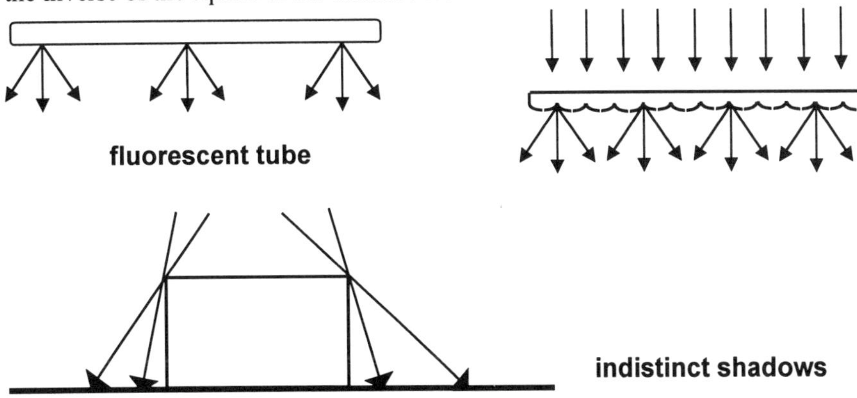

Fig. 7.40 Extended sources, like fluorescent tubes, and sunlight scattered by clouds, lead to indistinct shadows

A more complicated case is that of the extended source. Many real lights have a finite size – they subtend a significant angle from the viewer's position – and so light from a number of different angles will reach a single point on a surface (see Fig. 7.40). An example of this type of light is a fluorescent strip light and the sort of illumination which this type of source produces is called diffuse. It is not necessary for the light source to be large if there is some other mechanism of diffusing the light. Sunlight is diffuse on a cloudy day because the clouds act as a secondary source of light, scattering it in many directions. Whereas point light sources tend to produce harsh, clearly defined shadows and shading effects, diffuse light sources produce much less clearly defined shadows. In reality most situations are a mixture of the two types, as for example when diffuse daylight on a dull day is supplemented with a reading light close to the surfaces of interest and acting as a point source. Very few scenes which are artificially illuminated show no shadows at all though natural lighting outdoors often does. That component of the illumination which is the same on all surfaces is called the 'ambient' light. The simplest realistic model for 3-D imaging is to use some ambient light so that all surfaces can be actually seen and a minimum of one point source or spot-light (a parallel beam) to produce differential shading.

Types of surface

Another set of variables that affects the final image concerns the properties of the surfaces which make up the objects being modelled. One obvious property of a surface is its colour but the reflective properties are important also. A smooth shiny surface acts like a mirror in reflecting the light in one direction only. This is called 'specular' reflection and produces the shiny appearance of glass or a polished metal but it can also produce mirror-like reflections of other objects. A rough surface, on the other hand, reflects light in all directions, a process called scattering, and this produces a dull, matte effect. Many surfaces have properties part way between these two extremes. Other parameters include patterned surfaces, textured ('bumpy') surfaces and transparent (or semi-transparent) surfaces which act like lenses or prisms. Of course not all surfaces are flat and so allowance must also be made for curved surfaces

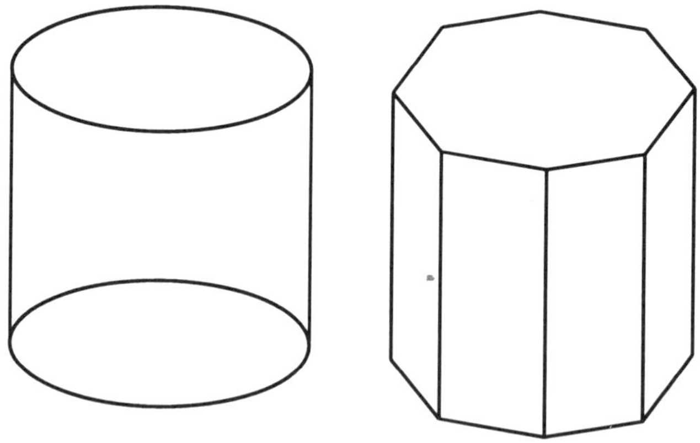

Fig. 7.41 *A smooth cylinder is approximated using Gouraud shading*

There are two basic approaches to the representation of surfaces: constant shading and varied shading. Constant shading is really only suitable for flat surfaces where the light strikes the surface in the same way at all points and where the observer receives the reflected light in the same way from all points. Under these conditions it is possible, knowing the relative orientation of the surface to the direction of the illuminating light rays, to calculate how much light will finally reach the eye of an imaginary observer. This information, together with data about the colour of the surface and its reflective properties is sufficient, in principle to produce a shaded, coloured image of that surface.

Curved surfaces can be treated by the same method as long as they are broken down into a large number of small polygons (usually triangles) – each polygon being treated as a new surface with its own unique angle to the light rays – but the problem is that unless these are extremely tiny polygons the edges will be seen. It would be better if a sudden change in light intensity across the boundary of polygon with its neighbour could be smoothed away. This is the principle of varied (or interpolated) shading. The process of interpolation involves calculating data values which lie in-between known values (as compared with 'extrapolation' which means calculating data values which lie outside the known range). Both processes imply that the data values change in some smooth, predictable manner and this is justified in the case of a smoothly varying surface.

Gouraud shading (sometimes called 'intensity interpolation') treats a curved surface as a series of flat surfaces and then mathematically smoothes the shading so that the edges seem to disappear. In Fig. 7.41 the first shape is the true cylinder which is required. The second shape is a crude approximation to a cylinder, made from a series of flat panels. If the flat surfaces are uniformly shaded it is obvious that the shape is not a true cylinder. If the number of flat surfaces is increased it looks more like a true cylinder but 'banding' effects may result. The eye can be very sensitive to small regular changes in intensity. The Gouraud algorithm first calculates a single value of shading for each flat surface but then calculates a series of intermediate shading values for that surface in such a way that the 'joins' disappear. The calculations are based on the diffuse value of illumination only so that no highlights are created.

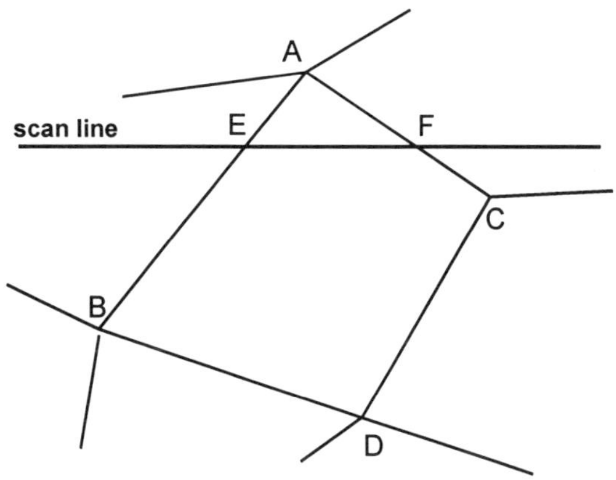

Fig. 7.42 *Gouraud shading, using interpolated values*

First, for each polygon, a single value of shading is calculated (as in the constant shading method). Then, shading values of the vertices of each polygon are calculated. For example, in Fig. 7.42, the shading value for vertex A of the central polygon, is calculated by averaging the values of the four polygons that meet at that point; the shading value for vertices B, C, and D are calculated in a similar way from the polygons that meet at those points. The next stage is to calculate values for all the pixels along the edge of the polygon by interpolation (between the values at either end). Interpolation between A and B, for example, gives values all along that edge, including the point E (where one of the scan-lines intersects with that side of the polygon). The same process is used to calculate the intensity at F (based on the intensities at A and C). Finally these intensities (at E and F) are used to calculate the intensity values for all the pixels which lie between E and F. This is done for each scan line which crosses this polygon and for each polygon which makes up the solid.

Gouraud shading produces the appearance of a smoothly curving object even though the calculations are based on a series of flat polygons. The edges of the polygons disappear, as long as the polygons are reasonably small. Gouraud shading, however, does not produce very good highlights – these are the mirror-like shiny regions of a smooth object which is illuminated with directional light.

Phong shading involves considerably more calculation but is capable of producing much better highlights with directional lighting. Phong shading uses a similar interpolation technique to Gouraud shading but with two important differences: it takes into account specular reflection (as well as diffuse reflection) and it calculates the orientation for each pixel before working out the reflected intensity at each pixel. Remember, Gouraud shading calculates the shading value at each vertex, based on a uniform value for the whole of a polygon. In other words, relatively large areas of the surface are treated as if they had the same direction to the light, which is not true for a curved surface. Phong shading uses extrapolation to calculate values for direction for each pixel and then calculates the shading value taking into account the specular properties of the surface.

Ray-tracing

The techniques described so far for generating images of surfaces can produce some quite realistic images but cannot cope with everyday effects such as shadows and mirror images. The best images are produced by a different approach – ray tracing. In principle this involves tracing, mathematically, rays of light from the light-source to every point on each surface in the set of objects that makes up the scene, and thence to the eye of the observer. *En route*, each ray of light will undergo a number of 'events' – such as reflection, scattering, absorption – but each of these is predictable, according to the laws of physics and the known properties of the surfaces – and so appropriate calculations will eventually establish what intensity and colour that ray will be when it finally enters the eye. On this basis a realistic image can be created – one with highlights on shiny surfaces, shadows and mirror-like reflections. However, many such rays will never enter the eye of the observer and so this approach will produce a great many wasted calculations. An alternative approach, therefore, is to trace the rays backwards from the observer's eye using all the information already specified, to discover if it finally intersects with a light source. This is permissible because the laws of optics are valid for rays of light travelling in either direction. The purpose of doing it this way is to avoid calculations concerning the very many rays of light which in every real situation do not end up in the eye of the observer. This method involves one set of calculations for every pixel in the final image rather than for every possible ray of light emerging from a source of light. When the 'ray' is traced back to a point other than a source of light then the corresponding contribution to that point in the image is zero since we have shown that no light can have reached the eye from this point.

Surface pattern and texture

Both Gouraud & Phong shading (particularly Gouraud) can produce rather synthetic-looking surfaces which have the bland appearance of plastic. Greater realism can be achieved by representing the patterns of colours and the fine structural detail (the 'bumpiness') of the surface. These two characteristics are often considered together under the term surface 'texture'. The texture of a surface can be represented by modifying Gouraud or Phong shading methods by the addition of a 'mapping' process. Mapping involves transferring a two-dimensional representation of colour or height variations onto the three-dimensional shape of the object, modifying the final colour of each pixel in the process. This means that the final colour of a pixel on a surface polygon will depend not just on the light falling on that pixel, and the general orientation of the surface at that point, but also on the colour and height of the mapping pattern. It has been likened to pasting wallpaper on a wall. This wallpaper effect is fine for some surfaces but is not very realistic for many others – for example, the wood effect can look like cheap veneer or a plastic surface stuck onto the wood. A better solution is to map a three-dimensional surface onto the object. This is more like modelling the grain of the wood (in this example) in three-dimensions and 'carving' the block to the shape of the modelled object. This 'bump' mapping can be done by photographing a real surface, illuminated so as to produce shadows, and using this as the texture-map. This is not wholly satisfactory as the shadows will not be in the right places when wrapped round some of the surfaces. To do it properly a 'displacement-map' must be produced. A map of the measured displacement of each point on the surface, above or below some standard height, is produced and this is then mapped onto the surface of the object.

Finally the subject of surface quality must be re-introduced. Many attempts at computer modelling produce rather synthetic results because the surfaces appear too regular. Real surfaces are not only rough but each substance has its own characteristic type of roughness – for example, those on knitted garments, animal hair, bricks and tree bark. As a result methods have been devized to mathematically simulate the texture of real surfaces. These usually involve a degree of randomness deriving from a mathematical random-number generator but must also have some sort of structure in order to produce the proper sort of roughness; very few surfaces have a totally random, unstructured roughness. One method which has been used involves a type of mathematics called fractal geometry. This can be used to break up a large smooth area into a number of smaller areas, a process which can be repeated as many times as necessary, to produce the surface elements of a required kind. If a regular repeated algorithm is used this can produce beautiful but largely regular patterns of unending complexity (see the Mandelbrot set in Fig. 6.9, Chapter 6). If, however, a random number generating component is introduced into the algorithm it can produce a large number of similar but slightly different components which can mimic, for example, the facets of a rock face, the leaves on a tree seen from a distance or the surface of a cloud.

Exercises for the Reader:

(1) Using the first BASIC program in the section on Text-Only Displays as a model, write a program to print all the members of the character set in green (or any other chosen colour). Hint – use a loop and remember that every *alternate* byte is for the character code.

(2) To show that the attribute bytes act independently of the character code bytes, add to the above program a short delay (using a SLEEP statement) and some extra code that then changes the colour of one or more of the characters already displayed.

(3) The ASCII characters whose codes are in the range 179–218 contain the component lines, corners and intersections that are used to make up single and double-line rectangular boxes. Check the truth of this statement with a modified version of program 1 above and identify which codes produce which shapes. (Hint, write your modified program so that it displays the characters 20 to a line, with 7 blank spaces in between each, to make it easy to identify each shape and calculate its ASCII code. Cheats can simply look up an ASCII code table!). Then use this knowledge to display a single-line rectangle and a double-line

rectangle – with or without dividing lines according to taste – all using POKE commands as before.

(4) Write a program, in two-colour, bit-mapped CGA mode, to switch on each of the eight pixels which are controlled by one byte, in turn. Once turned on, each must stay on, and they must be appear from right to left.

(5) Write a program to produce the same effect as the previous program but in four-colour bit-mapped CGA mode. This should turn on each of the four pixels controlled by one byte (all in one of the four colours – for example, all in white or all in magenta). The default palette is: 0 for black, 1 for cyan, 2 for magenta and 3 for white (00,01,10 and 11 in binary).

(6) Using the point-plotting statement (it is PSET in BASIC) write an implementation of Bresenham's algorithm to draw a straight line.

(7) Write two programs to draw a filled rectangle (oriented horizontally/vertically): (a) in the first case the filling should be the same colour as the boundary; (b) in a second program the filling should be in a different colour. Restrict yourself to using only two graphics statements: the *straight line* and *point plotting* statements (i.e. don't cheat by using the B and F options on the LINE statement!).

(8) Using a two-colour mode for simplicity, write a program which draws a circle (using the circle-drawing statement provided in BASIC) and then flood-fills it, using the PEEK and POKE statements. The algorithm is discussed in some detail in the text.

8

Graphics Programming

8.1 Introduction

The earliest programming languages provided no facilities for graphics because main-stream computers had no graphics hardware. The only exceptions were the small character-sized symbols (like tiny rectangles and other shapes) provided in the character set and useable in text-mode – as described in the previous chapter. As computer hardware developed, however, modifications of traditional languages – like BASIC and Pascal – were made, so as to incorporate extra, graphics, statements. A few examples of these were introduced in the last chapter. Everything changed, however, when GUIs (Graphical User Interfaces) like Microsoft Windows came to dominate the scene. Traditional languages had been designed to operate in a CLI (Command Line Interface) environment, where the interface was a very small, often trivial, part of any program. Now it was increasingly expected that every program would have a graphical interface, with windows, scroll bars, pull-down menus and the like – and with mouse-interaction as well. Suddenly it seemed that the problems of writing the program had become trivial compared with the problem of writing code for the interface. For a while there were only rather specialized solutions to this problem but now traditional programming languages like Pascal and BASIC are available in a form that automates the production of standard GUI facilities like menus and buttons. In this chapter we will look at one of these languages (Visual BASIC) from two points of view: first, how it is used to produce the graphical interface (for any program) and, second, how it is used to write programs that produce graphical effects. In this latter respect it is little different from traditional forms of the language – like QBASIC or Pascal.

8.2 The Visual BASIC Environment

Fig. 8.1 shows the working environment of Visual BASIC (to be referred to from here on as VB). It consists of a group of horizontal bars at the top of the screen (the Title bar, the Menu bar and the Toolbar) together with a number of floating windows. The two most important windows are the Toolbox and the Properties window. The other window that is visible in the figure is a blank window (called a Form) on which the program elements are to be placed. One is created automatically when VB is run and others can be added by clicking the appropriate icon on the icon bar.

The Toolbox consists of a series of icons, each one corresponding to an object (called a Control in VB) and these Controls are the standard items that are used in GUIs – buttons that can be clicked using a mouse, check boxes, selection lists, dialogue boxes and so on. Designers of GUI systems – like Apple and Microsoft – have established standard ways of interacting with the GUI, so that users of such systems can easily transfer their skills from one application to another, and so it follows that programmers are encouraged to use these visual tools in a standardized way. This means that the programmer does not expect to make decisions about, for example, the exact shape of an Option Button or the placement of a Minimize button on a window. These are already prescribed as part of the definition of the GUI. All the programmer is required to do is to choose which control is wanted, where it is to be placed and, in some cases, to choose cosmetic details like the colour or the font.

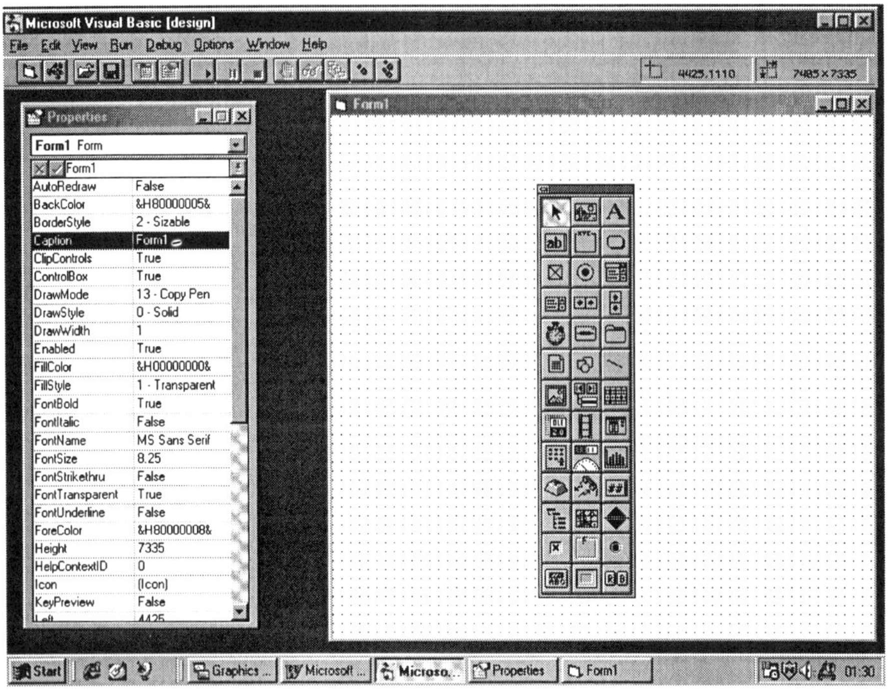

Fig. 8.1 *The Visual BASIC Environment showing the Toolbox, the Properties Window and a Form*

As a result, all the programming required to have a fully operational button or a scrolling list has been done already. The programmer simply chooses the control, using the icons on the Toolbox, and drags it into position on a form. It is just like using a drawing package and, in a sense, that is all that this part of the procedure is – drawing the interface.

The next stage is to choose the properties of the control. Some will be the sort of cosmetic properties already mentioned – colour and font. Some will be more functional, such as visibility (will the control be visible to the user when the program is first run?), will it be enabled (can it be used, or does some condition have to be satisfied before it is operational?) or what is its default state (will an Option button be selected or blank?). All of these are chosen by means of the Properties window (see Fig. 8.1). Whenever a Control is selected, the Properties window displays all the properties of that particular sort of Control and each property can have its default value changed – usually by a double-click, sometimes by choosing from a drop-down list.

8.3 Event-Oriented Programming

So far we have said nothing about computer code and yet we already seem to have started creating an interface for our program. In traditional programming the programmer tended to spend 95% of the effort on designing the structure of the program and writing and debugging the code – and to do that first. Only when everything seemed to work alright did the question of the interface arise and the last 5% of effort was devoted to adding it. An interface, in the Command Line Environment was whatever was required to enable the user to input information and to see the results – a few prompts and a few text output statements together with some text-based control features such as "Enter new data : Y/N". By its very nature, programming in VB is quite different; it is important to think about the interface at a very early stage. There are three reasons for this. First, GUIs tend to offer the user much more control over the way the software is used, simply because graphical environments provide more scope for change. The environment itself can be tailored to the user's requirements. For example, with many applications the user can choose which menu bars ("Toolbars") are displayed at any time (and where) and can add or subtract items from icon bars. Second, applications running under graphical environments tend to offer more options in the core-code of the program, simply because the user can access these options so easily. For example, users can "cut-and-paste" data between different applications in a simple and intuitive manner. Third, graphical environments are "event-driven". Code is triggered when the user presses a button or slides a scroll bar. It is this last point that defines the order of events in programming:

- decide upon the functions the software will offer;
- choose how the user will access these functions i.e. design the interface;
- create the interface:

  (i) place appropriate Controls on a series of windows (Forms)
  (ii) write and attach units of code to the Controls.

These code units are triggered when the Controls are activated.

8.4 The Syntax

This chapter cannot pretend to take the place of a textbook on programming principles or of a training course on programming in VB but it is instructive to examine the basic structures of VB through a few simple examples.

Example 1

This is a program in which clicking a button leads to some text being changed. The simplest possible case involves a Command Button which has some text on it (see Fig. 8.2) – this text is set in the design phase using the Properties Window. Clicking the button, when the program is running however, changes the text.

Programs are attached to a Control by double-clicking on that control. This brings up the 'Code Page' for that form (see Fig. 8.2). A Code page is a window associated with the current active form which displays the BASIC code which has been attached to each control on that form. At any time the code displayed is that which is attached to the selected control – in this case the button. All pieces of code are treated as 'Sub routines' (the BASIC equivalent of Procedures in Pascal) and so the

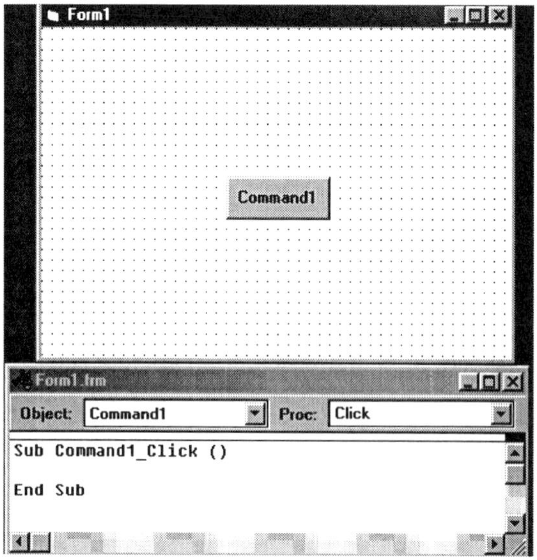

Fig. 8.2 *A Form with a single Control (a Command Button) together with the appropriate Code Page (lower window)*

beginning and end of the sub-routine are already provided. In this case the default name of the Command Button has not been changed (it is still Command1) and so the code end-points will be:

Sub **Command1_Click** ( )

End Sub

The words Sub and End Sub define the start and end of the routine. 'Command1' is the *name* of the control. This shouldn't be confused with the *caption* on the button (the words written on it) – because these can be quite different. The *name* of a Control and its *caption* are different properties.

Click is the default event associated with a command button. This is the event most likely to be used. The two pull-down lists ('Object :' and 'Proc :') at the top of the Code Page can be used to show other controls (if any) which are on the form and alternative events which could be associated with the current control (for example, *double-click*). The space between Sub and End Sub is provided for code to be added. The way in which this must be done (the "Syntax" of the language) is:

Control_Name. Property_Name = code

In other words, we write the name of the Control that is to initiate some change, followed by a 'Full-stop' ('Period' in US English), followed by the name of the property that is to be changed by the event, followed by an 'Equals' sign (strictly speaking it is an assignment operator). On the right of that is placed some valid VB code. In this case we wish the caption on the button to change when it is clicked so we write :

```
Sub Command1_Click ( )
Command1.Caption = "New caption"
End Sub
```

Caption is a property of a Command Button and "New Caption" is the value we wish it to take when the event is triggered (the string must be inside quotation marks).

When run, the program does nothing until the Command Button is clicked by the user (with the mouse). Until then, the caption we see on the button is the one we assigned it in the design phase, via the Properties Window. When the button is clicked, however, the code associated with it is triggered and the original caption is replaced with the words 'New caption'.

Example 2

In the first example, clicking a control produced a change in that control. More often programs are written to produce changes in some other object – such as closing a form, opening a new form etc. A very simple example would be to change some text, not on the Command Button but on the form. For this we place a second Control on the form – a 'Label'. (See Fig. 8.3.) A label is a piece of text that the user

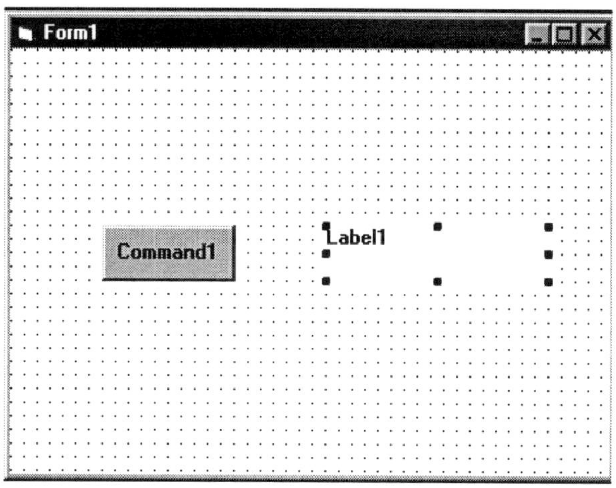

Fig. 8.3 *A Form with a Command Button and a Label*

of the program cannot normally change. It is used for offering guidance and instructions to the user. [There is another type of control – called a 'Text Box' – which is used when it is intended that the user should type in or change text.] The label has the default name of *Label1* and its caption is set to 'Old Text' using the properties window. The following code is then attached to the command button:

```
Sub Command1_Click ( )
Label1.Caption = "New Text"
End Sub
```

The first line determines that it is still the clicking of the Command Button that will trigger the code but the second line ensures that it is the caption on the Label that is changed this time, not the caption on the Button.

Example 3

The power of VB lies in two features. First, all the standard controls we associate with GUIs – forms, buttons, menus, even complete dialogue boxes and message boxes – are all pre-programmed and can be summoned up at the click of a button. Second, each of these controls has a wide range of properties, most of which can be

Fig. 8.4 *A Form, a Command Button and a Picture Box*

set in the design phase but can also be changed in run mode under program control. This third example shows how easily a very simple multimedia-style event can be produced. The program involves a form (every program needs at least one of them), a Picture Box and a Command Button (see Fig. 8.4). A Picture Box is a simple rectangle which contains a picture – which can be chosen in the design phase. In this case a picture is chosen and placed in the box but the *Visible* property is set to false. The code that is put on the command button is:

```
Sub Command1_Click ( )
Picture1.Visible = True
End Sub
```

When the program is run the picture box is 'there' but not seen; its *Visible* property has been set to False in the design phase. When the button is clicked, however, its *Visible* property is changed to True and so it becomes visible. It should be easy to see how this sort of facility could be used in an interactive program where the user chooses, in reading an encyclopaedia article for example, whether or not to view an associated image.

8.5 Other Controls

The power of VB in creating a GUI is best demonstrated by the ease with which such items as Menu Bars, Dialogue Boxes and Message Boxes are created.

8.5.1 Menu bars

Menu bars are created using the 'Menu Design' window (a menu option) – see Fig. 8.5. The menu headings are simply typed into the Caption box. Placing an ampersand symbol (&) in front of any letter in the menu heading will result in a line being placed under that letter when the application is run, indicating that a keyboard shortcut is available. For example, &File will produce File when run, indicating that the File menu can be selected with Alt-F.

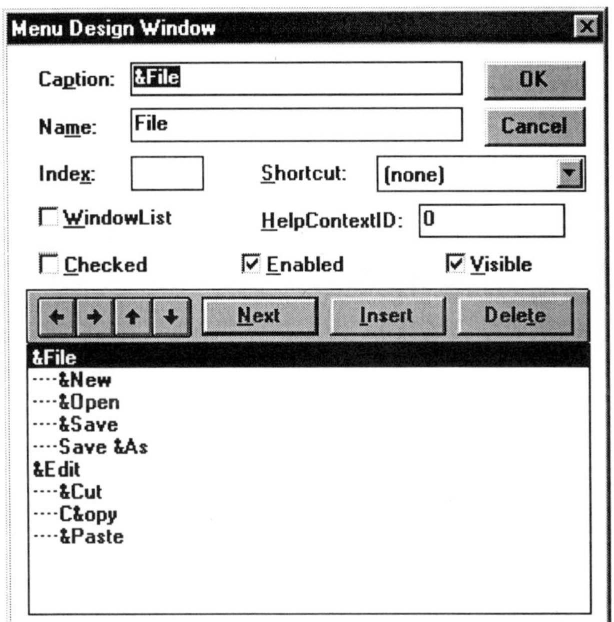

Fig. 8.5 The Menu Design Window

Each menu will have a number of menu items in it. These are created simply by typing a list of their names under a menu heading – indented to indicate that they are subsidiary parts of that menu. Sub-menus can also be created repeating the same process of indentation. Finally there are facilities to set a *Checked* and *Enabled* option for each item in a menu. *Checked* means that a tick appears against the item – usually indicating that that it has been selected (either as a default or because it has been chosen by the user on some previous occasion). *Enabled* means that it can be seen in black (and can be chosen) as opposed to disabled, where it appears in grey and cannot be chosen. Usually, both of these are changed under program control.

8.5.2 Dialogue boxes

VB can create five different Dialogue Boxes using one common command – called The Common Dialogue Box (CMDialog). A Dialogue Box Control is placed on a form – together with whatever other control will be used to activate it (often a menu item). For simplicity a Command Button is used in this case. The Dialogue Box Control will be invisible at run time but the following code will produce a visible box once the Command Button is clicked:

```
Sub Command1_Click ( )
CMDialog1.Action = 3
End Sub
```

There are six different values of *Action* :

0	No action
1	"Open" file Dialogue Box
2	"Save As" file Dialogue Box
3	"Colour" choice Dialogue Box
4	"Font" choice Dialogue Box
5	"Printer" choice Dialogue Box

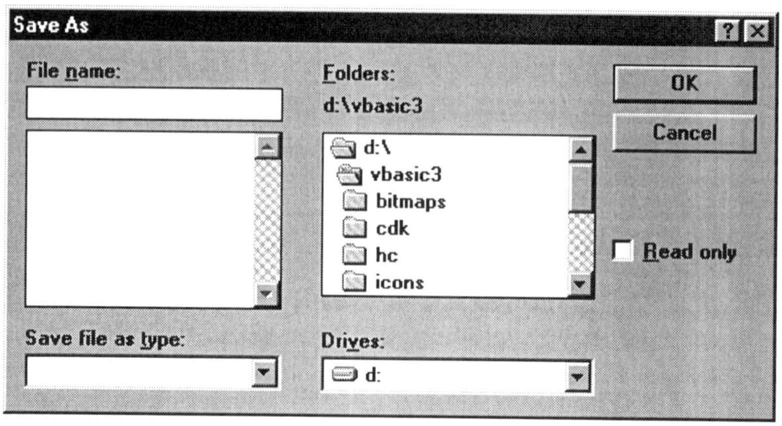

Fig. 8.6 *A "Save As" Dialogue box is created with a single line of code*

In Fig. 8.6 the value of *Action* has been set to 2 which produces the standard "Save As" Dialogue Box. The Common Dialogue Box provides a beautiful example of how much can be achieved with minimal effort. A complicated structure, with scrolling windows, command buttons and other features, is created with a single line of code. It should be remembered, however, that a Dialogue Box will do nothing without code, but most of the hard-work is already done.

8.5.3 Message boxes

Message Boxes can be created in a similar way:

```
Sub Command1_Click ( )
MsgBox "Message", n + m + o, "Title"
End Sub
```

The only difference is that there is no Message Box Control to be placed on the form. "*Message*" is any text string which is to appear in the Message Box, "*Title*" is the caption for the box and the numbers n, m & o have the following values:

n = 0 : displays an OK button only
n = 1 : displays OK and cancel buttons
n = 2 : displays Abort, Retry and Ignore buttons
n = 3 : displays Yes, No and Cancel buttons
n = 4 : displays Yes and No buttons only
n = 5 : displays Retry and Cancel buttons

m = 16 : displays a stop sign icon
m = 32 : displays a question mark icon
m = 48 : displays an exclamation mark icon
m = 64 : displays an i (the information message icon)

o = 0 : the first button is the default
o = 256 : the second button is the default
o = 512 : the third button is the default.

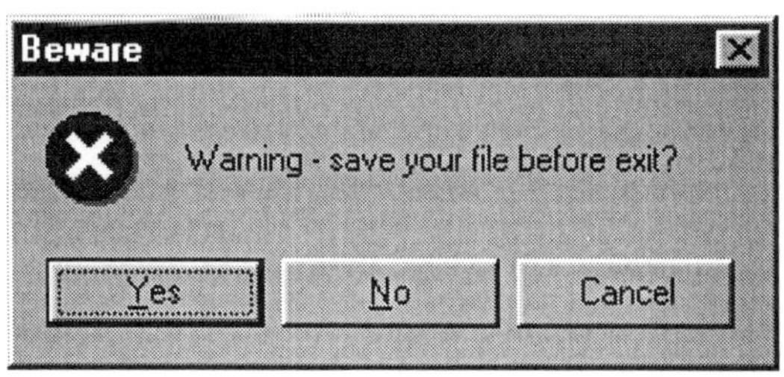

Fig. 8.7 *A Message Box*

As an example, see Fig. 8.7 where the *Message* is "Warning – save your file before exit?" and the *Title* is "Beware". In this case the values of *n, m & o* are 3, 16 & 0 so that the Box has *Yes*, *No* and *Cancel* buttons, a *Stop* icon and the first button is the default. Note that the values of the numbers *n, m & o* are so chosen that they can be added together and the total used instead of specifying them separately.

8.6 Colour

In Windows' applications (including VB) certain features like scroll-bars, menus and icons appear in colours which are determined by Windows itself. The Windows GUI has a default colour scheme but it also offers a number of alternative colours schemes and a facility to customize one's own. As a result the programmer cannot change the colour of, for example, a command button, though 3-D command buttons can have an icon attached to them. Many other Controls, however, can be

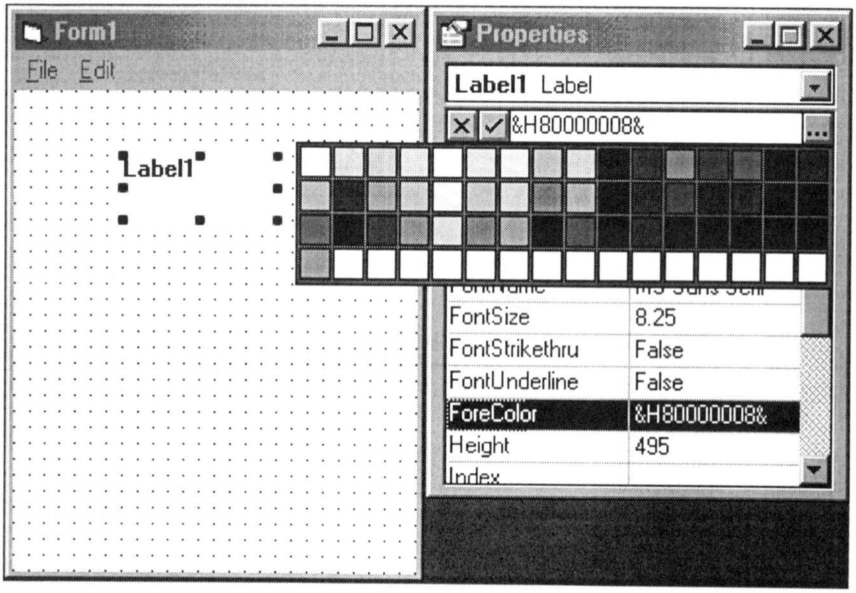

Fig. 8.8 The colour property of the Label Control can be chosen from a palette or specified using a colour code

displayed in a wide range of colours. When the colour property of a control is double clicked a colour palette appears (Fig. 8.8) containing 32 colours. Up to 16 more colours can be added to this using a Colour Palette menu item. More precise control can be obtained, however, by specifying the exact proportions of Red, Green and Blue in the colour required. In the properties window, the colour is specified by means of an eight digit hexadecimal number which has the form:

&H00FF00FF&

The &H at the beginning and the & at the end have no effect on the colour; this is specified by the last six of the eight hexadecimal digits sandwiched in between. The first two digits are always 00 and are not used. The next two digits signify the amount of Blue, the third two the amount of Green and the last two the amount of Red. The maximum values in each case are FF (which is 255 in decimal) and the minimum, 00 (0 in decimal). It can be thought of as : &H00BBGGRR& where B = Blue, G = Green and R = Red.

8.7 Writing Graphics Programs

We now turn to the question of how to write code to produce graphics effects (quite separate from the interface itself). VB has similar graphics features to those in QBASIC and Pascal, for example. Since graphic objects must be located on the screen the first thing that must be mastered is an understanding of Co-ordinate systems.

8.7.1 Co-ordinate systems

To locate objects on the screen a 2-D co-ordinate system is used with the default zero-zero point (the 'origin') in the top-left corner. A number of different unit systems are available : pixels (the numbers on a screen, of course, will vary according to the graphics mode being used), points (72 per inch, as used in the printing industry), inches, millimetres, centimetres, characters and 'twips' (1/1440 of an inch or 20 per point). These are chosen using the *ScaleMode* property (e.g. *ScaleMode* = 3 will choose pixels as the unit system).

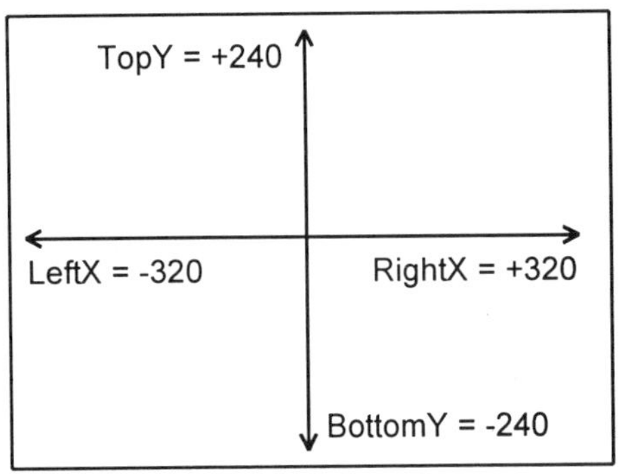

Fig. 8.9 *Specifying the Co-ordinate System*

The origin of the co-ordinate system can be changed from the default setting using the *Scale* method. It is used as follows :

Scale (*LeftX, TopY*) – (*RightX, BottomY*)

where *LeftX* designates the smallest value of x that is allowed, *TopY* the largest value of y, and so on. So, for example, to place the origin of the co-ordinate system in the middle of the screen using pixels as the units of measurement (and a VGA screen set at 640 × 480):

LeftX	=	– 320
TopY	=	+ 240
RightX	=	+ 320
BottomY	=	– 240

(see Fig. 8.9).

8.7.2 Colours

At any stage of a graphics program the programmer is working with a minimum of two colours – the foreground colour and the background colour. The foreground colour is the colour that will be used to draw any shape that is required; the background colour is the colour of all the other pixels on the screen (except, of course any other shapes that might have been drawn already). Many languages use a system of setting the foreground colour first and then issuing a statement to draw a shape (it then being drawn in this chosen colour). This colour is called the 'current colour' – the one that will apply to any objects drawn, until its value is changed. This can be a time-saving technique (for the programmer) because a large number of shapes can be drawn in one colour without having to specify that colour over and over again. The alternative is a system in which the drawing colour is specified as part of the shape-drawing statement. VB allows both these approaches. In QuickBASIC one way of specifying a colour is to use:

Color (*Foreground*, *Background*)

where *Foreground* and *Background* are codes specifying the foreground and background colours. There are three equivalents in VB :

BackColor
ForeColor
QBColor (*ColourCode*)

The first two are used in the form already described as the normal syntax for VB:

Object.BackColor = colour_code
Object.ForeColor = colour_code

The third is used in a different way; it is associated directly with a statement to draw a shape. For example, for a straight line:

LINE $(x_1, y_1) - (x_2, y_2)$, *QBColor* (colour_code)

The *colour_code*, as its name implies, is a code that specifies which colour is to be used. Details concerning the 16 colour code values can be seen in the VB Help system.

An alternative, for users who want to make use of the much larger range of colours available in modern displays, is to use a different colour code system: *RGB* (*red*, *green*, *blue*). This is reminiscent of the system described in an earlier section for assigning colours to controls in the properties window. Thus, for example, a line can be drawn using:

Object.ForeColor = RGB (*red*, *green*, *blue*)

Here, the foreground colour is set to a value specified by the values of *red*, *green* and *blue* (each of which takes values in the range 0 – 255). It is important to recognize that the red, green and blue codes are given in the reverse order from that used in the properties window.

8.7.3 Plotting a point

The basic building block of the dot-matrix display is, of course, the dot or point and therefore the irreducible minimum of a set of graphics statements is one which will display a point at any of the allowed positions on the screen. QBASIC uses:

PSET x, y, *colour_code*

where x and y are the co-ordinates of the position and VB uses the equivalent method:

Object.PSET x, y, *colour_code*

which draws a point on the specified object (a form or a picture box for example).

8.7.4 Drawing lines, rectangles and circles

The line drawing method has been used already. Its full form is:

Object.Line Step $(x_1, y_1) - (x_2, y_2)$, colour_code, B F

A number of these 'new' features are optional. The *Step* keyword, for example, allows the programmer to indicate that the end point co-ordinates are specified relative to the start point (not in absolute units). If B is used then a rectangular box is drawn instead of a straight line. In this case the co-ordinates signify the diagonally opposite corners of the box. If F is used then the box is filled in the same colour as the box.

Circles are drawn using:

Object.Circle Step (x, y), *radius*, colour_code, *start*, *end*, *aspect*

where x, y specify the centre of the circle, *start* and *end* allow partial circles to be drawn (the starting and ending points are specified using angles) and *aspect* allows ellipses to be drawn.

The width of any line can be set with:

Object.DrawWidth = Size

8.7.5 Clearing the screen

It is important to be able erase graphics and QBASIC has a CLS (clear the screen) facility. The equivalent in VB is:

Object.CLS

where the object can be a form, an image or a picture box.

8.7.6 Loading and saving pictures

Existing images which have been saved as files can be loaded into a form or a picture box using:

LoadPicture (*string*)

where the *string* is the name (and location) of the picture. For example:

Picture1.Picture = LoadPicture ("C:\clipart\dog1.BMP")

will load the file called dog1.BMP (which is stored in the subdirectory C:\clipart) and place it in the Picture Box control called Picture1. Its *Picture* property is now specified by contents of the file dog1.BMP.

The process is reversed using :

SavePicture Picture, string

where *string* is, again, the name and location of the file and *Picture* is the property of the Image box or Picture box where the image information is to be found.

8.8 Specialized Graphics Languages

It can be seen that a programming language like VB, though excellent for producing general-purpose programs to run under Microsoft Windows has very few graphics facilities: only points, straight lines, boxes and circles. It is clear that these are very limited – only enough to create a few simple bar charts, pie charts or simple diagrams really. Anything more sophisticated would involve an enormous amount of tedious programming. There are three options: graphics applications, operating system level graphics routines and specialized graphics languages. The majority of computer users are quite content to use one of the many types of graphics application software (discussed in an earlier chapter) but the reader might wonder what language was used to write those applications? Although the vast majority of computer users are content to create newsletters using DTP software, draw diagrams using illustration software, design machinery using CAD software, play computer games and create charts and graphs using presentation software, a small minority must master specialized graphics programming facilities in order that such applications software can be created. This last section is designed to give an introduction to this type of programming facility. First a few words about the facilities provided by operating systems.

8.8.1 Operating systems facilities

Operating systems (OSs) are usually thought of as systems software that handles routine matters like accessing peripherals and maintaining filing systems but increasingly they also have to handle graphics routines. If they did not, then the programmer would have to do an enormous amount of programming that would be repeated over and over again in many different applications. When screens displayed only text this was a fairly simple matter, but now very large amounts of data are routinely processed for graphics screens and bit-mapped printers and the operating system is the natural place to handle these demands – at least, all the basic operations. The Mac and the Windows OSs have features that support both 2-D and 3-D operations. 2-D features have been part of both OSs since their conception but 3-D features are a more recent addition. These routines, provided as extensions to the OS, are invaluable to the professional graphics programmer.

The basic facility provided in Windows is the GDI (Graphics Device Interface). This takes care of the screen display – the fonts and colour management, for example – and printer services. In fact some printer manufacturers take advantage of the GDI software provided with Windows to keep the price of their cheapest printers down. A GDI printer is one that relies entirely on the computer for all the processing required to turn a page description into a bit-map – activities, which in a more expensive device, are handled by the processor and memory installed in the printer itself. More recently, 3-D graphics processes in Windows software have been catered for by two rival standards: Direct3D and Open GL. Direct3D is Microsoft's 3-D standard and OpenGL is a version, for Windows, of a standard that has been used for some years by Unix-based workstations. Both of these need special 3-D video cards to get the best results but increasingly 'standard' video cards are being supplied with 3-D as well as 2-D acceleration features (see the chapter on hardware).

The equivalent software systems for the Mac are called QuickDraw and QuickTime. QuickDraw and QuickDraw GX look after standard 2-D functions such as basic screen drawing, printing and type management. QuickDraw3D looks after 3-D processes like wire-frame modelling and rendering. QuickTime handles video and sound clips and file compression.

8.8.2 The languages

Modern programming languages like Pascal or C are usually said to be procedural, which means that they can 'call' procedures, which are modules of code which perform particular specialized tasks. This modular approach is an ideal way of extending the basic facilities provided by the language – either by programmers writing their own procedures or by buying sets of procedures (or both). Specialized programming languages are in fact standard languages which are used in conjunction with libraries of graphics procedures. Ideally, these are hardware independent (sometimes called 'device independent') so that programs can be written that will run on any collection of display, input and printing devices. This requires that 'device drivers' are available for each input/output device – pieces of software that interface between the graphics code and the individual devices. Ideally the graphics procedures are also written to conform to agreed graphics standards which also makes for portability from one hardware system to another. The best-known standards are GKS (Graphical Kernal System) and PHIGS (Programmer's Hierarchical Interactive Graphics Standard), which is an extension of GKS. The graphics facilities offered by such systems are defined so as to be language independent also, with a 'language-binding' for each language (such as FORTRAN or C) which enables that language to access the graphics facilities of the package. This means that a programmer who has mastered a standard language like C can in principle write graphics programs without much extra effort by becoming familiar with the graphics routines available in the add-on library. The following gives some examples of the 2-D features of PHIGS:

8.8.3 Point and line plotting

The equivalent of PSET (used in QBASIC and VB) is:

SetPixel (x, y, intensity)

To reverse the process and retrieve a colour value there is a function :

GetPixel (x, y)

In addition to a simple point, it is possible to display small characters in a specified position, as in a graph for example, where the data points might be marked using an asterisk or small rectangle. This facility is called a polymarker :

PolyMarker (n, Pts)

Here, *n* indicates the number of markers and *Pts* signifies an array which contains a list of all the co-ordinates specifying the positions of the markers.

Line drawing is more sophisticated than in BASIC. It is done with a polyline function:

Polyline (n, Points)

A polyline is a sequence of connected straight lines. The co-ordinates of the end-points of the line segments are held in a two-dimensional array (*Points*). The value *n* corresponds to the number of co-ordinate positions.

The type of line – its thickness and colour and whether it is continuous or dotted and, if dotted, what the dot pattern is to be – can also be specified. These features of the line are called its attributes. *Attribute* is the term used to specify the secondary characteristic of a graphics primitive, such as the width of a line, the height of a character or the size of a marker. The appropriate function for the type of line is:

SetLineType (lt)

where *lt* is an integer which specifies the type of line. The width of a line is specified using:

SetLineWidthScaleFactor (lw)

where *lw* (the line width parameter) indicates the width of the line relative to a standard width. The colour of a line is specified using:

SetPolyLineColourIndex (lc)

where *lc* is the colour code. The significance of any particular colour code depends on the palette or CLUT (Colour Look-Up Table) as discussed earlier. A CLUT can be set up using:

SetColourRepresentation (ws, ci, colourptr)

where *ws* specifies the output device that is to be used, *ci* the colour index (the colour code) and *colourptr* the three intensity values of red, green and blue to be associated with the colour index.

8.8.4 Area-filling

Closed geometrical shapes can be created with *PolyLine* (already discussed) to create polygons, *circle* and *ellipse* functions. Filled shapes can be created using *FillArea* (which generates filled polygons), *FillCircle* and *FillEllipse*. What is needed, however, is a method of defining the type of filling to be used. This is where the power of a language like PHIGS is seen, since it provides considerable control over the fill-patterns using:

SetInteriorStyle (fs)

The value of *fs* distinguishes between hollow, solid fill, pattern fill and hatched fill. Hatching is a system of parallel lines, sometimes overlapping, and at various angles used engineering drawings and maps.

The particular fill pattern is chosen using:

SetInteriorStyleIndex (pi)

The size of the basic pattern element can also be set with:

SetPatternSize (dx, dy)

The starting point of the pattern can be set with:

SetPatternReferencePoint (position)

8.8.5 Bundled attributes

Another powerful feature of this type of graphics language is that of 'bundled attributes'. If a program is to be hardware independent it has to cope with the fact that different output devices have different capabilities. Some printers can print in colour, others only in black. Some display devices have much higher resolution than others and different numbers of colours. What is needed is a way of specifying a graphics program that will run on a different set of output devices without going through the program and altering all the attribute definitions. The solution is to group together in a table all those attributes that will depend on the output hardware in one particular installation. A table of bundled attributes defines, for one particular graphic primitive, how those attributes are to be interpreted by a particular output device and is called a bundle table. A set of tables can then be established, one for each type of installation likely to be met, thus ensuring that the programmer can define how one standard piece of software should be implemented under differing hardware situations.

8.8.6 Text

The handling of text provides another example of the power of a specialized graphics language. General-purpose microcomputer languages provide only very limited control over the display of text. This is partly because of the limitations of the first raster-scanned monitors which had a rather poor resolution and that meant that the in-built character set was very simple in design, each symbol occupying a rectangle made up from a small number of pixels. Normally, in text-only mode, characters of only one type-face are available. These have a fixed size and can be used in only one orientation (the normal one of horizontal, left-to-right). In contrast, in PHIGS, text can usually have many attributes. The following is fairly obvious:

SetTextFont (tf)

The fonts can be specified as bit-maps or as vectors (made from polylines and splines).

Text colour is specified using	SetTextColourIndex (tc)
Text height is specified using	SetCharacterHeight (ch)
Text width is specified using	SetCharacterExpansionFactor (cw)

This latter can be used to change the aspect ratio of a character since it does not change the height of the character. SetCharacterHeight is used under more normal circumstances when there is no intention of changing the aspect ratio since it scales the width by the same factor as the height.

Character spacing is specified using:

SetCharacterSpacing (cs)

The orientation of the characters is specified using SetCharacterUpVector (upvect) where *upvect* has two values which together determine the angle at which the characters are drawn.

For characters in horizontal or vertical alignment a separate statement can be used:

SetTextPath (tp) where *tp* has values of *right*, *left*, *up* or *down*

The alignment of the text can be controlled with:

SetTextAlignment (h, v) where *h* has values of *left*, *centre* and *right* and *v* has values of values of *top*, *bottom*, *half*, *cap* or *base*.

8.8.7 Co-ordinate systems and view-ports

One of the irritating but necessary chores of graphics work arises from the need to work with a number of different co-ordinate systems. The simplest example of this is the scaling factors needed to change from one co-ordinate system to another. For example, if a diagram of a piece of machinery is to be created, then measurements of that machinery will have to be made in, say, metres and millimetres. The display screen will almost always be much smaller than the machinery and so the measurements will all have to be scaled down by some suitable factor in creating the display. When a final drawing has to be made from the computed output using a pen plotter, for example, a new scaling factor will have to be used to fit the dimensions of the plotter.

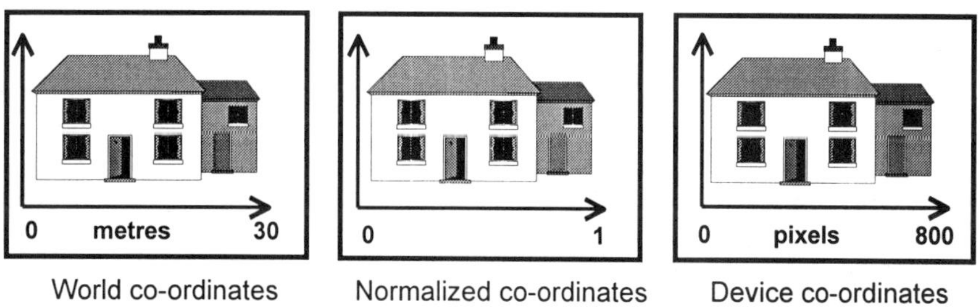

Fig. 8.10 *Three different co-ordinate systems*

In order to automate this process graphics languages allow for the use of a number of different co-ordinate systems. Measurements of an object are entered in those units which are most appropriate – a piece of machinery in metres, a map in kilometres, a micro-chip in micro-metres. These are called world co-ordinates – the co-ordinate system most suitable to the world which is being represented. A display device, a printer or a plotter, on the other hand, would each have its own co-ordinate system – these are device co-ordinates. As an intermediary between the two there is a third possibility – normalized co-ordinates, which are arranged so that the maximum dimensions are unity (Fig. 8.10). Once these co-ordinate systems have been defined the procedure is as follows. Information about the world to be modelled is entered in world co-ordinate units. This data is automatically converted into normalized co-ordinate data for the purposes of calculation and manipulation in the computer. At the output stage the display data or printer is then converted into suitable display co-ordinates. All the conversions are performed by the graphics software without further intervention.

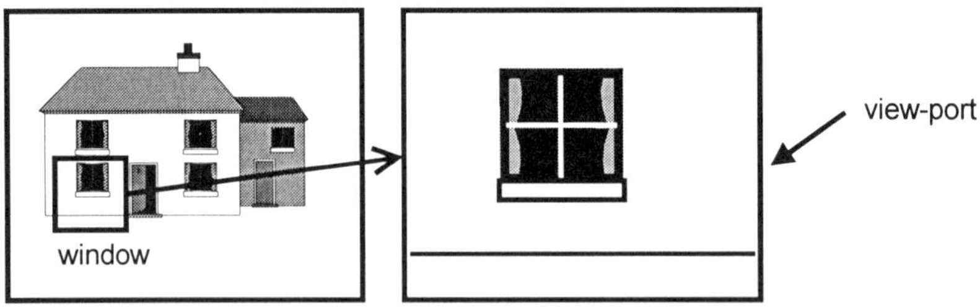

Fig. 8.11 *A window and a view-port*

The idea of a window is now commonplace because of its use in GUIs. It is a rectangular portion of a two-dimensional display, to which certain types of information are restricted. The idea can be given a specialized meaning in the context of different co-ordinate systems. A window is defined as a rectangular area in a world co-ordinate system. A rectangular area in a display co-ordinate system, however, is called a *view-port* (see Fig. 8.11). What this does is to make a conceptual distinction between a limited region of an object (a window: what part of an object is to be displayed) as opposed to the limits to the viewing process (the view-port: where the display is to be). Sometimes the view-port fills the whole of the display system in which case we tend to forget its existence. What we see depends only on the window. On other occasions the view-port only occupies part of the display. There may be other view-ports on the screen and some may partially overlap others, obscuring what is in them.

In brief then, the window determines what is to be displayed and the view-port determines where it is to be displayed. To take an example from the experience of viewing a real object like a building: the selection of which part of the building is to be seen – the front, the back, a small part of the building from close up or all the building from far away – is determined by the choice of window. Whether this image of the building is seen as a tiny picture in one corner of the display or fills the display or is partly obscured by another image – all these are determined by the choice of view-port.

The process of converting data from a window to a view-port is called mapping. The mapping process can take a number of different forms. The most obvious one is 'clipping' and this is the operation of removing those parts of an image which lie outside a particular chosen window. It is of course fundamental to the idea of a window, which is a limited region of an object. Other mapping methods can be used to achieve effects such as to simulate the movement of the observer. For example zooming is a form of mapping where progressively smaller and smaller windows with the same centre are mapped onto a single view-port. This gives the same effect as a zoom lens on a camera and produces the impression of an observer moving towards the object or vice versa. Similarly panning is achieved by progressively moving a fixed-size window across the object, again mapping on to a single view-port and so generating the effect of a camera or viewer moving in front of the object.

This whole approach of distinguishing a window from a view-port is complementary to a similar distinction between the object and the observer. It helps to separate into two distinct processes the modelling of the object from the viewing of the object. Modelling consists of building up information about the object until it is fully defined as a set of data. Viewing the object involves determining what that object would look like from a particular point in space and with a particular set of viewing restrictions. What determines the view of the object is the choice of window and the mapping method used between window and view-port.

8.9 Scripting Languages

Early in the chapter it was mentioned that most computer users are quite content to use graphics application software to create their graphics effects – rather than the laborious process of programming. In fact these are not the only alternatives – there is a middle way called scripting. Scripting is really another term for macro language programming. Many applications software programs offer some form of macros. The simplest form is that in which a sequence of key-strokes are recorded and saved under a name, to be re-used at any time. For example, in a word processor, if the user is continually performing a number of operations, either with dedicated function keys, normal keys or menu selections it can be very time-saving to switch on the macro facility and record them in a simple file. The file can then be associated with a particular key-combination. Pressing that key-combination then re-runs that recorded sequence of events. Good macro facilities, however, offer more powerful options. The macro is treated as just another computer program that can be edited or supplemented using classic programming techniques like loops and branches to produce much more powerful effects than can be created by recording key-strokes. What we have is a specialized programming language that is particular to one piece of application software. It operates within the setting of that application – it cannot be used on its own – and it draws from the specialized features of that software.

This approach has been applied to some types of graphics application software – particularly CAD and Multimedia authoring software. Some early multimedia packages, for example, were entirely script-based; the only way to create a multimedia presentation was by writing a program. Some current packages are now entirely icon-based; the only way to create a presentation is by means of a graphic metaphor. Some modern packages, however, offer the best of both worlds. Much of the routine work is done by icon-based methods but the more complicated effects are created by adding script. Here is a simple example (a branching structure), drawn from Lingo – the scripting language of MacroMedia Director :

```
on mouseDown
        if the clickOn = 1 then
                goto "London"
        else if the clickOn = 2 then
                goto "Paris"
        clsc if thc clickOn = 3 then
                goto "New York"
        else if the clickOn = 4 then
                goto "Tokyo"
        else
                nothing
        endif
end
```

Anyone who is familiar with Pascal or a similar language will recognize the basic structure. The context is a multimedia application that offers information about cities of the world. The labels "London", "Paris" etc. refer to other parts of the multimedia program which display video clips, for example. The clickOn event refers to the user clicking a range of possible options, probably with a mouse. The form of the code is entirely standard; the details, however, are determined by the facilities of this particular multimedia authoring package.

8.10 The Way Forward

Computing has changed enormously in the twenty, or so, years since the advent of the desktop computer. In the early days 'computing' almost equated with 'programming' and this meant it was, at best, a specialist activity for the technically-minded. Now the computer has almost become a commodity item like a stereo or a video recorder and for the vast majority of the millions of new users 'computing' now means 'applications software'. This change has come about for a variety of reasons but would probably not have happened without computer graphics – in the form of the GUI. Intuitive graphic interfaces have helped to break down the barrier between the machine and the user.

The technical changes that have occurred during this period have been so great that it is tempting to think we must be reaching the limit of what is possible, or necessary. After all, it was perfectly possible to have written a book in the early 1980's using an Apple II computer with one 360 K floppy disk, a monochrome text-only screen and a 1 MHz, 8 bit processor. All that the modern 450 MHz, 32-bit, 16.8 million colour, 8 Gigabyte HD monsters really add to that task is to help the author visualize what the printed product will look like and to make it much easier to add illustrations. Why do we need any more? What extras would we want to add ? Many would argue that we have already added too much. Software takes up too much disk space, has too many complicated 'features' which no-one ever uses or can figure out how to use and that the constantly up-dated hardware specifications produce little net gain for the user. Can any imaginable developments in computer graphics offer the sort of real improvements that came with the first GUIs?

Well, crystal-ball gazing is a notoriously unreliable occupation but it is possible to think of three areas where computer graphics could help the user of the future. The first is in the ill-defined area of multimedia. Strictly speaking multimedia implies 'many media', of which graphics is only one, but the visual tends to be the dominant sense and it is possible to imagine greatly-enhanced graphical environments that are much closer to reality than the current style of GUI. Most current GUIs are based on a crude representation of an office environment with, often, unrecognizable icons that need a label to explain what they are supposed to be – surely a failure to implement a basic principle of the GUI? Suppose that, with the use of realistic 3-D modelled images, and possibly, virtual reality-style feedback, the user could actually inhabit a computer-generated but recognizably 'real' world? What possibilities would that open up for the software designer and for the user? It should, in principle, mean that in many cases no computer skills at all would be needed to perform any computer-based task that mimicked a real-world task. The user would already have all the necessary skills – acquired in the real world – and now usable in the synthetic world. Using a computer would be much more like playing a modern computer game. The much-talked-of 'transparent' interface would be a reality. No-one would notice the interface any more, which, surely is the long-term aim of an interface designer?

The second possibility is perhaps nearer the present state of affairs. The huge growth of software 'features' has led to a condition often called the '80-20 rule' (80% of the features are used by only 20% of the users) and these unused features make it more difficult for the average user to find their way through this dense undergrowth of obscure tricks. The software is 'too clever by half'. Suppose software could be designed that began (as far as the user was concerned) with very few, basic features but which grew with the user? One method would be to make software modular – the user would buy and add extra features, as desired, to a very basic starting set of facilities. Another approach, however, would be to include all the features in the software from the outset, but to create an interface that hid most of them from the user – until they actually wanted them. A further extension of this principle would be a 'design-your-own interface'. Why should interfaces be imposed on the user? Each of us works in their own way – why not let us re-arrange our software so that it works the way that suits us? This principle would inevitably involve an imaginative use of computer graphics since design, for most of us, is a very visual activity. We, the users, could become the software designers of the future.

The third possibility is, perhaps, the least ambitious way to use computer graphics and therefore the most easily implemented. Help systems tend to be very word-based, like a printed manual transferred to the screen. What we all want, from time to time, is for someone to 'just show me how to do it'. The rapid growth in processing power and storage capacity should soon make it possible to create help systems which are based on a range of digitized videos – a real person showing us how to do something (together with a sound track). On-line help could contain what are, in essence, a series of mini training videos, but under the user's control.

Only time will tell whether any of these ideas will come to fruition, though the first signs of the user-designed interface are already with us. Some interfaces already allow the user to remove or add icons to their icon-bar, to change keyboard short-cuts or to alter the colours used in the display. These are fairly trivial, but still useful forms of user-based interface design. Perhaps none of these will become the next Big Idea but one thing is surely certain – that computer graphics has still a big part to play in whatever is to come.

Exercises for the Reader:

These exercises assume that the reader has access to a copy of VisualBASIC.

(1) Write a program, based on Example 1, such that, clicking a Command Button changes the font of a piece of text (use a Label). Now change the code so that the colour of the text changes instead.

(2) Extend this idea by creating a form with a piece of text on it, together with three Option Buttons (labelled "Red", "Green" and "Blue") – the labels on the Option Buttons should be in the appropriate colour. Write code for each Option Button such that when the program is run, and one of the Option buttons selected, the text changes to that colour. (Hint: remember the method of coding colours using Hex numbers.)

(3) Write a program, based on Example 3, such that, clicking a Command Button makes a picture seem to move from one point on the form to another. The word 'seem' is used because the program requires two copies of the picture (in two different Picture Boxes) to be placed on the form. Initially one is visible and the other invisible. Clicking the Command Button reverses this – the visible becomes invisible, and vice versa.

(4) Create a "File" menu on a form with the following items: New, Open, Close, (A Separator Bar), Save and Save As .. Indicate in the usual way which characters in each menu item can be used as keyboard shortcuts. Write code for the "Save As .." option that brings up the appropriate Dialogue Box. [Notes: (a) a Separator Bar is created by using a dash symbol; (b) each item in the menu must be given a name as well as a caption; (c) you will find, on running the program, that the Dialogue Box must be Cancelled before the program can be halted.]

(5) Use the menu created in the previous exercise and add, to the Open item, code that will produce a Message Box. The box should have the Title: "No Response" and the Message: "Disk Drive Not Ready". The symbol on the message box should be an Exclamation mark; the buttons should be "Retry" and "Cancel" (the first being the default).

(6) In the main text concerning the three variables *n*, *m* & *o*, used in Message Box it was said that these numbers can be written separately (for example: 2 + 48 + 256) or added together (306). How can this be so? Why are not the individual values of *n*, *m* & *o* lost when added together?

(7) Create a form which is Maximized when run (Maximized and Minimized are two of the three possible modes of the WindowState property of a Form). Set the co-ordinates so that the origin is in the bottom-right corner of the form and the units are pixels. Create a simple bar chart with 5 bars – each of them in a different colour and filled. They should be 50 pixels wide and spaced 50 pixels

apart. Choose any suitable values of height (all different). The bar chart should appear when the form is clicked.

(8) Use the circle and straight line statements in VB to draw a "match-stick man". The origin of the co-ordinate system should remain in the bottom-left corner of the form but the units should be inches (consult the Help system for the code). The head should be filled and light red in colour; the rest of the figure should be in light blue. The lines should be 3 pixels wide. (Note: since Circles – unlike Rectangles – have no 'Fill' option, a little ingenuity will be needed to fill the head).

Further Reading

Computer Graphics (General)

Most general-purpose text books on Computer Graphics have a strong orientation to algorithms but these also contain other very useful material.

"Computer Graphics" (2nd ed.) J. Foley, A. van Dam et al. (Addison-Wesley) 1996
"Introduction to Computer Graphics" Foley et.al. (Addison-Wesley) 1994
"Computer Graphics" R. Salmon & M. Slater (Addison-Wesley) 1987
"Computer Graphics" (2nd ed.) Hearn & Baker (Prentice Hall) 1994

Hardware

"Effective Colour Displays" D. Travis (Academic Press) 1991
"High-Resolution Graphics Display Systems" J. Peddie (McGraw-Hill) 1994
"Input Devices" ed. S. Sherr (Academic Press) 1988
"Output Hardcopy Devices" ed. R. Durbeck (Academic Press) 1988
"Peter Norton's Inside the PC" (7th ed.) P. Norton (SAMS) 1997
"Peripherals for Computer Systems" A. Bradley (MacMillan) 1991
"Real World Scanning & Halftones" D. Blatner & S. Roth (Peachpit) 1993

For up-to-date information on hardware developments, consult also the more technical computer magazines and manufacturers' sites on the Internet.

Software Applications

There are many books on specific software applications, which act as supplements to the software developers' manuals, but very few which attempt to review the general principles. Here are two:

"Using Computer Graphics" M. Richardson (Chapman & Hall) 1995
"Computer Graphics in Application" G. Marshall (Prentice Hall) 1987

Colour

"Color Publishing on the Macintosh" K. & S. Baker Random House (1992)
"Computer Generated Color" R. Jackson et al. (Wiley) 1994
"The Desktop Color Book" (2nd ed.) M. Gosney & L. Dayton (MIS) 1994

Fonts

"Computers and Typography" R. Sassoon (Intellect) 1993
"Encyclopedia of Typefaces" Jaspert, Berry & Johnson (Graphic Books Int.)
"The Fonts Coach" C. Robinson & D. Gray New Riders Publishing (1993)

Graphics Files

"Encyclopedia of Graphics File Formats" J. Murray (O'Reilly) 1994
"Graphic File Formats" Brown & Shepherd (Prentice Hall) 1994

Algorithms

"3-D Computer Graphics" (2nd ed.) A. Watt (Addison-Wesley) 1993
"An Introduction to Ray-Tracing" ed. A. Glassner (Academic Press) 1989
"Integrated Computer Graphics" B. Mielke (West Publishing) 1991
"Procedural Elements for Computer Graphics" D. Rogers (McGraw-Hill) 1985

A Glossary of Computer Graphics

Accelerator card

Printed circuit card that plugs into the computer main motherboard to accelerate the performance of graphics operations. Uses a special graphics 'co-processor' which performs graphic operations more efficiently than the general-purpose microprocessor which is at the heart of the computer and to which all graphics operations can be delegated.

Active matrix LCD

An LCD display (q.v.) which has a transistor with each liquid crystal, whose function is to turn the crystal on and off. These LCDs are more difficult to manufacture than 'passive matrix' LCDs and therefore more expensive but achieve higher contrast because the crystals do not begin to relax between refresh cycles.

Additive colour

Colour monitors and colour printing processes create a wide range of colours by combining three or more primary colours in various proportions. Colour monitors use an emissive process, in which the primary colours (red, blue and green) are emitted by coloured phosphor dots on the screen. When these three different coloured rays of light combine, they do so by a process of addition. The light which enters the eye is a mixture of these three primaries. Colour printing, however, uses an absorptive process. Natural or artificial illumination, in the form of white light (which is a mixture of all the colours of the spectrum) is reflected off a mixture of primary coloured dots on the paper. In doing so, some of the spectral colours are absorbed and the perceived colour depends on whatever wavelengths are not absorbed. When absorptive primary colours (cyan, magenta and yellow) are used to produce secondary colours they mix by a process of subtraction, each removing different wavelengths from the, originally, white light.

Aliasing

The result of digitizing a continuous shape into a series of discrete dots in a rectangular matrix. For example, an oblique straight line becomes a series of small steps. Anti-aliasing techniques are methods of reducing this effect.

Alphanumeric

A graphic shape which is either a letter of the alphabet or a number.

Ambient light

That part of the illumination of an object which applies equally to all surfaces in the object (as opposed to directional light which illuminates some surfaces more than others). It is caused by diffuse illumination (q.v.).

ASCII code

A numerical code for storing alphanumeric characters; the letters stand for: American Standard Code for Information Exchange.

Aspect ratio

The ratio of the width to the height of a graphics display or other image.

Background colour

When graphic objects are created they are placed 'on top' of a contrasting colour. This colour is the background colour. The colour of the graphic objects is the foreground colour.

Balloon help

A help system used in some graphical user interfaces (q.v.) in which a cartoon-like speech bubble (balloon) appears on the screen whenever the mouse is pointed at an object, to explain the function of that object.

Bit-map

A way of representing a digitized image in the memory of the computer. In its simplest form, each pixel in the image is represented by one bit in memory. For example, a bit set to 0 indicates a black pixel and a bit set to 1 indicates a white one. If more colours are used then more than one bit is needed for each pixel. The term 'map' indicates that a simple one-to-one relationship exists between the object being represented (the image) and the representation (in memory), as in a geographical map.

Bit-mapped font

A font which is represented as a set of bits, rather than as a more general description of the shape of the letters.

Body text

The type of font which is used for the majority of the normal text in a document – the 'body' of the text.

Bold

A thicker, blacker version of a font (q.v.) which causes the characters to stand out from the surrounding normal text.

CAD

Computer-Assisted (or Computer-Aided) Design. Software used for designing and drawing, usually in the context of engineering design.

Cathode-ray tube (CRT)

A glass vacuum vessel used in traditional computer displays and TV sets. A beam of electrons is fired from an electron gun, through a vacuum, and is absorbed in a fluorescent layer on the inside of the face of the tube. This layer emits light to form a glowing image. The beam is scanned across the face of the tube in a 'raster' pattern – a series of closely-packed parallel lines, its brightness being modulated to form the bright and dark regions of the image.

CCD

Charge-coupled device. A semiconductor device which is sensitive to light. They are used in document scanners and digital cameras.

Cel

A component of an animated image. In traditional animation, parts of the image are drawn onto transparent celluloid (hence the short form: cel). A number of cels can be placed on top of each other and the result photographed. By this means, unchanging parts of the animation can be separated from the changing parts and only drawn once.

CGA

Colour Graphics Adapter. The first graphics system used in IBM-PC computers. Had a maximum resolution of 640 × 200 pixels (two colours). At a reduced resolution of 320 × 200 pixels, four colours were available.

CGM

Computer Graphics Metafile. One of the many standard ways of storing a graphic image.

Character set

A complete set of alphanumeric characters in one particular font.

Clip-art

A collection of digitized images which can be incorporated into a computer graphic image.

Clipboard

A temporary store for a portion of an image which has been 'cut' (removed) from one image, ready to 'paste' into another.

CMYK

Cyan, magenta, yellow and black. The first three are the absorptive primary colours used in printed images (see additive colour). Black should not be required in printing because a mixture of the first three should produce black but in practice the quality of the black produced this way is often unsatisfactory.

Colour separation

The process of separating the three or four primary colour components from a colour image, in preparation for the printing process. See *Additive colour* and *Process colour*.

Colour look-up table (CLUT)

A table which relates the colour codes, stored in the refresh buffer, to the specification of the colours, in terms of their R, G and B components (see *RGB*).

Compression

A technique for storing computer data in a smaller amount of memory than would normally be required. Some compression techniques are designed so that no data is lost in the process (loss-less compression); others are designed to achieve higher levels of compression at the expense of losing data ('lossy' compression).

Continuous tone image

An image, like a photograph, which consists of such a large range of 'tones' (shades of grey or colour) that they shade imperceptibly, one into another. In contrast, a digitized image consists of a limited number of distinct shades. See *Grey-levels*.

Contrast

The ratio of the maximum to the minimum intensity of an image.

Control points

A set of points which is used to control the exact shape of a curve.

Co-ordinate system

A way of specifying the position of a point in space. The perpendicular distances (the x and y distances) to two right-angled axes are used in the 2-D Cartesian co-ordinate system. A third distance (the z distance) is used in a 3-D version of this method.

cpi

Characters per inch. Used to specify the density of mono-spaced printed characters.

Cursor

A small graphical symbol, used in conjunction with a pointing device, like a mouse, to indicate a position on the computer display.

Descender

The tail-like part of a character like p, y and j which descends below the line which designates the bottom of the majority of other characters.

Desktop publishing (DTP)

The use of special software and high-quality printers to produce printed material using a desktop computer. For best results the laser printer is used for the production of proofs (q.v.) and the final result is produced on a commercial-quality output device, like a typesetter, for use with a litho printer.

Diffuse illumination

Light which, because it has gone though a series of reflections or scattering processes, shines in all directions and so illuminates objects very evenly. Natural light is diffuse when the sunlight is scattered by clouds. Artificial light is diffuse when special glass diffusers scatter the light and when there are many different lights illuminating the same object. See *Directional illumination.*

Digital camera

Camera in which the film has been replaced with a 2-dimensional array of CCDs (q.v.). This produces a digital representation of the image without further processing; it requires no intermediate processing of film or secondary digitization process.

Directional illumination

Illumination, usually from a small source of light or spotlight, which illuminates some surfaces much more strongly than others because of its very specific direction.

Display buffer

Another term for a refresh buffer (q.v.).

Display device

A device, such as a CRT monitor (q.v.) or LCD (q.v.) which produces images based on computer data.

Dithering

A method, used by computer printers, of simulating grey-levels based on the use of large numbers of tiny black dots. Those areas where there is a high density of dots look darker than areas where the density is low. The method depends on the use of dots which are too small to be seen individually. Colour tones can be simulated in a similar way using cyan, magenta, yellow and black dots. See *Halftone.*

Dot matrix

A rectangular array of dots. Most computer printing and display devices produce images based on such an array. One particular type of impact printer has acquired the name of 'dot-matrix printer'.

Dot pitch

The pitch of a CRT display (q.v.) is a measurement of the separation of the coloured phosphor dots or stripes which are used to create the image. The closer the dots are together, the more detail that can be displayed on the CRT. The best CRTs have a dot pitch of about 0.22 mm (millimetres). This means that the red phosphor dots (for example) repeat themselves every 0.22 mm.

Dots per inch (dpi)

The number of dots which are printed or displayed by a computer printer or display device per inch. For example, most standard laser printer produce 600 dpi but a standard CRT monitor operates at about 60 –72 dpi.

Drum plotter

A pen plotter in which a pen is moved over a piece of paper fixed to a cylinder (drum). See *Flat-bed plotter.*

DTP

See *Desktop publishing.*

Dye sublimation printer

A printer which produces very high quality continuous tone colour images by a process of subliming dyes which mix and condense on the paper to produce intermediate tones. Sublimation is the process whereby some substances, when heated, turn from the solid phase directly to the vapour phase without melting to form a liquid.

EGA

Enhanced Graphics Adaptor. An improved display interface for the IBM-PC computer which superseded the CGA. Resolution of 640×350 (16 colours).

Electron gun

The device in a CRT (q.v.) which produces a high-velocity stream of electrons. These are fired at the face of the CRT and are absorbed in the phosphor layer, which then gives out light.

Electronic publishing

The production and distribution of documents in electronic form (e.g. on floppy disks, CD-ROMs, via intra-nets or via the Internet).

Encapsulated PostScript (EPS)

A file which contains a description of an image created in the page-description language PostScript.

Extended light source

A light source which, because it is large (e.g. a fluorescent strip light) produces a diffuse illumination because most surfaces on an object receive illumination from some point (probably more than one point) on the source. See *Point light source.*

Extrusion

See *Lofting.*

File format

The particular way of saving a file. Graphics files are saved in many different formats. See *CGM, PCX, TIFF.*

Fillet

A term used in CAD (q.v.) to describe the process of turning a right-angle join, between two straight lines, into a curved edge.

Filter

An algorithm which is used to process computer data. Photographic retouching software can be used to apply filters to images which change their appearance. In this case the term is used by analogy with a coloured filter which can be used to change the appearance of a photograph.

Flat-bed plotter

A pen plotter in which a pen is moved over a piece of paper fixed to a flat surface (bed). See Drum plotter.

Flood fill

A process used in drawing or painting software in which a colour or pattern is used to fill all the space enclosed by a chosen boundary of a specified colour – as if water were filling a container. Also called a 'Seed Fill'.

Folder

A term used in the Macintosh GUI (q.v.) and in Windows-95 and 98 to describe a symbol which represents what would be called a 'sub-directory' in most other, non-graphical operating systems. The analogy is with a cardboard folder, used in a filing cabinet, to store a number of documents which are to be kept together.

Font

A set of typographic characters with the same style or design. The term is often confused with the similar term 'typeface'. A font is usually taken to be a particular subset of a typeface. For example the typeface called 'Times' exists in many different sizes and in both bold and italic forms (q.v.). One complete set of characters in the Times typeface, of one particular size and form (for example italic), is a font.

Foreground colour

See *Background colour.*

Fractal

A type of mathematical function which is used to produce graphic shapes of a natural kind – for example to model the shapes of trees, rocks and clouds in computer-generated images. Fractal equations have also been used to produce very elegant abstract patterns which contain endless detail as they are magnified and also to compress files.

Frame

A rectangular shape which is used as a border for a graphic.

Frame-grabber

A hardware device which is used to digitize an image from the stream of images produced by TV and video systems.

GEM

Graphical Environment Manager. A GUI (q.v.) produced by the Digital Research Corp. The term is now used to designate the graphic file format (q.v.) used by it to save images (with the file extension IMG).

GIF

Graphics Interchange Format. A graphic file format (q.v.) developed for use by CompuServe for storing and interchanging images over the Internet.

Graphic tablet

Flat drawing surface, attached to the computer, which detects the position of a special pen (a 'stylus'); used for inputting drawings and other graphic information. A special version of the stylus – called a 'puck' because of its resemblance to a hockey puck – equipped with a transparent plate and cross-hairs, can be used to input position more accurately.

Grey-levels

Tonal variations of grey between the two extremes of black and white.

Grid

A rectangular array of dots or lines on a screen which can be used to help align objects drawn on the screen. See *Snapping*.

Graphical User Interface (GUI)

A pictorial system which enables a computer user to control software by means of small images (called icons) by means of a pointing device (usually a mouse). The ideas were developed by the Xerox Corp. but were first commercially successful in the Apple Macintosh.

Graphics mode

Many computers can operate in two different modes. In one, only a limited set of characters can be displayed on the screen. This is called text-only or character mode.

In the other, every pixel on the screen is under software control and so a wide range of graphics can be displayed. This is graphics (or 'true graphics') mode.

Greeking

When text is displayed by DTP software at such a low magnification (or with such small characters) that the screen is not able to reproduce it in readable form, then it can be 'greeked'. This means that the outline of each line of text is displayed as a grey bar, in order that the layout of the page can still be seen even though the text cannot be read. Greeking text will speed up the display of a page whenever changes of view are required.

GUI

See *Graphical User Interface.*

Gutter

The white space between two columns of text.

Halftone

An image which is reproduced using dots to represent continuous tones (q.v.). This is the normal method of printing photographs in books, magazines and newspapers. The halftone is created from a continuous tone image by photographing it through a fine mesh (a screen) which breaks it up into dots. See *Dithering.*

Handle

A small black square at the corners of a selected graphic object, frame or window.

Hard copy

A copy of a computer graphic image (or other file) which has been printed on paper.

Hertz (Hz)

A measure of frequency. One Hz means one cycle or operation per second.

Hidden line

A line which is part of a drawing of a 3-D object but which should be hidden from the observer because other parts of the object obscure it. In using a computer to create an image of a 3-D object, initially all the lines are drawn, and then the computer calculates which lines should be hidden, and removes them from the display. In different views of an object, different lines are hidden. The same terminology is applied to surfaces – for example, 'hidden surface' removal.

High resolution

An image which is displayed in very fine detail is said to be a high-resolution image. The same terminology applies to displays and printers. See *Resolution.*

HSB colour system

A method of specifying colour which uses three variables: Hue, Saturation and Brightness. Hue corresponds to the wavelength of the light and therefore to the name of the colour (e.g. red, blue, etc.); Saturation (or chroma) represents the strength or purity of the colour, sometimes called the purity or intensity (as if mixed to varying degrees with white); Brightness corresponds to the relative lightness or darkness of the colour (as if mixed to varying degrees with black). There is a similar system called the HLS (or HSL) colour system which uses Hue, Lightness and Saturation. See CMYK and RGB colour models.

Hue

See *HSB colour system* above.

Icon

Small stylized picture used in Graphical User Interfaces (or GUIs – q.v.). An icon is usually used to represent a piece of software or hardware and is used by clicking, double-clicking or dragging. Clicking makes the object associated with the icon active. Double-clicking will run the software represented by the icon. Dragging the icon over another icon causes it to interact in some way with the function associated with that icon. For example, dragging the icon representing a file, over the waste-basket icon, causes the file to be deleted (thrown away).

Impact printer

A printer which produces its output by a process in which an object hits a ribbon onto a piece of paper, so transferring ink. See *Dot matrix.*

In-betweening

Part of the process of producing animated pictures which involves creating large numbers of images which correspond to small stages in between the beginning and the ending of a movement of one of the cartoon characters.

Ink-jet printer

A printer which produces images by spraying very fine jets of ink from a large number of tiny nozzles in a moving head.

Input device

A computer peripheral (q.v.) which is used to enter information into the computer. Examples include the keyboard, mouse and scanner. See *Output device.*

Interactive graphics

Computer graphics in which the user sees an almost instant response to any input. All modern graphics systems are designed to be interactive although some systems still have an appreciable time-lag between input and system response (usually seen on the screen).

Interlacing

A system used in many CRT monitors (q.v.) and TV sets in which the raster lines which create the image are not laid down in strict sequence. All the odd lines are first laid down, followed by all the even lines, interlaced between them.

Inverse video

See *Reverse video.*

Isometric projection

A type of perspective drawing of a 3-D object in which the lines are drawn parallel to each other, rather than to a vanishing point, as in true perspective.

Italic

A font (q.v.) or character in which the, normally, vertical components of the characters are slanted.

Joystick

An input device (q.v.), looking like the joystick of an aeroplane, used to position the cursor on a display device.

JPEG

Joint Photographic Experts Group. Name of a standards' body which has given its name to a lossy compression standard. See *Compression.*

Justification

The process of introducing small extra spaces into a line of text to make it line up at the right-hand end. Typewritten text is left justified only, leaving the right end ragged, so no extra spaces need be introduced. Printed text is frequently right justified also (often simply referred to as justified but more properly, fully-justified).

Text can also be right justified (or aligned) with a ragged end at the left. Text which is force-justified is fully justified even in a line which ends with a hard return.

Kerning

A term used in typography to designate the moving of the component letters in certain character pairs closer together than they would normally be. This is done when the shape of certain pairs is complementary, so that they naturally fit closer together, and look better, especially in large font sizes, as in headlines.

Landscape

The orientation of a rectangular document or display when the width is larger than the height – as in a landscape painting. See *Portrait.*

Laser printer

High-quality printer which uses a computer-controlled laser beam and optical scanning device to discharge a charged light-sensitive drum. The drum attracts toner (special ink particles) to the charged regions which is then transferred onto paper to form the final image.

LCD

See *Liquid Crystal Display.*

Leading

Pronounced 'ledding'. The space between lines of text. Derives from traditional printers' method of separating lines of moveable metal type with thin strips of lead.

LED

Light-emitting diode. A semiconductor device which emits light. Is used in certain types of 'laser' printer as a replacement for the laser.

Line art

A graphic which consists of lines and is stored in a vector format. See *Vector*

Liquid crystal display

An alternative to the CRT (q.v.) as a display screen in computer monitors. The screen consists of thousands of tiny separate liquid crystals which can be individually turned off or on. The crystals act as a type of light-switch or gate. When light is let through, a pixel is lit. Otherwise the pixel is dark. For colour screens, each pixel has three liquid crystals, each with its own red, green or blue filter. See *Active matrix.*

Lofting

The process by which a 2-dimensional shape is extended into the third dimension to produce a 3-dimensional shape. Also called 'extrusion'.

Look-up table

See *Colour look-up table.*

Loss-less

See *Compression.*

Lossy

See *Compression.*

LZW

Lempel Ziv Welch. A type of loss-less compression (q.v.).

Mask

A method, used in graphic drawing and painting software, of protecting parts of the image from being changed. Also: a component of a colour CRT.

Menu

A series of options which can be chosen from a list; part of a GUI (q.v.).

Mono-spaced font

A font (q.v.) in which all the letters have an equal spacing. Those letter which are naturally narrow are artificially widened by the use of large serifs (q.v.). These fonts are designed for systems, like typewriters, which can only place characters in fixed positions regardless of the actual character being printed. They tend to be harder to read than proportionally spaced fonts (q.v.).

Morphing

The process of gradually changing one image into another by a series of small steps.

Mouse

A small plastic box which can be moved over a flat surface. The movements are conveyed to the computer and used to move a cursor (q.v.) on the screen.

Multimedia

The combination of a variety of different media of communication, such as graphics, sound, video and animation to enhance the quality of communication.

OCR

Optical Character Recognition. The process whereby a piece of software interprets the graphic file created when alphanumeric characters (q.v.) are scanned using a document scanner (q.v.), recognises the shapes and identifies the characters.

Orphan

A typographer's term for one or two lines at the beginning of a paragraph which occur at the end of a page or column and so look unsightly. See *Widow*.

Output device

A computer peripheral (q.v.) which is used to present information to the outside world. Examples include the screen and a variety of printers. See *Input device*.

Page description language (PDL)

A type of computer language which is concerned with specifying the layout of a page of text and graphics. The description of the page is independent of the exact characteristics of the printer which will produce the hardcopy. This means that a graphic file, which contains the computer code, can be sent to a variety of printers and each will produce an identical image, within the limits of its capability. The printers must, however, contain a language interpreter which can translate the code. The best known example of a PDL is PostScript.

Page printer

Unlike some printers which use a small moving head and lay down text and graphics in a series of horizontal bands, a page printer produces the whole page in one operation.

Paint software

An application package which is designed to enable an artist to create paintings electronically, using a mouse.

Palette

A collection of colours which is available within a graphics package. The number depends on the hardware and can vary from 2 to 16.8 million. Often more than one palette is available, but only one can be used at a time. Each palette corresponds to a different colour look-up table (q.v.)

Pantone colour system

A system of standardizing printed colours by the use of 'swatches' of colour cards which show how the chosen colour will look when printed – often quite different from its appearance on a computer display.

PCX

A widely-used graphic file format (q.v.).

Pel

A short form of 'pixel'. See *Pixel.*

Pen-plotter

A device which draws lines under computer control using a mechanical arm and a pen. See *Drum plotter* and *Flat-bed plotter.*

Persistence

The time that the glow on a CRT (q.v.) lasts before fading away. Because of the fading effect the display must be regularly refreshed.

Perspective

The effect whereby objects appear to get smaller as they recede into the distance. See *Isometric projection.*

Phosphor

The special lining on the face of a CRT (q.v.) display which glows when irradiated by an electron beam.

Photo-typesetter (or Typesetter)

A device for producing high-quality output, suitable for use as a printing master, using a laser to record directly onto photographic emulsion.

Pica

A measure of the size of type. One pica is equal to 12 points; 72 points are equivalent to 1 inch.

Pixel (or Pel)

A picture element. One of the many dots used in forming a computer graphic image.

Pixellization

A graphic effect in which a digitized image is represented with fewer than the original number of pixels. Each of the larger pixels is derived from a number of smaller, original, ones by an averaging affect.

Point

See *Pica.*

Point light source

A very small source of light which gives very directional illumination. See *Extended light source* and *Diffuse illumination.*

Pointing device

A peripheral input device which can be used to point to the display.

Polyline

A series of straight lines joined end-to-end.

Portrait

The orientation of a rectangular document or display when the width is smaller than the height – as in a portrait painting. See *Landscape.*

PostScript

See *Page description language.*

Primitive (or Graphic Primitive)

A basic geometrical shape from which more complicated shapes can be constructed.

Process colour

The combination of cyan, magenta, yellow and black 'separations' to produce intermediate colours in the printing process. See *Spot colour* and *Colour separation.*

Proof

A low-quality print which is produced for careful inspection and correction before the higher-quality final product is made.

Proportional spacing

Spacing between individual letters in a typographic font which is appropriate to their natural shape. See *Mono-spaced font.*

Puck

See *Graphic tablet.*

Raster

A method of displaying information on the screen of a CRT (q.v.). The electron beam is moved across the screen in a series of closely-packed horizontal parallel lines (a raster) and pixels are illuminated or switched off in a rectangular array.

Ray tracing

A process used to create a realistic image of a 3-D object. The laws of optics are used to calculate the paths traced by a large number of rays of light as they reflect and scatter off the object and enter the eye of the observer. The colour and intensity of the rays when they finally enter the eye are calculated from the types of interaction they undergo in the process.

Refresh

The images created by most computer display systems fade rapidly and need to be recreated or 'refreshed'. See *Refresh buffer*

Refresh buffer

That portion of the computer's memory which is set aside to store data specifying the image to be displayed on the screen. This information is needed in order that the screen, as it fades, can be refreshed regularly. See *Refresh.*

Registration

When colour images are printed by repeated application of the four or more primary colours (e.g. cyan, magenta, yellow and black) to a sheet of paper it is important that the colours match exactly. Special marks called registration marks are printed on the edge of the paper which can be cut off at the end of the process, and are used by the printer to adjust the machine to ensure that this matching process is exact. See *Additive colour.*

Render

A term used to describe the process in which software creates a realistic image of a 3-dimensional object by ray-tracing or other methods. See *Ray tracing.*

Resolution

A general term used in science and technology to describe the amount of detail to be found in a set of data. In computer graphics it is applied to the amount of spatial detail in an image and is therefore one measure of the quality of that image.

Reverse video

Also called inverse video. Characters have their normal foreground and background colours reversed. For example, white-on-black characters become black-on-white.

RGB colour model

Red, green, blue model. A method of specifying additive colours by the proportion of the three primaries which combine to create it. See *Additive colour.*

Rubber-banding

An aid to drawing objects on a screen with a mouse. A flexible line or rectangle is displayed on the screen to show where the object will be placed. The rubber-band shape is fixed at one corner or end but can be stretched by dragging the mouse until a suitable position is reached.

Sans serif

A serif is a term used in typography to describe the small hooks and decorations which are placed on the end of characters in certain typefaces. These are called serif typefaces. Plainer typefaces which have no serifs are called sans-serif typefaces (sans means 'without' in French).

Scan

A rather general term which means to move methodically over something. Used in the context of a document scanner to digitize a printed image. Also used of the electron beam in a CRT (q.v.) to move in a raster fashion over the face of the tube.

Scan conversion

The process whereby a vector description of an object is converted into a form suitable for use in a raster-scan display device or printer which needs a bitmap of the image. See *Bit-map* and *Vector.*

Screen capture

Sometimes called screen dumping. The process in which a copy of what is seen on the screen is captured in a graphic file for printing (as in a manual or textbook).

Screen font

A font which is used to display on the screen a good imitation of the font which the printer will use in producing hardcopy.

Scroll bars

Bars on the side of a scrollable window which can be dragged using a mouse to cause the contents of the window to scroll.

Seed-fill

Another term for flood fill.

Serif

See *Sans serif.*

Shading

The use of different tones to create the natural effect of light and dark on a solid object.

Snapping

The effect in which objects which are drawn on a screen are attracted to a rectangular grid pattern in order to automatically ensure good alignment. See *Grid.*

Spatial

Relating to space. See *Resolution.*

Spot colour

An alternative to printing colours by the mixture of three or four primaries in different proportions. A spot colour is a specific colour, chosen from a range of printing inks, which is used either in addition to process colours, or as a substitute, where only a few colours are required. Spot colour is a better method of producing solid blocks of colour. Process colour is better at producing a large range of shades. See *Process colour.*

Subtractive colour

See *Additive colour.*

Super twist

An improved type of liquid crystal which produces more contrast in LCD displays (q.v.).

Super-VGA

See *VGA.*

System font

The bit-mapped font of characters which is supplied with the computer hardware and used for routine display of text.

TIFF

Tagged Image File Format. A widely-used graphic file format.

Text-only mode

A mode in which the computer displays only text, and a limited range of other characters, in the system font (q.v.). See *Graphics mode.*

Thermal wax printer

A dot-matrix printer which uses a ribbon with a special waxy ink which is melted by heating the pins in the print head. See *Dot matrix* and *Impact printer.*

Tiling

A way of arranging windows in a GUI (q.v.) so that they do not overlap but sit side-by-side like tiles.

Toner

A special type of ink, in the form of a powder, which is used in laser printers. The toner is attracted to charged regions on the photosensitive drum. See *Laser printer.*

Toolbox (or Toolkit)

A small 'floating' window made up of icons in a rectangular array. Each icon represents a tool or utility for use in a graphics program. See *Icon* and *Window.*

Touch-screen

A transparent screen which is placed over a computer monitor and which is sensitive to touch so that choices from a menu can be made without the need for a keyboard or mouse.

Tweening

Short for in-betweening (q.v.).

Typeface

See *Font.*

Vector

In computer graphics, a line of any sort. Hence vector images are stored as a set of lines, as opposed to bit-mapped images which are stored as a set of dots (pixels) in a rectangular array.

VESA

Video Electronics Standards Association. A body which sets standards associated with video which has given its name to an (obsolete) way of interfacing video cards (q.v.) to a computer via a bus.

VGA

Video Graphics Array. A display interface for the IBM-PC computer which superseded the EGA. It had a standard resolution of 640 × 480 (16 colours). Has largely been superseded by an enhanced version called Super-VGA (S-VGA) which offers a number of higher resolution modes and more colours, the exact number depending on the amount of video buffer RAM supplied. All S-VGA cards offer at least 800 × 600 resolution and most offer 256 colours.

Virtual Reality

A form of highly-realistic simulation of a 3-D world created by a computer. 3-D stereoscopic vision involves the use of special helmets which present slightly different views of this imaginary world to each eye and also provide the computer with feedback as the user moves his/her head. Some systems use special gloves to provide feedback of hand movements also.

Widow

A typographer's term for one or two lines of text at the end of a paragraph, which occur at the top of a new page or column and so look unsightly. See *Orphan.*

Window

A rectangular, re-sizeable frame which contains text or graphics and is an important feature of GUIs (q.v.). Note: 'Windows' is the trade name given by Microsoft to its GUI which operates in conjunction with its MS-DOS operating system.

Wire-frame

A simple representation of a 3-D object in which the edges of the planes which make up the object are shown as lines, as if made from wire.

WYSIWYG

'What You See Is What You Get'. A type of display which attempts to represent exactly what the final printed graphic will look like.

X-axis

In the Cartesian coordinate system, measurements in the horizontal plane are designated with the letter x and the corresponding axis called the x-axis. See *Co-ordinate System*.

X-Y Plotter

Another name for a pen-plotter. See *Flat-bed plotter* and *Pen-plotter*.

Index

A

B

C

D

E

F

G

K

L

M

N

O

P

Q

R

S

T

V

W

X

Z